Efrem Zimbalist

A Life

Roy Malan

Efrem Zimbalist

A Life

Roy Malan

AMADEUS PRESS
Portland • Cambridge

Frontispiece: Sketch by Oscar Levant

Published in 2004 by

Amadeus Press, LLC
512 Newark Pompton Turnpike
Pompton Plains, New Jersey 07444
U.S.A.

Amadeus Press
2 Station Road
Swavesey
Cambridge CB4 5QJ, U.K.

For sales, please contact

NORTH AMERICA
AMADEUS PRESS, LLC
c/o Hal Leonard Corp.
7777 West Bluemound Road
Milwaukee, Wisconsin 53213 U.S.A.
Tel. 800-637-2852
Fax 414-774-3259

UNITED KINGDOM AND EUROPE
AMADEUS PRESS
2 Station Road
Swavesey, Cambridge, CB4 5QJ, U.K.
Tel. 01954-232959
Fax 01954-206040

E-mail: orders@amadeuspress.com
Website: www.amadeuspress.com

Printed in the United States of America

Library of Congress Cataloging-in-Publication Data

Malan, Roy.
  Efrem Zimbalist : a life / by Roy Malan.
     p. cm.
Includes bibliographical references (p.   ) and index.
Discography: p.
  ISBN 1-57467-091-3 (hardcover)
  1. Zimbalist, Efrem. 2. Violinists—Biography. I. Title.

ML418.Z94M3 2004
787.2'092—dc22

2003025107

For Jascha Brodsky and Vladimir Sokoloff, who loved Zimbalist as much as I did; for my dear parents, and for my son, whose middle name is Efrem.

To all who helped, my sincerest thanks. Extra special gratitude to my father, without whose encouragement this project would not have been undertaken, and to Eve Goodman, Amy Biancolli, Ralph Weiss, Kathy Jackson and David Abbott, without whom it would never have reached completion.

Contents

Foreword by Josef Gingold ix

Preface xi

A Note to the Reader xii

Prelude xv

1. Promising Beginnings (1890–1901) 1

2. St. Petersburg Proving-Ground (1901–1902) 7

3. Classroom and Palace (1902) 17

4. Student Life and Rimsky-Korsakov (1903–1906) 27

5. Prizewinning Graduate (1906–1907) 35

6. Luftpause in Alt Wien (Summer 1907) 43

7. Promise Fulfilled: Berlin (Fall 1907) 47

8. European Kudos (Fall–Winter 1907) 53

9. London and Joseph Fels (1907–1908) 61

10. A Temporary Base (1908–1909) 69

11. Return to Russia (1909–1911) 83

12. America and Alma: Love at First Sight (Fall 1911) 99

13. Trying the New World On for Size (Winter 1911–Spring 1912) 111

14. Marriage and a Changing World (1912–1914) 121

15. Manhattan Family Hearth (1914–1920) 133

16. High Living (1920–1932) 153

17. Discovering the Orient (1922–1928) 183

18. A New Career: Globetrotting Professor (1928–1933) 205

19. Soviet Invitation—and Personal Tragedy (1933–1938) 217

20. Mary Louise Curtis Bok and the C.I.M. (1938–1947) 245

21. Winding Down (1947–1968) 267

22. Productive Retirement (1970–1978) 295

23. Coming to Terms with Bach—and Mortality (1978–1985) 319

Postlude. Zimbalist's Violin Mastery and Influence 333

The Zimbalist Students 337

Discography 339

Bibliography 353

Index 357

Foreword

Mr. Roy Malan's biography of 'Zimmie,' as Mr. Zimbalist was affectionately known to his friends, is a critical life story of one of the greatest musical personalities of the twentieth century.

The author, a close friend and student of Zimbalist, depicts his long and glorious career with love, knowledge, insight and understanding. Mr. Malan's extraordinary research and detailed care make this book one of the best musical biographies I have ever read.

My congratulations and heartiest thanks to the author, whose book is a joy to read and one that I would certainly recommend to book lovers everywhere, be they musicians, music students or the general reading public.

Josef Gingold
Distinguished Professor Emeritus of Music
Indiana University, Bloomington

Preface

Efrem Zimbalist's impact was manifold: influential, brilliant solo violinist bringing to countless people (notably throughout Asia) artistry of a kind never before experienced; intuitive teacher molding many fine violinists to occupy key positions for further dissemination of his principles; head of one of the finest and most productive of music schools, adding again to the diffusion of his ideals. The important thing is that he was so successful in making his musical ideals America's, and the world's, too. His step-daughter Marcia Davenport's words are perfect in describing an often-overlooked manifestation of these ideals: 'I think it would be most remarkable if you were to find a symphony orchestra, American or foreign, which does not include among its member musicians those first-class, leading professionals who studied at the Curtis Institute of Music under the aegis of my "Papouchka."'

I studied at the Curtis Institute under Zimbalist, who taught there from 1928 and was director from 1941 to 1968. After my graduation, and his retirement, we both ended up on the West Coast. For six years (although I lived in San Francisco and he in Reno, Nevada), I kept visiting and playing for him, and we became good friends.

In April 1979, Zimbalist received a cassette of an eighty-ninth birthday tribute by the Pittsburgh NPR station. When I played it for him, I couldn't help noticing his grimaces. 'Where did they get this rubbish?' he wondered. For years, when asked to consent to an authorized biography he had replied, 'When I'm dead someone will write something.' I turned off the tape. 'It's your fault,' I ventured. 'You won't let anyone get the facts straight while you're alive to substantiate them.' A few days later I received a phone call in San Francisco. 'I've been thinking about what you said the other day,' he said, 'and I think I would like to have a book written.' 'Wonderful,' I replied, 'who will do it?' 'I think you should — you know as much about me as anyone does.' I secured his permission to interview him on tape and we began, with a bit of a head start (I had been jotting down his yarns for some time).

In 1962, on one of Zimbalist's trips to Russia, his interpreter started taking notes for a proposed Soviet biography. But progress was slow, and by his last trip, in 1970, after which they lost contact, she had only got as far as his childhood years. I was reminded of an American journalist's frustration when at the time of Zimbalist's U.S. debut, in 1911, he tried to interview him: 'If only he were loquacious,' he complained, 'but Zimbalist is most aggravatingly laconic, and teams of horses couldn't drag another word out of him!'

For me it wasn't quite that bad, though I remember one session when Zimbalist's cigar went out. Relighting it, he commented, 'I'm talking so much that my cigar objects.' I, too, was sometimes stymied by his reticence to elaborate. Once I pressed him more than usual. 'I can't tell you any more,' he resisted. 'This is a theme without variations.' What impressed me about the interviews was that, although over the years he had told some of the stories many times, not once did they vary in detail.

There was an initial draft in 1991, with revisions up till yesterday. My life has been immensely enriched by coming into contact with some of the most inspiring and colorful characters one could ever hope to meet. To all of them, and to dear Mr. Zimbalist, who didn't live to see the project completed, my eternal gratitude.

Roy Malan
North Pond, Maine

A Note to the Reader

Zimbalist's accompanist Samuel Chotzinoff, in his autobiographical *Day's at the Morn*, spelled Zimbalist's words phonetically in an attempt to capture his colorful pronunciation. I have spared readers any such efforts. In first-person accounts throughout the pages to follow, Zimbalist's words will be used as transcribed from tape recordings. The reader can supply the inflections—the warm voice rich with Russian intonation (Zimbalist's gentle accent was present to the end of his long life) and the infectious deep chuckle that was never far from the surface. There was also that delightful look of incredulity when he learned something new ('No, you don't *mean* it!')—and his eyes twinkled merrily in later years when, to quote his student Michael Tree, 'he would light up a favorite pre-Castro Havana, disappear in a cloud of smoke and allow his mind to drift back.'

Prelude

This chronicle begins at a pivotal point in the passage of violinistic time, some two hundred years after a recognizable violin first emerged from murky origins. Slowly a galaxy of virtuosi came into being, culminating in Italy in a supernova named Nicolo Paganini, whose spin-off satellites and comets criss-crossed the universe in brilliant orbit. Their luminescence dimmed by the end of the nineteenth century, with no sign of a succeeding galaxy. Yet the dawn of a new era was at hand; all the makings lay dormant at a location in the cold northern hemisphere.

Alchemy was about to lend a hand…

CHAPTER 1

Promising Beginnings

(1890–1901)

Rostov-na-Donu in the Ukraine from early days considered itself a cosmopolitan bastion of culture. In the early 1900s it was a prosperous city of about 100,000, with handsome buildings, good schools and fine shops, including the latest ladies' fashions from Paris. Normal travel within city limits was by droshky and horse-drawn tram; automobiles were few. Among Rostov's most imposing buildings was the Smalov Theater, home of the Ukrainian Opera Company, where in addition to drama and opera, orchestral concerts and ballet were regularly staged. The conductor for all these events was Aron (Alexander) Zimbalist, an accomplished musician. His training, undergone wholly in Russia, had provided him with a good enough stick technique to gain the respect of his musicians. But it was his quiet dignity, his pleasant manner and, above all, his incorruptible sense of fairness that endeared Aronchik to all with whom he came in contact.

Alexander Zimbalist had married a local girl, Maria Litvinoff, and they lived in comfortable rented quarters not far from the Smalov Theater. It was in this warm, cozy home that their first child, Efrem, was born on 9 April 1890.

Zimbalist père, although trained as a violinist, no longer drew a bow himself, owing to his demanding duties wielding the baton; so demanding, in fact, that young Efrem never heard his father play. An upright piano was a fixture in a subsequent home, however, and it is possible that the toddler heard his father play a note or two at the keyboard. Efrem's earliest musical exposure was provided by his mother, who crooned somber folk tunes and lullabies to him. Although not a musician herself, Maria Zimbalist adored music and attended all Alex's performances, a habit she resumed with the baby in tow as soon as that was practical. So Efrem was bounced on his devoted mother's knee to symphony and opera from his very earliest consciousness. Later, he accompanied her to her favorite plays.

As early as age two Efrem began to give indications of a remarkable ear and memory. When he was three a visiting physician friend predicted that Efrem would become a great musician, an opinion based on phrenology and the shape of the toddler's ears. Around this time evidence of perfect pitch was discovered, and one of Efrem's favorite amusements was to sing or pick out on the piano complete melodies heard on his latest visit to the opera house. Later he astounded visitors by performing long arias complete with lyrics. Alex presented his son with a quarter-sized violin some time between his fourth and fifth birthdays, and instructed him, with infinite patience, in the rudiments of left- and right-hand positions. He enrolled Efrem at the Imperial Music School at age five.

The school was a branch of the great Imperial Conservatory system, whose main bodies were in St. Petersburg and Moscow. The curriculum at the highly rated Rostov branch, headed by the energetic pianist M. L. Pressman, was comprehensive and days were long. Efrem's violin teacher, the first of many, was Professor Chabban. In addition to violin lessons there was the usual kindergarten fare, gradually laced with doses of the three Rs and rudimentary geography. Efrem loved books and read early, making random selections from his father's extensive library of classics, and Alex read to him daily from the *Riech*, Rostov's excellent newspaper, which featured essays by prominent literary figures. Efrem enjoyed hearing his father read these; this early exposure to literature eventually led to a costly fascination with fine books.

His mother walked him to and from school every day. In fierce winter weather she hired a droshky. At day's end she usually found him across the street at Belski's music store, whose proprietor captivated him with yarns of the celebrated names in music. Papa Zimbalist sometimes fetched his son after school and gave him a treat in the form of French pastry, ice cream or a piece of fruit. A loving father in an age when children were often soundly thrashed, he never laid a rough hand on his children. He had few disciplinary problems with his firstborn, who was placid and good-natured from the start.

On Saturdays during spring and summer the downtown stores on Sadovaya (Garden) Street closed at two. Then what seemed fully half the population congregated to enjoy promenading along those five acacia-lined blocks. Maria would take Efrem, and the sounds of the 'gypsy' bands singing Russian folk songs, accompanied by balalaikas and bayans, stuck vividly in his memory. Maria and her son continued their regular visits to the Smalov Theater but Efrem, no longer content to cling to his mother's skirts, would break away and run down the aisle to the edge of the orchestra pit, where he mimicked the waving of his father's arms, much to the audience's amusement.

Efrem's school routine left little time for the leisure enjoyed by other children, but he never complained. He enjoyed singing in the school chorus and learned sections from the popular Russian operas. The students performed them with piano since the Imperial School taught no wind instruments and had no orchestra. Most visitors to the Zimbalist household were musical colleagues of Alex's or Efrem's fellow students. His favorite playmate was the pianist Eugene Lutsky; this association extended into a professional one in later years.

Alex also kept a busy schedule. Between opera, ballet, providing incidental music for drama, summer variety theater and orchestral 'pops' programs, he worked year-round. When Efrem was about six a pattern developed that continued throughout his youth: Alex sent him and his mother off by train to summer in the Caucasus at the beautiful Kislovodsk Kürsaal. Musically it was no vacation for Efrem. His little fiddle, now a half size, was packed along with his toys. After a few summers an enterprising proprietor hired him to play for the guests at his fashionable hotel, and it became a tradition for Efrem to entertain appreciative crowds with his latest display pieces several times a week.

Young Efrem's rapid mastery of his fingerboard led to concert appearances in Rostov and environs from the age of seven. One was at a charity concert organized by Grand Duke Constantine in nearby Novocherkassk. The audience was ecstatic, and Efrem was called up on stage to receive a presentation from the effusive Grand Duke, who had been informed of Efrem's voracious reading habits. Efrem opened the bulky package backstage: it contained a two-volume leather-bound edition of *The Arabian Nights*. With characteristic modesty, believing himself unworthy of so extravagant a gift, Efrem handed the volumes over to an aide and went home. This inherent simplicity was fostered by his parents. When button-holed by admirers of his son's prowess, Alex limited his response to a smile and mumbled 'Thank you.'

Work began on the construction of Alex and Maria's own home on the wooded edge of town, four blocks from the river Don. The completed house contained about five rooms and boasted the modern conveniences of a bathtub and coal heating. Alex was particularly proud of a contrivance installed in two of the larger rooms: a naked bulb dangling from the ceiling which, at the mere touch of a button, emitted a magical luminescence. It was one of the first homes in town to enjoy the luxury of electricity. The family moved in when Efrem was about nine, its number having swelled with the birth of new brothers and sisters (Alex and Maria's progeny eventually numbered seven, four girls and three boys). The all-important samovar was one of the home's first installations, and Maria served the children their tea sweetened in the Russian way, with jam. Other standard fare included kapouska with black bread and fish from the nearby river; smoked salmon was a special treat.

Efrem's ear, miraculous memory, natural finger dexterity and high degree of intelligence were enough to produce brilliant results without endless drudgery; he practiced but an hour a day at best, just enough to prepare his lessons. The summer after his ninth birthday, his father was approached by a colleague, a concertmaster for a small touring company that presented Italian operas. An upcoming tour was in the planning stages, he told Alex, and he needed a good 'second konzertmeister' to share the first stand with him. Would Alex (who himself was making almost 400 rubles a month as early as the turn of the century) allow Efrem to fill the post, for a monthly stipend of 100 rubles? The young violinist had never played in an orchestra before, but he had observed his father's orchestra for years and was a good sight reader. Alex discussed the invitation with Maria and Efrem, and gave his permission. The boy was off, away from home by himself for the first time, for almost two months.

At any rate, that was the version Zimbalist told the author late in life; but a close friend, also late in life, gave a different version: at the age of nine Efrem had run away from home and looked about for employment, at which time he was offered the touring opera company position. (When queried, Zimbalist merely said, 'They could get me very cheap!')

Things started out well enough. To reach the rehearsal site, Efrem took a short cut through an orchard and emerged with his shirt stuffed full of apples, a favorite fruit all his life. The repertoire (*Rigoletto* and *Traviata*) he knew by ear, and by the second or third time through he had memorized everything and no longer needed to watch the music. To stave off boredom he turned his attention to the singers on the stage, which unfortunately played havoc with his duties as a page-turner. Very soon, familiarity led him into contentious ways. During a *Rigoletto* rehearsal a discussion arose among the senior musicians concerning a fine point in the score. When Efrem contributed his two cents the conductor fixed him with a fiery eye and asked if *he* would care to conduct. The young upstart jumped onto the podium and successfully rehearsed the disputed spot by memory, to the astonishment of all. Worse followed. The combination of excitement, hard work and hours consistently past his bedtime led to drowsiness, and it didn't take long for the young assistant concertmaster to fall fast asleep during a performance. Efrem was awakened by a smart rap on the head, and Alex was summoned to escort his somnolent son home.

When he was ten Efrem faced yet another new teacher at the beginning of the school year, and the only one to make a lasting impression on him: Professor Salin. Salin prepared Efrem magnificently for the most decisive period of his formative years, putting him through his paces, with the help of the immortal Kreutzer, Rode and de Beriot, and assigning him such blockbusters as the Goldmark Concerto and Vieuxtemps's No. 4 in d minor. His prize student had recently moved up to a three-quarter size instrument, from which he was drawing full, sweet sounds, a foretaste of the characteristic qualities his mature tone displayed.

In late 1900 the Imperial School was visited by two famous musicians from St. Petersburg: cellist Verzhbilovich and pianist-conductor Siloti, who had heard rumors of an extraordinary talent there. Efrem hadn't played more than two lines before the two men exchanged glances; Siloti finally stood up and said to Salin, 'What's he doing with you? He should be with Auer.' The legendary Leopold Auer of the St. Petersburg Conservatory enjoyed an unequaled reputation throughout Russia. Director Pressman was informed, and Siloti had a talk with Efrem's parents. Their expectations were coming true. Their son was about to fly the nest.

CHAPTER 2

St. Petersburg Proving-Ground

(1901–1902)

From the moment the decision was made, preparations for departure seemed endless. Salin continued to drill his pupil, with the aim of impressing Professor Auer. Efrem was slightly less lackadaisical about his practicing, and Alex and Maria did their best to bone him up on the necessary dos and don'ts. But the actual packing took no time at all, even with the few new outfits his mother had added to his wardrobe, and in early October 1901, Maria and her eleven-year-old son were on a train bound for St. Petersburg. Station stops during the two-day journey were a source of fascination to Efrem; he enjoyed hearing the unknown names called out as he was drifting off to sleep.

They arrived in St. Petersburg early in the morning and proceeded to an inexpensive hotel near the center of town. The clerk there peered at Maria over horn-rimmed half glasses. 'From Rostov, eh? The boy looks like a student.' This elicited a nervous nod. 'You plan to stay long?' The meaning of his words was clear to Maria, although they passed over the boy's head: talented students of all nationalities were welcomed at the St. Petersburg Conservatory, but the parents of Jewish children from out of town were not allowed to reside in the capital. Maria assured the man that her business was of short duration.

Efrem helped carry their bags upstairs and remained in the room to practice, a mute clamped onto his violin, while his mother, having first tenderly kissed his forehead, headed to the famous Imperial Conservatory, a short walk away. School officials confirmed Efrem's admittance and also his audition with Auer at his home the following day. Maria took down the address and then turned her attention to obtaining suitable housing for her child, for the Conservatory had no dormitories. She found the local boardinghouses uniformly grimy and returned downhearted to the hotel, where Efrem was distractedly playing scales. News of the imminent meeting with Auer spurred his efforts, and after a meal, he played for his mother the Goldmark Concerto, the first movement of which he had chosen for the audition. Then, tired out by his journey, he fell fast asleep.

Next morning a droshky deposited them at Auer's address at the agreed hour. Maria rang the doorbell and a sour-faced housekeeper showed them in. The great professor, with the barest modicum of geniality, listened while Efrem, with suitable composure, played the first movement of the Goldmark. Evidently satisfied, Auer gave them instructions on arrangements to be made at the Conservatory and showed them out. His report of the audition to director August Burnhardt came into Zimbalist's hands fifty years later: 'Ear excellent, a great talent and very musical. Son of a musician from Rostov. I accept him in my class as a scholarship student.'

It was a considerably more hopeful mother that held her son's hand on the droshky returning them to their modest hotel, and Zimbalist later recalled no difficulties surrounding his arrival in St. Petersburg. But Auer, in his autobiography, explicitly described one particularly chill autumn morning: 'My servant ushered in Zimbalist and his mother, shivering with cold. When I enquired the reasons for their early call, the boy began to cry. He told me that he and his mother had spent the night on the streets [and] had come in to warm themselves and ask for my help. It was a question of a permit allowing her to remain in the city for a few days.' Auer thereupon wrote the chief of police a letter, 'stressing the wretchedness of the poor mother, who was merely looking for a place where she could leave her child,' and emphasizing 'the boy's great talent.'

As a result of this intervention, Maria was permitted to remain in the capital a week, in which time she settled on a pensione that Auer recommended, not far from the Conservatory. It was a multistory red brick house, with separate rooms for each resident and three meals provided daily by the proprietress. Terms were reasonable, and everything was soon agreed. Upstairs, Efrem's room contained the essentials—bed, coatrack, desk, chair, and a washstand below an ancient veined mirror. Maria completed the furnishings by unfolding the music stand that had traveled with them from Rostov. While she unpacked his things, Efrem looked out the window at the city that would be his home for six winters.

Maria and Efrem next attended to remaining business at the Conservatory. Always a sobering sight, this grand building, with a student body of some two thousand, seemed especially awesome that day. The Zimbalists were taken to the Inspector's office, where Efrem was assigned courses—general academic studies (amounting to high school equivalency), music theory and solfège. These averaged three to four hours a day, plus violin classes. It was decided to defer the start of the required piano proficiency course. No fees were due, thanks to Auer.

School would begin in a week. Preparation for his busy schedule, combined with fascinating novelties encountered at every turn, diverted Efrem until it came time for Maria to say goodbye. Auer gauged her feelings at this parting: 'How her heart must have grieved when she was obliged to leave this inhospitable city, to trust her child to the keeping of strangers, and to face the depressing prospect of never being able to visit him when her mother love prompted.'

Efrem settled into the pattern of classes, and from the start, his ear and memory helped him excel. Solfège and dictation proved especially easy; a favorite trick was to solfège Paganini's 'Moto Perpetuo' at breakneck speed. His fabulous memory made equally light work of the academic subjects. To speak with him in later years was to encounter a top-flight intellect reflecting a lifetime of study. The truth is that, while a voracious reader, he was educated by practical firsthand experience—a true student of life. Nalbandian, Auer's assistant, continued where Salin left off, feeding Efrem the long succession of scales and etudes every would-be virtuoso must digest, which technical matters did not interest Auer himself.

Auer's class, the raison d'être, met twice a week. Still relatively in his performing prime, Auer was a hale and hearty fifty-six and freshly divorced; he occupied a large flat on the fashionable English Prospect and employed a full-time housekeeper, a super-efficient German woman whose unpredictable receptions kept visitors in mortal dread of her. Auer was on the short side and so carried himself perfectly erect, drawing attention away from his paunch, the result of a fondness for good food and port. He ate, drank and dressed well; more often than not he wore a bow tie and sported a gold watch-chain across his waistcoat. Long, starched

French cuffs framed his smallish, delicately tapering hands, and Efrem was especially impressed that Auer's thick coat was lined in ermine. The face, beneath a bald pate, was dominated by a prominent nose, offset by a well-trimmed goatee and ruled by Auer's captivating eyes. Smoky black, their gaze ran the gamut from benevolence to searing censure. All in all, the impression was of the grand seigneur.

He was notoriously stingy, even though he received 3,000 rubles a year from the Conservatory and a like amount for his duties as soloist to Tsar Nicholas II, a position he had also held under the two previous tsars. His income was further swelled by concert fees, both as recitalist and as frequent concerto soloist. Then there was his quartet, the St. Petersburg, which in 1901 consisted of Walther, Korguiev (both former students) and the cellist Verzhbilovich, whose tone Zimbalist always considered unmatched. Auer also conducted symphony concerts and ballet. Efrem once watched Isadora Duncan dance Beethoven's Seventh Symphony as Auer gamely kept pace on the podium.

How did Auer manage all this? Actually, his official load was not heavy: his entire teaching commitment consisted of but two master classes on Tuesday and Thursday afternoons, he never gave private lessons, and his position as soloist to the Tsar involved nothing more than the occasional ballet solo (his presence being required only long enough to depose concertmaster Walther for the duration of the solo). While attentive to these duties, he was above all a temperamental artist who, to uphold his reputation, practiced a minimum of three hours daily to keep his playing in top shape. According to Zimbalist, he was a truly great violinist, 'the first I ever heard.' He vividly recollected Auer's 'Kreutzer' Sonata and the 'incredibly beautiful' way in which he played the slow movement of Spohr's Ninth Concerto.

Auer's eagerly anticipated annual recitals in the Maryinsky Theater were strictly classical in content—he was a true disciple of his teacher Joachim—but he usually ended them with something more frivolous by his friend Henri Wieniawski. Encores often included a demonstration of Auer's beautiful spiccato in Paganini's 'Moto Perpetuo,' played *with* repeat. His tone, while not large, was exquisitely polished and elegant, his style and technical command impeccable.

Auer's classes lasted from 2 to 4 p.m. Zimbalist well remembered the double doors that enclosed his third-floor studio. The long room was sparsely furnished: a chair next to a table where the master sat, close by a grand piano (hardly ever touched during lessons) and, arranged around the wall, a row of chairs where the students sat while they waited for Auer to pick a 'volunteer,' a system that resulted in undeniable favoritism. While Zimbalist, in looking back, rated all his classmates that first year 'good players,' the only one besides himself to gain subsequent renown was Joseph Achron (of Hebrew Melody fame).

Auer had taught at the Conservatory for more than thirty years, since taking over Wieniawski's post in 1868. The Tsar had recently knighted him for outstanding work. Where were his early products to warrant this? The many students he turned out were competent enough violinists, some occupying teaching posts at the various cultural outposts, but it fell to future virtuoso pupils to propel Auer's name like a shining comet around the musical globe. Efrem was the first such great talent to reach Auer's care, and the Professor treated him accordingly. Indeed, fairly often, after class (which invariably ended as punctually as it began) Auer invited him home for supper.

Zimbalist related how the journeys to Auer's flat went. 'Let's walk,' Auer would say as they emerged from the Conservatory, ignoring the waiting droshky. They'd set out on foot, Efrem carrying his battered little case and the Professor puffing on a cigarette, with the droshky in discreet pursuit. After about half a block the procession came to an abrupt halt, and Auer turned to the driver, who quickly drew up alongside.

'Would you like me to drive you home, Professor?'

'How much?'

'Twenty-five kopecks.'

'I'll give you ten.'

'Twenty.'

'Too much. Come Efrem, let's walk!'

The pantomime was repeated at each block, and unless the penny-pinching Professor was unusually tired, they arrived at his comfortable home on foot. Auer was his most personable at these meals and always saw that his housekeeper fed Efrem generously. On one occasion she served the biggest fish Efrem had ever seen, and he enjoyed the obvious relish with which Auer dug in, first tucking a large napkin, biblike, behind his wing collar.

All Zimbalist remembered Auer giving him in the way of technical advice was to begin his practice sessions by drawing long bows on open strings. The youngster must have taken this advice to heart, judging from the reputation he acquired later for having the 'longest bow' in the business. Auer also insisted on another basic: slow practice. 'In public play at tempo, at home, slowly.' Prone to moodiness, he could sometimes be harsh, at other moments more kindly, but he was seldom encouraging and summarily passed over students who were not playing to his liking. 'Shoemaker!' he thundered, 'you should be peddling shoelaces instead of studying music!'

Soon Efrem was introduced to the current demands of the repertoire: concertos by Spohr (Nos. 2, 6, 8 and 9), Viotti No. 22, Mendelssohn, Bruch (g and d minor), Vieuxtemps (Nos. 4 and 5), Wieniawski d minor, Ernst, Paganini No. 1, Joachim's Hungarian Concerto (first movement only), with possibly a Mozart concerto or Beethoven romance thrown in for good measure, and finally the Beethoven, Brahms and Tchaikovsky concertos. Equally basic was an assortment of operatic fantasias by virtuoso-composers. 'Auer also showed me many new things in the Goldmark Concerto, and I remember wondering at how so "old" a man could still play!' Auer was actually just cresting his peak, and for the next six years was clearly to demonstrate this to his class, and to the public at large.

Eight to ten students made up Auer's class at any given time, violins at the ready in open cases on chairs beside them, or at their feet. When called to take one's turn, one could expect to play for about twenty minutes if doing well; if not, an early retreat to the practice room. Almost invariably there was no piano accompaniment—Auer didn't play the piano. Only occasionally did he have a senior student sit down to provide a bass line. He responded to timid questions or criticized performances by grabbing the student's instrument impatiently (he never brought his own violin into class) and playing the spot in question. He could always toss off the most complicated passages with ease—and then would return the instrument disdainfully, as if to say, 'That's how you should have played it and see that you do so the next time.' Auer's Russian was far from perfect (his native tongue was Hungarian). As a result, he wasn't always successful in making himself verbally understood by Russian students; it was from his playing that the youngsters often learned. 'His method was designed to scare us into practicing,' said Zimbalist. And Auer could be brutal. 'He had been complimentary about the Goldmark and gave me a new concerto to learn. At the second class I was a little afraid, because I hadn't practiced much. I put the music on the stand and played the first movement. After I finished, without a word he lifted the stand and music, opened the door and threw them out into the corridor. Then he took me by the collar and threw *me* out too.'

Taken all together, was Auer really a great teacher? He was, if one believes in a teacher who produces brilliant results, regardless of the manner in which these results were produced. The so-called older style of teaching, epitomized by Auer, worked best for those students capable of solving their own technical problems. The less talented were sometimes manacled for the rest of their playing days by technical shortcomings that hadn't been instinctively eliminated or analyzed at lessons. Today a master teacher is expected not only to make technical and musical competents out of average talents but also to enter into the psychological aspects of a student's developing personality. According to Mischa Elman and others, this modern approach has done nothing but raise the level of mediocrity. Still, one cannot deny that through the brilliance of his students Zimbalist, Elman and especially Jascha Heifetz, Auer affected irreversibly the direction violin playing took in the twentieth century.

It was not until the formidable Ivan Galamian reached his full stride in the latter half of the century that the all-pervading influence of the 'Russian school' began to fade, ending up by the time Galamian died in 1981 as an outdated style of marginal impact. The mainstream of violin playing had moved on. In actual fact, although all violinists will be permanently influenced by the Russian legacy of virtuosity, starting with Auer's products and continuing on through Oistrakh and other Soviet masters to the present day, Auer didn't consider himself of a particular school. Never did he instruct any of his students to hold their bow in the 'Auer' fashion.

What characterizes the 'Auer' or 'Russian school,' technically speaking, is when the right index finger contacts the bow above the second joint from its tip. The ring and little fingers are usually held straight rather than curved on the bowstick, and all fingers are kept fairly close together. Early photos of Auer show that his bow-grip owed to the German (Joachim) school of his formative years, and while holding his fingers tightly together on the stick, he definitely had a lower index contact point, nearer the nail end, than as just described as the 'Auer' grip. Before the advent of Heifetz in 1910, his students had a variable index contact point, the only factor in common being this tendency to hold the fingers close together, a generally accepted policy that was handed down by Joachim, Vieuxtemps, Sarasate, Ysaÿe and Ole Bull. Exceptions were Isolde Menges, a later student of Auer, who held her bow with widely spaced fingers, and Heifetz classmate Toscha Seidel, whose third and fourth fingers were curved in a 'modern' way. The situation changed markedly with Heifetz's reign; his brilliance inspired wholesale imitation, including the individual way in which he held the bow. Zimbalist heard Heifetz before Heifetz studied with Auer and bore witness to the fact that Auer changed nothing in his playing: 'He knew when to let well enough alone.' Yet outside observers naturally assumed that Heifetz's outstanding success owed something to the non-existent 'Auer' method.

Even as astute an observer as Carl Flesch, in his *Art of Violin Playing*, spoke of the 'Auer bow-arm' as an acknowledged, defined entity. During the later part of his teaching career, he went as far as advocating this bow-grip to his own students. Heifetz declared that Auer had no method; Auer once told little Jascha, 'Play it with your nose if you like—you'll make it sound right!'

Very shortly after he began his studies at the Conservatory, Efrem was approached by another young violinist, Volodya, whose father was Rimsky-Korsakov—a household name in Russian musical circles and one well known to Efrem. Volodya invited him to their house to play chamber music, and the next Wednesday afternoon Efrem made his way to the Rimsky-Korsakov home, not far from his own quarters. He wasn't sure how to react if the great man himself answered his knock and so was pleased when Volodya opened the door. He took him into the living room and introduced his mother and sister Nadia, who sat knitting, and his cellist brother Andrei, just graduated from the University of Heidelberg. Rimsky was in his study working, as usual. The boys pointed down the hallway warily, telling their guest no one could enter the room but Father, especially when he was composing. Efrem was also introduced to a younger third boy, Vitold Portugaloff, with whom he was to become good buddies; Vitold entered the Conservatory nine years later to study with

Auer. They set up for quartets, with little Vitold on viola. Volodya reached under the piano and pulled out a large stack of music. One title caught Efrem's attention: 'Oh, I've never heard that!'

They decided to try it. Volodya distributed the parts, seated himself behind the second violin stand, and they began. After half a page, footsteps were heard in the hall. The music continued and the door finally swung open; a tall, thin man with a long feathery beard and tiny eyeglasses stood solemnly framed in the doorway. 'Who wrote that bad music?' the tall figure inquired. 'You did, Papa,' laughed Volodya.

Beethoven's Op. 18 came next, then a Brahms quartet, which Rimsky admitted liking after initial coolness. (Brahms was generally out of favor among the Russians of his day.) At supper Efrem was struck by the composer's simple dignity. Moved to meet an eleven-year-old so completely on his own, Rimsky accepted Efrem into his home as another son and encouraged the boy to talk about his accommodations, his family and his background. Although the kindly composer didn't say much (this turned out to be the norm), when Efrem bade him a respectful goodbye, the look in Rimsky's eyes went straight to his heart. Efrem was delighted when Volodya and Andrei suggested getting together regularly, and for several years the chamber music readings became a weekly event. Efrem acquainted himself in this way with the vast classical quartet repertoire and was later to cherish these get-togethers above all other St. Petersburg memories.

Things at the pensione were working out fine. Alex sent 50 rubles a month for his son's keep, with a few extra for pocket money, which Efrem spent at the fruit stands and bakeries he passed during his ramblings. He was developing two life traits: self-sufficiency and a strong independence of mind. A shy sensitivity gave way to calm assurance—a distinctly Zimbalistian composure that extended from the small trials of daily existence to larger tribulations. These changes were noted by his family when he returned home for the summer break; he had proved a poor letter-writer and there was much catching up to be done. And there were old chums to visit, which Efrem did on his new bicycle, a welcome-home present. But as usual, his services were required at the Kislovodsk Kürsaal, where he was to be accompanied by the resident summer orchestra whose concertmaster, Lev Zeitlin, was a former Auer pupil; so he left for an

extended stay in the Caucasus, with Maria and the younger children
joining him later.

Listeners who heard Efrem's playing spoke of vast improvement, and
the concerts that summer of 1902 were very successful. At season's end
there was just enough time for a little bicycling in Rostov before setting off
for his second year of adventures in the capital.

CHAPTER 3

Classroom and Palace

(1902)

Efrem faced an expanded curriculum at registration that fall. Both chamber music and orchestra had been added, as well as a foreign language, either French or German. Auer advised the latter; it was his own second language and useful to musicians since Berlin was considered the musical world's heartbeat. Then there were harmony and counterpoint; Efrem was assigned to the most prestigious class, conducted by Anatoly Liadov, which was supposed to meet twice a week in 'the classroom under the clock,' named for the enormous clock that hung over the door. But the lazy Liadov often failed to show up. If Liadov was seldom to be found, composition professor Alexander Glazunov's corpulent figure was a familiar sight at the Conservatory; attired in a black frock coat and striped trousers, he would make his way busily up and down its corridors, shaking hands with faculty, students and staff alike and leaving wafts of fragrant cigar smoke in his wake. Rimsky's was another constantly felt presence at the Conservatory; he was very proud of his top student at that time, the young Igor Stravinsky. Zimbalist regretted not being a Rimsky student: 'I made a terrible mistake in not asking him to take me into his class.' But the Wednesday afternoon chamber music sessions continued at Rimsky's home, where Fima, as he was fondly nicknamed, was always welcomed as one of the family.

Among the Conservatory's most respected faculty members was Annette Essipoff, Theodore Leschetizky's second wife (three of his four marriages were to pianists; he considered Annette 'the best pianist among my wives'). She took a special interest in Efrem's progress, and he was thrilled when the grande dame asked him to join her in a reading of

Beethoven's 'Kreutzer' Sonata. (Her student Isabelle Vengerova turned the pages, as she later reminded Efrem.) But playing in the Conservatory orchestra (he shared the first stand with Joseph Achron) afforded Efrem what he considered his most useful learning experience. Close scrutiny of sounds produced by the various instruments was the beginning of his self-taught mastery of orchestration.

Big names on the musical scene seemed to pop up at every turn. Anton Arensky studied scores in the Conservatory library, Camille Saint-Saëns played the organ part in his Third Symphony with Siloti's orchestra, and once on the Nevsky Prospect Efrem was approached by a bearded, bespectacled man in the immaculate uniform of an army officer. It was César Cui, and he asked Efrem to play a little piece that he had just written. 'We went to his house—and the little piece was the "Orientale," which I read with him at the piano,' Zimbalist remembered many years later.

Auer selected a full-size violin for Efrem from the Conservatory's stock. The finest it contained, it was nonetheless not a very distinguished instrument. He used it for the next five years. That second year Efrem studied Lalo's 'Symphonie Espagnole' and delighted Auer with his innovative fingering at letter D in the Scherzando, slurring the repeated notes in one bow, articulating them with finger substitutions instead of bow changes. 'Who showed you that?' 'Nobody.' 'Let me see it again!' Auer arranged for him to play the Lalo with the orchestra in Helsinki under Robert Kajanus, a friend of Auer's. Jean Sibelius attended the concert and asked Kajanus and his triumphant young soloist to dine with him. With this favorable introduction to the Finnish public, Efrem was invited to return annually during his student years.

A classmate introduced Efrem to his tympanist brother, Artur Strok. Artur played for the Italian Opera Company, whose productions were staged in the Conservatory's Grand Theater, and he would sneak Efrem into the orchestra pit to attend performances whenever he wished. Strok set up an extra chair next to his tympani, and when the lights were lowered for the conductor's entrance Efrem would quickly slip into it. From this ringside perch, the youngster feasted on the great voices of the age— Tamagno in *Otello*, Tetrazzini, Masini and Cavalieri. The very first opera he heard in the capital was *Faust*, with baritone Matteo Battestini, then teaching at the Conservatory, tenor Anselmi and Swedish soprano Sigrid Arnoldsen as Marguerite. His whole life he recalled the impression her entrance made on him when, flutelike, she negotiated the opening notes 'without the slightest hint of portamento.' Efrem attributed a strong influence on his phrasing to the 'incomparable' Battestini, whose bel canto style permanently affected his playing; throughout his career Zimbalist played with vocal lyricism and treated virtuosic passages as coloratura.

Efrem's friend Strok had opened a can of worms. Efrem became an opera addict, going to the Grand Theater every night—except when he was given a student pass for a concert or the Imperial Opera or Ballet. (Of all aspects of St. Petersburg's artistic life, ballet was the least popular among the general populace, but, as the Tsar's special love, was heavily subsidized. 'Only the intelligentsia cared for it. Which was good for me,' Zimbalist reminisced. 'Vast numbers of free tickets were always available to students.') Theater too became one of his loves. It didn't take long before his face was familiar to ticket-takers at the door of every hall in St. Petersburg, and he didn't have to do much talking to get himself admitted free of charge to almost any event he wanted to attend. But there were no free tickets for Chaliapin's performances. When the celebrated basso appeared at the Maryinsky Theater, Efrem had to spend his precious pocket money to gain admission.

Efrem relished exposure to works by long-established Russian masters like Glinka, Tchaikovsky and Dargomisky, and he heard many of Rimsky-Korsakov's lavish operas. Rimsky had a reserved box at the Imperial Theater and would take Efrem and his sons to matinees. A member of the famous 'Russian Five,' Rimsky introduced Efrem to compositions by its other members—Mussorgsky, Borodin, Cui, and the group's leader, Balakirev. Another composer whose works Efrem hadn't heard before was Wagner. He didn't even know the name until Karl Muck came to conduct an all-Wagner orchestral program.

St. Petersburg, with its plethora of artistic riches, brought with it nonstop excitement, but the constant late nights were bound to have an effect on the twelve-year-old Efrem, and his work soon began to suffer. (When asked in later years if so much theater-going interfered with his schooling, he quipped, 'On the contrary, my studies interfered with my theater-going.') Never given to hard practicing, Efrem found the prospect even less enticing when it meant arising early after a late night, and he got into the habit of sleeping until ten or eleven, just in time to get to class. Auer noticed the dropping off of Efrem's production level and at first was gentle in his chiding—a patience probably stemming from recognition of the difficulties of so young a boy living away from home. But the Professor's Magyar temperament soon snapped back to its volatile norm, and then Efrem got it in the neck: 'Out! And don't come back until you are properly prepared!' After such outbursts Efrem usually missed several classes before returning. In looking back he put it succinctly: 'I was a pain in the neck for Auer.' He had also stopped going to Nalbandian. The only thing about Auer's assistant that impressed Efrem was his spectacular staccato—Nalbandian astounded his students by playing Kreutzer's second etude in one machine-gun upbow, then played it again, downbow.

Auer's scarcely ecstatic annual accounts to Alexander Zimbalist continued through much of the remainder of Efrem's school days. As late as 1906, when the Canadian Kathleen Parlow enrolled in St. Petersburg, she reported being 'scandalized' by several of the boys in Auer's class: 'They were so talented and so lazy! Auer really worried, especially about Zimbalist.' But a diagnosis of idleness didn't reach the heart of the matter, namely that Efrem's active mind thrived on a variety of stimuli, not just violin playing. In looking back on this period of growth and learning, Zimbalist had mixed feelings. While he regretted Auer's disappointment, he felt that the only thing lost was an earlier honing of his fabulous virtuoso technique. In exchange he gained a musical acumen that was the groundwork for the uncommon diversity he demonstrated in his subsequent career.

Auer's interest in the welfare of his young student never flagged. He rated Efrem his most intelligent student and lived to enjoy the fruits of his disheartening labors in watching his worldwide success. And despite all, throughout his student years the boy's devotion to his master was constant. Unknown to Auer he would sneak into the Maryinsky to hear his ballet solos, accompanying the exquisite configurations of Kschessinska, Karsavina, Geltzer and Pavlova, in the creations of Petipa and Fokine. At these events, Auer, the Tsar's soloist, with violin in hand and wearing a flowing cape, would stride majestically down the center aisle to enter the pit. (The conductor was Riccardo Drigo, whose name Auer brought to a wider audience thanks to the transcriptions he made of several of his compositions, played and recorded by most of his students.) Auer was in fact unaware that Efrem virtually lived in the theater and was informed of this only years later when he had moved to the United States. By this time the two were close friends, and Zimbalist had the pleasure of being able to square an old account by affording the aging Auer every possible type of assistance.

In presenting his first star pupil, the Professor had a strange notion. When Efrem was judged ready to give his first publicized recital in the capital, Auer billed him as 'Arno' because, he said, 'No one will come to hear an Efrem Zimbalist play.' This billing turned into a joke — at least half the audience already knew 'Arno' by his true name. The concert was a big success, but the stage name was dropped.

Auer would invite Efrem to share his box at recitals given by visiting celebrities. It was in this way that Efrem heard the legendary performers of that era, beginning with Jan Kubelik, whose St. Petersburg debut sold out the day it was announced. As Ševčik's star pupil, dubbed 'the second Paganini,' he had been creating a furor wherever he went, and his arrival on the Russian scene was no different. He played the Paganini D major concerto on an orchestral program and then a few days later gave a recital with piano. With unassuming grace and immobile stance, Kubelik played in a manner that had never been heard before. His total mastery of finger dexterity in every conceivable diabolical conformation was nothing short of miraculous. He not only performed the fiendish Émile Sauret cadenza to the Paganini Concerto but even added his own embellishments to increase its technical demands. As Zimbalist recalled, 'He received only polite applause when he stepped onstage, since most people hadn't heard him play. After he finished the Paganini there was nearly a riot! He was the most perfect technical machine I have ever seen. In his double harmonic playing, for instance, there was absolutely not the slightest hint of difficulty or imperfection. And he knew the fingerboard so well that he never had to "prepare" notes, even in the highest registers. The very idea of his making a mistake was just unthinkable, quite out of the realm of possibility.' After the Sauret cadenza Efrem turned to a wide-eyed Auer. 'Professor, how does he do it?' 'I don't know,' came the disarming reply.

Two weeks later Auer took Efrem to hear another recital, this time by the great Pablo de Sarasate. It was a tragic contrast, the result of poor planning. Sarasate walked out from the wings to a house that was not even half filled: no violinist, no matter how preeminent or firmly entrenched, could follow Kubelik at that point in his meteoric career and expect to draw an equal crowd. From his box seat beside Auer, Efrem clearly saw the hurt that gripped the Spaniard's handsome features. As his accompanist perched tentatively behind the keyboard, Sarasate paced back and forth surveying the scene, in earnest contemplation, it seemed, of canceling the entire evening. Perhaps it was the thought of the bundle of rubles stashed in his case backstage that finally prompted his decision (he always insisted on being paid in cash, and in advance), for he lifted his violin and launched into the Mendelssohn Concerto, tossed off to perfection, very fast and with a wonderful elegance and lightness of style. A sonata followed, but it was after the intermission that the veteran master truly came into his own, in a series of his Spanish dances. 'I remember as if it were yesterday,' Zimbalist said in his nineties. 'The vitality, charming simplicity and character in his playing of these little masterpieces, and above all his rhythm, remain indescribable.' Sarasate offered the same encore Kubelik had given, the E major prelude by Bach. He performed it at a frantic clip, bowed graciously and never played in Russia again.

Eugène Ysaÿe came to St. Petersburg every season and left Efrem with the image of 'an immensely cultivated and grand style. He played just the way his teacher Vieuxtemps must have played.' Ysaÿe's usual concerts were sonata programs with Raoul Pugno, whose artistry and bulk matched his own. Zimbalist particularly remembered their playing of Beethoven's c minor sonata. It was at these duo-recitals that he was introduced to the French and Belgian works that were Ysaÿe staples and not otherwise heard in Russia at the time, such sonatas as the César Franck and Gabriel Fauré. Sometimes Ysaÿe was heard in the more virtuosic kind of violin recital, accompanied by his brother Theophile.

The most profound impression made on Efrem was by an artist who was later to become one of his dearest friends, Fritz Kreisler. When he played in St. Petersburg in the early 1900s, in his youthful prime, Kreisler was presented on the sort of mixed program that is looked at askance today: Serge Koussevitzky conducted an overture and accompanied Kreisler in a concerto by Russian composer Jules Conus; the remainder of the concert was with piano accompaniment. It was the first time Auer had heard Kreisler, and from the first note he and Efrem were transfixed. The Professor normally skipped going backstage after concerts but this time, overcome, he made an exception. Efrem followed and watched him enter the artist's room. The crowd parted deferentially as Auer, in a manner at once dignified and humble, went over to the perspiring artist, busy putting

away his instrument. Kreisler turned to meet him with characteristic kindness. Auer, hand outstretched, announced his name. Kreisler's face lit up in
delight, and he threw his arms into the air. 'Harriet!' he shouted excitedly
to his wife. 'Come, Harriet! Come here and meet the great Professor Auer!'

In November 1902, on one of his periodic tours of southern Russia,
Auer was accosted in Elizabethgrad by a man with a young son who had
journeyed several hundred miles from Odessa, where the lad was a student
at the Imperial Music School. The man, Saul Elman, said that Auer had
heard his son Mischa at school the year before and had raved about him,
which didn't ring a bell. He explained that in order to afford their trip from
Odessa he had been obliged to sell part of his wardrobe and concluded by
stating that he would gladly make any further sacrifice, as long as Auer
would accept the youngster into his class.

Auer agreed to an audition before moving on to his next concert stop,
and early the next morning, while packing his suitcase, he listened to
Mischa. The Professor's reaction was positive, and the Elmans made plans
to continue on to St. Petersburg where, on his return, Auer had once again
to smooth difficulties for the parents. He brought the full weight of his
influence to bear on the detested Interior Minister Vyatcheslav de Plehve
(who was assassinated in 1904), and the entire Elman family were granted
permission to reside in the capital. So it was that before Christmas break
Efrem met and heard the brilliant boy from Odessa. 'He played exquisitely
and had an absolutely extraordinary violinistic gift,' Zimbalist remembered. Mischa proved not only sterling competition but also the source of
some unforgettable memories.

One particular incident stuck in Efrem's mind, not only as an example of
Mischa's thrilling violin playing but also as a sample of Auer's mercurial
temperament. In class the new student played Joachim's arrangement of
Brahms's Hungarian Dance No. 7 in his inimitable manner. At its conclusion the Professor was unable to contain his enthusiasm. He bounded out of
his chair and, in what one supposes to have been a gesture of hearty
approval, punched Mischa forcefully in the midriff. An audible gasp escaped
the spectators' lips as the boy, taken completely by surprise, fell flat on his
back. Auer's attitude to all this, after ascertaining that the violin was undam-
aged (an Amati, gift of a royal patron), was utter indifference. If it didn't
seem to faze him the incident certainly made an impression on the class.

Elman was a conscientious, hardworking student from the first. Auer

assigned him the Paganini D major concerto. In its last movement a succession of descending tenths (involving a large stretch) initially seemed
impossible for Mischa's small hand. But so determined was he to master
them that he practiced until his hand ached. In class he proudly performed
the passage perfectly, with tears of pain running down his cheeks. Mischa
kept his nose to the grindstone in large part because his father was in constant attendance, and the boy was afraid to incur his wrath. Saul Elman
would escort his son to the door of Auer's studio every Tuesday and
Thursday, wait outside and, when the class ended, whisk Mischa back to
his practice room — the all-too-familiar stage parent. Owing to Saul's
rigidity, Mischa and Efrem never were close friends, but there was certainly
no ill-feeling between the pair, whom some observers saw as rivals. True,
the two couldn't have been more different. While the outstanding quality
of Efrem's playing at that time was its natural elegance, it was Mischa's
emotional fire that left no heart untouched.

Auer was only too happy when Grand Duke Alexander (the Tsar's
brother-in-law) requested that the talented boys come to the semi-myth-
ical Tsarkoe Selo to play for him at the Catherine Palace. So was Papa
Elman, but he wasn't invited. Mischa's normally solemn demeanor
changed noticeably aboard the special train sent to transport him and
Efrem the fifteen miles to the engagement. Wearing his customary cap and
a wide grin, he was free from parental supervision for the day and bubbled
over with jollity. A luxurious carriage awaited them at the station, and as
it conveyed them to the residence of the Grand Duke, they must have felt
as close to royalty as two young boys ever could.

In a room filled with lilies in tall Chinese vases, they were given a light
snack on arrival, with the promise of a more substantial repast later. Silver
finger bowls were provided, which led to an embarrassing blunder:
thinking that a gourmet cold consommé had been set down before them,
Mischa downed one before Efrem could stop him. But the concert went
well. Two of Tsar Nicholas's daughters were in attendance, the Grand Duke
expressed delight, and all seemed pleased. In a long, polished hall, beneath
huge chandeliers, a banquet awaited them, laid out in buffet style. Steering
clear of the finger bowls, Efrem and Mischa gorged on chicken, lemonade
and pastries. Soon it was time to leave, as they had been promised home
before nightfall. Back on their special train the boys mirthfully rehashed
the day's events. Mischa, as any twelve-year-old might be tempted to do, at

one point threw the window open and stuck his head out. The result was the immediate loss of his cap. He turned to Efrem, his face the picture of terror. 'Papa, he'll kill me! What will I do?' Efrem racked his brain while his companion sobbed uncontrollably; Mischa refused to return home without his cap. Their only resort, Efrem decided, was to seek Auer's advice.

At St. Petersburg station a droshky was waiting to take them home. Efrem asked the driver to take them instead to Auer's apartment. Their knock was answered by the Professor himself, scowling at the sight of Mischa's tear-stained face. 'Professor, may we please talk with you?' Efrem's tone was serious. 'Come in,' sighed Auer. He heard the tale of woe and, in a rare show of generosity, gave each boy a five-ruble gold piece.

A mad dash to a downtown haberdashery turned up an almost identical cap, and Papa Elman never did notice the difference.

CHAPTER 4

Student Life and Rimsky-Korsakov

(1903–1906)

Efrem successfully passed the end-of-year exams and was back in Rostov in June 1903. He had brought his friend Vitold Portugaloff along, and they looked forward to weeks of fun before Efrem was due in Kislovodsk. But it didn't turn out that way. Efrem toppled from his bicycle, injuring his right index finger. It jutted out at an angle and couldn't be moved. Maria was wise enough not to touch the damaged digit and rushed the boy to a nearby physician, who proved neither knowledgeable nor gentle, grabbing Efrem's hand and manipulating the finger back and forth. The boy shrieked and dropped to the floor in a dead faint. The pain was awful enough, but the diagnosis was worse. 'His finger is badly broken, Madame. The only thing to do is amputate.'

Maria wanted a second opinion, and luckily Alex arrived home for the midday meal with Vitold's father, a prominent St. Petersburg physician, who had come to Rostov to visit his son. He examined Efrem, advised against amputation and referred the anxious Zimbalists to an outstanding specialist near Kislovodsk. 'If anything can be done, Pavlov is the one to do it.' (The legendary Ivan Petrovich Pavlov would win a Nobel Prize in physiology in 1904.) On Portugaloff's advice Maria and Efrem took the next southbound train. Thirty minutes after their arrival at the surgery, Efrem emerged with a plaster cast from his fingertips to his elbow and orders not to have it removed for twelve weeks. 'Well, no practicing and no kürsaal concerts for you for a while,' said Maria, over a comforting glass of tea.

Three lazy months followed. Efrem passed the time in Kislovodsk by swimming, stepping up his already huge capacity for reading and meeting new friends. While he was taking the sun at his hotel one morning an attractive family approached. The man, a Mr. Schloezer, introduced himself, his wife and a delicately beautiful daughter, Tatiana, who looked in her early twenties. Music lovers, they looked forward all year to Efrem's summer performances and were shocked to hear of his accident. Concerts or no, they decided to get better acquainted, and Efrem accepted an invitation to dinner. It was during his visit to their charming home that he realized the daughter was *the* Tatiana Schloezer, the girl for whom Alexander Scriabin had left his wife and four children — a scandal on the tip of everyone's tongue. Of course, the virtuoso pianist turned composer had long been linked with the scandalous. When he took up with Tatiana Schloezer, he told his wife that she must accept the affair as her 'sacrifice to art.' Although Efrem was to strike up a good friendship with the Schloezers, he never did meet the controversial suitor.

Back in Rostov, with only weeks to get ready for his return to the capital, Efrem watched tensely as Dr. Portugaloff unveiled his arm. The healing of the finger was pronounced perfect, much to the family's elation, but rehabilitation was painfully slow. Back at school Efrem bumped into Joseph Achron and informed him of the summer's mishap and his apprehension, which increased in direct proportion to the proximity of Auer's classroom. The lesson began. With a feigned air of confidence, Efrem embarked on his assignment. Halfway through he noticed a smirk on the Professor's face and braced himself for a tongue-lashing liberally laced with sarcasm. Auer put his hand on the boy's shoulder: 'Fine. You have made good progress.' Efrem took his seat, catching Achron's knowing look and wink.

The established routine resumed its flow: classes, concerts, orchestra and chamber music practice, visits to the Rimsky-Korsakovs' home, ice skating parties, and the inevitable opera, ballet and theater attendance. There was one keen disappointment. The Tsarina had organized a charity concert at which the celebrated Adelina Patti, the Queen of Song, would sing. This most durable of all nightingales was reported still in magnificent voice, and Efrem desperately wanted to hear her, but the theater's doorman dared not sneak him in — every seat had been sold and, with the entire Imperial Family in attendance, he was being more conscientious than usual.

The highlight of 1903 was a pair of concerts planned by the Moscow Conservatory, in November, to mark the tenth anniversary of the death of

Tchaikovsky. The moving force behind this tribute was Vasili Safonov, director of the Conservatory. Safonov, respected as director, pianist and conductor, had succeeded Nicholas Rubinstein, the school's founder. Safonov wanted to include Tchaikovsky's violin concerto and looked to Auer to recommend a soloist. The Professor chose Efrem.

The Tchaikovsky Concerto had been written in spring 1878, in Switzerland. Tchaikovsky returned to St. Petersburg that fall and presented Auer with a printed copy, dedicated to him. Auer was somewhat miffed that he had never been consulted; in his own words, 'When I went through the score in detail, I felt [that] it called for a thorough revision since in various portions it is quite unviolinistic and not at all written in the idiom of the strings.' Auer didn't finish his promised revision until shortly before the composer's death. In the interim the concerto had been attempted then abandoned, leading to its 'unplayable' stigma. Adolf Brodsky, a second-echelon violinist, had persuaded Hans Richter to let him give its première with the Vienna Philharmonic, on 4 December 1881. Hanslick, Vienna's notorious critic, killed the performance in a few words: 'Tchaikovsky's violin concerto brings us face to face for the first time with a revolting idea: May there not also be musical compositions which we can hear stink?' Brodsky played the unfortunate piece again, in both Moscow and in London, where critics called it 'somnolent and wearisome.' Tchaikovsky, bitter toward Auer, insisted that the dedication be changed to Adolf Brodsky and had Auer's name expunged. When Auer finally published his 'improved' version in 1893, he himself began to play it and to teach it to all his students. Indeed, it was inseparably associated with them.

On the overnight train journey from the capital to Moscow Efrem studied the scores of Tchaikovsky's D major string quartet and his piano trio, which were to constitute the second part of the program. Safonov joined Efrem and cellist Brandukov in the trio. Special accolades were accorded this performance, which was repeated in several cities, adding to Efrem's rapidly widening reputation.

In summer 1904 Efrem met his new brother, Sascha, destined to be a cellist. In Kislovodsk the Schloezers welcomed Efrem back, and everyone was happy at the resumption of his performances. That summer, Alex and his older son discussed the political climate, which was far from tranquil, especially in St. Petersburg. Russia had been at war with Japan since February. In August St. Petersburg reverberated to a three-hundred-gun salute, marking the birth of the long-awaited Tsarevich Alexis and vividly reminding every citizen of the continuing strength of the monarchy.

The tenth anniversary of the death of the revered founder of the St. Petersburg Conservatory, Anton Rubinstein, was observed that autumn by a concert of his orchestral works in the Grand Theater. Auer, who had been a friend of Rubinstein's, thought his violin concerto should be included. He had once played the piece, but it had since fallen into obscurity. To refresh his memory on its merits, the Professor brought a copy into class and called on Elman to read it. Notwithstanding his enormous talent, young Mischa was not a proficient reader, and Auer turned to Efrem. 'You try it,' he said. Efrem's reputation for sight reading stood him in good stead, and Auer assigned him the Rubinstein Concerto. After the concert Rubinstein's widow expressed particular appreciation of his playing, saying how much she wished Antoscha could have heard it. (The first and second themes from this concerto were summoned to mind by Zimbalist in his nineties, a remarkable instance of his musical memory, since in the intervening seventy-five years he had neither heard nor played the piece.)

Also that season Efrem performed Lalo's 'Symphonie Espagnole' at a benefit concert organized by Glazunov. Two legendary figures joined him on the program: Feodor Chaliapin and Josef Hofmann. 'Hofmann was No. 1 on the Russian concert platform then, because he had been a protégé of Rubinstein's,' Zimbalist recalled. That meeting with the twenty-nine-year-old pianist was the beginning of a friendship lasting fifty-two years.

Meanwhile school continued as usual, and at one of the few sessions to which Liadov showed up, he assigned the class a thorny counterpoint exercise. Efrem, unable to do it, excused himself and went out into the hall, where a lanky youth with blond hair was leaning against the wall. 'Sergei, can you help me?' he begged. With the completed exercise hidden under his coat he reentered the 'classroom under the clock.' Sitting beside him was his old pianist friend from Rostov, recently enrolled in St. Petersburg, Eugene Lutsky, who was also having trouble with the exercise. 'Copy this,' Efrem volunteered. Efrem was the first called on to bring his work up for correction. Liadov pored over it for a while, then growled, 'Good — ten.' Lutsky's turn came after many intervening students. With a mere glance Liadov snarled, 'I've seen this before — zero.' 'What a memory,' Zimbalist laughed later. (The lanky blond who had saved Efrem's skin was freshman Sergei Prokofiev.)

But the pattern of his education was about to be rudely shattered. In December 1904 the Russian army was soundly defeated by the Japanese at Port Arthur. Tsar Nicholas's popularity plummeted, especially in Jewish circles and among the country's student youth. The revolutionary fervor felt throughout the country heightened to a frenzy after the Tsar's troops opened fire on thousands of workers, women and children, led by the young priest Father George Gapon, who had converged on the Winter Palace to present a petition. About a hundred died and many more were wounded. Although the Tsar wasn't at the palace that icy January morning, he was blamed and nicknamed 'Bloody Nicholas.'

Auer's reaction was understandable, considering his background and loyalties. As court soloist throughout three reigns, he knew on which side his bread was buttered: he was an arch conservative and staunch imperialist. In his autobiography *My Long Life in Music*, he describes events thus: 'The students [at the Conservatory] followed the example set by the university students throughout the country. They elected a committee and declared a political protest strike. A few among the professors sympathized with the students and stopped giving their courses; others, on the contrary, came regularly and attended to their duties, paying no attention to the fact that only a fraction of their pupils assembled in the classroom. As for myself, who wished to have nothing to do with politics, I belonged to the latter class, which was regarded with suspicion by the strikers, who picketed the stairs and halls leading to the classrooms.'

While the military were barricading the streets, inside the Conservatory Efrem was named corridor sentry. Although not an admitted activist, Efrem was involved; a senior student and gentle rebel, his assistance was sought in dissuading students from attending Auer's class. Several sentries threw stink bombs into classrooms, making attendance impossible.

A committee comprised of the directorate of the Russian Musical Society and the Art Council charged Rimsky-Korsakov with the difficult job of settling differences with agitated pupils. Rimsky sympathized with their grievances; he considered director Burnhardt tactless and cowardly. After a few weeks he wrote a public letter to the daily paper *Rus*, taking the committee to task for not understanding the students and arguing that the existence of the committee itself was unnecessary since the students' wish for self-government was justified. In his autobiography Rimsky wrote, 'If one were to believe the conservatives among the professors and the direc-

torate of the Russian Musical Society I myself was possibly the very head
of the revolutionary movement among the student youth.'

A subsequent committee meeting degenerated into name-calling on
both sides and resulted in the dismissal of both Burnhardt and Rimsky-
Korsakov. In protest, faculty members Glazunov, Liadov, Essipoff,
Verzhbilovich and Blumenfeld resigned and the Conservatory had, finally,
to close its doors. There was a loud clamor of public outrage combined
with support for Rimsky-Korsakov. Students, with Glazunov's help, determined to stage a performance of Rimsky's new opera *Katschei besmertni*
(Katschei the Deathless) at Kommissarzhevskaya's Theater in March 1905.
Glazunov agreed to conduct. During one orchestra rehearsal, he was
stymied by the students' difficulty in playing a section in 5/8. The composer was consulted. 'It's easy, my children,' he told them. 'Just think of my
name: Rim—sky—Kor—sa—kov, Rim—sky—Kor—sa—kov.' His
suggestion solved the problem. Efrem developed a fascination with 5/8—
few of his mature compositions escaped a section in this meter.

'Rimsky always appeared very solemn,' Zimbalist reminisced. 'But once,
while I was having supper at his home, he came in laughing loudly—it
was the only time I ever saw him laugh. He said he had just talked to
Andreiev, the conductor of a famous balalaika orchestra. Andreiev had
performed for the Tsar and told him that in *Katschei* Rimsky had used the
balalaika. The Tsar was very fond of balalaika music; it was his reply that
made Rimsky laugh so much: "Well, it's about time!"'

By October 1905 the country was paralyzed, and instability at the
Conservatory continued. For two months early in 1906, Efrem replaced the
second violinist in the Grand Duke of Mecklenburg-Strelitz's private
string quartet. Unaccustomed to playing second violin, he was reprimanded for counting rests by tapping his foot, but he otherwise enjoyed
what time he spent rehearsing and performing at the Grand Duke's palace,
near St. Petersburg.

Meanwhile many students took private lessons with their teachers and,
under Glazunov's supervision, spring examinations were held. But the
school did not fully reopen until fall 1906, when Rimsky-Korsakov and
the rest of the faculty returned. In his autobiography Auer commented
on the new director, Glazunov, who had remained neutral during the con-
flict: 'A man of open and generous disposition, [he] later leaned [toward]

the side of the students, which won him boundless popularity. [For] myself, grown old under the ancient regime, I made no sacrifice to my convictions, [which] awakened the antipathy of some and... the esteem of others.' Any sympathy Glazunov may have harbored for the Marxists had tarnished by 1917; a few years later his disenchantment prompted him to flee to Paris, where he died an unhappy and disillusioned man.

Whatever form Efrem's involvement in the student uprising took, Auer's belief as to its extent resulted in a very painful experience for the sixteen-year-old. Once things settled down under Glazunov's pacifying hand, Efrem, violin in hand, opened the door to Auer's studio just before 2 p.m. on a Thursday. One report has him wearing a red shirt. The students, assembled inside, readied themselves for the storm. 'Oh, and what are you doing here?' Auer asked in an offhand tone.

'Professor, I've come to have my lesson.'

'You are no longer a student at this school,' thundered Auer and he rushed over to throw the terrified youth out. The door slammed. Efrem stood frozen in the dark space between the double doors. Sounds of a violin being tuned mocked him as he stepped out into the hallway and headed dejectedly toward the central staircase. He had descended only a few steps when the full impact hit him, and he collapsed in tears. But there was a footfall on the stairs, a hand laid gently on his shoulder, then a compassionate voice: 'Fima, what's wrong?'

Efrem's blurry eyes made out the beloved bespectacled face and long beard. As Rimsky-Korsakov listened to the details of the incident, his anger mounted. 'Come with me,' he said, taking Efrem by the hand and leading him downstairs. A clear demonstration followed of the high regard in which the great Rimsky-Korsakov was held. He marched into Glazunov's office and confronted him. 'Sascha,' he said, 'See that Efrem is reinstated.' Glazunov nodded. It was as simple as that. But the coup de grace was delivered in the hall outside the office when Auer, too, came to talk to Glazunov. He saw Rimsky and came over to pay his respects, completely ignoring the weeping lad beside him.

'Nikolai Andreyevich, how *are* you?' he inquired with both hands extended. His approach met with the back of Rimsky-Korsakov's coat.

'Come, Fima,' said the soothing voice, 'let's go home.'

Rimsky put his arm around Efrem and led him away. Auer, with his hands still outstretched, was nonplussed. But when the reinstated student entered his studio the following Tuesday the Professor was all congeniality. Not the slightest mention of the affair was ever made, and lessons continued as if nothing had happened, except that Efrem was more conscientious, a happy outgrowth in view of his not-too-distant graduation.

CHAPTER 5

Prizewinning Graduate

(1906–1907)

One day in his last year of studies at the Conservatory, Efrem was practicing before a lesson when the door opened to admit Glazunov and,
behind him, Felix Blumenfeld, the distinguished piano professor.
Glazunov was carrying a bulky manuscript.

'Good to see you practicing, Efrem,' he said, his eyes twinkling. 'Please
do forgive the disturbance.' His sentences had a way of trailing off into
near inaudibility and a soft chuckle. 'I've just finished the first draft of a
concerto for Auer, and would not like him to see it until I'm satisfied that
the piece has some value. So I wonder if you would be good enough to
read it through for me? Professor Blumenfeld will play an accompaniment
from the orchestral score.' Soft chuckle.

It was not just that Glazunov remembered Tchaikovsky's experience
with Auer. Underneath his kindly warmth there lurked an insecurity and
veiled unhappiness, from which he periodically escaped by drinking;
during these bouts his office door was locked for days, and empty bottles
on the doorstep were promptly replenished by sympathetic staff. Finally
Glazunov would emerge, immaculately proper.

Efrem sight-read the difficult concerto as accurately as he could.
Glazunov, puffing on his ever-present cigar, expressed satisfaction,
inquired into its violinistic feasibility and made a few changes. A short time
later he presented the work to Auer. The entire violin class attended its first
performance, given by their Professor in the Grand Theater with the composer conducting. The performance was not without incident. After the
opening theme and first episode there occurs a section in fancifully bowed

sixteenth notes that lasts for a full page and has become one of the literature's notorious technical hurdles. The difficulty lies not only in the
physical endurance required to maintain the brilliance of the bowing
pattern, but also in memorizing the passage's intricate twists and turns in
obbligato support of the woodwind melody. Auer foundered on one of
these florid maneuvers, and the whole thing ground to an embarrassing
halt. Always in command, he appeared not the slightest taken aback. Violin
and bow in his left hand, he grandly reached into his vest pocket and withdrew a gold watch attached to a long, ornate chain. He studied its face for
some moments, then mounted the podium to find a starting place on
Glazunov's score. The music resumed. But the identical trap snared Auer
again, and it was only after a second consultation with his timepiece that
the unlucky Professor was able to vault the hurdle. When the concerto
ended the composer was much applauded and Auer soundly hissed,
although witness Sergei Prokofiev believed this to be for political reasons,
not because of the memory slips.

Auer never played the Glazunov Concerto again. In fact, he had Efrem
learn it to replace him in its Moscow première. It was a calculated move.
Times had changed, and an almost feudal rivalry between St. Petersburg
and Moscow musical circles had replaced the amicability of the
Rubinsteins' era. 'The performance was a big fiasco,' Zimbalist recalled.
'They hated the concerto. Auer was very clever in not going himself!'

But he continued to teach the piece. By this time Canadian Kathleen
Parlow had joined Auer's class, and he taught it to her too. She was taking
the required piano course that Efrem continued to shirk. Although Efrem
couldn't see submitting to lessons, he sometimes settled into a practice
studio and experimented with chords and progressions. Often these
sessions exceeded the amount of time he spent on violin practice. Parlow
told a humorous story about his piano playing: 'Once I was to play the
Tchaikovsky Concerto for my lesson, when in walked a tall and very stout
gentleman. There was instant silence and the boys stood. Auer beckoned to
me to come forward. Mr. Glazunov had found some free time, Auer said,
and had come to hear me play *his* concerto. Fortunately I had obeyed
orders and memorized it. As there was no score available Zimbalist sat
down to play the accompaniment as best he could from memory. Evidently
his efforts did not satisfy the composer. Out of the corner of my eye I saw

that huge person sit down on the piano bench and gradually push "Zim" from it without missing a note.'

In his last year, in preparation for graduation, Efrem was assigned two great warhorses of the repertoire, the Brahms and Tchaikovsky concertos. These, together with the Glazunov, became his signature tunes.

Auer had also taught his revision of the Tchaikovsky to Elman, who played it with brilliant success in his 1904 Berlin debut and, in March 1905, in London. After that Mischa didn't return to St. Petersburg except for a short visit. Although he worked with Auer for two more summers, in Ostend and London, Elman never felt he owed the Professor any appreciable debt for his successes. On the contrary, he accurately credited his scintillating debuts with fanning Auer's reputation into full flame. Its radiance was further enhanced a few years later with Efrem's emergence into international prominence. The stream of foreign students into Auer's St. Petersburg class swelled, becoming a torrent stemmed only by the 1917 revolution. Aside from Parlow these foreigners included Americans Eddy Brown, Richard Burgin, Max Rosen, Thelma Given, Roderick White, and Ruth Ray, the English Isolde Menges (first to record the Brahms Concerto) and the brilliant Dane, Cecilia Hansen.

Zimbalist recalled with a happy smile one chamber music afternoon that last year at the Rimsky-Korsakov home when he found himself wandering down a corridor and stopping before 'the door,' which was invariably shut. Unaccountably, it now stood open, revealing Rimsky-Korsakov's dimly lit inner sanctum, and Efrem slipped across the threshold and made for the desk, where his eyes fell on a manuscript page dotted with notes in a meticulous hand. At the other end lay a pile of completed pages and what looked like a title sheet. Having seen all there was to see, he rejoined his friends, who were impatient to play a Haydn quartet. 'Volodya, what is "Coq d'Or"?' queried Efrem. 'Why, I haven't a clue,' was the puzzled reply. 'Why do you ask?'

Efrem told him he had seen the name on the title page in his father's study. Volodya and Andrei exchanged concerned glances. 'Fima,' Volodya said tensely, 'don't breathe a word of this! No one but Father goes into that room. We never know a thing about his latest works until he announces them. How lucky you were not to get caught. Now don't forget, keep your mouth shut.'

Rimsky never heard a performance of *Le Coq d'Or*, his last opera. But
when Zimbalist finally heard it, years later in New York, he gave full expression to his feelings by writing 'Coq d'Or Fantasy' on themes from the opera.

Efrem was extremely busy. Joseph Achron had graduated at the end of
the previous year, and Efrem had taken over his concertmaster's chair. He
kept up independent harmonic and theoretical studies and, with or
without Liadov, was increasingly drawn toward composition. It was here,
in St. Petersburg, that he began work on his Op. 1, a violin piece intended
for Professor Auer. A warmth was developing in Efrem's relationship with
Auer that would grow right up to the older man's death, but clashes were
inevitable between such different natures: Efrem's imaginative, susceptible
to new influences and easily seduced away from long hours of practice;
Auer's purposeful, self-disciplined and inflexibly authoritarian.

As that graduation year unfolded Efrem played more often in class than
ever before, and there were many extra lessons at Auer's home followed by
suppers, during which they put their heads together in some hard discus-
sions about what should happen after graduation. Auer considered Berlin
the logical launching point for his career: Mischa had started with a recital
there; then, as a respectful gesture, he had played for Auer's teacher,
Joachim. Successes had followed in London, and the young artist was now
well on his way. It seemed a tried and true plan, and Auer set about making
similar arrangements for his next star presentation. He wrote to Joachim,
telling him of his high hopes for Efrem.

Meanwhile Efrem took the preparations for his graduation in stride,
save for the realization, a scant week before final examinations, that he
would be expected to pass the long-deferred piano proficiency test in order
to graduate. He had never taken a single piano lesson, but he got hold of a
book of Beethoven and barricaded himself in a practice room, coming to
grips with a few selected pages. At the examination he could barely play the
scales requested of him. Quizzed as to what he *could* play, he announced
the first movement of Beethoven's F major sonata and played it very
acceptably, passing the test. The fact that he was able to pull this off is
testimony not only to his musicianship but also to his natural aptitude for
the keyboard. His piano technique in later years, while not of virtuoso
caliber, was always expert enough to be the source of much pleasure both
to him and to those whom he accompanied.

The violinistic requirements for graduating involved playing a concerto with the orchestra and a recital with piano. Since Efrem was also a contender for the prestigious Anton Rubinstein Prize (awarded once every three years), the requirements were much more severe. First he would play for the professors and a small audience of musical celebrities, who would determine his eligibility. Auer suggested the Glazunov Concerto and Christian Sinding's 'Suite' in a minor, a favorite of his.

This first round was in the smaller of the Conservatory's two halls, used for chamber music performances. Glazunov, pleased to have his concerto included, offered to spend a few hours on it with Efrem and ended up playing the accompaniment at the performance, where he demonstrated his dry sense of humor. Just before the second section a simple modulation takes place to prepare for D-flat major, while the violin resolves from an open G to an A-flat. Aware of Efrem's well-known propensity for holding long bows, the composer decided to play a joke. Embarking on the appoggiatura open G, Efrem was startled by a succession of unfamiliar chords that meandered in and out of several keys before finally resolving to the dominant of D-flat, as written. When Efrem turned toward him Glazunov was grinning mischievously. (Zimbalist considered the published piano reduction of the score—not actually Glazunov's doing— 'very poor.' He worked out an improved one, which he often used.)

Rimsky attended the performance with his friend V. V. Stasoff, a popular writer on art and music. Both were hearing Glazunov's concerto for the first time and were enthusiastic about the piece and about Efrem. Stasoff put his hand on the young soloist's head and announced, 'You are going to be a great man!'

Efrem had gained the approval he needed. Auer could now turn their full attention to perfecting the Tchaikovsky as well as the Brahms Concerto, which had been selected for the Rubinstein Prize second round and the Berlin debut. The latter stimulated an increase in the amount of time Efrem spent with the violin, but it didn't lessen his abiding dislike of practicing, and he never put in nearly the hours that one might expect, given the importance of the demands placed on him. Their very seriousness triggered in him a laissez-faire indifference, and indeed the rest of his life was characterized by a mildly hostile attitude toward the pretensions and trappings of a public career. He shunned the histrionics of his profession and was occasionally criticized by those who failed to appreciate his cheerful and enviable philosophy: 'Let's see what happens,' it whispered, 'after all, whatever the outcome, it's not the end of the world.'

By the time graduation finally arrived all the Zimbalist hallmarks of style and sound were firmly established: a golden tone produced by one of the smoothest and most elegant bow-arms ever drawn, the brilliant fluency of left-hand passagework and, above all, a patrician nobility of interpretation. On the urging of Auer, Artur Nikisch attended the Brahms Concerto performance. Afterward Nikisch's mesmeric eyes bore right through Efrem: 'You played wonderfully,' he said. 'We must work together in Leipzig.'

Eighteen graduating participants took part in the final public concert in the Grand Theater; Efrem's performance of the Tchaikovsky was viewed by many as a revelation. The jury's unanimous verdict was boldly scrawled across their report: 'Incomparable.' A newspaper reviewer declared, 'One would be hard pressed to find in Europe the equal of this seventeen-year-old fully ripened master.'

GRADUATION PROGRAM, ST. PETERSBURG, 1907

The Rimsky-Korsakovs were among the backstage crowd, scarcely concealing their pride, and Glazunov, who seemed particularly moved. He squeezed Efrem's hands and kissed him on both cheeks; on returning home he sat down to pen a note to Auer congratulating him on Efrem's prowess and stating his opinion of the performance: 'A colossal talent. Phenomenal musical feeling. His interpretation was inspired, full of mood. His playing made a shattering impression on me, beyond comparison. Words fail me.'

Auer's reply: 'I agree with the Director's opinion, but I must say that during the last two years he missed a great many lessons, which probably accounts for his achievements.' (Many years later Zimbalist was given these notes.)

At commencement Efrem was awarded the gold medal for violin playing and the Rubinstein Prize for distinguished studentship. Monetarily the Rubinstein award amounted to 1,200 rubles, which Efrem offered to his father. Alex refused it, suggesting that Efrem use it for his career in whatever way was advisable. The next morning Efrem went to see Glazunov. 'This is the most money I have ever seen in my life. What should I do with it?' Glazunov smiled and didn't hesitate in his advice: 'Professor Auer told me you are going to Berlin—good. It shouldn't cost you more than half the amount to have an agent rent a hall and make all the publicity arrangements. As to the remainder: you heard Kubelik when he played here. Just at present it seems to be the fashion to take a few lessons with his teacher Ševčik.' Soft chuckle. 'Now don't take this the wrong way, and above all don't tell Auer, but I think that such a course might enhance your technique. There should be plenty of money to spend a month or two in Pisek with Ševčik, before going to Berlin. And one last thing,' he added fondly, 'if everything goes as well as we all expect, you will be blessed with a wonderful career. If not, there is always a job waiting for you here as a professor.'

CHAPTER 6

Luftpause in Alt Wien

(SUMMER 1907)

Efrem took Glazunov's advice. His independence long since absolute, and not relishing the prospect of a long, hot train ride to Rostov, Efrem instead headed straight for the Portugaloffs' summer place at Viipuri, a little port on the gulf of Finland, to rest up for a few weeks. Mid-July found a refreshed Efrem steaming out of St. Petersburg's railroad depot, this time heading southwest and eventually crossing the Prussian border at Braniewo. Little did he know he would not visit his native land again until 1909, and thereafter only at brief, widely spaced intervals. Efrem crossed the Czech border during the night and arrived at Prague's central terminal next morning. Already a confident traveler, he quickly exchanged rubles for Czech currency, bought a ticket and settled himself on the next train for Pisek, a bucolic village where Otokar Ševčik, the great violin pedagogue of Prague, owned a summer house.

Efrem quickly established himself in the village, the sound of scales and general violinistic drudgery drifting from almost every window. He found his way to the Ševčik home, where an assistant assigned him an appointment with the master. Back at his boardinghouse Efrem was served a simple supper, which he ate to the accompanying chorus of would-be Kubeliks who practiced right through the dinner hour and late into the night, when a weary Efrem finally laid his head on the pillow.

Ševčik, a bachelor, was totally dedicated to his teaching duties. The venerable professor's grim, unadorned studio at the Prague Conservatory was described by students as resembling a waiting room at a railroad station. His Pisek studio was equally drab; it contained no furniture except for an upright piano, a chair by the keyboard and a music stand. The walls were completely bare aside from a large portrait of his friend, violinist Willy Hess. On top of the piano was a dusty violin case, permanently open, housing Ševčik's modest instrument. But unlike Auer, he never took a violin into hand at lessons and was customarily seated at the battered upright, thumping out an accompaniment to a concerto or rendering chordal support for his volumes of exercises. The format of their teaching also differed. Auer almost invariably taught by the class, whereas ninety-nine percent of Ševčik's lessons were private, with only the occasional master class when an end-of-year student recital was in the works.

From 7 a.m. (the hour he preferred to teach his most promising pupils, to get them used to performing at peak level under disadvantageous conditions) until late in the evening, Ševčik drove his students. He allowed himself an hour at midday to eat—his doctor had him on a diet of plain vegetarian fare—and walk along the river. Apart from this the only break from his grueling schedule was on Saturday evenings, when he put on his snappiest attire and, surrounded by disciples, relaxed at the Hotel Dvořáček, discussing his students' strengths and weaknesses at great length. The name of his most famous graduate, Jan Kubelik, always figured prominently. Outside of these weekend discourses Ševčik was sparing of words and quietly spoken. He displayed impatience in his studio only when a student was suspected of laziness—something he could never condone. He used a stout walking stick to emphasize his disapproval. 'Again!' he'd bark, giving the stand a sharp whack.

Although hordes of hopefuls flocked to him, the 'Ševčik craze' proved limiting. Certain of the pedagogue's products did, undeniably, become fine musicians. Erica Morini's playing always evidenced a natural and irreproachable musicianship, and Kubelik himself was a more cultivated musician than his pyrotechnical reputation has credited him. But the majority of Ševčik's students, subjected to endless dry technical exercises, emerged with a lopsided emphasis on left-hand dexterity and hampered by a small, underdeveloped tone, distinctly short on expressive content. Somewhere along the way, all musical feeling seemed to have been drained out. Ultimately the Kubelik technical ideal could not be equaled. The closest runner-up, Jaroslav Kocian, achieved considerable technical command and was billed 'the second Kubelik' on vaudeville tours of the United States.

Ševčik received Efrem with special interest (Glazunov had sent a letter;

they had met when Ševčik taught at the Kiev Conservatory). Efrem launched into the Glazunov Concerto, and Ševčik, unfamiliar with it, elected not to tackle the piano part. He sat and listened, making no comment until the end of the piece. Then he announced his verdict: 'You have a certain amount of facility, which serves you in such works as the concerto you just played. But, do you play *Paganini*?' Efrem admitted to very little Paganini in his repertoire. 'That is where I can help you. Kubelik practiced ten hours daily to acquire his Paganini technique. You could do it in six.' Ševčik, recognizing in Efrem his most talented raw material since Kubelik, even offered to waive his lesson fees. While Efrem put away his violin, Ševčik directed him to a shop in the village that sold his authorized method. He prescribed the manual on double stopping, the fourth volume. 'You don't need the first three volumes. After a few days of practice, come back and see me.' What stuck in Efrem's head was the part about six hours a day of practice. Knowing his work habits one can imagine his horror.

Efrem dutifully bought the prescribed volume, and after lunch he retired to his room to begin work. At first he was struck by the cleverness behind the exercise patterns, but his interest quickly flagged, and that night, rest came with difficulty; he tried to read himself to sleep with some Dostoyevsky but found his mind enmeshed in a morass of Ševčik fingering formations. Next morning, he made six hours of practice his goal, but after lunch it became clear that his fingers, while supple and graceful, lacked endurance. His hand ached, and he began to wonder if he was practicing correctly. 'You're doing fine,' Ševčik told him at the next day's lesson. 'Don't worry about the aches and pains. Your arm will get used to it.' The old adage that it's not doing any good unless it hurts!

Ševčik continued finger drills and added Paganini's 'Le Streghe,' packing Efrem on his way with a description of the magnificent impression Kubelik always made with the piece. Efrem found it a challenge but had it under his belt in a few days (later in his career he often played and taught Kreisler's version of it). Ševčik responded to his continued complaints of pain by showing him a half-dozen ways to work on left-hand pizzicato. This was the last straw, and by the end of the second week, Efrem's fingertips were sore, his arm was killing him and, worst of all, he seemed to have completely lost the easy facility he had counted on as a birthright. Disconsolately he pondered his best move. Escape he must, and the looming Berlin concert would be the excuse. He told Ševčik that, while he had benefited from even so short a period of lessons, he must leave for Berlin to make arrangements for the debut. The master was surprised, but when they shook hands he wished Efrem well and a snapshot was taken. Efrem wondered what Auer might have said of the whole episode — had he known about it.

Efrem hoped that a complete rest would heal his offended digits, and so he packed his bags, paid his bills and left for Vienna — the perfect place for an enriching escape from responsibility. There his German studies stood him in good stead, and he hired a carriage and went straight to the opera house to hear *Die Meistersinger*, the famous prelude of which he had heard in St. Petersburg. Now, the entire masterpiece thrilled him like nothing he could remember; his only complaint was that Felix Weingartner took the prelude too fast.

Happy as a lark, Efrem stretched his schillings to cover a full month's stay in the city, whose glittering attractions delighted him at every turn. His daily routine was not very different from the one he had kept in St. Petersburg. He rose late and spent daylight hours reading or wandering around town, treating himself to Viennese pastries and other delicacies. The fascinating shops displayed everything from elegant clothing to exotic fruits he had never seen. Sometimes in the afternoons he visited art galleries but invariably, at dusk, he made a beeline for the theater to hear opera or Viennese operetta, his newfound passion — such bonbons as *Ein Walzertraum*, *Der Tapfere Soldat* and others by Oscar Straus and the like. He also found time to attend concerts; Alfred Reisenauer's playing of Shülz-Evler's 'Blue Danube' was a stunner.

This carefree schedule soon cured Efrem's overexerted musculature. After three weeks he took his violin from its spot behind an armchair and rattled through Sinding's 'Suite' without the slightest effort — his fingers had returned to their usual suppleness. It was time to get back on track for the Berlin debut, but he went slowly, practicing no more than half an hour a day, with a day off every now and again to be sure not to overdo things.

By mid-September 1907 Efrem's funds had dwindled. The agent's fee covering rental of the hall and advertising in Berlin had been paid by Glazunov's office, but living expenses there had to be considered. Like it or not, the state of the exchequer dictated an end to his pleasant Viennese existence. Efrem allowed himself two more evenings at the Carl Theater. Then, gathering together his worldly goods, he departed for the German capital.

CHAPTER 7

Promise Fulfilled: Berlin

(FALL 1907)

Following an impressive trade fair in 1896, Berlin had grown to a city of close to two million residents and had also accelerated its artistic pace, considering itself since the turn of the century equal in musical importance to London, Paris and Vienna, the more established leaders. Certainly many musical events were presented by the Royal Orchestra and the Royal Opera, both under Richard Strauss, and the newer Berlin Philharmonic which, under Artur Nikisch's direction, was possibly the best orchestra in the world. Recital halls, too, resounded constantly to the tones of the most celebrated artists on the circuit. On the concert advertisement page of the *Berliner Tageblatt* the announcement of Efrem's appearance was flanked by such names as Leopold Godowsky, Emil von Sauer, Henri Marteau and Erno von Dohnányi playing sonatas, Elena Gerhardt and Artur Nikisch in lieder recital, and Nicolai Medtner in a program of his own works. A raft of local names, too, were advertised in various performance formats — and all this to take place over a period of just days!

Berlin was, for that time, a very modern city. Many considered it the most American of all European cities. Yet there lingered in its atmosphere a stubborn vestige of small-town narrow-mindedness, reflected in its press. Berlin had no newspaper that ranked with the *Times* of London, the *New York Times* or *Le Figaro*. Still, at the outset of one's career it was deemed important to receive the sanction of Berlin critics.

Soon after his arrival Efrem was ensconced, on Auer's recommendation, at the Hotel Sans Souci, a favorite of traveling artists. In the morning, he was awakened by violin sounds very close at hand. He clapped his ear to the wall and heard 'a wonderful musician with unbelievable facility and beautiful tone' playing in the next room, practicing two of Auer's Beethoven transcriptions, 'Turkish March' and 'Chorus of the Dervishes.' On his way to breakfast, Efrem passed the concièrge's desk. 'Excuse me, but could you please tell me who is registered in Room 43?'

'Herr Enesco, sir.'

Efrem didn't know the name, but Georges Enesco's playing, which continued nonstop throughout the day, deeply affected him. (He soon learned the extent of the Romanian's reputation in Europe and was sorry they never actually met.)

After breakfast Efrem presented himself at the Hermann Wolff offices, the management agency that had been engaged on his behalf. Wolff himself, a musician and critic turned impresario, had died in 1902; his flourishing business was taken over by a sister, who had previously helped out at the box office and seen to the artists' accommodations. It was she that Efrem met. A dumpling of a woman, severely dressed, Frau Wolff's appearance belied her reputation as Europe's top manager, but her no-frills speech and way of fixing one directly in the eye upheld it.

Frau Wolff's general plan for Berlin debuts, including the one that had launched Mischa Elman three years earlier, was a debut in two parts. 'In the world's musical capital,' she explained, 'a young newcomer from out of town cannot expect to draw any kind of a house without first passing muster with the local experts.' This august body consisted of the cream of musical society (if not musical, then at least social) and of course the critics. The plan was to give a pre-debut recital for them, followed ten days later by the official debut, hopefully to a packed house attracted by intervening favorable press notices. The intimate Bechsteinsaal had been booked with Rubinstein Prize funds for Monday, 28 October; here Efrem, with a pianist supplied by Frau Wolff, would play for the bigwigs. Wolff had already collaborated with the Philharmonic Society in jointly sponsoring his official debut on 7 November; at this, Efrem would appear with the Philharmonic on the stage of the Beethovensaal under the baton of Ernst Kunwald in a blockbuster program, comprising both the Glazunov and Brahms concertos and Sinding's 'Suite,' seldom heard in Germany at that time.

Efrem signed an agreement, and Frau Wolff promised to arrange for an accompanist. 'I'm glad you arrived in plenty of time,' she said. Efrem mentioned that he also intended to play for Joachim. 'In that case,' she shook her head solemnly, 'you didn't arrive early enough. Dr. Joachim died in August.' Efrem had keenly anticipated the honor of meeting him, and this news cast a brief pall over things. (When Efrem left St. Petersburg Auer had given him letters of introduction to Joachim, Paderewski and several other influential friends; fearing further disappointment, Efrem now threw them all out.) But the delivery of a warmly inscribed photo from Rimsky-Korsakov soon lifted his spirits, as did his first exposure to a world-renowned violin shop, Hammig and Sons, Berlin's biggest violin dealership.

All the trappings of the trade greeted Efrem on entering—from the delicious whiff of solvents and varnishes to the high ceilings and wooden beams that make a violin's tone sound richer. The inner sanctum was just visible from the glass-topped counter, its workbenches strewn with fascinating tools. The 'violin shop' remains a captivating enclave; then as now, the proprietors of these unique establishments, adept at playing on musicians' heartstrings, are capable of making more 'happy marriages' or breaking more hearts than any matchmaker.

Efrem set his case down on the counter and was presently greeted by the excessively rotund and jolly Walter Hammig himself. The new set of strings Efrem requested were handed over; as he put them away Hammig peered into Efrem's case. Efrem took out his violin, still the same mediocre instrument of Conservatory years, and began playing to test the bow hair. Hammig's eyes popped open. From Efrem's pronunciation he knew he was a foreigner. From the look of the youth's equipment he had taken him for student. Instead here was an artist. 'What are you doing in Berlin, my boy?'

'I'm here from St. Petersburg to give a debut recital.'

'Do you intend to play a Berlin debut on that box?'

'It's all I have.'

Hammig was aghast. 'There's no way you can play that violin,' and he disappeared into a side room, returning with an instrument of exquisite finish and spotless appearance. 'Try this,' he said. The young Russian did as he was told. Efrem's eyes lit up as his bow drew forth its first Cremonese vibrations. Hammig's eyes glowed. 'I see you like it. It's a Lorenzo Guadagnini, made in 1745.'

'But I can't afford a violin like this.'

'Then I'll lend it to you for your recital. And I'll rehair your bow gratis.'

Damp-eyed and speechless, Efrem watched as a handsome case was brought out and set on the counter. 'Use the bow inside until yours is ready,' Hammig advised. 'And just leave your little violin here. We'll exchange again after the concert.' Finding his tongue at last, Efrem was effusive. Hammig shrugged lightly. 'Think nothing of it. A great artist deserves a fine instrument. And get me a ticket to the recital!' he smiled as he hurried off to his workbench.

That afternoon Efrem practiced harder than he had for weeks, enjoying every note. He adjusted quickly to the Guadagnini's dimensions and found its tone and response ideally suited to his style. During a practice break, he laid the instrument on the table at an angle that caught the twilight and pored over every detail of the violin's beauty.

Efrem's pleasure in practicing made for a quieter stay in Berlin than in Vienna. There were still visits to museums, art galleries and theaters, only fewer. He got his first taste of Shakespeare at Max Reinhardt's Deutchestheatre, seeing *Hamlet*, *King Lear* and *Merchant of Venice* (Rudolf Schildkraut's Shylock captivated him). He also went to a recital by Willy Burmester, a special favorite of the German Empress, who had his arrival in towns heralded by a military fanfare. Many uncomplimentary anecdotes have been circulated about Burmester, most concerning his arrogance, but all Zimbalist remembered about the recital was 'all those small pieces.' Burmester played entire programs of nothing but his light, lusterless arrangements of the classics.

About the middle of October Efrem's curiosity was piqued by press notices concerning the revival of Strauss's controversial opera *Salome*, under the composer's own direction. Its first performance (Dresden, December 1905) had more than raised eyebrows, and the tremors were still being felt throughout the musical world (the 1907 production at New York's Metropolitan Opera was withdrawn after only one performance). Despite Strauss's commanding stature in Berlin, the city's planned restaging of *Salome* ran into problems with the Kaiserin: the star of Bethlehem, she stipulated, was to rise in the sky following the deaths of Jokanaan and Salome. Strauss was forced to make the pious concession.

Richard Strauss's name was familiar to Efrem, even if his music was not, and he bought a ticket for opening night. The Staatsoper was packed beyond capacity. In a charged atmosphere the crowd impatiently awaited the appearance of the maestro, and the eminent Emmy Destinn, who was singing the title role. Strauss at last stepped unpretentiously onto the podium and acknowledged the tumultuous applause. 'He looked like a first-rate barber—one would never have guessed that he was a musician,' Zimbalist laughed. From *Salome*'s first chord the young Russian was shaken. The performance was an unqualified success, cheered to the echo. Strauss relaxed his undemonstrative manner enough to kiss Destinn on the cheek; of the famous 'Dance of the Seven Veils' Zimbalist said only, 'Destinn was of ample proportions.' He spoke further in retrospect: 'I was flabbergasted by the opera and didn't understand anything about the music. It was so strange to me that I couldn't sleep all night.' Open as always to new ideas, he bought a piano score early the next morning and spent hours scrutinizing it—a conspicuously Zimbalistian move. He even spoke with the pit musicians and later retold a yarn from the first horn player, who had approached Strauss during a rehearsal with a question: 'Herr Strauss, my part is not clear. Am I to play B-flat or B natural, please?' The composer didn't even glance at the score. 'It makes no difference, my friend.'

In Zimbalist's own mature compositions the influence of Strauss is pronounced. Strauss was the first 'modern' composer Efrem had ever heard; Debussy's and Ravel's works were unknown to him. *Salome* was a real shocker; its harmonies and orchestral textures profoundly impressed Efrem's musical sensibilities. Not all traditionally reared musicians were as open-minded; 'For a pig's mess like *Salome*,' Max Bruch wrote in an acrid letter to a colleague after hearing the same performance of *Salome*, 'I have no words.'

Frau Wolff wrote Efrem, announcing that his accompanist for 28 October would be Herr Emile Frey and relaying particulars for their first rehearsal. The pre-debut recital was not advertised, but Frau Wolff enclosed publicity for his November appearance, which would run daily in the *Tageblatt*. Efrem soon after found himself before a tailor's mirror, trying on his first evening concert dress. Closely cropped curly brown hair framed his solemn yet gentle face, dominated by arresting blue eyes. (One journalist in the 1930s ended her interview thus: 'Anytime Mr. Zimbalist doesn't know what to do with his big blue eyes I will be glad to have him look my way.') Efrem and pianist Emile Frey met at the appointed time. Frey was an old pro; that first rehearsal, like the two that followed, was low-keyed, and before he knew it, Efrem, wearing his new outfit, was taking the fateful ride to Bechsteinsaal.

The recital was scheduled for seven; Efrem arrived two hours early. (This was a habit throughout his career; eventually he might even arrive after lunch and practice in the hall until half an hour before curtain.) A doorman showed him backstage and turned on some lights. The late October air was crisp, and Efrem was glad the hall was comfortably heated. He unpacked, stepped onto the dimly lit stage, and began to practice, pacing back and forth. His warm-up procedure had broadened to show traces of Ševčik's influence; Vladimir Sokoloff, Zimbalist's last accompanist, was intrigued by the complete absence of any musical extracts in his warm-up before concerts: it was scales and exercises only.

Frey joined Efrem at 6 p.m. to test acoustics, and about half an hour later Frau Wolff bustled in. 'Your reputation has preceded you,' she said. 'A good number of uninvited music lovers are coming in.' At precisely 7 p.m. Efrem strode out to meet them and the critics.

He began his program with the Vitali Chaconne in Auer's arrangement, which became (with the occasional substitution of a Handel sonata) the standard violin recital opener for the next four decades. Wieniawski's 'Légende,' Riccardo Drigo's already well-known 'Harlequin's Serenade' (again arranged by Auer), and Sinding's 'Suite' followed. He ended with the Glazunov Concerto, accompanied—in accordance with prevailing recital etiquette—by a piano reduction of the orchestral score (an unacceptable practice today).

The assemblage responded noncommittally to Vitali's Chaconne, but by the end of the hour it was clear what the press's comments were likely to be. Warm applause from the music lovers' sector left no doubt that the Russian newcomer had won over what one writer described as 'the most critical and blasé audience in the world.' 'Efrem, you're a success,' beamed Hammig as he rushed backstage; since he had lent Efrem the Guadagnini, Hammig had taken him out for splendiferous dinners and taught him how to appreciate good German beer and that specific kind of Berlin humor characterized by ceaseless puns. Frau Wolff's comment was coolly managerial: 'Tomorrow's papers will tell the tale.'

Efrem wasn't sure what his own thoughts were. He felt he hadn't played particularly well but that he had done his best. As he put the Guadagnini back in its case Hammig suggested a bite of supper at Kempinski's, an establishment that was a household name to Berliners. Leaving the hall with Hammig and Frau Wolff, Efrem found a whirlwind of well-wishers waiting to greet him. He smiled readily as he shook hands and, later, over a tray of oysters washed down with German champagne, he felt almost buoyant.

UPPER LEFT: Age twelve.

LEFT: Leopold Auer as he looked when Zimbalist came to study with him. They often communicated in German, until they were both living in the United States.

ABOVE: Age six. (Courtesy Nadya Tichman)

ABOVE: Glazunov and Rimsky-Korsakov, inscribed to Zimbalist in March 1905, following the student performance of *Katschei*.

RIGHT: Age seventeen, London.

UPPER LEFT: With Ševčik in Pisek, summer 1907.

LEFT: Joseph Fels.

BELOW: Richard Strauss.

LEFT: Age eighteen, Europe.

LOWER LEFT: Jascha Heifetz as he looked when Zimbalist first heard him.

RIGHT: Artur Nikisch in action.

BELOW: Caught in action by a sketcher during the first American season, 1911.

LOWER RIGHT: Alma and Efrem with Marcella Sembrich (right) at her estate on Lake Geneva, summer 1913.

ABOVE: On the doorstep of 10 Cornwall Terrace with Mary Fels, Alma and John Powell, 1913.

UPPER RIGHT: Alma snapped this picture of her fiancé on board ship to England, spring 1914.

RIGHT: Wedding picture, Cornwall Terrace, 15 June 1914.

UPPER LEFT: Recording the Bach 'Double' with Kreisler, Camden, N.J., 14 January 1915.

CENTER LEFT: Norfolk (Connecticut) Festival, June 1915. Left to right, Carl Stoeckel, Zimbalist, Frederick Stock, Kreisler, Damrosch (carrying the viola he loaned Kreisler for the Mozart 'Sinfonia Concertante,' and that Zimbalist bought).

LOWER LEFT: Maria Virginia makes her first 'public appearance' at Lake George, aged less than two months.

Upper left: Damrosch, Zimbalist and Kreisler on tour, 1915.

Center left: The Kreisler party and Heifetz arriving at Fishers Island, 1919.

Lower left: At the beach.

CHAPTER 8

European Kudos

(FALL–WINTER 1907)

Efrem was awakened just before noon next day, 29 October 1907, by an energetic knocking at his door. The bellhop handed him a message: Frau Wolff had phoned and wanted him to stop by her office. He was there in an hour. She handed him a rave from the *Borsen Courier*: 'Not for some years has the reviewer listened to the playing of a newcomer with such pleasure.' Efrem's technique, poise and maturity were praised. 'The success of the Philharmonic concert is a foregone conclusion,' she said. 'Afterward you will leave on a local tour—I am working on the rest of Europe.'

Efrem strolled back toward his hotel. He stopped at the Schwarze Ferkel, a favorite hangout for writers and actors, and ordered a cup of coffee and two Napoleons—this was not a day for half measures. Efrem sipped his coffee and gazed out at the stream of pedestrians passing by. The majestic row of linden trees were losing the last of their leaves, strewing the pavement with gold (it wasn't too many years before these beautiful trees were removed to allow better viewing of Third Reich military spectacles). 'Patrisaiche!' (Amazing!), he muttered to himself. 'It's absolutely amazing.' He smiled, picked up his fork and attacked a Napoleon. 'Guess I'm not going to be a professor just yet!'

One day, in that week before his first rehearsal at the Beethovensaal, Efrem was invited to the home of the *Tageblatt*'s editor for lunch. 'Would you like to play a little music?' his host asked after dessert. 'I didn't bring my violin,' Efrem replied.

'I have a violin you can use.'

'I have no pianist.'

'I will play the piano.'

Out came a Strad, and a very creditable rendering of Brahms's A major sonata ensued, a nice sample of the cultivation of Berlin's upper crust. 'Music was a part of every German's general education,' Zimbalist recollected. It was also at the editor's home that he first heard the miracle of musical reproduction via the phonograph. He listened, astounded, to Caruso's voice and Sarasate's playing.

Efrem's first rehearsal with the Berlin Philharmonic was on Monday morning, 4 November. Efrem shook hands with concertmaster Anton Witek (whose smile of welcome, together with bows tapping on stands, indicated a relaxing of the orchestra's notorious austerity—word about the latest wonder 'aus St. Petersburg' had traveled fast), and he found the genial Kunwald to be a competent musician. Kunwald didn't know the Glazunov Concerto and was grateful for Efrem's pointers; he was even amenable to Efrem's few requests in the Brahms, a work he probably felt he knew at least as well as his young soloist did. The orchestra members too were very supportive—Efrem's pleasant, unassuming manner invariably invited friendliness—and it was agreed there was no need to meet again till the dress rehearsal, on the day of the concert.

On concert night, 7 November 1907, Frau Wolff noted gratefully that *Der Tag*'s blurbs had spurred brisk box-office activity. She came backstage and found Efrem, in full concert dress, ensconced in an overstuffed armchair. He had arrived at half past five to practice, and after dressing he had sat down to contemplate the pre-concert hustle and bustle that surrounded him. Orchestra members were starting to arrive, and periodically one of them came over to offer words of appreciation and good wishes; he found himself wondering what the life of a professional orchestral musician would be like.

The Beethovensaal concert began with Sinding's 'Suite,' with piano accompaniment; Zimbalist and Frey were warmly received when they appeared. As a program opener the Sinding is nothing short of spectacular: its first movement consists entirely of brilliant moto perpetuo sixteenth notes played presto and spiccato. One of the perennially dazzling jewels in Zimbalist's technical crown was his spiccato—according to Boris Schwarz in *Great Masters of the Violin*, some of the fastest spiccato he had ever heard. So Efrem jolted his listeners out of their seats from the word go, and they thundered their approval. Later in his career Zimbalist, with blithe logic, performed the 'Suite' with its order of movements reversed, to save the first movement's brilliance for last.

Next the Philharmonic members took their places for the Glazunov. Kunwald shook Efrem's hand before following him on stage. The soloist's affinity for the colorful concerto was evident throughout, and the Berliners showed no hint of being blasé, their enthusiastic applause completely engulfing the final chords.

After intermission it was the Brahms Concerto. Comparisons between the playing of Elman and Zimbalist, the St. Petersburg marvels, were already rife; it was generally felt that Zimbalist, at seventeen, was a much more seasoned musician than Elman had been when he appeared in Berlin at the age of thirteen. This maturity was evident in the Brahms, and a 'storm of applause' rewarded Efrem's performance. After several curtain calls he offered an encore, Bach's unaccompanied Prelude and Fugue in g minor — a lengthy choice after such a program, but substantial concerts were then de rigueur.

Backstage a long line of admirers stretched down the corridor outside the greenroom. Among the first to approach Efrem was a small bespectacled man with a sharply pointed beard, Christian Sinding himself, who expressed delight. A beaming Hammig stood by throughout, and when everyone was gone he embraced Efrem, who suddenly looked sad. 'You are thinking you must give back the Guadagnini,' Hammig put the words into his young friend's mouth. 'Well, you don't. You will obviously enjoy a worldwide career. You will earn plenty. Keep it and pay me when you can.' He bundled Efrem into his coat. 'Tonight it is not Kempinski's. Tonight we dine at the Adlon!'

The next day, Frau Wolff handed Efrem an itinerary for a tour of eight German cities, at 600 marks per concert. This sounded like plenty to Efrem, even when Frau Wolff made it clear that fifteen percent would go to her. There was more good news. 'This just arrived from England,' she said, handing over a sheet of paper that bore the letterhead Karl Junkermann. 'Karl is an associate of mine in London — he handled Kubelik's debut. First you will tour Germany. Then I will collaborate with Karl's agency in presenting you to the British public.' Frau Wolff gave Efrem an advance on his fees to settle the Sans Souci bill. Suddenly he felt very wealthy: that evening Hammig would be *his* guest at dinner.

Reviews of the Philharmonic concert were mixed. The *Tageblatt* was positive but testy: 'The young Zimbalist is a very good violinist, with a clear tone, energetic bowing and solid technique, but he didn't convince me of his inner artistry in the Brahms.' The *Zeitung*, by contrast, spoke of Efrem's beauty of tone, earnest interpretation and 'sensational rendering' of the Brahms, concluding, 'We are compelled to recognize that indefinable something which we are wont to call the "divine spark" of genius!' The *Norddeutsche Algemein*'s critic was patronizing: 'He could have used a little more temperament, although his technical virtuosity has been reliably educated under Professor Auer.'

Like it or not, Auer's 'new Russian school,' in the persons of Elman and now Zimbalist, was turning the musical world on its ear. What audiences found so striking in hearing Auer's products was first and foremost the sound they made: a far more mellifluous and vibrant tone than was then the norm. While proclaiming respect for each student's individuality, Auer nevertheless placed one demand on all: 'Sing, sing, sing on your violin—it is the only way in which to make its voice tolerable to the listener.' This singing owed partly to a more liberal use of vibrato. Auer's teacher Joseph Joachim and others of the older generation preferred to save vibrato for the more expressive notes in phrases. Joachim practiced what he preached: his records display an almost total lack of it; where additional melodic or harmonic stress is needed, he adds a thin, fast tremor. As head of the Hochschule for thirty-eight years, Joachim had established the Berlin school, characterized by a tone today regarded as unacceptably dry, inexpressive and hard—the result not only of Joachim's beliefs regarding a spare use of vibrato, but also to the low-elbow, high-wrist bowing he advocated. (Some scoffed that so awkward a technique could only be mastered by practicing inside a telephone booth.) St. Petersburg–trained violinists used higher right elbows for a deeper sound.

Tones of Joachim's generation simply didn't throb—the exact word often used to describe Mischa Elman's tone. Sarasate's, even with its somewhat more continuous vibrato, was a small tone, on the thin side. Ysaÿe's was perhaps the warmest of its time. But both Elman and Zimbalist used a wider, more colorful vibrato. A continuous vibrato is now considered basic, with contrasting effects produced by withholding it altogether, or highlighting other phrases by adding to its width and intensity. (As an old man Zimbalist laughed, 'The violinists I heard when I was young saved their vibrato for expressive notes. Nowadays violinists consider it expressive *not* to vibrate!') Strangely, Leopold Auer, in his book *Violin Playing As I Teach It*, sticks by his teacher Joachim's dictum on vibrato, calling it 'an effect, an embellishment, which can reduce a program of the most dissimilar pieces to the same dead level of monotony by peppering them all with the tabasco of a continuous vibrato!' Auer's advice on vibrato, it seems, went unheeded by his hot-blooded young disciples, and their use of it showed a marked step toward the present.

Auer's progeny departed from previous trends on another point: their use of a more refined and expressive portamento, which, simply put, is a way of connecting notes. These connections, or slides, are produced by certain fingering combinations. The Auer school helped introduce the art of vocally inspired slides that beautify the music. Although some criticized these portamenti as mere violinist gratification, they should have taken a closer look at the slides of a decade earlier, when they were used as functional, incidental by-products of getting from one position on the fingerboard to another. Even when violinists of the mid-1800s used slides to assist phrasing, they could seldom provide the intended warmth, owing to lack of a sympathetic vibrato. Then along came the Auer students, with their luscious slides that added a new warmth of expression. Auer called the portamento 'one of the most telling of violin effects, when used with restraint, in the proper way at the proper time.'

Another characteristic of Auer's teaching was noted by the *Tageblatt* reviewer when he referred to Efrem's 'energetic bowing,' which could more accurately have been described as 'bow speed.' All the Russians used bow speed in varying degrees to provide stress and accent. This lent an element of sweeping contour in phrasing. The great Jascha Heifetz developed bow speed to a particularly fine point, using it with enormous brilliance in conjunction with his preferred slide—in which the arrival finger is used for sliding rather than the departing finger, as was customary before. Zimbalist's bow speed was marked by vital, personalized attacks in which a burst of speed slightly followed the bow's contacting of the string.

When one mentions terms such as warmth, vibrancy and color the name of Fritz Kreisler immediately springs to mind. Where did he fit into the overall picture? Certainly in his own way he epitomized the so-called Auer hallmarks. He was even occasionally—and incorrectly—labeled an Auer student in older music reference books. Since Kreisler had been around for a while before the Russian influx, championing a warm (then so-called French) vibrato, why were the sounds of the Auer school considered so fresh? For one thing, Kreisler's early career was somewhat checkered. After the waves he made winning the Paris Conservatoire's Premier Grand Prix at age twelve subsided, he somehow wasn't subject to the kind of hype that accompanied Auer products. And his easygoing personality didn't demand it. Although he had become a hit in Berlin as early as 1899 and was a fixture there, his career elsewhere took a long time to attain the level of exposure and acclaim it ultimately enjoyed. According to Carl Flesch, before 1900 Kreisler's overtly sensuous, vibrant style was not fully appreciated—the public wasn't ready for it. The fact that the newly emerging stars from St. Petersburg were stylistically along the same lines helped to tip the scales, as together they shaped public taste. Berlin, fancying itself the world's musical center, was cautious about new violinistic trends, and a percentage of its musicians found the Russians' approach unpalatable. Gerhard Masur, in his book *Imperial Berlin*: 'The hostility aroused by an innovation in the realm of literature and the arts was so violent that it required a good store of courage to praise the men and women who dared to open new windows on the world.'

An impact on the development of violin playing equal to Auer's did not occur again until the middle of the twentieth century, when Ivan Galamian's products started to make their effect. Auer and Galamian are both stellar figures in the annals of violinism. Both elicited controversy. Productive change is always criticized, doubtless prompting Zimbalist's oft-voiced observation, 'When one is criticized, one knows one is doing something right.'

Frau Wolff, used to the Berlin critics' barbs, never dwelt on reviews. Efrem himself was amused by them and was led to pose the question many an artist has asked: could all these critics have been at the same concert? His Berlin debut was an undeniable success—the Philharmonic immediately reengaged the young Russian to join British conductor Landon Ronald in performances of the Tchaikovsky Concerto and Lalo's Symphonie Espagnole—yet this early experience of the vagaries of critical opinion, added to his natural modesty, led to his lifelong aversion to publicity. (Zimbalist's pianist Vladimir Sokoloff stated that during the twenty-seven years they traveled together, Zimbalist never looked at a single review.)

A few days after his 7 November concert Efrem set off from Berlin's

central station on his first tour. Many of the cities in which he played—
Brunswick, Hamburg, Bremen, Hanover, Dortmund, Düsseldorf, Cologne
and Bonn—were connected to his own musical and violinistic
antecedents. Brunswick was the birthplace of Ludwig Spohr, whose concertos Efrem had studied with Auer. Next came Hamburg, full of Brahms
associations, still sensed by any musician who visits the city. How much
more clearly must Efrem have felt them a scant ten years after Brahms's
death. In his recital there Efrem included Brahms's Hungarian Dance No.
20, arranged by Joachim and taught him by Joachim's pupil Auer, making
him a link in historical continuity difficult to imagine duplicating today.

Frau Wolff, working for her fifteen percent, had made all travel and
hotel arrangements for him, so getting from place to place was simple and
pleasant. Efrem would check into a hotel, where he was awaited by the
local representative of Frau Wolff's network, and meet with the local
pianist for a rehearsal. If he was to appear with orchestra, contact would
have been made with the conductor. Then he would take off and cover the
town's length and breadth on foot. His command of German had grown
quickly, and everything fascinated him, every fact and figure; the history,
population, chief attractions and sources of revenue of each new place
were neatly cataloged in his inquiring mind, over time creating a startling
font of information he tapped throughout his life. He also enjoyed the
local cuisine—his tastes in food ran to simple fare. The plain wursts with
red kraut, and some bread and cheese, were his favorites, and at dinner he
sometimes enjoyed a stein of German beer (his alcohol consumption was
always very circumspect). Along with these learning experiences came a
sharp lesson: the morning after his Düsseldorf performance Wolff's agent
delivered his fee. Just about to leave his room, Efrem left the cash out in
plain view, later to find it stolen.

In Hanover, where Auer had studied under Joachim, Efrem played the
Brahms Concerto, with Joachim's cadenza (he later wrote his own). Next
came a recital in Dortmund; Efrem decided to add the Paganini 'Witches
Dance,' which he had tangled with under Ševčík, as a test to measure the
extent to which his natural, pre-Pisek, facility had returned. The results
were flawless, and with added confidence he began practicing Paganini's
caprices, and the first concerto (in Wilhelmj's version). The orchestra in
Düsseldorf was good, and his concert rewarding.

Cologne's *Tageblatt* spoke of Efrem's rich, warm, intoxicating tone, his

musical maturity and ability to touch an audience: 'It is years since a violinist met with a success equal to that of Zimbalist.' Another Cologne
paper nourished a comparison between Zimbalist and Elman that survived for a time: 'Zimbalist must be considered the greater of the two
because, in addition to his amazing virtuosity, the musical life in him pul-
sates more freely.'

The first thing Efrem did in Bonn was to visit the house in which
Beethoven had been born. It affected him deeply, and critics found his
recital imbued with 'an uncommonly noble beauty of tone and interpretation.' One of the most appealing qualities of Zimbalist's art was already
making itself felt: much mention was made over the years of his dignity
and nobility — a kind allied not with austerity, but compassion.

His German sojourn ended with Efrem's reengagement with the Berlin
Philharmonic under Ronald. By the time he was on the Ostend train, his
thoughts had turned to London, and soon the youth, violin case in hand,
boarded the ferry that would carry him across the English Channel. The
early December sky was overcast, the breeze cool. Efrem buttoned his coat
tightly as the Belgian coast disappeared from view. Europe had been good
to him.

CHAPTER 9

London and Joseph Fels

(1907–1908)

Efrem, realizing he would soon be at a distinct communicative disadvantage, spent most of the two-hour Channel crossing cudgeling his brain for the few English words it contained. Disembarkation and customs posed no problems — his baggage was still but a single suitcase and his violin. On the boat-train he had a cup of strong English tea and some fruitcake ('tea' was among the few English words he knew), and he presently found himself, British pounds in pocket, directing a hansom to the hotel that Frau Wolff had booked for him. Even after Vienna and Berlin, London's noisy bustle was marked, and the cab driver seemed pitted against great odds in his efforts to advance along the narrow, twisting thoroughfares. At length they arrived at the hotel in Mayfair. Efrem was relieved to finally arrive in his pleasant upper-floor room; he drew aside the shutters and looked out over a city poised for its first winter snow. Dinner that evening, with a German-English dictionary beside him, offered more diligent practice for his crash course in the English language. Ever adaptable, within a couple of weeks he was able to make his wishes clear in this complicated new tongue, even if for some time he listened more than he spoke, and always with his easy, benevolent smile.

On presenting himself at Karl Junkermann's Regent Street offices next morning, he was glad to discover that his agent was conversant with all the world's musical languages. They spoke in German, with the occasional English word thrown in. Efrem would debut in London on Monday, 9 December, at Queen's Hall, a sumptuous concert venue with superb acoustics. The program would open with Weber's *Oberon* Overture, followed by the Tchaikovsky Concerto; in the second half would come Sinding's 'Suite' with piano, and the first, fourth and fifth movements of Lalo's 'Symphonie Espagnole' with orchestra. The rousing (and, one would think, unnecessary) finale would be Strauss's 'Don Juan.' Announcements of this London Symphony concert, with conductor Landon Ronald and 'featuring the Russian violinist who made such a sensational debut in Berlin on November 7,' had been running on the front page of the *Times* for a fortnight, stirring wide interest.

With barely a week before the big event, Efrem was forced to practice rather than sightsee. Some work on the Lalo was necessary, and there were rehearsals with Charlton Keith, his English accompanist. He was also pleased to see Landon Ronald again. Besides being an important conductor, Ronald was an excellent pianist, much sought after as an accompanist (in which capacity he acted for Zimbalist on a few occasions); he was so con-scientiousness with every detail of the orchestral accompaniment, Efrem had nothing to suggest. After rehearsing they simply shook hands and smiled, to the clatter of musicians' bows tapping approval on stands.

British orchestras were already acquiring their reputation for excellence. From the mid-1800s these ensembles had been undergoing consistent doses of European orchestral discipline, as meted out by such stellar figures as Felix Mottl, Anton Seidl, Hans Richter and Artur Nikisch—not to mention Henry Wood's tireless groundwork. The London Symphony had been formed three years previously as a disgruntled offshoot of the Queen's Hall Orchestra, when its conductor, Wood, abolished the 'deputy' system (this had allowed for the sending of substitute players to rehearsals and performances—hardly conducive to interpretive cohesion). Having emerged as the London Symphony, the renegade band decided to run things themselves, hiring guest conductors by democratic vote—a facet of control that many symphonies exercise to this day. Landon Ronald was hired as resident conductor and succeeded against all expectation in molding a disciplined and responsive orchestral sound, the finest Efrem had so far encountered. (English orchestral players, for all their spirit, tend to take discipline with more good-humored grace than their European counterparts.)

His London debut was Efrem's first formal afternoon concert. After the morning run-through, he was served Cornish pasties and tea in his dressing room. He sipped a cup as he changed into what was, for him, novel concert attire: a rented morning coat, grey waistcoat and striped trousers. He began warming up, strolling over to the window while playing. From it he watched London society arriving in the hall's main carriageway. The exquisitely civilized elegance of it all, that overriding British sense of order-liness, fascinated him. A steward knocked on the door to announce 'Five minutes,' and presently strains of the Weber overture could be heard. Shortly before its last bars, a second knock alerted the soloist, and Efrem was ushered downstairs just as Landon Ronald returned from his bow.

Ronald wished Efrem luck with a pat on the back and a smile. Their appearance onstage was greeted with loud, prolonged applause. So much for cold English receptions. Stimulated by this welcome, Efrem played at his peak. The debut was an enormous success; as reported next day in the *Times*, Efrem's 'remarkably fine violin playing' roused the audience to immense enthusiasm.

For Efrem the big time had arrived, and he was about to gain lasting access to a new stratum of society. Among the post-concert greenroom throng there appeared a man, sixtyish, and a middle-aged woman, both of Lilliputian dimensions, who spoke to Efrem first in English then, with better results, in German. Their name, the man said, was Fels, and he and his wife were Americans. Just over five feet tall, Joseph Fels exuded extraor-dinary energy and vitality, and was clearly in charge; his bald head capped an active face imprinted with shrewd intelligence. Mary Fels was even smaller, and her manner contrasted entirely. A strange vagueness of delivery made all her statements come out sounding more like questions, perfectly corresponding to her washed-out complexion and prematurely white hair. But behind this pale facade was great warmth, and the couples' mutual devotion was obvious. 'You must be starving,' Mrs. Fels ventured faintly. 'Come and have dinner with us.'

Efrem declined, not feeling up for socializing. He struggled to explain, but Mr. Fels wouldn't take no for an answer. 'Nonsense!' he spoke enthusi-astically, and to the point. 'You can learn English from us. We'll wait for you to change.'

Joseph and Mary Fels' unaffected friendliness at dinner that evening won Efrem's affection. The trio hit it off instantly, and all seemed reluctant to part. At evening's end, Mr. Fels took the ball again. 'You must be our guest at Elmwood. How soon can you come?'

Efrem stared. 'Elmwood?'

Mrs. Fels explained that it was their home, situated in Bickley, in the Kent countryside, about an hour from London by train. Efrem agreed to come for the weekend. Directions would be mailed to the hotel, and he would be met at Bickley station that coming Friday.

Next day, 10 December 1907, Efrem walked over to Junkermann's office; the *Times* review was on Junkermann's desk when he entered. 'The name of Zimbalist,' Junkermann said, 'is on the tip of every music lover's tongue. Many engagements will be forthcoming.' A repeat of the debut program in Birmingham, the Tchaikovsky Concerto in Manchester, and the Brahms in Cologne were scheduled, and Efrem had already been invited to give drawing-room soirées in several elite homes. Junkermann thought these were a good idea, both for the additional exposure and because they provided more money than Efrem's regular concert fee. One such was at the home of a socialite noted for the excellence of her musical salon; on this particular evening she had engaged several prominent artists. The soprano, greatly upset that her accompanist had not materialized, made an eloquent appeal to a famous solo pianist, who was also on the program. He declined, pointing out icily that he was a soloist, not an accompanist. Efrem overheard the conversation and, without introducing himself, quietly sat down at the piano. His playing so delighted her that she offered him the position as her regular pianist — and her embarrassment can only be imagined when the time came for Efrem's solo turn. One audience member expressed the general wonder audibly: 'By Jove, the piano chap is going to perform on the fiddle!'

Junkermann also advised that Efrem acquire a secretary, E. M. Geller, who had just left the employ of Mischa Elman, living in London now. Efrem and his new secretary soon became good friends, and Geller issued a statement to the press: 'Zimbalist is absolutely without affectation and combines a most sympathetic personality with charm and magnetism; far from being in the slightest degree spoiled, he is so natural in his manner that it would be impossible to judge from this criterion that he is an artist' — a much-encountered observation over the years.

Directions from Joseph Fels arrived at the hotel, as promised, and that Friday, Efrem headed out for his weekend in the country (his first ride on the famous Underground), accompanied by Geller. The Felses met them at Bickley with a hansom, and they rode a couple of miles along muddy lanes before arriving at Elmwood. The house was set on a sprawling acreage;

rose gardens extended from its front to a distant copse of elms, and Joseph Fels's personal creed was embodied in the words engraved over the front doorway: 'What I spent I had / What I saved I lost / What I gave I have.' Clearly the Felses were wealthy, and the generosity they would lavish on their new friend was to show no bounds. Efrem sensed immediately there was a lot more to them than money, and his intuition was eventually confirmed. At the first lunch Efrem met Walter Coates, the Felses' permanent houseguest, whom they had taken under their wing thirteen years before; Coates had largely taken over the day-to-day running of Fels's business affairs, freeing him for his humanitarian concerns.

The weekend was a constant delight. But there was a studious side to it. Although fluent in German, Fels decreed that only English be spoken during the visit, and he and his wife added daily to their seventeen-year-old guest's vocabulary. Geller promised to carry on the Felses' good work when, on Monday morning, Efrem left Bickley with a slightly less faltering grip on the King's English.

Efrem and Charlton Keith traveled to Birmingham together. Midland cities of the time tended to be unpredictable in their response to new artists, but Birmingham treated Efrem, again under Ronald, very well, adopting him as a favorite. In Manchester Efrem was to play with the great Hans Richter. Lionized in England, Richter had conducted the first performances of Wagner's *Ring* at Bayreuth; in light of this Teutonic background, Efrem wondered how the venerable maestro would treat the Tchaikovsky Concerto. Richter's manner during rehearsal and at the performance was as formidable as his appearance. He was moody and unpleasant at times, but he brought things off with a minimum of complication — and as little flair. After the rehearsal they spoke in German. Richter's eyes twinkled behind the minuscule, rimless spectacles that were almost lost on his huge face. 'Marvelous!' he enthused. 'You are not only a virtuoso, but also such a good *musician*.'

It happened that Russian violinist Adolf Brodsky lived in Manchester, where he was a professor at the Royal College of Music. Richter, who had conducted Brodsky's première of the Tchaikovsky, invited him to hear Efrem's performance. Having made sure that the integral part he had played in the concerto's emergence was thoroughly understood, Brodsky became charming in the extreme, happy that 'his' concerto was gaining wider acceptance. He had heard the Auer version in 1904, at Elman's Berlin debut. At that time he was understandably disapproving, but now he grudgingly accepted some of Auer's changes.

Today, with the dwindling of the Auer-influenced old-timers, one hears more and more young performers playing the concerto in the original version. This is partly because the Tchaikovsky Competition, held every four years in Moscow, demands the urtext. Original versions, good or bad, have attained something of a chic status in the current mania for 'authentic performance practice.' However, there will probably always remain the courageous few who study works with an unprejudiced ear and the security to make decisions based on musical conviction rather than archaic historicism. Such players concur that Auer's cuts in the last movement of the Tchaikovsky Concerto mercifully do away with the irritating impression of a phonograph record having become stuck interminably in the same groove.

Efrem and Richter rode together on a southbound train, chatting easily the while. Richter himself was returning to London to the Herculean task of preparing Wagner's *Ring* cycle for presentation in the 1908–09 season, the first complete production in English. Efrem promised to attend, hoping that his English would by then be equal to the task — a comment that drew a hearty chuckle from the conductor. He offered Efrem reengagement in Manchester the following season.

In Cologne Efrem played the Brahms Concerto with respected Brahms conductor Fritz Steinbach, and though the occasion was a success with audiences and critics alike, it was Steinbach's praise that pleased Efrem most. Steinbach introduced Efrem to two young brothers — one his concertmaster, the other his timpanist. They were the Busch brothers, Adolf and Fritz, also recently graduated. Steinbach and the Buschs took Efrem sightseeing, and they spent many pleasant hours talking shop together over meals prepared by Frau Steinbach.

Among Efrem's accumulated mail at his London hotel was a note from the Felses, asking him to phone. Geller helped him place the call — another first for Efrem — from the concièrge's desk. Mrs. Fels answered, delighted, and insisted that he join them again in Bickley that weekend. A heavy snow had left the city's pavements under inches of slush, and Efrem was only too glad to exchange them for Elmwood's glowing hearth: he'd decided there was something about the damp cold in Britain that even Russian winters couldn't match. Once hearthside, Mrs. Fels showed him a review of his

Queen's Hall debut in the January 1908 issue of *Musical Times*, which ran in part: 'The newcomer possesses musical talent and executive facility extraordinary for his years even in these days of youthful precocity.... That Zimbalist will become an artist of the first rank there can be little doubt.'

Evening lessons in English vocabulary continued around the fireplace at Elmwood. The days included a little practicing and composing. Efrem was busy on a piece along baroque lines, 'Suite in Alter Form,' that he intended to dedicate to Auer. The weekend extended into a full week. Over dinner one evening Mr. Fels had an idea: 'We so enjoy having you around, young fellow, that I think you should consider making this your home. How would that suit you?'

'You know you have become almost like a son to us,' added his wife.

Efrem was touched at the prospect, but certain practicalities intruded. In his faltering English he answered slowly, hoping not to offend. 'That would make me so happy. But I travel often to Europe. So I must live in London. Bickley is too far.' His hosts had to agree with this logic.

Efrem left next morning, to rehearse for a 16 January performance of the Brahms and Glazunov concertos with the London Symphony under Landon Ronald; for the obligatory solos with piano he was throwing in Tchaikovsky's 'Serenade Mélancolique' and Paganini's 'Witches' Dance.' The concert was not devoid of added interest. Efrem had met a musician friend of Geller's, Johann Kruse, an Australian who owned a 'most perfect Strad.' Kruse offered Efrem use of his prize for the concert, and the allure of playing on a Stradivarius ultimately won out over Efrem's allegiance to his old friend, the Guadagnini. But a severe shock resulted. At the end of the program Efrem replaced Kruse's instrument in its case in the artists' room and went out for his final bow without the violin. 'Imagine my fright,' Zimbalist recalled, 'when I returned backstage to find both the case and violin missing.' He drove off at once, in great distress, to Kruse's house, where he found to his intense relief that the owner of the Strad was himself the 'thief': Kruse had entered the artists' room just when Efrem was making his way back to the stage and, being in a hurry to get home, had taken the instrument with him, never dreaming what anxiety his hasty action would cause. 'I suppose it was better than taking the violin away before the concert,' Zimbalist laughed.

Press response to the concert was of the sort that henceforth greeted Zimbalist performances almost without exception. From the *Times* of 17

January 1908: 'Zimbalist created his atmosphere from the very first moment he drew his bow across the strings, one of poetry tinged with dignity and self-restraint, and by the ease with which he accomplished everything he brought his audience to a pitch of great excitement.' But the supreme compliment was paid him at his hotel early the next morning. He had barely arisen when there was a knock at the door. Outside stood Fritz Kreisler. With a smile Kreisler graciously (and unnecessarily) introduced himself. Then, in the warmest manner, he congratulated Efrem on his successes and welcomed him to London. His own concert commitments, he regretted, had taken him away at the time of his colleague's December debut, and he had returned to London too late to attend Efrem's latest concert. 'But I did so want to meet you.' Efrem was moved to tears. Despite a fifteen-year difference in their ages, the two were to become lifelong friends, sharing a passion for first editions, chess, fine violins and vintage wines.

In early spring 1908 Efrem embarked on his first 'Harrison' tour. Each season, prominent entrepreneur Percy Harrison engaged three artists to give concerts in larger cities and provincial towns throughout England, Wales, Scotland and Ireland. As may be imagined, such a group of 'artistes' touring together for weeks could easily result in the bruising of fragile egos, and smoothing out rough edges often required the patience of Job and unlimited tact. Luckily the appropriately named 'Daddy' Harrison was possessed of both, and succeeded in maintaining a sense of camaraderie among his musicians. Efrem's fellow artists on the 1908 tour were Wilhelm Backhaus and the effervescent Frieda Hempel, on whom Efrem developed a mad crush. Programs followed the potpourri formula of the day, with arias and instrumental solos interspersed. He and Backhaus didn't play together since sonatas were not at all the thing on such tours. But he enjoyed playing with one of England's most respected musicians, Hamilton Harty, who accompanied his and Hempel's solos.

Incidentally, the well-known limitations of British cuisine daunted Efrem not a bit — he was introduced that spring to what he considered two high delicacies, Scottish kippers and Stilton, which remained his favorite cheese for life.

CHAPTER 10

A Temporary Base

(1908–1909)

Efrem's first appearance back in London was at a Royal Amateur Orchestral Society 'smoking concert,' where, during the performance, the use of tobacco was allowed both in the auditorium and on the stage. His Royal Highness George, Prince of Wales, was present and asked Russian ambassador Count Paul Benckendorff to bring the artist for royal accolades. After introductions and congratulations, the Prince of Wales attempted to engage Efrem in the usual small talk. But the embarrassed violinist was seized by nervousness—he couldn't understand a word. Staring blankly, he turned to Benckendorff for help. 'Your Highness,' the ambassador interposed, 'Mr. Zimbalist's English is not too good as yet. Would your Highness allow me to serve as interpreter?'

Prince George agreeably addressed his question for Efrem to the count. 'What did he say?' Efrem asked in Russian.

'I haven't a clue either,' muttered Benckendorff. 'Just say "yes" and smile.'

As a result of the prince's enthusiasm, Efrem was engaged to play at the Russian embassy for a banquet honoring the dowager Empress Marie Feodorovna (Dagmar), Tsar Nicholas's mother, who was in London visiting her sister, Queen Alexandra. Prince George thought the Empress might enjoy being entertained by her adopted country's latest musical prodigy. The banquet was also attended by Princess Victoria, daughter of the King and Queen. Queen Alexandra proved kindness itself; her simple statement that Efrem put her 'in Heaven' by his performance of a Chopin nocturne remained a glowing memory. Pleasantries were also exchanged with the dowager Tsarina, a meeting that had a useful sequel two years later.

But a more immediate result followed. While on tour in the Midlands, Efrem and his accompanist Hamilton Harty received a telegram: 'His Majesty King Edward wishes you to perform for League of Mercy Benefit Albert Hall 24 May [stop] Advise of availability [stop] Paolo Tosti' (Tosti, of 'Mattinata' fame, was a professor at the Royal Academy of Music and coordinator for His Majesty's musical events). They wired back that they were, indeed, available.

Efrem returned in high spirits to a capital showing welcome signs of spring. Geller showed him the performance lineup for His Majesty's charity concert. The roster read like a Who's Who of Britain's favorites — Antonio Scotti, Edna Thornton, John McCormack, Ben Davies, Sir Charles Santley — and heading the list were two names that raised Efrem's pulse rate: Nellie Melba and Enrico Caruso. Both an orchestra and pianists (Landon Ronald, Hamilton Harty, and Tosti among them) would provide accompaniments for the artists.

On 24 May 1908 an audience of more than ten thousand packed the Royal Albert Hall. From the stage the distant recesses of the circles, not to mention the upper galleries, looked so far away that Efrem was sure no one seated there would hear a note he played. They did hear him, of course, but, thanks to the abysmal acoustics, many seconds after the patrons seated on the main floor did. His contributions were Tchaikovsky's 'Serenade Mélancolique' and Brahms's d minor Hungarian Dance. Then he stood in the wings to hear the living legends close up. After an encore (the sextet from *Lucia* — and what a cast) the entire lineup took curtain calls — one newspaper recorded fully a dozen. Barely having caught their breath in the wings, they were ushered off to a room adjoining the royal box, where they were to be received by His Majesty. An aide presented the artists with little boxes containing royal tokens of esteem as His Majesty conversed, briefly but graciously. When Efrem received his gift (he and Caruso got emerald stickpins) the King addressed him in a tone that reflected polite interest — and his heritage: he spoke with a German accent 'thick enough to cut with a knife.'

Just days after the affair Efrem had a delightful surprise. Mrs. Fels appeared at his hotel with exciting news: 'We have bought a place in London, just so that you can stay with us!' This was partly true, since the Felses wanted to get Efrem out of the clutches of Geller, whom Mary considered a spendthrift and an unhealthy influence. But Joseph Fels's own travel demands were increasing; for him too a London pied-à-terre was more convenient. Efrem packed immediately, and they left in a hansom for No. 10, Cornwall Terrace. (In later years Zimbalist liked to joke that he visited the Felses for a weekend and stayed for three years.)

At this point a glance at Joseph Fels's background is in order. He was born in Virginia of immigrant German Jewish parents. At fifteen he left school to work with his father, a small-scale toilet-soap manufacturer, in Richmond, then Baltimore. In 1881 they set up in Philadelphia, where Joseph's brother Samuel joined as a junior partner. Even at that early stage the brothers showed a zeal for social improvement by providing a clean, well-lit and comfortable environment for their factory workers. Business flourished; following Joseph's purchase of a process involving naphtha in the production of laundry soap, it skyrocketed. Fels-Naphtha was born, and Fels eventually sent his products to every part of the civilized world, making a fortune in the process.

When he moved to England in 1901 to widen export trade, his relocation also brought him into easy contact with humanitarian leaders he admired, among them pioneering Socialist leader and Member of Parliament George Lansbury. Fels bought thirteen hundred acres at Hollesley Bay and six hundred more in Essex for the use of the unemployed. From 1905 his name was inextricably linked with the Single Tax cause, the principles behind which—that land is a gift of nature; that all men have an equal right to its use; that it is unfair for a few to acquire great wealth by holding land that increases in value—were originated by American social reformer Henry George. Joseph Fels was a key advocate for the movement, giving platform addresses wherever an audience could be had, and he spent more than $100,000 annually after 1905 on promotion, with additional sums donated to the cause in various foreign countries. He once stated, 'We can't get rich under present conditions without robbing somebody.... I am proposing to spend my money to wipe out the system by which I made it.'

For Efrem, meeting the Felses constituted not only an entrée into society but also, more importantly, access to some of the most active and influential minds of the day. This, added to the Felses' disdain for anything that smacked of prejudice, was an invaluable education.

Furniture movers, workmen and deliverymen from Harrods were busily engaged in the finishing touches of setting up house at No. 10,

Cornwall Terrace, a spacious two-story mansion fronted by Corinthian columns. 'As you can see, things are far from settled,' cautioned Mrs. Fels. 'Still, let me show you around.' They climbed the circular staircase from the entrance hall and came to Efrem's room, directly above the front door. It commanded a panoramic view of Regents Park and, like the rest of the house, was elegantly appointed in the finest Edwardian style. 'It's like a dream,' Efrem gasped.

'Think nothing of it,' laughed Mrs. Fels. 'We are so pleased to have you. I feel that this will be a happy place.' Her prediction was borne out. The travel-weary eighteen-year-old could at last enjoy a home base between tours.

The Felses' courtship had been an interesting one: While traveling in Keokuk, Iowa, as a salesman, Joseph met a distantly connected branch of the Fels family. Although he was twenty-two at the time, he was struck with Mary Fels, then a pretty nine-year-old. Nine years later they married, having meanwhile corresponded and met at rare intervals. But it had been a difficult decision, first involving 'two years of inner inquiry . . . with reservations as to the conduct of [our] united lives,' in Mary's words. Perhaps these reservations hinged on the couple's blood ties, albeit far removed, which in turn could explain, despite Joseph's love of children, their not having any of their own, and Mary's fondness for 'adopting' young wards, Efrem being the latest in the series. Mary was soon doting on '[her] boy Zimbalist with his dear broken English' like a favorite son, much as she once had on Walter Coates.

The orderly routine at Cornwall Terrace was a good influence on Efrem, providing both structure and time for relaxation. Sometimes he made use of the Felses' private dock to row on the lake in Regents Park. There was also sightseeing—he had been too busy until now. Two places of interest just around the corner were visited right away—Madame Tussaud's waxworks and the Royal Academy of Music. The latter's pretentious but grizzly exterior reminded him immediately of the St. Petersburg Conservatory. He discovered that some of the occupants were as grizzled, with ornate mustaches and beards abounding. Johann Kruse, along on the visit, introduced Efrem to the principal, the reputable Alexander Mackenzie. Mackenzie asked Efrem to look at 'Pibroch,' a rhapsodic suite on Scottish themes he had written for Sarasate in 1889, and scrawled an inscription to Efrem across the score's cover. Efrem gladly embraced the charming work in his repertoire.

Visits to the Tate Gallery and, commensurate with the improvement of his English, to London's theaters, added richness to his enjoyable new British lifestyle, and Efrem's circle of acquaintances grew, thanks to the constant social round at 10 Cornwall Terrace, where H. G. Wells and George Bernard Shaw were welcomed to tea regularly. At chamber music parties around town, Efrem met violist Lionel Tertis, English pianist-composers Cyril Scott and York Bowen and American pianist-composer John Powell. After completing his studies with Theodore Leschetizky, Powell, like Efrem, had made a successful Berlin debut, and was making London his head-quarters while doing the European circuit; a mutual interest in composition forged a friendship between the two. According to pianist and scholar Roy Hamlin Johnson, both Powell and Zimbalist were charter members, with pianist Benno Moiseiwitsch, in the Fresh Air Art Society, a London-based group devoted to 'reason and sanity in art.' This organization, with its quasi-ethical-aesthetic-philosophical overtones and ultra-conservative leanings, was somehow tied in with Powell's and Moiseiwitsch's interest in the Deutsche Weiner Turnverein in Vienna, a strongly nationalist group whose motto was 'Frisch, Fromm, Froh, Frei' (fresh, pious, happy, free). Critic and poet Karl Berger recorded that Powell and Efrem attended FAAS meetings in Vienna, but Zimbalist later claimed no recollection of the group.

Early in summer 1908 Efrem went to the Palladium to see Harry Lauder, a favorite of his. During intermission he strolled around the foyer with the crowds, the emerald stickpin he had received from King Edward only weeks before adorning his four-in-hand tie. When he resumed his seat he discovered that the emerald had been neatly clipped from its pin. Thoroughly crestfallen, he rushed home to use the Felses' phone.

'I telephoned Scotland Yard, and I said, "I want to talk to the Chief." I told him I had received a present from the King and that it had been stolen. Do you know, the Chief came right over to the house. He listened to the story, looked at what was left of the stickpin, and said he would do his best. But I hadn't much hope. I thought to myself, "One little emerald—seven million people in London—goodbye emerald." Two days later I got a call from him. "I can lay my hands on the emerald, if you will agree not to prosecute," he said. "Certainly I agree," I said. So he brought it to me. I just couldn't believe it. I asked him, "Will you please tell me how you found it?" He told me he knew, by the way it had been clipped, which gang was responsible. Through certain sources he communicated with the leader of the gang, promising not to prosecute if the emerald were surrendered, and pointing out that the stone was a present from the King and of great value to me. So I got it back and had the stickpin repaired, only to lose it for good a few years later, when my bag was stolen while on a train in Italy. That bag also contained treasured photographs of Strauss, Nikisch, Richter and others, all inscribed to me.'

Engagements were pouring in, which pleased Junkermann, and everywhere the concerts were triumphs. Efrem was pleased too, although there were times when he felt busier than he wanted to be. In late June 1908 he was once again crossing the Channel, en route to Holland and Scandinavia. This time he enjoyed the companionship of the Felses, who had decided to come along to 'keep an eye on business.' Fels himself was not particularly fond of fine music (although he had advised the adolescent Mary Fels to study music, 'the most essential part of a civilized education'), but he often whistled his shrill approval at Zimbalist's performances. On this trip, he addressed Efrem's nagging anxiety about not owning a true concert instrument. 'Are you satisfied with that violin from the Berlin dealer?' he asked. Efrem told him how much he loved the Guadagnini. 'When we get home I'll get in touch with the man,' Fels said, letting the matter drop.

Efrem appeared with the Concertgebouw Orchestra in Amsterdam and The Hague, conducted by the fabled Willem Mengelberg, who lived up to his proverbial loquaciousness. A fiery 'virtuoso' conductor of short, rotund stature, he was nicknamed the Napoleon of the orchestra. Efrem played the Tchaikovsky; Mengelberg, a firm believer in tampering with scores, gladly agreed to Auer's cuts. 'Ein Heldenleben,' a Mengelberg specialty, finished the program. Strauss had dedicated it to the conductor in 1899. It was Efrem's first hearing of the work, and he was very affected by it.

Back at Cornwall Terrace Fels contacted Hammig, as promised, and sent him a check for the equivalent of $3,000 — the Guadagnini was Efrem's. And Mary Fels, who had all along urged him to write the occasional letter to Rostov, now suggested it was time he began thinking about paying his homeland a visit. Efrem pointed out that his endless stream of engagements wouldn't allow for such a trip in the near future. He did not mention the main reason for his reluctance to return to Russia: the fear of military recrimination. At that very moment he should have been fulfilling the obligatory stint in the Tsar's army required, at age eighteen, of all eldest sons. (Only-sons were excepted.) He had come of age that past April but hadn't even registered; for several months he had been in consultation with Russian ambassador Benckendorff on the subject. He suffered recurrent visions of being shunted off to the barracks the minute his feet touched Russian soil. Nonetheless, in a letter to his parents, Efrem tentatively proposed returning home in fall 1909. Alex Zimbalist responded joyously, and Junkermann, who had been communicating with Efrem's old tympanist friend Artur Strok (who was getting his feet wet as a concert manager), began organizing appearances in several cities.

Efrem and Auer had kept in touch without Mary Fels's prompting, and Auer's continued interest had pleased him. But abruptly the Professor stopped writing, ignoring all notes, including one telling of the proposed Russia return. Indirectly, Efrem discovered the reason: Auer had caught wind of his lessons with Ševčik and was angry. Efrem was miserably embarrassed and decided to wait and talk to him in person.

Summer 1908 was taken up with resort appearances: Blackpool with Landon Ronald and Bournemouth with the amiable Dan Godfrey's small but excellent orchestra. Bournemouth's quaint charm captivated Efrem, and he vacationed there for a week before returning to Queen's Hall for his first appearance with Henry Wood at the Promenade Concerts series. A throng of music lovers (especially students) still queues for hours to buy inexpensive tickets for these renowned concerts; the season's Last Night has become something of a national institution, when a packed house, standing at patriotic attention, joins forces in the singing of 'Rule, Britannia!' The energetic and flamboyant Wood liked Efrem, and they appeared together many times over the next decade. Efrem became friends with Wood's young concertmaster, Albert Sammons, who in time developed a reputation as Britain's greatest violinist.

The fall 1908 season included a return to Holland and first appearances in France and Belgium, where, in Brussels, Efrem met one of his earliest idols, Eugène Ysaÿe. This giant (physically as well as artistically) attended Efrem's recital and invited him home for a late supper. He, too, owned a Lorenzo Guadagnini and was interested to try out his colleague's. Zimbalist recalled his trepidation when Ysaÿe picked it up: 'He looked as powerful as a bear, and his fingers were at least one third thicker and longer than mine. I thought he would put one of them right through my

little violin.' There followed a lengthy tour throughout Germany and
Austria, organized by Frau Wolff.

On 3 December Efrem returned to Manchester for a performance of the
Bruch g minor concerto with the Hallé Orchestra under Richter. Efrem
well remembered this concert as it included the première of the first symphony by an English composer: Edward Elgar's Op. 55. Richter introduced
his players to the work: 'Let us now rehearse the greatest symphony of
modern times, written not only by the greatest English composer, but by
the greatest modern composer of any country.' Zimbalist recalled Elgar
nervously pacing back and forth at the dress rehearsal.

There was a jolly Christmas at Cornwall Terrace. Soon after, Richter
launched the first complete *Ring* cycle in English, and Efrem, as he had
promised him, was at Covent Garden on opening night. King Edward and
Queen Alexandra were in the royal box.

The top of Richter's bald head appeared in the pit, and he began laboriously working his way through the orchestra to the podium. At first sight
of him, his adoring public jumped to their feet. Improved though Efrem's
English comprehension was, it didn't prove a match for the way a language
can suffer under singers' diction. But the music overwhelmed him. He had
never observed the maestro in the opera pit before, and soon noticed
something strange: Richter periodically disappeared. One instant he was
fully visible, waving his arms in his inimitably deliberate way, the next altogether gone from view. Mystified, after the curtain Efrem went over to the
pit, where a violist was packing up his instrument. In his best English Efrem
inquired: 'Vy the conductor keeps going avay?' The violist pointed to a stool
next to the conductor's desk. 'At the beginning of each act a full pint-o-
bitter stands on it,' he chortled. 'By the end you can be right sure 'tis empty!'

Soon Auer arrived to hold his widely advertised London class — mainly
English students with a few from the Continent. Efrem visited the
Professor following the afternoon session, but Auer was very cool and their
conversation strained. He had found out about the Ševčik debacle in the
worst way: happening on a few lines of Berlin publicity stating that Efrem
was arriving in the capital straight from Ševčik's class. Efrem tried to make
amends by presenting him with the first draft of 'Suite in Alter Form,'
inscribed across the top 'Prof. Leopold Auer gewidmet' (they still communicated in German). Auer relented, though not without stressing how
much his feelings had been hurt, and they went to tea together.

A relatively quiet couple of months ensued—time to reacquaint himself with London pleasures, practice some new music, and visit with John Powell and other friends. He also attended a few concerts and thrilled again to the bewitching sounds of Kreisler's violin. Kreisler included on his program some of the famous 'Miniatures' he claimed to have resurrected from manuscripts found at a monastery in Avignon; these little gems entranced Efrem.

Following Kreisler's lead, he had become a regular performer not just at soirées but at private concerts held for the entertainment of guests at parties in London's swankier mansions. He often played at the Waldorf-Astors, but his introduction to such lucrative employment was at another famous home. Junkermann, who had booked Efrem there for twice his customary 100 guinea fee, asked how it had all gone. 'Fine, except for the audience,' Efrem reported. 'They talked and laughed all the way through.' His manager smiled and told him that Sarasate had appeared at a similar venue near the end of his career. Well off and very tired of these affairs, Sarasate had asked the hostess for the astronomical fee of 1,000 guineas. His intention was to discourage her—instead she unflinchingly accepted his terms. However, the grande dame had a condition: equating musicians with hired help, she asked him not to enter through the front door. She would have the butler meet him at a side door, where he would be shown in through the kitchen, to the drawing room. After playing his numbers, she stipulated, Mr. Sarasate would kindly retrace his steps, leaving without disturbing her guests. 'In that case,' the relieved artist had replied, 'my fee will be only 500 guineas.' Efrem, already familiar with the tedium of post-concert chitchat, appreciated the story.

In April 1909 Richter invited Efrem to lunch with him—they were to repeat the Bruch Concerto in London, along with the Glazunov. At the maestro's favorite seafood restaurant on Regent Street, they enjoyed the best sole Efrem had ever tasted. Richter, between sputtering mouthfuls, brought up business. 'My young friend, why do we have to do the g minor again? I have just received a much more interesting piece by Bruch, perhaps his finest work for violin. Do you know it?' He reached into the ample expanse of his coat pocket and flattened out a wrinkled score amid the fishbones and buttered breadcrumbs that littered the table. Efrem had never heard of the piece, 'Scottish Fantasia,' which settled the matter for Richter. 'Good! Then we will play it together.' With the performance only two weeks away, Efrem had misgivings, but true to form, he learned it in two days, directly from the score, which he kept — ever after it bore disfiguring butter and Worcestershire sauce blotches, in mute testimony to that lunch on Regent Street.

Efrem made several cuts in the work, and at rehearsal Richter entered the adjustments into his score. This practice was commonplace at the time, with or without the composers' permission and Efrem, in fact, continued to employ it throughout his career.

Richter, standing with his soloist in the wings before the concert, mentioned that a few 'violinist friends' were present. When Efrem stepped out onto the stage the first eye he met was Auer's, front row center. On his right was August Wilhelmj and on his left, sitting regally upright, Émile Sauret. As Efrem tuned he caught Richter's knowing smile. It was one of the few occasions during his long career when he remembered feeling less than his usual nonchalant self.

Nervousness notwithstanding, he must have played well: Auer hurried backstage to pay compliments. Sauret followed, handlebar mustache waxed to perfection. Posture militarily erect, he divided his attention between the nineteen-year-old soloist and Auer, spouting an unbroken torrent of gibberish. Efrem thought he detected at least four languages, and could tell from Auer's amused appearance that he too was unable to make a word of sense out of the soliloquy. Sauret finally bowed elegantly from the waist, flashed a charming smile, and was gone. Efrem and Auer shared a good chuckle. A few days later the Professor sent Efrem a signed photograph, inscribed 'from your old friend.' All was forgiven.

On 13 May 1909 the *Times* reviewed the concert: 'Max Bruch's "Scottish Phantasie," which is generally made to sound peculiarly thick and ponderous, was galvanized into life by Zimbalist's performance.' It was an interesting program, bearing the imprints even at so early a point of that typically Zimbalistian eclecticism, and including, in addition to 'Scottish Fantasia' and the Glazunov Concerto, Tchaikovsky's Meditation and Scherzo for violin and piano (orchestrated by Glazunov) and the Bach Chaconne, with Schumann's uninspired piano accompaniment played on the organ. Critics said that the Glazunov was given with exactly the right combination of barbaric energy and passionate melancholy, but they pounced on the Chaconne, even in those more tolerant days. With the current passion for authenticity, to extract the Chaconne and perform it on its own is bad enough, to add an accompaniment surely the most flagrant heresy.

That spring Efrem was joined on a second 'Harrison' tour with mezzo-soprano Julia Culp and pianist Harold Bauer, who took an active interest in Efrem's composing. On tour he was working on his Polish and Russian dances; Bauer suggested adding a Hebrew dance. Efrem agreed, incorporating the Hebrew tune Bauer gave him, and the suite was published two years later as 'Slavonic Dances.'

It was a wide tour of Wales and the English provinces, including performances at such resort towns as Worthing, Penzance, Ilfracombe and Blackpool. The final concert was in the tiny village of Dewbury, Yorkshire. Efrem was to rehearse in London the next evening with Mark Hambourg for a concert at the Edinburgh Festival. Concerned for time, he hired a carriage to nearby Huddersfield station, but he arrived just as the express to London was steaming away. Rain was pouring down and the next express wasn't until late evening. Luckily his driver found a small inn where the proprietress made Efrem welcome. In return for her kindness he played for her guests, and many of them saw him off at the station that night. Fate added a postscript: at 9:42 that morning the train from Huddersfield was derailed near Friezland, killing two and injuring fourteen—it was the train Efrem had missed.

In June, with mixed feelings and the military question still unresolved, Efrem embarked on the long journey back to Russia. Before the Russian tour began, there would be concerts in Germany and Hungary and a short vacation in Kislovodsk.

En route in Berlin, Efrem attended a Philharmonic concert with Hammig and Franz von Vécsey (Joachim's protégé). Efrem had been attracted by the double-billing of Nikisch and a Hungarian violinist whose reputation was, to put it politely, controversial: Ferenc Hegedus. Possessed of means, Hegedus had engaged Nikisch and the Philharmonic to back him in three major concertos. To Efrem the star of the concert was Nikisch who, by continuously mopping his brow, gave signs that his wide reputation as the most adroit accompanist was being tested to the limit that evening. Efrem and Franz, between whom there was immediate mutual simpatico, compared notes on Hegedus's performance. Franz was excited that Efrem was visiting his homeland, Hungary; he made him promise to call on his teacher, Jenö Hubay.

Arriving in Budapest, Efrem checked into the Hotel Hungary. Awaiting him was a note from Hubay, inviting him to his home. Hubay couldn't have been more hospitable, and suggested visiting the Royal Academy of Music, where he was the director. The elegant stone building on Franz Liszt Place was then only five years old, but the institution itself was one of the oldest and most distinguished conservatories in Europe, attended by some 250 students from all over the world.

Hubay was then at the zenith of his career. He gave Efrem a guided tour, introducing him to faculty fellow David Popper (the world's No. 1 cellist); wherever the Grand Master went, he was greeted by the reverential bowing of heads. This exalted respect stemmed not only from Hubay's reputation as a dazzling virtuoso and his position as director. The handsome, bearded hero was also a musician of broad cultivation, having composed four violin concertos, two symphonies and four operas, the best known of which, *The Violinmaker of Cremona*, was then enjoying much popularity in Hungary. (Both he and his prize student Vécsey recorded an arranged extract from the opera.)

'He was very sweet to me, taking me all over for meals and sightseeing,' Zimbalist said in thinking back to the period, which made a lasting, multicolored impression. Hubay exposed Efrem for the first time to the unique, irresistible virtuosity of the Hungarian gypsy fiddlers. Zimbalist told the story: 'Hubay took me to a place under a bridge which crossed the Danube separating Buda and Pest, to a café where his favorite gypsy performed. He introduced me to the man, who stood in front of an orchestra. "What would you like him to play for you?"

"What does he play?"

"He plays everything."

"Well, he doesn't play Brahms, does he?"

"Oh yes. [to the gypsy] Play the Brahms Concerto for him."

'And he played the whole first movement with cembalo accompaniment!'

The musician was Dinicu, composer of 'Hora Staccato.' Efrem was also taken to hear a gypsy children's orchestra, where the average age was ten and one three-year-old had to stand on a chair to be seen.

Strolling around town, Efrem noticed a disconcerting billboard announcing his recital. The poster was headed in ten-inch banner lettering, 'Violin Recital,' while his name, in tiny type, was almost hidden among the ticket prices and general information near the bottom. Surely, he inquired of Junkermann, the reverse would have been more in keeping? His manager explained that 'Zimbalist' in Hungarian meant, literally, 'cymbal player.' 'If your name were on top people would think we are advertising a cymbal recital, and we wouldn't sell many tickets.' (One version of the genealogy of the Zimbalist name does trace it to Hungary. Another traces it to a German nobleman by the name of Zimbalmoshe who in ancient times settled in Russia and Russianized his name.)

The evening before his recital Efrem and Junkermann had dinner at the Hotel Hungary, where yet another gypsy violinist strolled. The fiddler gave special attention to their table. After dinner Efrem introduced himself. The man's eyes lit up. 'Mr. Zimbalist,' he said, 'I entertain here to earn a living, but my true love is for the masterpieces that you play. Could I ask a great favor?'

'I'll do what I can.'

'Then get me in to hear your concert.'

'I'd be happy to.'

'There's one thing, Mr. Zimbalist: I would like to be as close as possible, to watch your fingers. Do you think I might sit on stage?'

'That's easy to arrange,' said Efrem obligingly. 'Why don't you turn pages for my pianist?'

The man appeared backstage just before concert hour, in an ornate tuxedo. He followed Efrem and his accompanist on stage. First came the Glazunov with Efrem's own piano reduction. After only moments there was a minor commotion to his left, and Efrem glanced over to see his pianist diving to turn a page. Moments later the same thing happened. During intermission Efrem noted his pianist and page-turner in a heated huddle. In the second half all was quiet, the gypsy's captivated gaze riveted on the soloist's hands. Afterward he told Efrem that he had thoroughly enjoyed himself.

'I'm so glad,' Efrem replied. 'But you didn't turn a single page. Would you please tell me why not?'

'In the first half your pianist didn't tell me *when* to turn and in the second half he told me *not* to turn,' said the man matter-of-factly. He couldn't read a note of music.

CHAPTER 11

Return to Russia

(1909–1911)

Efrem was elated to arrive again in Kislovodsk, the beautiful spot associated with so much of his youth. He checked into the same old hotel, but with a significant difference: now, instead of entertaining the guests, he was taking the waters along with them and the many friends who welcomed him back. Summer concertmaster Lev Zeitlin was especially happy to see him, and the two spent many hours together. When Efrem spoke of a desire to expand his repertoire Zeitlin suggested the Sibelius Concerto, the Russian première of which he would soon give.

As a returned celebrity Efrem luxuriated in his hard-earned rest, soaking daily in hot springs over which the 18,510-foot Mt. El'brus towered. He renewed his friendship with Tatiana Schloezer's parents, who filled him in on all the latest details concerning 'l'affaire Scriabin,' and with his old schoolmate Eugene Lutsky, who was to be his accompanist on the tour. One evening in the dining room the pair recognized a fellow vacationer, Liadov, their harmony teacher from Conservatory days. The grumpy professor couldn't place them, but Efrem seized the opportunity to make a clean breast of it. 'Anatoly Konstantinovich, don't you remember the time Lutsky and I turned in the same counterpoint example in class? Neither of us wrote it—Sergei Prokofiev did.' 'Hah,' growled Liadov, 'I always suspected that he made money off you other students!'

Efrem's train had passed through Rostov on his way to Kislovodsk, yet he had felt no inclination to alight. His sense of independence, of having been on his own for so many years, had distanced him from the rest of the family. Efrem did eventually get to Rostov, where his parents introduced the younger children to their famous sibling. A brother, Samuel, had taken up the violin; he later switched to viola and did some composing. His brother Sascha was poised to begin his first year at the Leipzig Conservatory, studying cello under Julius Klengel. Alex was eager for Efrem's tales of travels and triumphs throughout Europe; he himself had never been outside Russia.

Efrem began his homecoming tour with a recital in his father's artistic habitat, the Smalov Theater. What seemed the entire population of Rostov turned out and took Efrem to their hearts with characteristic exuberance after the concert: when he appeared outside the stage door he was picked up by the cheering audience and carried home shoulder high. Concerts in Odessa and Kharkov followed. In Pavlovsk Efrem heard his friend Zeitlin's Sibelius Concerto. At the morning rehearsal he hated the work but changed his mind at the performance. He studied it, and it became one of the most requested pieces in his repertoire, as well as a personal favorite.

He played next in Moscow and Minsk. Before going on to St. Petersburg, he made a swing through Poland, Latvia and Estonia. His concert in Warsaw was attended by the Hilsberg family, whom he met backstage. Dismissing himself as a mere businessman, Mr. Hilsberg proceeded to his favorite topic of conversation, his sons. There were two present, one a banker and the other a pianist, Ignace. At home, he said, was the *real* wunderkind of the family—Alexander, an eight-year-old violinist who, he lamented, was lazy and steadfastly resisted all entreaties to practice. Papa Hilsberg proposed that Efrem come to dinner with his violin to stimulate Alexander's interest.

So the next afternoon Efrem visited the Hilsberg home. He set up in the music room and began practicing just when Alexander came home from school. The tones from behind the closed door immediately interested the boy. He was told that a great violinist was visiting and had wanted to do some work before dinner. The youngster was insatiably curious. Perched precariously atop a table and chair balanced against the door, Alexander spied on the visitor through the transom. A loud clatter in the hallway eventually brought Efrem to the door. The scene made him roar with laughter. 'You must be Alexander,' he ventured, locating a pair of startled eyes peering out from under the collapsed furniture. Efrem listened to the brothers play, and on his advice, their parents entered them in the St.

Petersburg Conservatory, where Alexander studied under Auer. Alexander Hilsberg's and Zimbalist's paths would cross again.

In Lodz Efrem met another future colleague when Isaak Rubinstein, local theater manager, introduced him to his pianist son Artur. Just twenty-one years old and fresh from his first U.S. tour, Artur was jolly company. Over a meal he fascinated Efrem with animated tales of the New World. Also present was violinist Paul Kochanski and Karol Szymanowski, with whose music Efrem was unacquainted. Artur enticed them all into playing poker well past midnight.

Efrem was invited to dinner at Auer's as soon as he arrived in St. Petersburg. The housekeeper, dour as ever, let him in, and a dinner of smoked sturgeon was served up. Auer, puffing on a fragrant cigar while sipping his after-dinner port, was friendly and clearly excited that Efrem's recital would include 'Suite in Alter Form.'

Efrem had been devastated at the news of Rimsky-Korsakov's death the previous year. His mind flashed back to Rimsky's prophetic words at their parting two years before: 'Goodbye dear friend. We won't see each other again.' They had kissed. And now, everywhere he was reminded of his privileged association with the departed master. He realized how much he had loved him. Zimbalist always credited him with more impact on his life than any other person except his first wife, at once formative musical influence and second father figure.

At the concert Rimsky's daughter and son Volodya sat in the front row in Symphony Hall. Beside them, looking gorgeous, sat Ekaterina Geltzer, the Imperial Ballet's star ballerina. The packed house also included Glazunov, Auer, Nalbanjian and the entire Conservatory faculty and student body. Efrem began with Bach's unaccompanied d minor partita, followed by the 'Suite in Alter Form,' which was warmly received; he also played a piece by his London acquaintance York Bowen. Paganini's 'Witches Dance' brought the program to a triumphant conclusion.

Auer was very complimentary. He urged Efrem to visit his next class to hear the new crop of talent, which then included Cecilia Hansen, Eddy Brown and Isolde Menges. The class still met at 2 p.m., and when, a few days later, Efrem entered the Conservatory at about 1:45, he was in for the experience of a lifetime. Although he could not have known it then, the event forever changed the course of violin playing and affected many a fine career, his own included.

Well aware of Auer's obsessive punctuality, he had allowed himself a little time to spare, opening the outer of the two doors to the Professor's studio at ten minutes to two. In the dark alcove between the doors stood a short man carrying a violin case. At his side was a young boy, violin in hand. The man spoke immediately, imploringly: 'You are Zimbalist—I heard you a few days ago. You have to help us.' He motioned toward the child and continued. 'This is my wonderful boy. Auer refuses to listen to him, but you could change his mind. I beg of you—give me two minutes and hear him play.'

The man's tone affected Efrem, which put him in a difficult position. He hesitated. 'I'd like to help you, but if I'm late for the class Professor Auer will be furious.'

'The class doesn't begin until two o'clock. You have five minutes. Please, just give us two.'

Efrem made a quick decision. 'If we can find an empty studio, I'll hear your son play a few notes.'

Luckily there was one right next door, and the eight-year-old, who looked for all the world as if he had stepped out of a Raphael painting, began to play. Indeed his angelic appearance and his performance of the Mendelssohn Concerto seemed inextricably linked. Two minutes lengthened into ten as Efrem, stunned, listened to the whole first movement. 'There was not a note or nuance out of place,' Zimbalist recalled. 'It was absolutely perfect.'

The class was in progress when, much to Auer's annoyance, Efrem ran in and grabbed his arm. 'Professor, come with me. I have just heard the most unbelievable boy. You *must* listen to him!' Auer drew himself up: 'Then bring him here.'

The boy's name was Jascha Heifetz. He played the Mendelssohn Concerto and a Paganini caprice, astounding all. The rest is history.

The full story is that when Heifetz's father first approached Auer about teaching his son, the class was already full. Since the successes of Elman and Zimbalist, Auer had been barraged by the hopeful parents of every prospective prodigy. Auer's irritability had increased with age. The more persistent the parent, the more disobliging he became. So when Ruvin Heifetz arrived, fresh out of Lithuania, Auer had Nalbanjian listen to little Jascha, saying it would be better for the boy to work in his assistant's class. This was not good enough for Papa Heifetz, and so he used leverage on

Zimbalist. After finally hearing Jascha, Auer, of course, immediately made room for him. He even went so far as to accept Ruvin (a violinist and his son's first teacher) into the class as well. Although Heifetz père was never an active member of the class, this authorization on paper was a bureaucratic ploy allowing him, as 'a Jewish student,' to remain in St. Petersburg with his son.

The blinding light with which Jascha filled Auer's studio that fall afternoon tended to put the members of the class who played after him somewhat in the shade. But Efrem was impressed by a young student sitting in to accompany that day, eighteen-year-old Emanuel Bay. He also remembered the beauty and vitality of Cecilia Hansen and the gifts of Miron Poliakin, as Jascha was to do. Poliakin was the lone member of the last group of Russian Auer students to return permanently to his country after the 1917 revolution and was considered a rival to the emerging David Oistrakh. The impression Jascha Heifetz made on Zimbalist remained 'vivid and unforgettable.' In his nineties, he could look back on at least eighty years of listening to violinists on all levels, and the only youngsters who were to approach the impression Heifetz made on him were Mischa Elman, Franz von Vécsey, Yehudi Menuhin and Oscar Shumsky, all about the same age when he first heard them.

While the musical success of Efrem's homecoming had been a foregone conclusion, in St. Petersburg he was called to task for his failure to register for military service. The explanation that spending time in the Imperial armed forces would damage his career was heard with skepticism, but a relieved Efrem was allowed to continue on to Norway.

Scandinavia was a fertile field ('lots of concerts and wonderful audiences'). Auer summered in Christiania (Oslo), and music lovers there were always interested in the latest prodigies from his atelier. In Stockholm Efrem found some short pieces by the violinist-composer Tor Aulin, two of which became signature tunes on his recital programs—'Humoresque' and the brilliant 'Impromptu.'

But Efrem's greatest honor was about to be bestowed in Leipzig. Dating from Joseph Joachim's performance of the Beethoven Concerto with Schumann conducting in the 1860s, he was considered the concerto's supreme interpreter and had played it in the Gewandhaus every New Year's Day. For two years following Joachim's death in August 1907 Nikisch, the Gewandhaus Orchestra's director, had, out of respect, scheduled no soloist

for the New Year's Day performances. But he had contacted Frau Wolff in
the interim, offering Efrem the distinction of being the soloist at the concert
on 1 January 1910. He suggested the Tchaikovsky Concerto, thus breaking
the time-honored tradition on two counts: a new violinist and a new concerto. Efrem's mind had raced back to the enthusiasm Nikisch voiced
backstage at the St. Petersburg Conservatory in 1907. Now Nikisch had
come through, and Efrem was simply thrilled.

Wherever he went, the dapper Nikisch was adored. His handsome face
was crowned by an unruly mop of dark hair, and the ladies in particular
were hypnotized by the curious brooding haziness of his eyes. He unfailingly complied when they wrote requesting one of his curly locks. A friend
once wondered that he had any hair left. 'Don't worry about me,' Nikisch
winked, pointing behind him. There, looking like a freshly shorn sheep, lay
his faithful black poodle.

Exceptionally charming, he knew how to get an orchestra's best with the
least effort, and without the slightest hint of unpleasantness. He believed
that it was only with the fresh attentiveness of his musicians that great
music could be made. Accordingly he never overrehearsed. A typical work
session began with unhurried stories of recent interesting experiences, or
exchanges with musicians: 'Is that you, Schultz? I had no idea you were a
member of this great orchestra. Do you remember when you and I played
under Liszt?' (Nikisch had been a violist.) Then, after removing his kid
gloves, he started work. Often he elected to briefly talk through the piece,
pointing out various pitfalls, rather than to play it all the way through, and
he usually ended the rehearsal with a friendly admonition: 'Tonight, gentlemen, I know as little as you what I might do. But if you would kindly
keep a close watch, I will try to make things enjoyable for both of us. And
now, we have worked hard—you won't mind if we stop a bit early?' Such
a conclusion invariably generated spontaneous applause; orchestra
members were ready to lay down their lives for the maestro. At performances they watched his baton like hawks. This was facilitated by the
overlarge cuffs Nikisch wore to focus attention on his small hands.
Nikisch's method, remarkably, accomplished both precision of ensemble
and the impression of an orchestra extemporizing in a trance.

Frau Wolff was waiting for Efrem at the station in Leipzig. She stressed
the magnitude of the Gewandhaus performance, assured him that all plans
were going well, and wanted to make sure that he was comfortable. Efrem

appreciated this thoughtfulness as an outward sign of the kind heart he had always suspected.

PROGRAM FOR THE TRADITION-SHAKING NEW YEAR'S DAY CONCERT,
LEIPZIG GEWANDHAUS, 1910

Efrem stepped on stage for the rehearsal, overcome. 'Welcome, my young friend. Nice to see you again,' Nikisch said as he took Efrem's hand. 'We have all been following your exciting progress, and look forward to a brilliant concert.'

'Thank you, Professor. It is a privilege.'

The oboe A sounded, Efrem tuned, and before long all were engrossed in the task at hand. At the concert Efrem's performance of the Tchaikovsky, his most inspired to date, met with an enormous ovation. After three curtain calls, Nikisch asked Efrem if he had any Bach for an encore. 'I do, Professor, but how could I play Bach after *Joachim*?'

'Go out and play it,' Nikisch prompted, with a gentle push.

The g minor Prelude and Fugue ensued, and the youth returned to the wings to receive Nikisch's effusions. In the conductor's room they talked about a repeat performance, planned for the next week in Berlin. An attendant started pouring champagne, and then came the inevitable stream of

fans, including Efrem's brother Sascha. Behind Sascha was a squat man
with a moon face who came right over and announced himself: Max Reger.
Efrem had heard of him. The reactionary composer removed a chewed
cigar from between his pudgy lips and, squinting through pince-nez bi-
focals, complimented him. 'Herr Zimbalist, you are a wonderful artist. I
enjoyed particularly your beautiful Bach playing.' And compliment it was,
taking into account Reger's regard for Bach (he was the first of the 'Back to
Bach' experts). Nikisch stepped over to accost his old friend: 'Ah, but Max,
you have never heard *me* play Bach.'

'Very fortunately not,' Reger growled, teeth clenched around his cigar.

'Efrem, give me your fiddle,' Nikisch requested and, taking it up, hacked
out a few bars of the Fugue. Reger squirmed. 'It was pretty bad,' Zimbalist
remembered.

Nikisch chortled, 'So hat Joachim gekrazt!' (That's how Joachim
scratched!), arousing Reger to hearty laughter—but not Efrem, who was
horrified at such disrespect.

Reger was flanked by two Russian champions of his works, critic
Alexander Schmuller (who had played his violin concerto) and pianist
Leonid Kreutzer. Both had graduated from the St. Petersburg Conservatory,
a decade earlier than Efrem, and Schmuller, who had also studied with
Auer, started to converse amiably in Russian. Eugene Simpson, correspondent for the *Musical Courier*, was standing by and suggested that a chamber
music session be organized. Another man was introduced as Leipzig's
leading surgeon; this Dr. Barban, a music lover and patron of the arts,
invited everyone to his home the following day for dinner and music-
making.

Schmuller and Kreutzer were there when Efrem arrived, along with
pianist Telemaque Lambrino, cellist Gdal Saleski, and an elderly physician,
Margulies. Barban expounded on his colleague's talent as a violinist,
stating that Margulies had been a favorite pupil of Wieniawski's before
taking up medicine to support his family. This was a new story to Efrem:
a budding musician who turned to another profession as a vocation yet
remained more enamored of music than many professional musicians.
Gdal Saleski, in *Famous Musicians of a Wandering Race*, described how
Zimbalist was modest enough to play second violin in the quartet that was
formed after dinner: 'We played several quartets of Mozart, Haydn and
Beethoven as well as the Brahms piano quintet with Leonid Kreutzer, and

later with Lambrino the quintet of Dvořák. . . . I had the opportunity to observe Zimbalist at close range. The gifted young man was the soul of the gathering and a charming gentleman. I also heard him that evening accompany Schmuller at the piano. He demonstrated an uncommon gift for accompanying.'

In Berlin Efrem returned to the Sans Souci. Performing with Nikisch in Berlin was just as thrilling as in Leipzig. Frau Wolff was there with news of fresh bookings. Hammig was there too and suggested that they all adjourn to a nearby beer garden, where Nikisch mentioned a concert he was giving the following week with Franz von Vécsey. Naturally Efrem wanted to attend, and at the Beethovensaal he found a ticket waiting for him, as Nikisch had promised.

Vécsey, very small for his sixteen years, appeared on stage. But his size, youth and quietness of manner didn't diminish the impact of his playing of the g minor concerto, written especially for him by Hubay. His tone had a great deal of character, its slight lack of sensuousness compensated for by the vitality of his bow attack. Whether or not the musical content of Vécsey's art equaled its violinistic brilliance was never satisfactorily established, because of his early retirement and mystery-shrouded last years. But the showpiece he played that day in Berlin admirably displayed his talent, leaving an indelible mark on Zimbalist's musical memory. He was quick to go backstage to express his admiration, and Nikisch invited the pair to join him for supper at his hotel.

Arriving at the Esplanade, Nikisch pointed out the dining room and excused himself to visit the men's room. Franz followed him, while Efrem waited in the lobby. A distinguished gentleman sporting a small beard and monocle came over. 'Aren't you Zimbalist?' he asked. Efrem nodded. 'I heard your splendid performance with the Philharmonic last week. You gave me much pleasure. I would like to do something for you. Have you ever been in a dirigible?' Efrem looked puzzled. The man smiled. 'Well, just get in touch with me whenever you feel like flying.' He thrust a card into Efrem's hand, tipped his hat and disappeared into the bar. Efrem's companions returned. 'What has you looking so astonished?' asked Nikisch.

'Professor Nikisch, what is a dirigible?'

'What on earth put such a thought in your head?

'A crazy man just talked to me about flying.'

'Which man?'

Efrem pointed. The man stood engaged in lively conversation, with a
large group of people surrounding him. Nikisch laughed. Pointing to the
name on the card he gleefully announced, 'That is Count Zeppelin!'
Efrem's eyes shot from the card to the celebrity in the bar, whose name was
on the tip of every tongue.

Ever since *Salome* Efrem had held Richard Strauss's name sacred and
considered the man himself on a par with the illustrious countrymen who
preceded him (Bach, Haydn, Mozart, Schubert, Beethoven, Schumann,
Brahms, Mendelssohn, Bruckner, Mahler) — the culmination of an
extraordinary flowering of German romanticism. How one country could
produce such boundless genius, its force dominating the musical world for
centuries, was inexplicable to Zimbalist. And now, before he made his way
back to London, he would play under Strauss's baton in Berlin! But he had
heard that Strauss was not charitable toward the works of living composers (especially of the Russians) and he was a little apprehensive about
the scheduled program: they were to do the Tchaikovsky Concerto.
Indeed, the only rehearsal (on the morning of the performance) did not
start out encouragingly. Strauss greeted his young soloist in a manner
more businesslike than friendly. His half sigh indicated his unwillingness
to go to any bother: 'Don't mind if the rehearsal doesn't go too well — I
don't know this work. But this afternoon I have a little time to look at it.
Tonight it will be all right.'

He tapped his baton and the rehearsal began. Things went so well that
Efrem would never have guessed Strauss was sight-reading the score.
There was a pause before the last movement to mark Auer's cuts, then the
concerto drew to a close. They shook hands. At the performance Strauss
conducted a spotless accompaniment of the Tchaikovsky — and he did it
without using the score. Afterward, he congratulated the astounded Efrem,
then shrugged, 'Well, the piece is not so bad after all.'

Backstage, Efrem was approached by a man who introduced himself as
'Pop' Adams. The man made an appointment to come to the Sans Souci,
where he explained to Efrem that he represented the New York Wolfsohn
Bureau, 'the biggest American management network,' and made annual
trips abroad to secure fresh talent for the agency. Efrem found it amusing
that, while he might represent the 'biggest,' Adams was the only man he had
ever met *smaller* than his beloved sponsor Joseph Fels. Whereas Fels's flattering beard and distinguished bearing enlarged one's perception of him,

Adams's pale complexion and anorexic tendencies made him appear even tinier. He came straight to the point, proposing that Efrem make a 1911 tour of the United States: thirty concerts at $300 each. 'At that time I was making more in Europe, so I told him I'd think about it,' Zimbalist recounted.

This was not his first American proposition. Plans for a fall 1908 tour under J. E. Francke's aegis had fallen through because of rumblings about Efrem's military service, although the official reason given was illness. In the long run this delay proved advantageous: Oscar Hammerstein had persuaded Mischa Elman to make a splashy New York debut at the Manhattan Opera House, with the Tchaikovsky Concerto, that same fall (Mischa had been excused from military obligations), and the New World probably couldn't have handled the simultaneous arrival of two young Russian sensations. By 1911 the increasingly music-loving American public would be ready for Zimbalist. He was ready too. In mulling over what he had heard and read about the United States three things came to mind: the Boston Symphony (then ranked by many as the world's finest), the Kneisel String Quartet, and—'I wanted to see the Grand Canyon,' he jested in 1979, 'so I signed!'

As a follow-up Adams sent Arthur Abell, Berlin correspondent for *Musical America*, to see Efrem. Abell impressed on him the futility of attempting a tour of the United States without the requisite publicity. It was then customary for artists to provide funds and publicity material—press clippings, photos, flyers, window display cards—to aid managers in promoting them; Efrem committed himself to a $1,500 advertising contract, which would make hefty inroads into his net. ('We called [*Musical America*] the "Revolver Journal"—they held a gun to your head, sparing you only if you paid them enough money.')

Before leaving Berlin Efrem went to an afternoon recital given by Henri Marteau, who had succeeded Joachim at the Hochschule. The impression made on him was not a favorable one. Other listeners reported a change in Marteau's style, from the French elegance that distinguished it prior to Berlin to the more pedestrian heaviness that characterized the playing Efrem heard. The Hochschule was still under Joachim's influence, perpetuated by his disciple Moser and others. Marteau had evidently fallen prey to this atmosphere.

In the foyer after the concert Efrem met the redoubtable Carl Flesch, who had recently settled in Berlin. Since they were heading in the same direction, Flesch suggested that they walk together. Flesch was highly opinionated. What he had to say about Marteau gave the distinct impression that he resented the Frenchman's engagement by the Hochschule, considering himself the logical choice for the post. As Efrem listened to Flesch expounding on one subject after another, he braced himself for a lecture on *his* shortcomings. But Efrem's playing was never mentioned, the monologue having finally settled on Flesch's own life and professional accomplishments, which he presently summed up: 'You see, I am a remarkable fellow. Without great talent I have achieved quite extraordinary things.' Pretty objective words.

Although Zimbalist later had great respect for Flesch's teaching, he offered a candid recollection: 'I heard many giants in my youth. Three who tried but didn't make it were Marteau, Burmester and Flesch.' He also heard J. M. Grün, Flesch's teacher. When asked how Grün sounded, Efrem quipped, 'Green is good for the eyes but not for the ears.'

Efrem arrived back in England, and that April, after celebrating his twentieth birthday at Cornwall Terrace, he left for a 'Harrison' tour of northern cities with Elena Gerhardt and Mark Hambourg. He returned to London for another successful appearance, on 25 May, with the London Symphony conducted by Alexander Chessin, an old colleague who had been director of the Imperial Music Society's concerts in St. Petersburg. The *Times*, next day, showed a good measure of the esteem in which the soloist was held: 'The young violinist who gave a concert yesterday afternoon in the Queen's Hall has already established himself in the affection of the English public, and has shown himself a genuine artist as well as a virtuoso of remarkable skill.' The *Times* also reviewed a subsequent recital, concluding humorously: 'Now that the custom of presenting flowers to lady performers has become so general as to become quite meaningless and often ridiculous, indiscreet enthusiasts are taking to giving them to men also [and when] Mr. Zimbalist, after his fine performance, had to accept a large bouquet, [he] did so with an air of embarrassment which enlisted one's sympathy.'

Zimbalist remembered the recital for an entirely different reason: 'During intermission Geller came backstage and said, "You must be quite a draw: Patti is in the audience!" I was very excited and just had to see her. After my last encore I managed to run round to the front of the hall to watch her getting into her carriage. Pulling my hat down low I joined the crowd and was all pins and needles as she came out. I saw an old lady on the arm of her very young husband, whom I was told was a Swedish baron. I stared. It was the only time I saw her, and I felt more keenly than ever my disappointment in not having heard her in St. Petersburg during student days.'

Efrem's first performance of the Beethoven Concerto was with the Royal Philharmonic that spring. He had been asked to play this masterpiece before but had always declined, not feeling ready—Auer had once told him that Ysaÿe had waited until he was over forty to meet the challenge. Efrem deeply loved Beethoven (he was horrified by Cyril Scott's dismissal of the Beethoven Concerto as 'nothing but an uninteresting succession of scales and arpeggios'), and the special dignity of his playing was perfectly suited to the music's eloquence. (In later years he ranked the Beethoven, Brahms, Sibelius, and Mendelssohn concertos the greatest in the repertoire, the latter having the most perfect form.)

Ysaÿe's student Louis Persinger, who heard one of Zimbalist's early Beethoven performances, described it as nobly beautiful. He distinctly remembered his legendary bowing control. In the slow movement, shortly after the second solo violin entrance, occurs one of Beethoven's most profoundly serene melodies. Its first four measures are played by many violinists in eight bows; those wishing to attempt a more seamless phrasing take them in four bows—Zimbalist spun it out majestically, and with singing tone, in just two. Persinger never forgot the feat, and when he heard Zimbalist play the concerto many years later in New York he was pleased to find his fabled bowing control unimpaired by the passage of time.

The Royal Philharmonic's manager, Francesco Berger, recorded his impressions of Zimbalist in *Reminiscences, Impressions and Anecdotes*: 'Efrem Zimbalist is one of the most remarkable artists I have known. Recommended by no less an authority than Glazunov, he created such an impression by his performance of the Beethoven Concerto at "the Philharmonic" that he was at once retained to repeat it during the orchestra's centenary in May 1912. [He is] in the front rank of living violinists, and many who heard him on the occasion I have mentioned, myself included, declare that in the whole range of their experience they have never listened to a nobler or more poetic rendering of that great work.'

Soon after Efrem's return to London, Nikisch arrived in town to play piano for Elena Gerhardt in a lieder recital, one of the things he enjoyed doing most. Efrem was there and saw her backstage. 'Elena, you sang so beautifully!'

'Hush,' she said, 'I won't accept any compliments in front of this magnificent lady.' Gerhardt motioned with great reverence toward the shriveled old woman who stood next to her. 'Allow me to introduce Pauline Viardot.' The eighty-nine-year-old Viardot was a piece of living history: her father had been the first Count Almaviva in *The Barber of Seville*; her brother Manuel Garcia had been the most celebrated singing teacher of the nineteenth century, and her sister was the legendary Maria Malibran, toast of the operatic stage, lover of Charles de Beriot and victim of a fatal equestrian accident at twenty-eight. Pauline Viardot was only months from her own end when Efrem met her.

The idyllic London spring of 1910 soon gave way to tribulations. In an interview a few years later, Efrem said, '[I had] no trials to speak of in England until after I became rather well known. Then they took the shape of numerous letters, from people whom I had never seen or heard of before. You have no idea what a lot of different proposals were made to me by this means, but I am sorry to say that most of them had some connection or other with money. Almost everybody who approached me appeared to be hard up, but they all had a first-class scheme for making a fortune, provided I would only lend them a bit to make a start with.'

Worse yet, his name figured in a paternity suit filed by a girl to whom Geller had introduced him at a concert reception. She claimed to be carrying Efrem's child. Knowing him to be thoroughly unsophisticated, and believing him to be a wealthy celebrity, she sought to take advantage. Confirming his naivete, he appeared before the bench without legal council. The initial hearing (which Efrem kept secret from the Felses) ended up in her favor, as the *Times* of 4 June 1910 reported in its criminal court columns: 'At Bow-street Mr. Curtis Bennett made an order on Efrem Zimbalist, a Russian violinist, who recently appeared at the Queen's Hall, to contribute five shillings a week towards the support of the illegitimate child of Miss Maud Sylvia Weaver, of Camden-gardens, Shepherd's Bush.'

'So I had to go to Fels, and he put the matter into the hands of his lawyers,' Zimbalist said. It took a while, but the ruling was reversed. Still, Efrem's faith in the goodness of mankind was grievously wounded. The experience made him more suspicious and world-wary, although throughout his life there remained in his makeup a touch of endearing gullibility.

Trouble continued with the Russian military authorities. Ambassador Benckendorff was being pressured to persuade Efrem to return to Russia. 'They seemed about to *make* me serve in the army,' Zimbalist remembered. 'Because of the uncertainty I couldn't accept engagements.' The situation was untenable, and Joseph Fels again came to the rescue. Having learned that the dowager Tsarina Empress Marie was making one of her frequent visits to her family in Denmark (her brother Frederick VIII was the Danish king), he traveled to Copenhagen and with considerable political deftness wangled an audience with her. He reminded the Empress how impressed she had been on hearing Efrem in London. He pointed out that it wasn't want of patriotism on Efrem's part but rather the prospect of losing momentum in a career he had worked so hard to build that made military service unattractive to him. (What an ironic turn of events: here was an envoy of well-known Socialist leanings begging an Imperial waiver for a former anti-Tsarist student demonstrator.) The dowager Tsarina was receptive, recalling that her son had done something to excuse Mischa Elman from service.

Fels wrote to an American friend in October 1910: 'I went to work for Zimbalist, our Russian violinist ward, to keep him from being forced to serve in the Russian army. Took me a week, and cost me some "massumon" too, but it's cheap all the same. "Z" is the greatest fiddler in the world today and America will hear him in 1911.'

In London Efrem received a letter from the Tsar exempting him from military requirements. When the Empress next visited Queen Alexandra, Efrem wanted to thank her. Ambassador Benckendorff picked him up in a gleaming carriage and escorted him to Buckingham Palace, where the Empress teased him mischievously. 'My dear young man,' she said, 'we didn't do it for you, but for fear that your hands might be hurt.'

On 10 November 1910 Efrem heard Kreisler's première of the Elgar Concerto under the composer's baton. Comparing notes afterward, Kreisler and Efrem were in agreement on two counts—the magnificence of the work and the impediment Elgar's conducting had been in its performance. Efrem bought the score and studied the concerto, though he never performed it, possibly because he spent the larger part of his productive years in the United States, where Elgar's music finds less favor. This is a pity since Zimbalist's style was ideally suited to the 'nobilmente' of the Elgar, and he himself considered it the last great concerto written for the violin. (In England, Albert Sammons became its major protagonist.)

Mary Fels's concerns about Efrem's upcoming American trip were reflected in a letter to her friend Horatio Connell, a baritone in New York under Wolfsohn management. She knew that the agency was looking for an accompanist for Efrem's tour and wanted to put in her two cents, in light of her continued misgivings about Geller. She asked Connell to keep an eye out for a pianist of fine character, explaining, 'My friend and protégé, Zimbalist, is an inexperienced and impressionable artist, and I think it of utmost importance that his accompanist in America should have moral and ethical qualifications in addition to being a fine pianist.' The Felses arranged for Efrem to be met on arrival and put up by their life-long friends, the Rosenbaums. Mrs. Fels was unable to make the trip over with him to attend his debut, which would take place in Boston, but she and her husband planned to arrive in time for the Carnegie Hall sequel.

First there was another tour of Germany. In Berlin, at the Sans Souci, a letter from Max Bruch was waiting. The composer had heard from Richter that Efrem was playing his 'Scottish Fantasia'—his letter begged for a visit and a performance of it. Efrem was only too glad to oblige, and called at the address given in the letter. A maid took him upstairs, where Bruch was in bed recuperating from pneumonia. He confided that Sarasate, dedicatee of the 'Scottish Fantasia,' had never cared for the piece. Without thinking to mention the cuts he had made when he first played it under Richter, Efrem began. Bruch, visibly affected, listened to the performance without a word, acknowledging each movement's close with a barely perceptible nod. At the end he reached out to press Efrem's hand. 'Thank you so much for giving me such pleasure—and your cuts were an improvement.' Such commendation from a figure as conservative as Bruch was the first of many instances where Zimbalist discovered composers, in general, to be flexible insofar as 'artistic liberties' are concerned.

On 9 April 1911 Efrem turned twenty-one. At 10 Cornwall Terrace, a big celebration marked his birthday and Schott's publication of his 'Suite in Alter Form' and 'Slavonic Dances.' That September he boarded the North German Lloyd Line's *Kaiser Wilhelm* and set sail for the land of fame and fortune, opportunity and, above all, the Grand Canyon.

CHAPTER 12

America and Alma: Love at First Sight

The Statue of Liberty was already welcoming voyagers to the harbor, but it was the New York skyline that loomed behind her that most excited Zimbalist after the ten-day crossing. He was met by the Rosenbaums, who helped him clear customs and bundled him into a taxi for the trip to Broadway and 106th Street — Zimbalist's first ride in an automobile. The West Side's wide streets were filled with a speedier bustle than he had ever experienced and, from the first, it got into his blood. He knew he was in the New World!

The Rosenbaums lived in a handsome brownstone. The doorman let them in with solemn deference, and a gleaming elevator (another novelty) whisked them all to the ninth floor, where the Rosenbaums occupied a corner apartment. The enormous high-ceilinged living room commanded a panoramic view of the tree-lined Hudson and the Palisades; costly paintings covered its walls, and a Hamburg Steinway filled the center of the room. Zimbalist settled in immediately and began to explore the alluring metropolis on his own.

Meanwhile Mary Fels's little scheme was hatching. Her letter to Connell had wound up in the hands of a Wolfsohn secretary's piano teacher, a young man by the name of Samuel Chotzinoff who was struggling to make headway in a fledgling pianistic career in order to support his poor Russian immigrant family. Secretary Dora Feller, a faithful student, was always on the lookout for his betterment, and Mrs. Fels received a letter composed by the two of them that presented Chotzinoff as an accompanist and artists' companion of vast experience, which he certainly was not. Also implied was an age upward of his twenty-one years. This letter had arrived in time for Mrs. Fels to discuss Chotzinoff with Efrem before he left London. Her intuition was that the pianist was ideal, and Efrem had agreed to hear him; but 'Pop' Adams, head of the Wolfsohn Bureau, had arranged for Zimbalist to try out half a dozen other pianists as well. The candidates were auditioned at the Rosenbaums' over several days. Chotzinoff's turn came toward the end, as he described in *Day's at the Morn*:

> Mr. Zimbalist came into the room. He looked exactly like his pictures—very youthful, very Slavic [and] he appeared completely at his ease. [He] pressed my hand warmly with both his hands, and said with the thickest of Russian accents, 'Excuse me, please, I did not mean to keep you vaiting. Sit down, please. I am so happy to see you. Vhat a *vahnder*ful country you live in!... But you are not comfor*table* in this chair. Let me bring you another one.... Perhaps you vould like some coffee? I tink it vould be nice to have a little coffee.' He pressed a button [and said to the maid] with the same pleasant earnestness, 'Excuse me, please, vould you be so kind, if it is not too much trahble, to bring perhaps some coffee.'... I was enchanted.

After coffee, Zimbalist said, 'Shall we play a leetle?' Already nervous, Chotzinoff became even more so when he sat down at the piano and, staring at the cover of the music in front of him, read, 'A. Glazunov— Concerto for Violin.' 'I was unaware that Glazunov had [even] written a violin concerto,' Chotzinoff wrote. 'All my work on the violin repertoire had gone for nothing.' Zimbalist allowed him a few minutes to look through the music, and they started to play. Chotzinoff did his best to keep pace with Zimbalist's rubati, and they ended together. Zimbalist smiled— '*Vahnder*ful!'—and engaged Chotzinoff on the spot. The pianist was almost in tears.

At an earlier dinner the Rosenbaums had also introduced their guest to the pianist André Benoist, whose name was later associated with such artists as Mary Garden, Ernestine Schumann-Heink, Kreisler, Elman, and Heifetz; Zimbalist engaged him to replace Chotzinoff for a few concerts during his early American tours. In contrast to Chotzinoff's colorful description of Zimbalist, Benoist in 1911 found the young Russian 'painfully shy.' Zimbalist's lifelong aversion to formal dinners did result in long silences at the table.

Many of the accompanists who had auditioned along with Chotzinoff played as well as he did, but Zimbalist's compassion ('poverty was written all over the boy's face') had taken the upper hand. The bright shine on Chotzinoff's shoes didn't hide the fact that they were falling apart. He was affected by the young man's situation, and his earnestness, perhaps more than by his pianistic abilities. After the audition Zimbalist invited him to lunch at a '*vahnder*ful' place he had discovered on a walk the previous day. Childs Restaurant was on 59th Street, and the pair walked down Broadway, stopping frequently for Zimbalist to gaze at the window displays; he finally made a stop at one store to indulge his fondness for brightly colored silk shirts, buying one pink, one blue and one mauve.

Zimbalist's enthusiasm for statistics amused Chotzinoff. Zimbalist asked him, 'Now, what do you think is the population of Japan?' Chotzinoff shook his head. 'No, really! What do you think?' When his accompanist made a guess, Zimbalist fixed him with an enchanting smile. 'Twenty millions? My dear friend, Japan has *hundreds* millions!' Further revelations concerned the annual bushels of wheat produced in the Ukraine and the number of stars in the solar system. This continued at Childs, which they entered after a few minutes spent on the sidewalk in front, watching through its window a cook flipping buckwheat cakes. Zimbalist had been drawn to the place because of the white tiles that covered its interior — the number of which he now decided to estimate.

At the Wolfsohn Bureau Adams gave Chotzinoff a datebook of Zimbalist's engagements for the upcoming tour and, taking a pencil and ruler in hand, sketched the tour's path across the continent on the large map on the wall beside his desk. The concerts were about evenly divided between orchestral solo appearances and recitals with piano, which meant Chotzinoff could expect about $60 a week, out of which all road expenses were to be paid. Although this was double Chotzinoff's previous income, Zimbalist contributed another $40 a week toward his pay and took care of both his accompanist's and his own traveling expenses.

Chotzinoff by now idolized Zimbalist. He lived only to serve him, and, on 1 October 1911, felt privileged to be asked to help his hero unpack at his new suite at the Prince George Hotel on East 28th Street. He looked admiringly at Zimbalist's expensive items of jewelry and fabulous wardrobe. In particular he admired his finely tailored dress suit, and said so.

Zimbalist guessed, correctly, that Chotzinoff didn't own tails and immediately offered him his own. 'Just your size,' he said. Although honored, Chotzinoff found it difficult to accept so generous a gift. Zimbalist insisted. He assured his colleague that he had taken the precaution of ordering several duplicates from the tailors at New York's exclusive Bell Brothers. The set of tails was complete right down to suspenders, an evening shirt with studs and cufflinks and black silk stockings to go with a pair of glossy patent leather shoes, also just Chotzinoff's size. Then Zimbalist reached for an afternoon cutaway at the back of the trunk and offered it as well. 'It will come in handy.'

Until Zimbalist started to fulfill an increasing number of social engagements on his own (which his new pianist resented) Chotzinoff dogged his steps, drinking in the entrancing manners and old-world aura with which the Russian succeeded in bowling over seemingly half the female contingent of New York. Waitresses in the 'leetle places' frequented by the two musicians were treated to an apologetic effusiveness that charmed their socks off.

Chotzinoff was worried that Zimbalist never practiced or showed any inclination to rehearse. The pianist spent virtually all day at the suite, where an upright had been installed for him. When he finished his own practicing and was too tired to travel crosstown to his East Side home, he spent the night on Zimbalist's living room sofa. All the while his host's violin rested untouched. Chotzinoff knew that the Boston debut was only weeks away, but nothing seemed further from Zimbalist's mind. His routine seldom varied: he arose late and luxuriated in a lengthy hot bath before ordering up breakfast. On the breakfast tray were messages related to the days' activities. Before he stepped out to explore the city, plans for the evening would be made. He had joined the New York Bohemians, and dinner was often at the club, or at the homes of new acquaintances. Most days were free for unhurried visits to used book stores, autograph dealers and antique emporiums. When he grew hungry he could always find a 'leetle place' for an inexpensive bite.

Zimbalist's suite at the Prince George was the center of the kind of hubbub that surrounds any celebrity. Chotzinoff was unnerved by the constant ringing of the telephone and ceaseless procession of bellboys, deliverymen and other callers; he was sometimes asked to answer the phone: 'Would you be so kind?' But most of the time Zimbalist answered, always unruffled, greeting callers as if they were long-lost friends even when he had never heard of them. He was besieged by photographers, parents with children carrying violin cases and delegations of Jewish charity organizations hoping for benefit concerts. He soon got into the habit of referring them to Chotzinoff, who became expert at polite but summary dismissals.

Chotzinoff viewed warily a heavily pockmarked man by the name of Davis, who came by to follow up on the advertising contract Zimbalist had signed in Berlin. He felt sure Mrs. Fels had had just such people in mind when she entrusted him with the chaperoning of her protégé, and he felt dismayed and powerless when Zimbalist received Davis warmly and listened intently to his every unconvincing word. Davis sent a writer from *Musical America* to interview his new client. This first American interview, accompanied by a candid photo, mentioned Zimbalist's shyness about his own accomplishments, calling him aggravatingly laconic, but it ended with the conviction that his 'frank, open, cheerful and cordial' smile— besides seeming 'always à propos, enlivening his occasional conversation and adding point to his protracted silences'—was of a kind seen but once in a generation.

Most people found Zimbalist charming and accommodating in the extreme. But there were some who didn't. Among callers at the Prince George were numerous poor immigrant Russians who claimed to be members of his family. (A newspaper report mentioned them waiting dockside as Zimbalist disembarked.) Some who said they had fled to the United States after the 1905 upheavals were probably legitimate, if far removed, relatives; others were simply gold diggers. Having left Rostov at so early an age and, in effect, severing any close family ties, Zimbalist couldn't recall having met or even heard of any of them, and they got no handout. Many harbored permanent resentment against him. 'In his success he turned his back on us,' a distant cousin told the author seventy years later. Zimbalist always considered his position perfectly justifiable.

Mischa Elman phoned, and they agreed to meet at the Russian Tearoom for lunch. This picturesque establishment abuts Carnegie Hall and in later years, when he lived just a few blocks away on Central Park West, became a favorite Elman hangout. The conversation, as usual with Elman, centered mostly around himself. (A typical Elman greenroom scene: after expounding at length on the high points of his performance, Elman turned the proceedings over to friends. 'Well, I haff talked enough about myself. What did *you* tink of my performance?') But during lunch at the Russian Tearoom Elman talked only briefly about his musical victories; instead he chattered on about his virtuoso female conquests. Zimbalist made a mental note that his colleague had turned frisky out from under Papa Elman's watchful eye, and he found the whole conversation rather silly.

His unpleasant litigious experience in England had left Zimbalist somewhat suspicious of the opposite sex, despite Chotzinoff's impression that women found him irresistible. The press, of course, fostered this impression. Billed as 'the Poet of the Violin,' Efrem was portrayed as a 'Russian Romantic,' not only a musician but also a writer of poems and a play, *The Fateful Marriage*. Newspapers made much of his 'romantic' appearance, and *Musical America* went so far as to print an ode he had allegedly written for his first lady love: 'Oh my Queen of wintry snows, / Nobody in Russia knows / How completely I adore thee' — and so forth.

Chotzinoff continued his daily practice at the Prince George while Zimbalist was gone in Boston, astounded that his idol had not once picked up his violin before leaving. They had gone to Grand Central Station together and were met there by a man from the Wolfsohn Bureau, whom Adams had provided as troubleshooter for the trip. With the reassurance that ample time remained to rehearse for the Carnegie Hall recital and a cheerful wave, Zimbalist had left.

His arrival in Boston coincided with a spell of Indian summer weather. Olin Downes called on him at the Copley Plaza, to gather background material for a piece he was writing about the debut. Downes pressed him for his most meaningful experience in Europe. 'Hearing Emmy Destinn in *Salome*' was the unhesitating response.

On 27 October 1911 Zimbalist made his U.S. debut in the first American performance of the Glazunov Concerto, with the Boston Symphony under the direction of Max Fiedler. It was a decided victory. In its review the *Boston Globe* made much of Zimbalist's 'glorious tone, exquisite cantilena and faultless technique, as near perfect as any human violinist is likely to get.' Two leading critics noted the perfect accuracy of his intonation. The *Boston Journal* couldn't resist a comparison with Elman: 'The newcomer is quite unlike his compatriot Mischa Elman: Elman is a youth of leonine individuality, while Zimbalist is the master player, a sensitive interpreter, the creator of prodigiously pure tones.' Another critic wrote, 'Elman has the more pronounced violinistic instinct; Zimbalist is immeasurably greater as an artist and a musician, scorning anything approaching sensationalism.'

The Russians were also compared with their Austrian colleague, Fritz Kreisler. A piece appeared in *Vogue*, bringing up age-old questions about child prodigies. The writer ranked Zimbalist above Elman, but preferred Kreisler to both, guessing that the Russians had suffered from being pushed as wunderkinder.

One of Zimbalist's immediate and most avid admirers was Boston Symphony concertmaster Franz Kneisel. This much-respected musician's contributions had been an important factor in educating the musically unsophisticated America he had discovered when, as a youth of twenty, he arrived from Germany to assume his duties in Boston. He soon formed the celebrated quartet that bore his name and toured widely, bringing chamber music, often for the first time, to every corner of the country. He considered introducing the late Beethoven quartets to American ears a special mission.

Chotzinoff welcomed Zimbalist back from Boston as a conquering hero but was sorry to discover that he still showed no desire to practice or rehearse, just when New York's musical pulse quickened in anticipation of hearing the violin kingdom's latest sensation. It hadn't long to wait. On 2 November, Zimbalist played the Glazunov Concerto in Carnegie Hall with the New York Philharmonic; it was also conductor Josef Stransky's debut with the orchestra, as successor to Gustav Mahler. Within a week Zimbalist would join them again in the Tchaikovsky Concerto and was due to play his first Carnegie Hall recital on 10 November with Chotzinoff.

On the morning of the Philharmonic debut, Chotzinoff had to wake Zimbalist in order to get him to rehearsal on time. The violinist was completely unperturbed, taking the time to leisurely bathe and dress before leaving for the hall. When they arrived Stransky was peering out into the auditorium, looking for his soloist. Zimbalist shook his hand and started to play with complete absorption. The orchestra often strayed out of synchronization with him, and they stopped several times to regroup. At the end of the rehearsal Zimbalist shook hands with the concertmaster and Stransky, while the orchestra thundered its approval. He did not comment when Chotzinoff asked his opinion of Stransky's accompaniment.

In *The Great Conductors*, Harold Schonberg quotes Karl Muck (with whom Zimbalist was later to give his most memorable performance of the Beethoven Concerto): 'Stransky can do nothing, and the nothing he can do least is accompany.' Thankfully Zimbalist's tolerant temperament enabled him, the few times he played under his baton, to take Stransky's inadequacies in stride. But the orchestral musicians progressively lost respect for their maestro as they watched him run the Philharmonic nearly into the ground during his twelve-year tenure.

On the afternoon of the big day Zimbalist received visitors as usual, took a long walk and went out to lunch. He gave no indication of concern that he was about to make perhaps the most important debut of his career. The occasion attracted all New York's musical notables, including Arturo Toscanini and Emmy Destinn. (The famous opera star had chanced on Zimbalist's flattering mention of her in the press and had two dozen long-stemmed roses delivered to him backstage.) Chotzinoff, of course, was in rapt attendance, one of many standees at the back of the hall. The end of the Glazunov was greeted with tumultuous applause, and Zimbalist went out again and again to bow. Chotzinoff knew he was witnessing a triumph.

So did the critics. Among the raves was that of W. B. Chase in the *New York Tribune*: 'Mr. Zimbalist is a tone-poet [whose] playing, coming after the vast deal of fiddling we have heard lately, was refreshing in its artistic maturity and astonishing poise.' Richard Aldrich in the *New York Times* wrote that Zimbalist's poignant expression, beautiful tone and plastic phrasing had made the most of a perfunctory work, 'a singularly jejune piece, with little real inspiration.' (Ysaÿe refused to play the Glazunov because of the brassiness in the finale, likening it to circus-band music.) *Musical America*'s critic Arthur Farwell reported that the soloist was 'an instantaneous and genuine success of the sort that does not often occur in the concert world,' and fully expected Efrem to 'conquer the world like an Alexander.'

Among the notables who came backstage to greet the soloist was Franz Kneisel, in New York to give a 'late' Beethoven concert with his quartet (Zimbalist attended the concert next evening). Others who became close friends were Alexander Lambert, Frederick Steinway and Rawlins Cottenet, who as a member of the Metropolitan Opera House board of directors represented the Vanderbilt interests. Over supper at Sherry's this tall, aristocratic man told Zimbalist of his plan to organize a private recital at Mrs. Vanderbilt's and promised to send a violin piece he had composed.

By this time the Felses had arrived on the scene, and Zimbalist took them to meet Adams. This 'strategy summit' must have been something to see. Joseph Fels and 'Pop' Adams started in on negotiations, and Fels instructed Adams to pull out all promotional stops. To the campaign's central figure these tiny men made a droll picture, embroiled as they were in the formulation of a plan that he thought was blown out of all proportion, but Fels was finally satisfied.

Chotzinoff was much relieved when Zimbalist suggested they start preparing for the Carnegie Hall recital, and he attributed this stimulation of his colleague's sense of industry to the Felses' arrival. Adams had also scheduled a private concert, prior to the recital, at the home of General Edward P. Meany in Paterson, New Jersey. The joint artist would be the popular American soprano Alma Gluck, a name Chotzinoff certainly knew, but Zimbalist didn't.

To get to Paterson they were to take a ferry across the Hudson to Union City and a train through the New Jersey countryside. As they boarded the ferry, they passed Alma Gluck, sitting near the front door with her accompanist Arthur Rosenstein and a friend, Althea Jewell. Sitting down in the rear with Zimbalist, Chotzinoff settled in for the short ride. He noticed his companion's distracted efforts to read the afternoon paper. After a while he put the paper down and turned to Chotzinoff, and the classic story begins. 'Excuse me Samuel, but did you notice that pretty woman sitting up front?'

'That is Alma Gluck,' Chotzinoff answered.

'Very pretty,' Zimbalist reiterated, and Chotzinoff told him Miss Gluck's story. Alma Gluck, née Reba Fierson, was born in Bucharest; when she was still a small child her parents had brought her to New York. She was employed as an East Side stenographer when she married a Mr. Glick, by whom she had a daughter. Glick encouraged his wife's voice studies; she eventually sang for Gatti-Casazza and Toscanini, who persuaded her to change the 'i' in her name to 'u' and then engaged her for the Metropolitan Opera. She made a spectacular debut there and had since become a popular concert artist. 'Do you think she would mind if I went up and spoke to her?' Zimbalist got up, walked over to Miss Gluck and bowed with extravagant politeness. Miss Gluck's friend Althea switched to an empty seat beside Rosenstein so that Efrem could sit down next to Miss Gluck; he remained at her side all the way to Union City, where together they awaited the next train to Paterson. Again, they were seatmates.

In Paterson they were met by two automobiles. Zimbalist joined Alma Gluck, Althea Jewell and Rosenstein in the first; Chotzinoff, much to his chagrin, was herded into the second. Arrangements had been made for the musicians to freshen up at a nearby hotel; in the privacy of their room Chotzinoff asked Zimbalist's impression of Miss Gluck. 'Very pretty, very pretty' was all he said. She was already at General Meany's house when they arrived, tall and radiant in a white satin gown, her dark hair in a braid around her head, her hands encased in long white gloves, in one hand a small fan.

Zimbalist was convinced he had never seen any woman as beautiful. After starting the program he stood off to the side with Chotzinoff while Alma Gluck sang. Both were taken with the velvet purity and exquisite flexibility of her voice. But what affected them most — and it was this quality that endeared her to listeners — was her intimate delivery. She had the rare gift of leaving each member of her audience with the impression that she had been singing for them alone. In Zimbalist's case, that afternoon in New Jersey, the impression may have been an accurate one. Efrem disappeared into her dressing room at intermission. On the train going back they sat together, and on the ferry they wandered off to the railing to look at the New York skyline. When they arrived at the dock, Zimbalist and Miss Gluck got into a cab and drove away, leaving behind a dejected Chotzinoff.

A few evenings later Zimbalist took her out to dinner. Chotzinoff (who had arrived at the Prince George in the morning as usual) observed with mixed enthusiasm the smitten violinist's elaborate preparations for the date. After an extended hot soak in the tub he put on his finest full evening dress. Then in charmingly apologetic terms he asked his accompanist to telephone downstairs for a private car and chauffeur. Zimbalist called for Miss Gluck at her apartment, and, as Chotzinoff had feared, he took her to Childs Restaurant, the epitome of a tacky American coffee shop. Zimbalist next day was pleased to report that Miss Gluck had enjoyed watching the man behind the plate glass window tossing buckwheat cakes and was equally impressed by the plethora of white tiles. The evening ended with Zimbalist playing the piano for her at the Prince George. He introduced her to little known arias from Rimsky-Korsakov operas, including 'Song of India' from *Sadko*, which she subsequently added to her repertoire. They exchanged stories. She amused him with her account of having sung 'Das Lied von der Erde' under the composer's direction; Mahler had had to tell her to quit beating her foot. And Alma suggested another date: 'I'm having a few friends over for Sunday afternoon tea — won't you come?' To Chotzinoff, Zimbalist seemed delirious.

Decades later Alma Gluck still loved to tell *her* version of their first date, as quoted in Marcia Davenport's autobiographical *Too Strong for Fantasy*: 'For days he followed me around trying to persuade me to go out to dinner with him, showing up in his best clothes and handing me his card after the opera. I finally agreed. He picked me up in a taxi and we rode to Columbus Circle. When he pointed to Childs he said: "Madame, have you ever seen anything so beautiful?" We stood outside for a long time admiring it. Then he took me in and we had scrambled eggs.'

Cottenet often dropped by the Prince George to hear a bit of the now daily rehearsals, before taking Zimbalist out to lunch. His violin piece, 'Chanson Méditation,' had arrived as promised. Zimbalist and Chotzinoff played it for him, to his obvious pleasure, and to theirs. It was delightful. They were surprised when told that it was his only composition. The man was a font of entertaining gossip about all the impressive names in the social register, as well as the great artists he numbered among his close acquaintances. Talk got around to Fritz Kreisler, one of his 'dearest friends.' It was not until after Cottenet's death that Zimbalist learned the true story about 'Chanson Méditation.' Kreisler confided that Cottenet had yearned to impress his artistic friends with a show of personal creativity. Finally he had begged his old friend to help him out, and Kreisler had obliged — with the 'Chanson Méditation by Rawlins Cottenet.'

Carnegie Hall was sold out on the afternoon of 10 November 1911, and chairs had to be set up on stage behind the piano. Alma Gluck occupied the box nearest the stage; the Felses and Rosenbaums occupied one lower-tier box; the Chotzinoff family were in an adjoining box, ready to witness their Samuel's hour of triumph. It was Zimbalist's, too. The dazzling ease with which he tossed off Paganini's 'Witches Dance' to end the program had the audience on its feet. Alma was at her most charming afterward, backstage; Fels was there too, congratulating Adams and attributing the packed house to all-out advertising. In line with his views on publicity Fels would later gladly absorb the difference in price when Zimbalist traded in the faithful Guadagnini for a 1716 Stradivarius Hammig had come across. While he had trouble pronouncing and even remembering the name Guadagnini, Fels knew the effect the name Strad had on the public. This particular example, the 'Titian,' was considered by some connoisseurs the loveliest-toned fiddle in existence. Zimbalist was proud to be able, in time, to repay Fels. (The price of the 'Titian' in 1912 was around $12,000. It is now worth millions.)

The Carnegie Hall program had included, aside from Paganini, Bach's solo sonata in g minor, standards by Brahms, Tchaikovsky and Drdla and a couple of interesting additions to Zimbalist's repertoire, a suite by York Bowen and 'Tallahassee,' written for him by Cyril Scott. Press reaction was unanimous. In the *Times* Aldrich wrote: 'The highest point of Zimbalist's achievement was reached in the Bach, which he interpreted with magnificent breadth, dignity of style, and easy command over all the awkward difficulties with which Bach's style besets the performer.' Irving Weil summed it up in the *New York Journal*, calling Zimbalist 'indeed, already, one of the very greatest of living violinists.'

CHAPTER 13

Trying the New World On for Size

Mary Fels invited Chotzinoff to forsake his practicing long enough to meet her downstairs in the tearoom of the Prince George for a chat. She had chosen an early hour when she knew Zimbalist would still be asleep. The candleglow highlighting Mrs. Fels's face as she leaned closer across the table lent her features more urgency than they usually possessed. She spoke in her hushed way. 'Things are going all right with Efrem, it seems? What is your opinion of his character?'

Chotzinoff rhapsodized. Mrs. Fels laughed, and told Chotzinoff how devoted she and her husband were to Efrem. She finished with an assessment of Chotzinoff's character: 'You look like a good man, Mr. Chotzinoff. Don't forget that I expect you to have the best influence on him.' Chotzinoff thanked her for the compliment and invited her, her husband, and Zimbalist to dinner at his home.

The Felses and their protégé made the trip down to East Broadway a few evenings later. Mrs. Chotzinoff had splurged as far as means permitted, and the occasion was a successful one, much to her son's relief. Joseph Fels carried on a lengthy one-sided conversation with Chotzinoff senior (who didn't speak English) on business matters and the Single Tax movement. Blintzes were served. Zimbalist, charming as ever, declared them the best he had had since leaving Rostov. He loved things simple and homely and missed them at the parties in New York's great houses, where he was often engaged to give private performances. Such 'privates' (Chotzinoff's term for musicales in posh homes) flowed on the heels of Zimbalist's initial success in New York. In looking back Zimbalist sized things up: 'If I had to depend only on the thirty concerts that had been booked, my first season would have been a deficit year.... Luckily there were many private concerts. They paid $1,000 each the first year. So I left New York a rich man!'

The first was in the home of a leading society figure, Mrs. Ogden Mills. Zimbalist's co-artist was the soprano Georgette LeBlanc, wife of Maurice Maeterlinck. Once considered a rival of Mary Garden, LeBlanc was clearly over the hill, and her singing reduced Chotzinoff to the giggles. A beautiful woman sitting next to him spread out her white ostrich feather fan to offer him cover. The pianist's embarrassment changed to awe when the woman with the fan introduced herself as the wife and model of artist Charles Dana Gibson: she was the original Gibson girl.

'Privates' followed at other glittering mansions: the Astors', the Belmonts', the Clarence Mackays'. When they played at the Cornelius Vanderbilts', a flunky in a cutaway took Chotzinoff's hat and coat and led him over to where the men stood chatting. Zimbalist was already among them, exuding the exotic touches that made 'foreign' artists so desirable at snobby gatherings. But the disillusioned Chotzinoff discerned few, if any, cultivated accents or bon mots in the conversational hum, and the blank gaze on most faces disconcerted him. He thought that Zimbalist looked out of place, his polite manners and dignity far exceeding what the occasion warranted. Perhaps Chotzinoff's observations of New York's elite bore a trace of prejudice. He openly preferred playing in wealthy Jewish homes, where the hosts displayed a high level of sophistication in their programming tastes and the applause was heartier; in Gentile houses, it seemed to him, often the only interest given the musical segment was its length, in order that the evening's other events could take place on time.

Perhaps Zimbalist and Chotzinoff did seem to meet more fascinating people in the homes of the Adolph Lewisohns, and the Jacob Schiffs, where the convivial environment made them feel at home and where they were valued far beyond their interest as curiosities. But Zimbalist couldn't help being impressed by the splendor of it all: 'On one occasion Mrs. Vanderbilt engaged Josef Hofmann and me to entertain "an important audience." The entire audience consisted of Mrs. Vanderbilt and her two daughters. Of course, she always did things on a grand scale. Another time I was playing an afternoon game of bridge with Cornelius and his wife. Suddenly she said, "We're having a few people over for dinner this evening. Won't you join us?" "But I have no time to change," I said—I was wearing an open collar and sport coat. "Oh, don't bother," she laughed, "stay as you are." Some 150 guests showed up for dinner. Every single man wore tails with stiff wing collars. After dinner two orchestras were set up at opposite ends of the mansion for dancing. This was their notion of "having a few friends over for dinner." One of the guests was Otto Kahn, president of the Loeb banking concern. I was introduced to him. When we shook hands I felt only two fingers. I asked Mrs. Vanderbilt about it, and she said, "Don't be offended—he always gives actors and musicians two fingers. It's bankers or brokers who get the whole hand."'

Chotzinoff, riding on Zimbalist's coattails, got to know Alma Gluck fairly well, and he remained an ardent admirer of her exemplary art. Gluck's daughter Abigail (Marcia Davenport), eight or nine years old at the time, remembered Chotzinoff tagging along when Zimbalist, invariably loaded down with toys for her, came calling. Once when Abigail was away at school in Peekskill her mother, Zimbalist and Chotzinoff arrived for a surprise visit and gave the students an impromptu concert. Whenever Gluck's regular accompanist was unavailable Chotzinoff stepped in, and he was later engaged as Abigail's piano teacher.

The Zimbalist-Gluck romance was top-priority gossip. Coincidentally an operetta called *Alma, Where Do You Live?* was enjoying a long down-town run, leading one wag to answer, 'Why, at Zimbalist's of course.' People relished the fantasy inherent in so sparkling a pairing of talents, but there were those who with raised eyebrows pointed out the difference in their ages (Gluck was six years older), plus the uncomfortable fact that, with seeming ingratitude for Glick's generous promotion of her career, Alma had divorced him—in those days a scandal on its own.

Zimbalist wasn't the slightest bit hesitant in making his intentions known, proposing almost immediately, if to no avail. He reminisced: 'Meeting Alma was the luckiest thing that ever happened to me. Her pos-itive influence was tremendous. Despite my successes and travels I was still, at twenty-one, an innocent young man. Meeting her not only helped me to mature, but also protected me from the darker sides of life, of which I was so ignorant. At that time I was completely open to influence and could easily have fallen into all sorts of hands. Alma was probably the most extraordinary person I have ever met. I was only sorry that she didn't agree to marry me sooner.'

One of Alma's objections was not that her suitor *was* too young but that he *appeared* too young. This he tried to overcome by taking up cigar smoking. 'I thought it would make me look older and more important,' he laughed years later, lighting up what he estimated was his 92,000th-some cigar. Likely the controversy regarding the year of his birth, started around this time, was a deliberate attempt to close the gap in their ages. The birth date question had nothing to do with reconciling the old Russian calendar: this was a matter of an entire year. Zimbalist confirmed having graduated at seventeen and having made his U.S. debut at twenty-one, but shortly thereafter newspapers and publicity releases were reporting 1889 as the year of his birth. The confusion was compounded by a review of his London debut that placed his age in 1907 at fourteen, instead of seventeen. Even Zimbalist himself became unsure of the year of his birth. Many years later, on a Russian tour, he found records of his age at graduation; they were consistent with the date on his passport and confirmed his actual birth date: 9 April 1890 (28 March, old Russian calendar). In any case, the age issue apart, Alma had considerable misgivings about being able to combine a busy career with the sort of marriage she wanted the second time around. It was a thorny dilemma, one she wrestled with for more than two years.

Zimbalist's cross-country tour began in Cleveland that winter of 1911. From there, Zimbalist, Chotzinoff and Mary Fels sped to Chicago overnight under bitter weather conditions on the Twentieth Century Limited; after the recital, at the Studebaker Theatre, Mary took them to an icy North Shore Drive for dinner at the home of an advertising magnate in her husband's organization. Next morning Zimbalist and Chotzinoff put her on a train back to New York and steamed on to Minneapolis, thence zigzagging southwest, hitting Omaha, Denver and such colorful smaller towns as Wichita and Colorado Springs, with its hot sulphur baths and TB sanitarium. The wheat fields of Kansas and Nebraska reminded Zimbalist of the Ukrainian farm belt. On longer stretches between stops Chotzinoff noted his colleague laboriously writing letters; he didn't know what a departure this was from the norm, but it didn't escape his notice that the letters were all going to Alma's New York address. At the Santa Fe terminal Zimbalist delightedly sighted several ten-gallon hats and fancied that a bona fide American Indian might be among the crowd. The West enthralled him, and he felt surer with every passing day that this new country of strange extremes would become his home.

Groves of orange trees heralded their arrival in Los Angeles, where the travelers took a four-day breather. Zimbalist seized the opportunity to engage in some unhurried shirt shopping; Chotzinoff spent his free time visiting local family. A sister-in-law, passing the disconcerting comment that Mischa Elman had presented *his* accompanist with a gold watch and chain, expressed surprise that Samuel didn't have one. Feeling slighted but confident that he knew his mark, Chotzinoff invited himself on a shopping spree with his idol. They entered a large department store, and while Zimbalist perused the silk shirts, Chotzinoff planted himself in front of the jewelry counter and began earnestly eyeing a tray of watches. It wasn't long before Zimbalist appeared beside him. 'I was going to give you one at the end of the season,' he smiled. 'Why don't you pick one out now?' Chotzinoff chose the biggest fourteen-carat watch on display and a matching chain, then pressed Zimbalist for an engraved inscription inside the lid. 'Oh, just have them write something,' Zimbalist said lightly. At dinner next evening Chotzinoff showed the family his new acquisition — and the inscription he himself had chosen for it: 'To My Dear Friend and Accompanist Samuel Chotzinoff with Love and Admiration from Efrem Zimbalist.' His only qualm was that, sooner or later, Zimbalist might ask to see it.

San Francisco made a greater impression on Zimbalist than any American city outside of New York; he always considered them the 'King and Queen of American cities.' He and Chotzinoff stayed at the St. Francis Hotel; shortly after their arrival they dined at the landmark Cliff House, from which they watched seals cavorting on the rocks below, and then stopped at Palisades Park to ride the roller coaster and have their pictures snapped on a donkey. Some days before his first San Francisco appearance Zimbalist took a ferry across the Bay to play in Oakland. The attendance was discouragingly small, but the turnout in San Francisco made up for it. It was the inaugural season of the newly formed San Francisco Symphony which, under the direction of Henry Hadley, was giving sold-out per-formances at the Cort Theater. Zimbalist played the Tchaikovsky Concerto to an overflow house.

At a subsequent recital Zimbalist had a happy reunion with Harold Bauer, who was accompanied by a frail old man. With obvious respect Bauer introduced his companion as Oscar Wile, a man whose teaching method both he and Paderewski admired. Chotzinoff was delighted by his name, and Wile straightaway suggested that he spend the week working

with him on pieces scheduled for an upcoming recital while Bauer showed
Zimbalist around town. Chinatown, having suffered much destruction
during the 1906 earthquake and fire, was bustling once again, and
Zimbalist loved it especially (Kreisler's visit to this section some years
before had inspired 'Tambourin Chinois').

The tour ended in San Francisco, and he and Chotzinoff headed back
East, Zimbalist looking forward to springtime in New York with Alma
Gluck. However, she was away on tour when he returned: constant
demands for Alma on the concert platform had induced her to abandon
the operatic stage in favor of recitals. Over the next few years a pattern
developed—as much as possible, Efrem scheduled his own concerts wherever Alma was most likely to be, and when they were in different cities he
tried to see her if free days in their schedules coincided. This once involved
a long journey for a single brief meeting. Conditions could not have been
less favorable, yet the suitor persisted.

That spring of 1912, just after his twenty-second birthday, Zimbalist and
Chotzinoff went to Camden, New Jersey, to make their first recordings.
Zimbalist had been contracted for ten sides by Calvin Childs, Chief
Recorder and Artist's Director for the Victor Company; terms were fifteen
percent royalties, with no initial fee. Childs played a major part in building
up Victor's prestigious Red Seal Catalogue, securing long-term contracts
with most of the greats—Caruso, Amelita Galli-Curci, John McCormack,
Alma Gluck, Emma Eames, Geraldine Farrar, Antonio Scotti, Kreisler,
Elman and Zimbalist; and he led the pre-electric Victor Company in its
competition with powerful rival Columbia for the world's celebrated artists.

By 1912, recordings by Elman, Kreisler and Maud Powell were already
best-sellers; because of his inexplicably early decline Jan Kubelik's
American recordings were not, but fortunately his talent had been captured at the height of its brilliance by the Societa Italiana di Fonotipia di
Milano, Columbia's Italian subsidiary. Of the older masters, Paganini,
Vieuxtemps, Wieniawski, Wilhelmj and Ole Bull regrettably went
unrecorded, and Joachim's discs, made only a few years before his death,
fail to give an accurate picture of his artistry: his intonation and facility at
that stage were scarcely representative. On the other hand Sarasate, at the
end of his career, made records that show no flagging of his technique.
Made for the Gramophone and Typewriter Company, they were the first
records Zimbalist had heard in Berlin in 1907, and they demonstrate how

lightly the concept of sound recording was taken by Sarasate: on two of the discs he can be heard talking—once to himself (when he purples the air in Spanish after coming to grief at the end of a ridiculously fast perform-ance of Bach's Prelude in E) and once instructing his accompanist to cut the slow section, in an otherwise wonderful performance of his 'Zigeunerweisen.'

Many recordings of the period sounded equally unrehearsed. One sup-poses that so outlandish an invention was taken as a passing fad—the thought that their efforts were being preserved for posterity's judgment seems not to have occurred to many of those early giants who stepped 'before the horn.' Then too, the restrictions and discomfort imposed by the acoustic 'horn' technique made recording prior to the introduction of electric microphones quite an undertaking. The technique was very basic: a large metal horn was suspended from the ceiling; connected from its small end was a flexible pipe that passed through a thick curtain to the etching machine in an adjoining room. Singers were instructed to face away from the horn on particularly telling high notes. Violinists had, on the contrary, to position themselves with their sound holes facing directly into the horn's mouth—their recorded tone had a tendency to fade out entirely in the higher reaches of the E string. The possibility of knocking against the metal rim had constantly to be guarded against. Balance prob-lems were usually handled by moving the piano into the furthest corner, or setting it up on a riser, so that its sonority was directed above the horn. Both solutions made ensemble between the musicians difficult at best. And then there was the duration problem: a timing run-through, often done just before recording, could result in arbitrary and hastily worked out cuts to whittle selections down to a prescribed length.

When one considers the likelihood of having to put up with these uncomfortable conditions for hours, in attempting to make a technically (let alone musically) perfect matrix of a single selection, the fatigue factor becomes apparent. Artists had to record a piece from beginning to end without stopping—unless ordered to do so for mechanical reasons, as they frequently were, by unseen technicians behind the curtain. Another often overlooked disadvantage was the mechanism's incapacity to provide immediate playback. If the artists were on tour they had to sign permis-sion for release, without knowing how things had actually sounded. All the more reason to admire those pioneer musicians who, without the aid of splicing, were able to produce countless three- or four-minute vignettes of magical brilliance, many unequaled since.

Zimbalist's 1912 session did not please him very much. He echoed the sentiments of many a musician on hearing themselves truly objectively for the first time: 'Do I really sound like that?' Nevertheless, we can get a clear picture of the artist at twenty-two. One notices his ringing tone first—those who find it more reserved than warm might note the advancement it represents over the dry Kubelik-Sarasate-Joachim tradition. The recordings also immediately give evidence of a deeply musical and natural interpretive gift, and of course brilliant technical facility combined with impeccable intonation. But their most endearing intrinsic quality is the striking individuality of Efrem Zimbalist's character itself: integrity and conviction fairly leap out of the old grooves.

Recorded at the first session were 'Humoresque' (Tor Aulin, v64241); 'Orientale' (César Cui, v64261); 'Long Ago' (Edward MacDowell, v64266); 'I Hear You Calling Me' (J. P. Marshall, v64330); 'Hebrew Dance' (Zimbalist, v64550); 'Serenade' (Franz Drdla, v64710; dedicated to Kubelik); 'Andantino' for unaccompanied violin (Max Reger, v64518). All selections but the last listed 'piano accompaniment by Sam Chotzinoff.' Most were of the lighter, more saleable encore type and were advertised in the Victor catalog as demonstrating the artist's 'invariably lyric quality, the frank envy of lesser men.' (It is rumored that there was an unreleased duet with Alma Gluck from this session, but there is no substantiating data.)

Two weeks later Zimbalist returned to Camden. Chotzinoff was indisposed, and Emanuel Balaban, a Russian friend, sat in for Pierné's 'Serenade' and Zimbalist's 'Russian Dance.' To complete the Slavic set Zimbalist recorded 'Polish Dance' with what passed for an orchestra but was really little more than a glorified brass band, augmented by a few woodwinds. This august group settled themselves into a remote corner, backs to Zimbalist, and played as softly as possible, eyes glued to a conductor strategically placed to relay the soloist's impulses. Despite such seemingly impossible logistics, 'Polish Dance' was Zimbalist's top-selling solo record. In succeeding seasons he steadily enlarged his recorded output, usually accompanied by Chotzinoff but also by Francis Moore and Alexander Lambert (Zimbalist always credited him as the only cultivated musician he ever met whose singing voice rivaled the inability of his own to carry a tune). Zimbalist's records, he modestly reckoned, sold 'wonderfully well.'

Some of the ones he made with Alma Gluck sold in the millions. But he considered only certain of the electrical recordings he made decades later to be decent representations of his playing—in particular, the Victor release of Ysaÿe's g minor solo sonata.

John Powell returned to native shores to find that Zimbalist had been spreading the word about the European successes of 'America's great composer.' Powell's hometown of Richmond, Virginia, was honoring him at its Spring Festival and had engaged Josef Pasternack to conduct an orchestra on 30 April 1912 with Powell as soloist in Liszt's E-flat concerto and Zimbalist premièring Powell's violin concerto. Zimbalist liked the work immediately, but he knew he could make it 'sound better,' more violinistic. His friend, however, resisted even the slightest change. 'He was not one of those nice composers who allowed me to do things,' Zimbalist laughingly recalled, 'but he did let me write the cadenza.' Owing to Powell's excessive fussiness at rehearsal, Pasternack ran out of time, and the eventual audience of nearly four thousand had to be content with hearing only the violin concerto's first movement. *Musical America*'s reviewer called Zimbalist's interpretation nothing short of marvelous: 'So great is Zimbalist's love for this work that, as he neared the conclusion of the movement, it was all that he could do to control his emotion and upon leaving the stage amid thunderous applause, his eyes were full of tears.'

But not for long. Alma was back from tour, and Efrem was able to spend a few days with her before he sailed for London in early May.

CHAPTER 14

Marriage and a Changing World

(1912–1914)

Zimbalist had hardly unpacked at Cornwall Terrace before he was hard at work again. He opened the Royal Philharmonic's centennial season on 23 May 1912 with the Beethoven Concerto; Artur Nikisch was on the podium and had requested him as soloist. Next evening Zimbalist joined the London Symphony under Leopold Stokowski. An electrified Queen's Hall audience on the night of Stokie's London Symphony debut included Nikisch, Elman, Elena Gerhardt, Sir Edward and Lady Elgar, and Joseph Szigeti. In his 1947 autobiography Szigeti mentions 'the feline suppleness of the orchestral support that the young [Stokowski] gave to Zimbalist's playing of the Glazunov Concerto.' Thus began a mutual admiration society that flourished for years; Stokowski always cherished a Mendelssohn Concerto they did together.

On the same day, 24 May 1912, eleven-year-old Jascha Heifetz was making his Berlin debut, to mixed reviews (one complained of a small tone). Auer felt that since Joachim's death the Berlin Hochschule had been overrun by conceited violinistic dwarfs professing to uphold the 'German school' tradition. So he had determined to show them what he, a more enlightened Joachim student, was producing in his St. Petersburg studio. He had worked with Jascha less than two years when he decided to present him in the Hochschule's concert hall; he knew that his revered master would have approved.

Zimbalist was in Berlin himself two weeks later to play the Brahms Concerto with Richter. Professor Auer, Papa Heifetz and Jascha were in the audience. So was Fritz Kreisler, hearing Zimbalist for the first time: he appeared backstage, full of praise, introducing his wife, Harriet, and inviting Efrem to lunch at their apartment. Conversation soon got around to the eleven-year-old sensation from Vilna. Zimbalist told Kreisler of his own first exposure to the nine-year-old Jascha. Kreisler had heard his Berlin debut and related that a few days later Jascha had played the Mendelssohn Concerto at the home of *Musical America* correspondent Arthur Abell for an audience that included Jan Kubelik, Bronislaw Huberman, Carl Flesch and Willy Hess. Kreisler himself had accompanied the boy at the piano and afterward made a famous comment to the assemblage of violinists: 'Well, gentlemen, we can now break our fiddles across our knees!' In 1980, when all their playing careers were long over, Zimbalist spoke modestly of the unpredictable nature of careers: 'Kubelik elbowed aside Sarasate, Heifetz edged out Elman and to some extent Kreisler. A few years later Menuhin badly jolted Heifetz's career, although it was a short-lived displacement. Me? I was never affected because I was just a small-fry.'

Zimbalist followed his Berlin Brahms performance with a recital that included Powell's concerto, which he was trying to popularize (some publicity even had him calling it 'the finest since Brahms'). To his dismay the piece met with adverse criticism. While in town he heard Paderewski's performance of the 'Emperor' Concerto and Busoni playing Liszt. Both made a strong impression on him. 'I heard so many pianists in my youth and they all seemed to play well, but a few stood out among the others,' he remembered years later.

With Russian composer Alexander Grechaninov Zimbalist explored the Rhineland and went horseback riding in France. Then he returned to Kislovodsk for a month's vacation spent studying the Sibelius Concerto and preparing for his next season in the United States. He began the trip back to New York in late August, stopping off briefly in Rostov before crossing the Atlantic. On board he did some performing at the keyboard, accompanying two European prima donnas en route to the Metropolitan, to the delight of fellow passengers Leopold Stokowski and his pianist wife, Olga Samaroff. In New York Zimbalist again took a suite at the Prince George.

His second season was beset by managerial complications. It all began the previous spring, with an unpleasant development at the Wolfsohn Bureau. According to Zimbalist, during the first decade-and-a-half of the century Elman was considered 'king of violinists throughout the land,' and although there were those who preferred Zimbalist or Kreisler, they couldn't approach Elman's overall popularity. Mischa guarded his popularity vigilantly. He had become wary when he read press reaction to Zimbalist's U.S. debut the previous fall, and toward the end of the 1911–12 season he had marched into Adam's office and delivered an ultimatum: 'You haff Elman, the greatest violinist in the world. If you keep Kreisler and Zimbalist you won't haff Elman!' It was Elman's jealous father who had put him up to it: he wouldn't allow his son to be managed by anyone who handled other violinists. Paradoxically, during this period Elman consistently praised Zimbalist and Kreisler when their names came up.

The unhappy Adams was forced to capitulate and traveled to London to break the news to Kreisler, only to receive the sharp end of Harriet's everhoned tongue. Kreisler signed on with Charles Ellis, distinguished manager of the Boston Symphony and four of the brightest stars in the artistic firmament—Melba, Geraldine Farrar, Paderewski and Samaroff. Ellis had had to get Melba's consent, which was no problem since Kreisler was not a soprano—and she admired him, even going so far as to answer when an interviewer asked her about phrasing: 'If you wish to learn about it, listen to the playing of Fritz Kreisler.' For his part, Zimbalist accepted an offer from Loudon Charlton, an experienced manager who, like Joseph Fels, felt that his introductory season could have been better handled.

Charlton started out by doubling Zimbalist's fee, and his blurbs pleased Fels but made the violinist squirm: 'Loudon Charlton has booked an extensive tour for Zimbalist [that] includes practically every city of importance from Boston to San Francisco. The Chicago Symphony is one of the important organizations to add Efrem Zimbalist to its list of soloists this season [and] there is every indication of the violinist's second American visit far outstripping the splendid record he made last season.'

Zimbalist decided to escape New York's September heat and his manager's feverish preparations for the upcoming season by paying Alma a surprise visit in Lake George, where she was still summering. His visit held more surprise than he had intended. He arrived in Lake George and asked to be directed to her cottage. As it happened, Mr. Archibald, cashier at the Lake George bank, was just on his way to see her about a banking matter. He offered Zimbalist a ride in his auto. En route the vehicle overturned on a sharp curve and went over a ten-foot embankment, 'badly hurting one of the violinist's fingers' (New York Star). Archibald suffered rib fractures. Both were taken to the closest hospital, fifty miles away in

Glens Falls, to which Alma was summoned. Zimbalist's injury was fortunately not severe, and with a few weeks of tender loving care he was
completely recovered.

The opening New York Philharmonic performance in October 1912
created such a buzz that it prompted a young hardware salesman named
Sol Hurok, just out of Russia, to hunt down Loudon Charlton. He
informed him that he was organizing entertainment for a Socialist Party
benefit at the New Palm Garden in Brownsville. Knowing Zimbalist was a
student during the 1905 revolution, Hurok wondered if he could be persuaded to appear at a cut rate as the special attraction. To Hurok's surprise
Charlton told him to call on Zimbalist at the Prince George. In *Impresario*,
Hurok wrote about the meeting: '[Zimbalist] listened to me with sympathetic courtesy. When I left him I had a contract in my pocket. The
contract specified $750 for the concert—it was not good business for an
artist to cut his fee, but Zimbalist had agreed to deduct $250 and call it a
personal donation to the Socialist Party.'

Hurok cleared $1,600 for his first entrepreneurial effort—the entire
affair was carried off brilliantly. Later that season, Hurok talked Zimbalist
into an appearance at the Hippodrome celebrating the fifteenth anniversay
of the *Jewish Daily Forward*, a Socialist newspaper. And Zimbalist agreed
to another Hurok idea: that arrangements for the season's Carnegie Hall
finale be placed in his hands—but only if he could clear it with Charlton.
Then the touring began.

What with all the concerts and talk of another Victor recording session,
Chotzinoff reckoned to earn twice what he had last season. Shortly after
they set out, for places near and far, he bared his heart, telling the embarrassed Zimbalist what wonders their collaboration had wrought for the
entire Chotzinoff family. The clan had even discussed the possibility of
moving to Staten Island, where there were more trees. Orthodox
Chotzinoff senior had not been impressed. 'I would rather see a few beards
than a whole forest of trees,' he told his son.

Zimbalist remembered early travel conditions only too well: 'The trains
were often undependable, sometimes four or five hours late. There were
times when we arrived in a town at 2 or 3 a.m. and had to sit all night in the
hotel lobby, or outside on the steps, until the desk clerk came on duty and
gave us rooms. Regular practice was impossible. But I tried to make it a rule
to arrive fully dressed at the hall hours before concert time to do a bit then.'

On 2 November 1912 Alma Gluck sang a typically varied recital at Carnegie Hall. She divided the program into four groups: the first devoted to older masters; the second comprising German songs; the third Russian and French (although she sang Ravel's 'Chanson Hébraique' in Yiddish); and the closing group American, including a miniature by Rawlins Cottenet. Richard Aldrich's favorable review in the *New York Times* contained an interesting line: 'At the end of [her Russian group] were two new songs by Efrem Zimbalist, who was present in a box.' Zimbalist had coached her in these additions to her repertoire. At this stage she learned the words purely phonetically; later she studied Russian, bringing to a total of eight the languages in which she was fluent.

An important performance of the season was with Walter Damrosch's New York Symphony Orchestra playing the Brahms Concerto as part of a Brahms festival. While festivals featuring a single composer are nowadays commonplace, at that time Damrosch's idea was unusual. He was 'Mr. Music' to the American public at large but especially to the estimated six million schoolchildren who listened weekly to his student broadcasts. They invariably began with his hearty, German-accented greeting, 'Good mornink, my dear children.' His endorsement was an important rung in the ascendency of Zimbalist's American career.

Another lasting musical impression was forged when Zimbalist played the Beethoven Concerto under Karl Muck in Boston. It was Muck's first season as director of the Boston Symphony—a post he held until being forced out of the country in 1917, suspected of spying for the Germans. The nasty, misanthropic reputation that Muck developed later was absent in his working relationship with Zimbalist: at the conclusion of the concerto, while the audience roared its approval, he stepped down from the podium to kiss his blushing young soloist on the head.

During this period, Zimbalist was interviewed by F. C. Fay of the *Musical Courier* for an extended piece that let the public in on some of the less obvious aspects of his personality. It mentioned his love of composing and contemporary composers and spoke of his fine collection of autographs, including a sheet of music by Liszt and letters from Robert Schumann, Rossini, Meyerbeer, Spohr, de Beriot, Vieuxtemps and Paganini. It ended with Zimbalist's worshipful opinion of Beethoven: 'The other day I met with a sad disappointment. I had found in a little New York shop a manuscript by Beethoven. I did not have enough money with me to pay for it, and had to go to the bank to get some. When I returned, an hour later, the manuscript was sold. Of course, I know that Beethoven lived, that he was a man, but I can't believe it! His music, one concerto for piano especially, is so superhuman, so far above the reach of human understanding, and yet so divinely simple and clear, that I can find nothing in me to respond to it but tears.'

Zimbalist, still championing the efforts of John Powell, gladly agreed to share his friend's New York debut recital on 25 February 1913.

Gluck and Zimbalist were frequently booked to appear together at 'privates,' which only fueled speculation concerning their marriage plans. But Zimbalist, even with his cigar or pipe as a prop, still couldn't persuade Alma. Her daughter Marcia Davenport, in *Too Strong for Fantasy*, gives clearest insight as to why this was so, even while acknowledging 'how deeply they were in love': 'From very early on, she wanted to [marry him but] her reluctance was rooted in the conviction that she could not create a real marriage whilst she was at the height of her career.... As an artist [Zimbalist] was her peer and she believed, her superior. But no violinist is the public idol that a young, beautiful soprano can be, and only John McCormack drew audiences and commanded fees as large as hers.'

Meanwhile Hurok was pulling out all promotional stops for Zimbalist's Carnegie Hall season closer. A woman who called to reserve two tickets inquired of the bemused Hurok: 'By the way, what kind of instrument *is* a zimbalist?' His answer: 'A Russian of great charm, which has blue eyes, curly brown hair, an interesting nose and a talent for playing the violin as easily as you and I recite prayers.' Hurok's ticket booths were shoeshine stands, bakery shops and spaghetti joints throughout the city. It's no wonder he sold tickets.

On 27 April 1913, Sol Hurok presented his first attraction at Carnegie Hall. It was a spectacular occasion, as described by the *New York Sun*: 'When three thousand had been seated and others turned away, [Zimbalist's] manager hastily arranged to have a flashlight photograph taken of the crowd—the big white smoke-bags hung above the boxes were objects of curiosity throughout the evening.' Zimbalist played some unfamiliar pieces—a Goldmark 'Aria,' a 'Quasi Ballata' by Alois Reiser, humoresques by York Bowen and Tor Aulin—to which he added his own 'Hebrew Dance' and some Kreisler numbers, including 'Chanson Méditation by Rawlins Cottenet.' Cottenet sat in a box near the stage, and the performance met with a spirited reception. From the *New York Herald*: 'Rain did not prevent the admirers of Mr. Efrem Zimbalist from filling Carnegie Hall last night to give the young Russian violinist a farewell that he ought to remember for the two years he will remain away from this country.' Mention was made of 250 fervent admirers seated behind Zimbalist on the stage, and Hurok's 'day job' boss, who attended the concert and was convinced that those fervent admirers were the entire Brownsville Socialist Party.

Despite the overwhelming success of the season, Zimbalist was no longer on smooth terms with Loudon Charlton. For some time they had disagreed on the boundaries of good taste in showmanship, and a month before Carnegie Hall there had been a big blowup. Charlton had agreed, without telling him, to have Zimbalist appear at the Lyceum with Sirota, the Russian cantor. William and Samuel Jonas, the presenters, agreed to pay Charlton $500 for Zimbalist's services and then engaged the hall. But Zimbalist did not show up on the appointed day, and the Jonas brothers claimed to have come up $2,000 short of their expected income. The matter went to court, where Charlton threw up his hands, saying that he had only acted as an agent and that a furious Zimbalist, informed only days before the performance, had refused to play on the grounds that to do so would have a negative impact on his career. Justice Smith sided with Charlton and slapped a judgment of $69.58 against the Jonas brothers, for court costs. 'Temperamental? Can't Blame Him' ran the headline of the *New York Telegraph*.

But with Hurok now in the picture Zimbalist was not unduly concerned about the Charlton incident. And Karl Junkermann and Frau Wolff had been besieged with bookings for him in England and Europe. Several New York newspapers saw Zimbalist's upcoming season as an answer to the ever-intensifying competition between him and Elman, claiming that the rivals had settled on a plan to keep out of each other's way: when one toured Europe, the other toured America.

Zimbalist's fee had become sizeable, and before leaving New York he cashed many large checks. But he withheld one check for seventy-five cents, as a souvenir of his second American season. It related to a benefit concert he had given at the Metropolitan Opera House. The artists were to receive half the box office take above a certain amount. Zimbalist jokingly told theatrical producer Daniel Frohman that unless he came to the concert he stood to lose half of Frohman's admission fee of $1.50. Frohman didn't attend, but next day sent his friend a check for the amount he would have gained by his presence.

Zimbalist, Alma Gluck and Althea Jewell traveled to Europe together in summer 1913. Alma had been working with Marcella Sembrich, who divided her summers between her estate on Lake Geneva and a villa in Nice. It was here they headed. Alma had been booked by Shulz-Curtius and Powell for a solo debut in London, and she wanted to spend the weeks beforehand getting some up-to-the-minute coaching. As Sembrich's guests, Zimbalist practiced, or played bridge with Althea, while Alma had her lessons.

In London they were welcomed by the Felses. There was a joint concert at the Royal Albert Hall, which Gluck and Zimbalist shared with Vladimir de Pachmann, the enigmatic Russian pianist whose odd behavior was matched only by his diminutive size. The organizing impresario introduced them before the concert. 'How do you do, Mr. de Pachmann?' Alma asked. 'Not at all well,' he answered, kissing her hand with flourish. 'In fact, I almost didn't come this afternoon.' He went on to elaborate on the unsettled state of his lower alimentary tract and described in detail, and several languages, how many times that morning Nature had called him. Alma simply laughed. Zimbalist blanched.

It was de Pachmann who was approached by a young lady pianist to whom he had just listened. 'Mr. de Pachmann, please tell me what you thought about my execution,' she begged. 'Ma chérie, I'm all in favor of it,' he beamed. 'He was inimitable in his playing of small pieces, especially Chopin,' Zimbalist said of him, 'but I never could decide whether he behaved so strangely out of stupidity or for a calculated effect.'

A week or two later Alma gave her solo recital. A *Times* review of the concert reports that she was not accompanied by her usual pianist: 'Perhaps [Gluck's] choice [of songs] would not have been specially attractive but for the charm of the singer, whose voice, style and presence is altogether gracious and winning, and her fortune in having Mr. Efrem Zimbalist for an accompanist.' Alma had included two of his songs, a 'cleverly written Revery,' and the 'Chanson Triste.' The *Telegraph*'s review was even more complimentary to her pianist: 'Mr. Efrem Zimbalist's piano playing, even heard in such close proximity to Mr. Paderewski's last week, proved in its own way equally satisfying.' Zimbalist himself was very modest: 'My piano playing seemed legitimate but it really wasn't—I had to simplify the Schubert and Strauss accompaniments and play them in my own way.'

Afterward Alma, accompanied by Althea Jewell, returned to her daughter and her summer retreat at Lake George. Zimbalist had concerts to play but later joined her there. They spent the fall back in England, based at Cornwall Terrace, while Efrem continued his European concerts. On 3 December 1913 Alma traveled back to New York with the Felses aboard the *Kaiser Wilhelm II* to be with Abigail for Christmas and to fulfill concert commitments in the United States. Reporters were waiting; *Musical America* asked her if she expected to marry that year: 'No, not this year. But next year I expect to be married ten times, on the stage. I am doing *Romeo and Juliette* at the Metropolitan!'

Stokowski's New York debut with the Philadelphia Orchestra was on 21 January 1914, a benefit concert that was to begin at 3 p.m.; Alma was the soloist, singing a Mozart aria near the beginning of the program. But, as one published account had it, 'Miss Gluck — a sweet name meaning bountiful and happy — was under the impression that the concert began at four o'clock. So at three o'clock she was sitting quietly at her home, munching a dietetic luncheon, consisting of a half a whole meal biscuit, and a vague vision of a glass of water. She was garbed in a wrapper.' At 3:10 Alma was startled by a loud pounding at her door and was informed in the messenger's stentorian tones: 'Mme. Gluck, you are keeping the critics and Maestro Stokowski waiting. The concert was to have begun ten minutes ago!' With a shriek of despair, she threw her clothes into a waiting car and dressed en route to the hall.

In February 1914, while on tax law business in Washington, D.C., Joseph Fels contracted pneumonia and died; Mary was at his side. Fels's death was a stunning blow to Zimbalist, who received the news while touring Russia. He admired him and had felt closer to him in many ways than to his own family. Fels must have felt equally close to his 'Russian violinist ward' for he reportedly bequeathed him a considerable sum of money, though Zimbalist denied it. His denial could have been what prompted Mary Fels's comment to Samuel Chotzinoff: 'Efrem was prone to take the people who loved him for granted.'

On 15 June 1914 Zimbalist and Alma Gluck were married in a quiet ceremony in the drawing room at Cornwall Terrace. Among the presents was a six-inch violin from Hammig, which he himself had carved to scale — an exact working replica of the Strad Zimbalist had bought from him (the bridegroom played 'Yankee Doodle' and 'Turkey in the Straw' on it). Another was an inscribed score of *Die Meistersinger* from Wilhelm Strecker, owner of the Schott music publishing company, 'To celebrate the entrance of a soprano into your life.'

Zimbalist gave a recital at Queen's Hall the very next day, and the *Times* was advertising a 'Song and Violin Joint Recital' for 27 June. Recently released recordings had freshened the public's recollection of Gluck's beautiful voice, but without a doubt what boosted ticket sales most was news of the wedding, and Shulz-Curtius and Powell foresaw a lucrative outcome.

Queen's Hall was packed on the 27th, and the newlyweds were loudly cheered. It was a wonderful send-off. For an extended honeymoon Zimbalist took an apartment at Richmond, one of London's most beautiful natural areas; the bridal couple was accompanied by Althea Jewell, who as Alma's dearest friend always traveled with her. The trio arrived to find the apartment piled to the ceilings with boxes. Among Zimbalist's wedding offerings was a huge cowhide suitcase filled with so much crystal and gold that it couldn't be lifted, and photographic equipment so elaborate that it required the attention of two experts to be used. Alma returned this last, for which her husband had paid 123 pounds, to the Eastman shop in London, taking in exchange numerous smaller cameras to give away to her friends (she told people to use her account at the shop, and after seventeen years, it still had a credit balance). Alma's wedding present to her husband was along more practical lines: a dozen monogrammed silk shirts special-ordered from Paris.

The ubiquitous Althea Jewell had an unusual relationship with Alma. A tall, attractive spinster with prematurely white hair and a perpetually joyful smile highlighted by three prominent gold teeth, she was Alma's dearest friend, constant companion and possibly finest influence during the troublesome periods of the singer's life. Abigail called her Aunt Alfy. Alma and Alfy between them were always capable of turning potentially disastrous situations into delightful escapades, accompanied by shrieking laughter. Once while in London Alfy lunched with George Bernard Shaw. True to her nature she talked and talked, ending her monologue with a question: 'Well, Mr. Shaw, what do you think of the intelligent woman of today?' 'Never met one' was the smooth reply. Alfy married late in life and outlived Alma by many years.

The honeymoon continued at a rented cottage in Chamonix, France, in the Pennine Alps, near the Swiss border. Paderewski had a majestic villa, Chalet Riond-Bosson, across the line in nearby Morges, and, toward the end of July, the honeymooning couple were invited as weekend guests. Josef Hofmann, already fascinated by automobiles (he was eventually to patent a shock absorber design) picked them up and gave them a ride to Morges. Talk over the billiard table, or during tea on the porch overlooking Mont Blanc across Lake Geneva, centered around the tensions gripping Europe. But these concerns didn't put a crimp in the lavish style at Chalet Riond-Bosson. On 1 August lunch was served as usual. At one o'clock the Master descended the staircase, greeting each person present with a few apt inquiries about their health and activities. He led the way to the dining room and, after seeing to everyone else's comfort, seated himself at the head of the table, which stretched from one end of the enormous hall to the other. Halfway through truffled pheasant the tall entrance doors swung open, and the major domo strode quickly over and whispered in his master's ear. Paderewski removed the silk napkin from his collar and rose. The emotion in his voice confirmed the fears of all present when he announced: 'German infantry forces have invaded Belgium and are advancing into France. Europe is at war.'

CHAPTER 15

Manhattan Family Hearth

(1914–1920)

Pandemonium erupted. Even as Paderewski spoke, all but his oldest servant dropped what they were doing to return to Germany and enlist. Dessert went unserved as the diners too made frantic plans — it was likely to be only days before unrestricted movement became impossible.

Zimbalist as a Russian citizen feared being captured, though Switzerland promised to remain neutral: even at that moment soldiers were marching into the house in Kreuth where his countryman Ossip Gabrilowitsch was staying (after going through all his papers, they dragged him off to prison). Neither did Zimbalist wish to fall afoul of the Russians, since he was of prime draft age and in wartime his military pardon was unlikely to be respected.

The Zimbalists were determined to return to the United States as quickly as possible. They made a hasty foray back to Chamonix for belongings; since France had declared war, the plan was to recross the Swiss border and head south through Italy. Their greatest immediate problem was financial — travelers' checks, letters of credit and even paper money were now invalid. Gold was the only accepted currency, and they had very little of it. Stalled in Chamonix, their reserves dwindled. For days Zimbalist wrestled with consulates for help with funds and travel arrangements. His wife bided her time exploring the picturesque little village and shopping with Alfy. Alma spent her last gold piece on a present for Abigail, from whom she had received a letter begging her immediate and safe return. Finally they were able to leave, via Turin, for Genoa, departure point for many boats bound for the United States.

At the French border guards separated the Zimbalists to search their baggage and persons; the fancy camera Efrem was carrying attracted the searcher's attention. Alma returned to find her husband, red-faced, attempting to explain in German (the only language besides Russian in which he was fully conversant). 'Es ist nur ein Apparat! Nimm es. Ich will es nicht!' (It's only an Apparat! Take it. I don't want it!). But the Apparat, in conjunction with Efrem's nervousness, nearly caused his and Alma's internment.

They considered themselves extremely lucky when the *Espagne* nosed away from land and headed toward open sea and the freedom of America, though the voyage was less than luxurious (Alma likened it to traveling in a cattle car). Even as they made their escape the Paderewski estate was becoming a haven for some fifty less-fortunate souls, most of whom had to sleep in tents erected on the front lawn. Among them were the Josef Hofmanns, Marcella Sembrich and Ossip Gabrilowitsch and his wife, Clara.

The honeymooners arrived back in New York a celebrated couple and began to live their role to the hilt. They bought a house on the West Side (315 West 100th Street), equipped it with every amenity Alma thought celebrated couples should enjoy (a cook, maid, butler and chauffeur to drive their new Hudson Deluxe) and surrounded themselves with sumptuous decorations and furnishings. 'We lived very grandly,' Zimbalist remembered with amusement.

While this was all well and good, Alma had serious misgivings about having Abigail grow up in so 'unnatural' an atmosphere. She had thought this all out simultaneously with her decision to marry Zimbalist. Their lifestyle could not, she felt, provide an appropriate environment for the healthy rearing of children: a simple family life, education in a good day school and the company of other children. Accordingly, Abigail was packed off to Philadelphia to join the family of Earl and Anna Barnes—recommended as people of 'unusual character' by Mary Fels—for the next seven school years. The Barneses, Alma was confident, would teach her daughter how 'real' people lived. To ensure this, Aunt Barnes (as Abigail had to call her) was handsomely paid. She enrolled the eleven-year-old in the Quaker school the Barnes children attended and generally subjected her to a liberal dose of the firm discipline Alma evidently believed she needed. Abigail hated it and lived only for the summers, when she would rejoin her mother and stepfather. (She was later to change her name to Marcia and marry the writer Russell Davenport.)

Zimbalist was elected to *Vanity Fair*'s Hall of Fame 'because he now shares along with his friend, Fritz Kreisler, the highest niche in the temple dedicated to the votaries of the violin; because he has always placed sincerity in music higher than mere perfection of technique; because his modesty is proverbial; because he is one of the worst living bridge players, and because no less a deity than Alma Gluck has consented to share his name.' One of the first things Alma did as Mrs. Efrem Zimbalist was to see to it that Adams reinstated her husband at the Wolfsohn Bureau (Elman then moved to another agency), and Zimbalist stayed with the Bureau until its doors closed (thereafter he was handled by Arthur Judson, then NBC Artists and later, in the 1940s, by Jack Adams).

Calvin Childs at Victor lost no time in capitalizing on a sure bet: recording the newlyweds together. Numerous beautiful discs of standards with violin obbligato were the result, among them 'Ave Maria,' Braga's 'Serenata' (with Eugene Lutsky at the piano) and Massenet's 'Élégie.' At these sessions the singer and violinist each had separate pickup horns; Efrem later joked that his was much smaller than Alma's: 'They didn't want me to play too loudly and spoil everything!' Most successful financially were songs in the popular vein: 'Sing Me to Sleep' (Greene), 'Fiddle and I' (Goodeve), and the Zionist hymn 'Hatikva.' But it was their recording of 'Old Folks at Home' that everyone adored. While rehearsing it for their joint recital in London, back in June, Zimbalist had found the obbligato poor; it occurred to him that Dvořák's 'Humoresque,' played at a tempo slightly slower than customary, perfectly fit Alma's melodic line. This is how they recorded it. The record, along with Alma's rendition of 'Carry Me Back to Old Virginny,' sold over a million copies the first year, resulting in a combined income for the pair high in the six figures—and this in days of no income tax.

What a joy these recording sessions must have been to two young artists in love. The most special for Zimbalist was when, at her request, he accompanied Alma at the piano in 'Swedish Cradle Song.' Following up on the unprecedented success of 'Carry Me Back to Old Virginny' and 'Old Folks at Home,' and catering to the public's faddish interest in black spirituals, Childs had Zimbalist record such solos as 'Old Black Joe,' paraphrases like Kramer's 'Chant Nègre' and Albert Spalding's 'Alabama' (dedicated to

Zimbalist), and 'Massa's in de Cold, Cold Ground.' The latter was one of Victor's streamlined presentations—Zimbalist was accompanied by a large string orchestra with celeste for added glitter, arranged and conducted by Josef Pasternack, the company's new music director.

Adjusting to the joy of married life and being lord of his own manor fully occupied Zimbalist during the early war years. These adjustments took up the slack that wartime created in concert schedules. He also busied himself editing two concertos for Schirmer's Library of Musical Classics, the Beethoven and Conus, which work he later condemned: 'I was too young.'

The *Lusitania*'s sinking grimly underlined ocean travel hazards. Enrique Granados, in America to supervise production of his opera *Goyescas* and to play for President Wilson at the White House, returned to Europe aboard the SS *Sussex*. He perished when it was torpedoed in the Channel. Wary artists living or grounded in the United States had to content themselves with scarce domestic engagements. When America entered the war and channeled most of its energies and funds to that end, even these became scarcer.

Alma Gluck's popularity was at its height during those years—she can be seen on fluttery period newsreels, visiting army bases throughout the country, bringing the soldiers much-needed song and cheer. But wartime conditions forced her to cancel many scheduled debuts in Europe, thereby affecting her career more than her husband's and ultimately limiting her renown outside the United States to her recordings. By the time World War I ended she had largely retired from touring.

Many of Zimbalist's friends from London days were affected by the war. Patriotic bitterness was rampant. The possibility of violence against those bearing German names prompted music publisher Willy Strecker's imprisonment (by his own request) at Alexandria Palace, where he remained for two years. And when Hans Richter returned the honorary doctorates he had received from the universities of Oxford and Manchester, *Musical Times* noted, 'The great conductor has not, however, renounced the fortune he has won in this country.'

Fritz Kreisler, who was a reserve officer in the Austrian army's Fourth Battalion, made a stand against the advancing Cossacks near Grodeck, south of Lemberg, in early September 1914. During a nighttime cavalry attack Kreisler received a bayonet wound in the right thigh.* He lost consciousness and awoke later to find that, although he had survived the charge, his fighting days were over; after some five weeks of recuperation he was exempted from further military service. Harriet Kreisler perhaps suffered more, for on 7 September a dispatch listed her husband as having been killed in action. She was beside herself until, two days later, she received a cable from Fritz telling her he was alive and would soon arrive in Vienna. On 24 November the couple returned to the United States. Kreisler walked with the aid of a cane and was eagerly welcomed back by a capacity Carnegie Hall audience on 12 December 1914. America was still neutral, and there was no sign of the unpleasantness that developed two years later, prompted by war hysteria.

Jacques Thibaud was also welcomed back when he returned to America after serving on the French side. One day he and Kreisler happened to meet on the street. Both were limping. Formerly fast friends, convention now required a response foreign to their natural inclination: they merely saluted each other and proceeded on their way. Thibaud, however, confounded convention by attending Kreisler's next concert and going backstage to embrace him afterward. Their friendship endured the rest of their lives. (An incorrigible practical joker, Thibaud loved going to Kreisler recitals and, knowing his colleague's dread of having to play 'Caprice Viennois' for the umpteenth time, starting up a call for it from the back of the hall in a high falsetto.)

Shortly after Kreisler's return appearance Zimbalist too was heard at Carnegie Hall, in the first of a series of recitals. In the *New York Times* Aldrich reviewed the second, a typically imaginative program that included Spohr's d minor concerto and Reger's solo sonata in a minor, given early in January 1915. He spoke of Zimbalist's exquisite taste and poise, and went on: 'Some might wish that there should be at times something more in him of impulsiveness and youth. It is [his] temperament not to wear his heart upon his sleeve.' These comments were timely: Zimbalist was just then feeling the impending sense of responsibility of a soon-to-be father.

A concert in Milwaukee soon after marked the first time Zimbalist and Kreisler played together. Their performance of the Bach 'Double' drew shrieks from delighted women in the audience. Zimbalist spoke of the association in glowing terms. The only problem arose with regard to assignment of the solo parts—both friends wanted to play second violin. (Kreisler ended up playing first.) Meanwhile Childs had persuaded Victor to attempt its first 'serious' recording venture—the presentation, on three twelve-inch sides, of the entire Bach 'Double' Concerto. It seemed to him that their two Russian violinists under contract, Elman and Zimbalist, would make an ideal pairing. When Elman vociferously rejected the idea, Zimbalist proposed Kreisler. The recording session was held on 14 January 1915, in Camden, with orchestral accompaniment reduced to a simple string quartet. The resulting discs sold well, encouraging Victor to record other complete major works.

Following the session the two artists had gone their busy ways, as usual without being afforded the opportunity of listening to a playback. Zimbalist acquired the finished product some months later and played it on his Victrola at home. He was appalled by the heavy portamenti he had employed in the slow movement. 'I thought I was being very expressive,' he grimaced in recollection, moving his left hand in an exaggerated imitation of the slides. 'But I was young. What a pity Fritz didn't tell me how awful it sounded!' Although Zimbalist hated the recording, it was a favorite in many homes. One was that of close friends John and Lily McCormack. Galli-Curci once visited them and was astonished to hear the McCormack children Gwendolyn and Cyril singing the entire first movement of the Bach 'Double' by memory. 'They had heard it so often from the record that it had sunk deep into their memories,' John McCormack reported. And when asked in later life to name his favorite recordings Kreisler had no hesitation in placing it at the head of the list.

(As an inquisitive student years later, the author asked Zimbalist about the fabulous Kreisler tone heard at close range. With great admiration he answered, 'When one stood very close to him one might think the tone a trifle harsh—he used mostly the middle of the bow and pressed—one could hear the friction. But from the first row back it was the most heavenly, ringing sound.')

The Bach 'Double' venture was such a success that the artists were engaged to repeat it at the Norfolk (Connecticut) Music Festival that summer. Damrosch, who was to conduct, didn't have to try hard to persuade them to add Mozart's 'Sinfonia Concertante,' with Kreisler tackling the viola part. How much did they rehearse? 'We played it through once, the cadenza twice maybe,' Zimbalist laughed. Percy Grainger heard the concert. Never a fan of Jewish violin virtuosi, Grainger fell completely under the spell of their Mozart playing and spoke of it for years. During the same festival Zimbalist premièred Chicago Symphony conductor

Frederick Stock's violin concerto, under the composer's direction. 'Stock was one of the great musical minds,' Zimbalist often asserted in later years. He considered the concerto one of the best showpieces in the repertoire.

The three-day Norfolk Festival was sponsored by Mr. and Mrs. Carl Stoeckel and held each June on the grounds of their estate, White House, nestled in the heart of a wood. Long, shady lanes bordered by fragrant flowering shrubs led to the Music Shed, the quaint building with unbeatable acoustics where concerts were held. Anne Homer, whose mother, contralto Louise Homer, often appeared there, described the whole affair (in *Louise Homer and the Golden Age of Opera*) as 'a kind of annual house party in the midst of an inspiring interlude of music. No tickets were ever sold to this so eloquently contrived event. They were all given away, and were so highly prized that audiences came from great distances to attend.'

The Zimbalists' arrival in Norfolk typified the style with which Alma did things. On the way their train ground to an unscheduled halt just outside New Hartford. The time estimate for repairs was not encouraging in view of the hour Efrem was due to rehearse with Kreisler and the orchestra. Undaunted, Alma picked up her valise and sunshade and led her husband into town, where they located a Ford dealer. She had Efrem plunk down $700 in cash, and within minutes they were putt-putting to their destination in a Model T. As they pulled up triumphantly in front of the Stoeckel mansion they were heartily applauded by Kreisler and Stock, who were standing in the doorway. Alma alighted and bowed grandly. All converged on the brand new 'Tin Lizzie' for a closer look. 'How about a ride?' Zimbalist offered. Kreisler and Stock piled in for a spin. 'We hadn't gone more than three blocks when we stalled,' Zimbalist recollected. 'None of us could crank the engine back to life, so Fritz and Fred rolled up their sleeves and pushed me back to the house.' This time there was thunderous applause.

Alma always associated the Norfolk Festival with Jean Sibelius, having met him there in 1909. She and Efrem had run into him again when he conducted his own works on a 1914 U.S. tour, establishing long-standing friendship. When Alma discovered that the composer and Efrem smoked the same brand of cigar, she organized a fund to keep Sibelius supplied for life, to which her husband contributed annually.

Together the Zimbalists made the far-reaching decision to christen the child they were expecting, which entailed their own conversion (the

Encyclopedia Judaica simply states that they 'left the Jewish faith'). Zimbalist had never displayed signs of being a religious man, but Joseph Fels's catholic views and constant efforts to see through a doctrine's outer shell for its deeper meaning had affected him at an impressionable age. Fels was sometimes called a 'Christian Jew'; once when he was asked what, if they were indeed God's chosen people, the Jews were chosen for, he shot back, 'To bring Christianity to the world.'

Zimbalist's own idealism was in all areas tied to a healthy pragmatism, and he was a realist in terms of advancing his career. So he fell in line with a trend of thinking prevalent among immigrants at the time, who thought that their success, and that of any offspring, would be better assured if they didn't appear too ethnic. (This trend became even more marked when 1917 Russian Revolution refugees started to flood into the United States—there were a great number of conversions as well as Americanization of Russian and Jewish names.) Zimbalist had married an American, was in the process of becoming a citizen himself and, like Alma, wanted any offspring to be raised as Americans. Efrem's and Alma's successes notwithstanding, they must have believed that as Christians their children would have an added advantage. (Several years before, Althea Jewell had persuaded Alma to send Abigail to a parochial school.)

The author is aware of Zimbalist's childhood witnessing of heart-breaking discrimination against Jews. I have also spoken to an anti-semitic colleague from his London days. Just how much all this affected Zimbalist's decision to conceal his heritage is indicated by his response when I put the question to him in 1980. I had never before seen him as ani-mated: 'To me it was unpleasant to be a Jew, and I didn't want my children to have the same experience. What is a Jew? Just a human being and, like any other, capable of being either a good or bad person. I've traveled all over the world and met countless good or bad people of every race and creed. Now, you ask, what kind of a "Jew" am I? I didn't go to synagogue, and I never learned Hebrew. My father wasn't orthodox. Yet while my mother and father lived, they knew nothing about my views on the subject. When they died, I said goodbye to the past. As far as I'm concerned, there has been no "Jew" in the family for sixty-five years. And my children are just "good people," plain and simple.' The events of World War II con-firmed his decision, and as with all Zimbalist's decisions, he stuck to it to the end. Once, in his twilight years, Zimbalist stopped an Israeli student for overemoting. 'The Jews were exiled thousands of years ago,' he observed. 'What's the point of crying about it now?'

People renounced their Jewish heritage for various reasons: Auer did it to assure his position as Soloist to the Tsar (according to Mischa Elman's father, he also encouraged his Jewish students to renounce theirs), Kreisler for his Catholic bride. A wicked story has Harriet Kreisler vehemently attempting to discredit the idea that her husband had Semitic roots. 'Why Fritz hasn't a drop of Jewish blood in him,' she snapped. 'Poor fellow, he must be very anemic,' countered Leopold Godowsky.

Summer 1915 was spent as usual at Lake George. Alma was very close to giving birth. When signs indicated the event was imminent, Efrem and the maid, doubtless not calmly, put Alma into the Hudson and drove her to the nearest doctor, fifty miles away in Glens Falls. In all the excitement no one noticed that their collie Droog (Russian for 'friend') had hidden under the back seat, and three times on what turned into an increasingly frantic trip Zimbalist had to stop and tend to the unfortunate car-sick puppy. Maria Virginia was born on 20 August 1915 and shortly after baptized an Episcopalian. Her parents took every precaution to keep her roots, and theirs, secret.

Many years later Maria's daughter Susan, away at college, phoned to ask permission to bring a boyfriend home for the holidays. Both she and her sister Jane had been raised Episcopalian, so she felt obliged to mention that the young man was Jewish. Maria was silent at the other end of the line; she had probably become aware of her Jewish heritage but decided to carry on the front adopted by her parents. She didn't let on. For what it is worth the public at large, and musicians in particular, never had any doubts (in March 1987 Josef Gingold played Zimbalist's 'Hebrew Dance' in a concert honoring Jewish musicians). And Marcia Davenport recalled that, long after her mother cut herself off from any Jewish identification, she would sing 'Hatikva' as an encore; when she sang it in Carnegie Hall, she received a standing ovation, and Jews wept.

One final thought on the subject: it is possible that a precedent for denial had been set earlier in the Zimbalist lineage to safeguard positions of importance in Russian society. Zimbalist once hinted at this when he told Curtis Institute accompanist Ethel Evans: 'I had no idea I was Jewish until I was ten.' This would have been just the time preparations were being made for his fateful move from Rostov to St. Petersburg.

America, fascinated as always by the doings of the rich and famous, was delighted with the addition to the Zimbalist family, and the press made the most of it, reporting that both Efrem and Alma had given up all professional engagements for the season, braving the loss of a small fortune in fees in order to devote themselves exclusively to their daughter. Barely months after Maria Virginia's birth one reporter estimated that so far her mother had sung her $150,000 worth of lullabies. A cameraman was hired to shoot home movies of Alma bathing the baby, father hovering at her shoulder and smiling proudly. Seeing these films, one can't help noticing the myriad nannies hovering about in immaculately starched white uniforms and bonnets. Many years later Zimbalist marveled, 'Alma was one of the most successful concert artists of her time but also the most wonderful wife and mother, all at the same time. How she did it is incredible to me.' All the maids and governesses doubtless helped.

The joy of those early days of fatherhood was tempered by the sobering tragedy of a world at war. Efrem had just taken out his first papers and became a U.S. citizen a few years later. Safely removed from his homeland and the battlefields, having formally cut any attachment to his roots, he nonetheless experienced a gnawing in his heart at news from the Russian front. Jews of the Pale of Settlement residing in the battle zone were declared German spies and were forcibly transported to the Russian interior in cattle cars, without food or water, and without any provision for housing once they arrived. Thousands died, the merest prelude to what was to come two decades later.

Zimbalist did honor his engagement in fall 1915 as soloist on Damrosch's New York Symphony tour—fifty concerts in roughly the same number of days, but the grueling schedule was lightened by comfortable traveling conditions: Damrosch hired a special private train, which literally became his musicians' home. This, along with their irrepressible sense of humor, kept morale high at all times. Zimbalist appeared on each concert, rotating concertos—Paganini, Bruch and Mendelssohn—and he and concertmaster David Mannes played poker nightly in the train's smoke-filled lounge car until the small hours.

One stop was Fargo, North Dakota, where the citizens attended the first symphony concert they had ever heard. At the Grand Opera House the orchestra launched into Joachim Raff's 'Lenore' Symphony. Zimbalist was sitting in the wings awaiting his turn when an inebriated cowboy teetered over, wanting to know what all the noise was about. Zimbalist explained that a symphony concert was in progress and the man immediately sat down and became serious. He listened intently until the orchestral sound grew to a big climax. Then, unable to restrain his enthusiasm, he grabbed Zimbalist by the knee and exclaimed, 'Goddammit, I *like* that music!' He settled down again as the music became quieter, but as the cymbals crashed and brass resounded at the peak of the next crescendo he sprang to his feet and yelled, 'I don't care if they all go to *Hell*, but they sure *can* play that music!' At dinner afterward Zimbalist laughingly told Damrosch the story, and they relived their own thrill at hearing symphonic sounds for the first time. The cowboy yarn soon made the rounds of the orchestra, and for the rest of the tour it would crop up, tailored to every situation and always drawing chuckles: Goddammit, I like this omelet; Goddammit, but this is a good hand, etc.

For Zimbalist the highlight of the tour was when Kreisler joined the happy band in Salt Lake City and San Francisco for Mozart's 'Sinfonia Concertante.' As before, Kreisler played the viola part, amazing everyone with the volume and richness of tone he drew from the small Deconet instrument he had borrowed from Damrosch. (Zimbalist was so taken with its sound he later later bought the viola.) Persistent rumor has it that the pair recorded this piece, with piano accompaniment. If so, it has yet to see the light of day. It certainly rivals in collectors' speculation reports of an unreleased Ysaÿe record of the Mozart G major concerto.

In March 1916 a musical happening crowded news of the Battle of Verdun off the front pages of Philadelphia newspapers: Stokowski fronted an augmented Philadelphia Orchestra, numbering 110 players, and a chorus of 958 singers in the American première of Gustav Mahler's Eighth Symphony. On 9 April the entire cast of 1,200 (including staff) journeyed to New York for a repeat at the Metropolitan Opera House, and the Zimbalists attended (it was Efrem's twenty-sixth birthday celebration). William Henderson's facetious review appeared in the *New York Sun* of 10 April: 'This is a piece of perfectly disinterested advice. If Philadelphia believes that Mr. Stokowski is essential to her musical development, let her decline to permit him to conduct great concerts in New York.' Another event that spring was the Zimbalists' acquisition of a summer getaway on Fishers Island, New York, a few miles off the Connecticut coast — a thirty-five-room shingled stone 'cottage,' Harbour Hill, overlooking Hay Harbor.

Its main attraction to Zimbalist was the billiard room in the basement; Alma kept her Lake George place as the occasional alternative retreat.

The United States entered the war in January 1917, and anti-German sentiments soon ran very high, forcing Fritz Kreisler to step down from public view—this despite the fact that for some time he had been playing concerts solely for the benefit of war-orphaned children. In Russia Tsar Nicholas's grip on the reins was loosening. The revolution that came in the wake of Russia's collapse filled Zimbalist with fear for the safety of his family, and he devoured the daily headlines, noting with horror the slaughter of Tsar Nicholas and his entire family at Ekaterinburg.

By far the most earth-shattering musical news was the U.S. debut of Jascha Heifetz on the afternoon of 27 October 1917. Without any doubt, Heifetz's emergence on the world stage redirected the course of violin playing. An instant sensation, he established by the sounds he drew from his violin the Parnassus to which all violinists who followed would aspire. Though familiar to most readers, the reaction of two eminent colleagues who shared a box at Heifetz's debut is too much part of the saga not to retell. The story goes that halfway through Elman, hearing Heifetz for the first time, mopped his perspiring brow. Leaning over to a friend on his left he muttered, 'Very warm in here isn't it Leopold?' 'Not for pianists,' quipped Godowsky drily. Within a couple of weeks Heifetz set in wax his classic recordings of many pieces from the famous debut, eternalizing the unprecedented perfection he had established.

Leopold Auer had spent the summers of 1915 and 1916 in a picturesque village in Norway, even more attractive because of its neutrality. The many students who accompanied him there combined study with outdoor recreation. One was the superb violinist Toscha Seidel. Born in Odessa in 1900, Seidel was a student at the Stern Conservatory in Berlin in 1912 when he first heard Heifetz play. Stunned, he immediately returned to Russia in quest of lessons with Heifetz's teacher. Seidel was the fourth in the quartet of great Auer students (chronologically by major debuts, Elman, Zimbalist, Heifetz, Seidel). Nathan Milstein's name is purposely omitted; his contact with Auer, just before the Professor's flight from Russia, was very limited.

Seidel, among the last of the great Auer students fully formed in Russia, was to have a sad career in the United States, where he arrived too soon after Heifetz's revelations to have an impact. This, compounded by an inability to handle his affairs intelligently, eventually relegated Seidel to chasing the Hollywood dollar. His sensuous tone made him the consummate background soloist for the romantic movies then being churned out. Owing possibly to envy, detractors claimed that he couldn't count very well, and the end of his career was clouded by frustration and bitterness. Ironically, in the 1950s, at Heifetz's request he served as concertmaster for some of the master's most spectacular concerto recordings. Seidel died in Los Angeles in 1962.

In summer 1917 Auer had set up headquarters in Saltsjobaden, Sweden, another charmingly neutral spot. That summer Auer helped Heifetz prepare his U.S. debut program, and Auer and Seidel gave a joint recital in a spacious hall that attracted several thousand people. In September Auer wrote his American student Ruth Ray: 'We decided not to return to Russia on account of the unpleasant circumstances, waiting till something better comes.... I am now again a traveling artist [and] am ashamed to be obliged at my age to do such business. In Scandinavia life during the winter will be difficult on account of the need for coal and food. The Swedish are not happy at all to see so many foreigners in their country. If necessary I shall go to America, as old Europe is blocked.' At the urging of Zimbalist, Heifetz and Kathleen Parlow, Auer embarked for New York from Christiania on 7 February 1918, arriving ten days later, seventy-three years of age, with his Stradivarius, two trunks, and his memories. He was accompanied by Thelma Given and her mother, Toscha Seidel and his mother and brother and Mme. Stein. The welcoming committee, a crowd of students and colleagues, included Zimbalist, Heifetz, Elman and David Hochstein (in uniform; he left for the French front in days, never to return). Before he knew it the Professor was hard at work again.

Auer's mysterious relationship with Mme. Stein bears passing attention. Originally the wife of Bogutska Stein, a pianist on the faculty at the St. Petersburg Conservatory, Mme. Stein left him and began to spend her time with Auer. In some accounts she is referred to as Auer's niece. When he died she was officially acknowledged as his widow, although it is not clear exactly when they married. Was it on arrival in the United States, to avert scandal in their newly adopted homeland? Another version has them marrying before leaving St. Petersburg, creating an equivalent scandal in Russian musical society.

Encouraged by his students, Auer gave a Carnegie Hall recital on 23

March 1918 and other successful concerts in Philadelphia, Boston and Chicago. On 7 June 1920 Auer gave a seventy-fifth birthday recital at Carnegie Hall for which he chose all his old favorites, including Tchaikovsky's 'Melodie' and Brahms's first Hungarian Dance. At a select party afterward Victor company technicians recorded the Professor playing these two short pieces. A limited number of copies were pressed, not for commercial release, and distributed among family and friends. The first four were labeled 'Victor Special Record' and given to Zimbalist, Heifetz, Elman, and Eddy Brown. They were inscribed by Auer 'To my musical children.'

These recordings give clear evidence of the elegance, charm and nobility of style that listeners never failed to mention when describing Auer's playing. They also demonstrate violinistic mastery largely undiminished by the passage of time—he was still in remarkably good technical and tonal trim. His record of the Brahms is a testament to the forward progression of violin playing. Joachim recorded the same dance when he was almost Auer's age, and the comparison between master and student is pointed: Joachim's technique is sloppy, his tone considerably drier and, despite the great master's lofty reputation as the 'purist' musician, his legato phrases rankle with their stomach-turning glissandos and rough bowing. Listening to the Auer version gives one the sense of having bridged more than a generation gap, of emerging into a world where more contemporary hallmarks are quickly recognized. One is carried away by the elasticity and freedom of phrasing associated with the so-called Russian School, and also its temperament and verve—indeed, all the qualities that helped endear it to audiences and entrench it for decades. After the theme's embellishment in double stops, Auer brilliantly arpeggiates before landing on a low G tremolando with the kind of vigorous accent, produced by exuberant bow-speed, that cropped up repeatedly in the playing of Zimbalist, Elman and particularly Heifetz. The source is evident.

Thanks to the name his disciples had established for him in America, scores of new students began flocking to his West Side studio to become legitimate 'Auer pupils.' He charged fees commensurate with the legend, wrote a method, edited many pieces for Carl Fischer (some say he delegated this editing to his students) and even authorized the sale of 'Leopold Auer Violin Outfits' for beginners. In a 1920 letter to Ruth Ray he wrote, 'By advice of my physicians (three of them) I am overworked and have to diminish the number of my lessons about a half. For that reason I charge 30 dolls. for a lesson and 35 dolls. for a hearing.' He added that hearings were without any guarantee of subsequent lessons and that those canceling lessons or hearings on less than three days notice forfeited their prepaid fees. By the late 1920s Auer's fee had risen to $100 an hour. In addition to his autobiography he wrote two widely selling books: *Violin Playing As I Teach It* (1921, now reprinted) and *Violin Master Works and Their Interpretation* (1925).

Only months after Auer's 1917 descent on New York, Alex and Maria Zimbalist arrived with their four daughters and two other sons. Likewise driven out by the revolution, they disembarked virtually penniless but devoid of Auer's earning potential. What part Zimbalist played in their flight out of troubled mother Russia he never told. He had grown apart from his family and kept a very low profile about them. It's known that he bought a house for the brood in Astoria and also provided monthly financial support until his brothers became active on the New York musical scene and could take over. Violist Samuel, the older, moved to the West Coast (he was *not* the Hollywood producer Sam Zimbalist), and Sascha joined the cello section of the Metropolitan Opera orchestra. Sisters Helen, Edna, Flora and Luba married and lived in the greater New York area.

Although geographically Astoria and Manhattan are not far apart, Zimbalist maintained an unnatural distance from his parents. He seemed loath to talk about them. Efrem Jr. does recall being taken to visit on rare occasions, and seeing Alex's bushy white mane adorning the front row at his father's concerts. When the lad was older, he and his sister determined to foster closer bonds with their grandparents. Maria took him to Astoria, but since neither grandparent spoke any English the effort proved unrewarding.

Zimbalist had been performing out of town on the historic Saturday afternoon of Heifetz's introduction to the American public (on his return Adams at the Wolfsohn Bureau had been quick to inform him of the sensational debut), but he, Kreisler and Kneisel hosted a Bohemians' club dinner in Heifetz's honor on 29 December 1917. The white-tie affair at the Biltmore attracted all the musical elite except Mischa Elman, who declined. The evening began with a one-act opera by Offenbach. Then came the food. Each course was served to a corresponding musical selection. Kreisler was his gracious self throughout, despite the fact that he was obliged to watch his once-adoring American public lavishing their affection on the sixteen-year-old newcomer from Russia. To their credit, neither Kreisler nor Zimbalist resented their younger colleague's success.

During the 1918 season Zimbalist persuaded Walter Damrosch to program the Hubay g minor concerto. Since being introduced to it by Franz von Vécsey ten years before he had performed it often in recital but never with orchestra. After the concert in Aeolian Hall, the *New York Post* found the concerto's musical value scant, concluding that Zimbalist must have chosen it 'chiefly because it gave him abundant opportunity to display his marvelous [virtuoso] skills.'

Alma, discovering that she was expecting again, wanted a release from her scheduled 1918 engagements. Adams wouldn't hear of it. The season had been heavily booked, and if she canceled she would be liable for breach of contract fines. Efrem Zimbalist Jr. was born on 30 November 1918 in New York. His father was on tour in Chicago. 'Some difference away,' he noted seriously to the press. Six weeks later, in January 1919, Alma set out on a nationwide tour. Since she would not be separated from her infant son she took him with her, chartering a private railroad car nick-named the Pioneer. She hired two Pullman employees to run the car, a maid, a cook, a nurse, her accompanist and his piano tuner. Althea Jewell came along too, and an agent from the Wolfsohn Bureau. When the Pioneer had a layover in a station near Philadelphia, Abigail popped in for a visit and pointed out to her mother that her three-year-old half sister Maria was in New York under the care of Nanny Staunton while Zimbalist himself was away on tour. This was exactly the broken-up pattern of life that Alma disapproved and had dreaded. Zimbalist's comment? 'After the children were born Alma hated to be away from them. But she still wanted to sing. She often said to me, "Make me stop." Of course I didn't even try.'

The season ended, and on 26 April 1919 the New York Bohemians honored her and Zimbalist with a dinner. Musical entertainment for the evening was provided by the Letz Quartet, giving the first performance of Kreisler's recently completed string quartet. Then Zimbalist took Alma and the children to Lake George for a few weeks of quiet before moving on to Fishers Island. Leopold Auer was resting up nearby, suffering from a heart condition compounded by painful gallstones. Zimbalist and the Professor had become very fond of each other. Zimbalist played for him and sought pointers on the upcoming season's programs, which included Frederick Stock's new concerto. 'He listened intently, sitting very close so

UPPER LEFT: Famous trio cooling off.

CENTER LEFT: Before dinner. Zimbalist, Harriet, Alma, Heifetz, Kreisler. After dinner came the Mendelssohn Concerto…

BELOW: Proud papa. In the nursery on East 72nd Street, 1920.

ABOVE: Arrival in Yokohama, 1922. On Zimbalist's right is Kyusaburo Yamamoto, director of the Imperial Theater in Tokyo, where concerts were held. Gregory Ashman is to Zimbalist's left.

LEFT: With his parents on the steps of the house he bought for them, Astoria, New York, 1920s.

Above: Zimbalist and Emanuel Bay entertaining Yamamoto in Atlantic City in the spring just prior to their 1924 Asian tour.

Upper right: Fishers Island, summer 1926. Ruvin Heifetz with student Efrem Jr. and his parents.

Right: With Nellie Melba on the steps of Coombe Cottage, 1927.

Drawing by Ruyl

The Buildings of
The Curtis Institute of Music

LEFT: The Curtis Institute as it looked when Zimbalist first saw it (from the 1927 catalog).

LOWER LEFT: In his library on his fortieth birthday, poring over first editions.

UPPER LEFT: Arrival in Yokohama, 1930. On Zimbalist's right is a famous blind Koto master. Trying to peer through the crowd (back row, far left) is Harry Kaufman.

LEFT: In performance with Kaufman, Osaka, Japan, 1930. (Photo from the New York Public Library)

BELOW: Leaving for Central and South American air tour, spring 1932. Left to right, Samuel Piza, Zimbalist, Theodore Saidenberg. (Photo from the New York Public Library)

Upper left: Being seen off by his wife and children on his 1932 Asian tour.

Upper right: En route to Japan, 1932. Captain Ito, to Zimbalist's right, hosting a special dinner on the promenade deck of the SS *Tatsuta Maru*. Saidenberg is on Zimbalist's left.

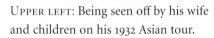

Center right: Zimbalist with his 1933 class and accompanists. Second row far left is Felix Slatkin. On Sokoloff's left is Iso Briselli.

Left: Press photo, rehearsing *Eugene Onegin*, 1935. (Photo from the New York Public Library)

LEFT: With Alma at the Tokugawas' Temple de Soleil, Tokyo, 1935.

BELOW: 'Re-Enacting the Life of Zimbalist' in a comic skit at a party in honor of the twenty-fifth anniversary of the violinist's U.S. debut. Left to right, middle row: Samuel Chotzinoff, Jascha Heifetz (as Zimbalist), Mrs. Zimbalist, Mr. Zimbalist, Marcia Davenport (as her mother, Alma Zimbalist), David Sarnoff (as a confidence man), Germaine Schnitzer, Marc Connelly, Nicholas Moldavan (as Gatti-Casazza). Front row: Pauline Heifetz (as a geisha), Mischa Levitzki, Mrs. Thomas Finletter (as Zimbalist's mother), Pierre Luboshutz (as Zimbalist's father). In the rear, wearing a top hat is Walter Damrosch as a Russian Grand Duke. New York, 9 December 1936. (Photo from the New York Public Library)

RIGHT: Ad for the 'Three Bs' series, 1938–39.

BELOW: Late 1930s publicity shot.

as not to miss a single note,' Zimbalist remembered. Whenever possible he would preview new programs for Auer, introducing him to the Sibelius Concerto and Ysaÿe's solo sonatas.

Alma meanwhile spent much time gardening, which she found took her mind off concert tours and railroad cars. Auer and Mme. Stein were enchanted with the Zimbalist children. Alma's colleague and friend Louise Homer was also summering close by. They had made many successful recordings together, their voices blending with a special affinity. From Anne Homer's biography of her mother: 'In New York, when she came to the house to rehearse, Alma [was] beguilingly modern and stylish, [but] in the summers [one] might find the pretty singer on her knees in her "victory garden," weeding the beans and wearing [her] "farmerette" outfit, a shapeless brown coverall and brown bandanna.'

Elizabeth Sprague Coolidge was a friend of the Zimbalists'. From Efrem's reply to a request for his participation in a festival in Pittsfield, Massachusetts (the embryo of Tanglewood), one gains a full measure of his then still quaint English:

> My dear Mrs. Coolidge,
> I have just returned back to the City and found your very kind letter and invitation to play at your festival. It would give me great pleasure to do so any other summer, but unfortunately, as I am not playing next Winter, outside of Joint Concerts with my wife (very few, only January and March [1920]) by playing at your wonderful festival I would offend many managers in the country, whom Mr. Adams refused my appeareance.
>
> May I assure you that it would give me great joy, if I possible could do it, and I hope you will be kind enough to ask me some other time.
>
> > With kindest regards, I am always
> > Most sincerely yours,
> > Efrem Zimbalist

As he had done when Maria Virginia was born, the proud papa was taking a season off to spend time with his son. (Incidentally, for all his life he pronounced 'appearance' exactly the way he spelled it here.)

Kreisler had thrown in the towel on 26 November 1917, in the midst of a U.S. tour. The only performances he had played since were in Boston, the following month, when he filled in for his ailing friend Franz in a series of Kneisel Quartet charity concerts. The first and second took place, but public disfavor against Kreisler necessitated canceling the last. Since 1915 the Kreislers had made summer visits to Seal Harbor, Maine, where they were among colleagues who didn't allow politics to interfere with their admiration for Kreisler's art or character, among them Gabrilowitsch, Godowsky, Josef Hofmann, Harold Bauer, Walter and Frank Damrosch, Stokowski and his wife, Olga Samaroff. The Zimbalists were among the staunch friends who stood by Kreisler through the bitterest period of his withdrawal, and he and Harriet accepted their invitation to spend summer 1919 with them at Fishers Island. Harriet brought along a friend, baritone Reinhold von Warlich.

It was a fun-filled sojourn at Fishers Island. At one point Heifetz visited for a little sun and surf. What did three of the world's star fiddlers talk about? 'Never about our careers — we were only too glad to get away from them,' Zimbalist recalled. Snapshots were taken of them on the beach and frolicking in the ocean. There were also evenings of music-making, far removed from concert pressures, when between pieces the celebrated violinists amused each other, and guests, with hilarious yarns. One evening they decided to play the Mendelssohn Concerto, each choosing a movement while one or the other took turns accompanying. 'Heifetz was a better pianist than I, but Kreisler was the best of the three,' Zimbalist later asserted.

Listeners retired to comfortable sofas, and the first movement got under way, Kreisler as soloist, Zimbalist at the piano and Heifetz turning pages. Harriet Kreisler ensconced herself front row center, contentedly sipping a horse's neck, her favorite beverage (a jigger of gin in a glass of ginger ale). It was evidently not her first of the evening, and it brought out the less pleasant side of her nature. That afternoon she had twice embarrassed her husband with a sharp reminder: 'Don't forget to *limp*, Fritz!' (although his wound had healed, she wanted him to cultivate a residual limp for sympathy). Now the gin unleashed her bossiness in full force, and after a few measures she started a running commentary — 'Too fast Fritz! ... Slow down Fritz! ... In tune Fritz! ... Too *fast*!' — the criticisms, be it noted, of a music-hater.

Zimbalist cringed and turned to Heifetz. 'What *are* we going to do, Jascha?' he asked in Russian. Heifetz shrugged. By the end of the movement they had formulated a plan. Zimbalist led Heifetz into the pantry, returning shortly with a fresh drink for Harriet, which she took without so much as a glance or a thank you. There was a gleam in the Russians' eyes as they watched Harriet's chatter gradually slow until she finally nodded off. Zimbalist and Heifetz exchanged knowing grins. They never told Kreisler the horse's neck *they* had fixed her consisted of an entire glass of gin with but a drop of ginger ale, and the performance resumed. Zimbalist played the second movement with Heifetz as pianist, and in the finale Kreisler accompanied Heifetz. Oh, to have been a fly on the wall!

That summer at Fishers Island Zimbalist and Kreisler also did some light reading. *Honeydew* by Joseph Herbert (an adaptation of the French farce *Les Surprises Divorces* by Alexander Bisson) particularly amused Zimbalist and gave him an idea. He suggested to Kreisler that they write comic operettas to while away the time. Kreisler loved the idea; he selected a story by William Le Baron, and they both got to work. Kreisler, with more time on his hands, finished *Apple Blossoms* in fairly short order; it ran for almost a year on Broadway. Zimbalist's progress was slowed by concert commitments, and in the fall he shelved the project until a forced vacation in Charleston, South Carolina (recuperation following appendectomy), finally gave him the chance to complete it.

Zimbalist's operetta, *Honeydew, the Scourge of the Sea*, 'a fantastic comedy,' premièred in Providence in March 1920 and opened on Broadway at the Casino Theater on 6 September. 'It had a very interesting piano score which the Remick Music Corporation published,' Zimbalist said. 'But when the "in-house" arranger orchestrated it for Broadway I was disappointed that he simplified it so much.' Joseph Herbert's story depicts the life of Henry Honeydew, a composer and confirmed impressionist, who lives for his art and winds up with two mothers-in-law, an ex-wife and his new wife under the same roof—his father-in-law is his first wife's husband, his uncle is now his father-in-law and on and on. 'An everyday love story that could happen anywhere,' Zimbalist chuckled drily. The show grossed $18,780 its first week and ran for seven months.

Alma, who never liked musical comedy and therefore disapproved of the entire thing, refused to so much as hum a tune from it. The most popular of these were 'Drop Me a Line Some Time,' 'Believe Me Beloved,' 'A Cup of Tea' and 'It's a Small, Small World,' still occasionally heard today. But Heifetz was a fan and attended the openings of both *Apple Blossoms* and *Honeydew*.

With the birth of their second child Efrem and Alma felt that they were outgrowing their West Side home. They moved to 101 East 72nd Street, near Park Avenue, an abode that was more of a mansion than a house. Naturally, the staff had to be expanded to keep pace with the added opulence. Alma engaged an extra housekeeper, a cook named Hannah and a butler of haughty demeanor named Ross, whose favorite line was 'It's just out of this *world*, Madame.'

Among the first items to decorate the walls of the music room was a much-worn Victor ten-inch disc, mounted with an inscription:

> To Miss Alma Gluck
> One of your records, entitled 'My Old Kentucky Home,' was taken to the battlefields of France by Headquarters Co., 307th Field Artillery A.E.F. during May 1918. So grateful were the boys for having your interpretation of this beautiful old song, it was unanimous with the company that you should have this record souvenir which furnished so much pleasure on the battlefield.
>   Offensives: St. Mihiel, Mense-Argonne
>   Minor offensives: Toul Sector, Prague, Grand Pre
>   Camden, N.J. 1919

The Hudson was traded in on a short-lived Rolls Royce. On its maiden journey, to dinner at the Plaza, English chauffeur George Ladd misjudged a turn and they almost skidded off the road. Convinced that the car was jinxed, Alma refused to ride another foot. She ordered Ladd to replace it with a more dependable vehicle. Next day he showed up in a top-of-the-line Rolls Landaulet, a beauty of some rarity even then. Between car waxing and chauffeuring duties, Ladd tried to improve Efrem's notoriously poor driving. One can well imagine the colorful exchanges that went on, King's English stretched to opposite extremes, behind the Landaulet's controls.

The stage was set for the distinguished gatherings and glittering parties that made an invitation to the house 'off Park Avenue' a much desired favor, and Alma Gluck and Efrem Zimbalist among the most celebrated hosts in the world.

---

* This 'official' version is based on Kreisler's personal account in *Four Weeks in the Trenches*. Whenever it came up Zimbalist evinced subtle but telltale indications that its veracity was to be doubted.

CHAPTER 16

High Living

(1920–1932)

The 1920s and early '30s were for Zimbalist a time replete with the greatest satisfaction in all areas. He enjoyed a wonderful domestic life, a large number of interesting and artistically rewarding concerts, a social circle graced by warm, stimulating friendships and (excepting the crash of 1929) carefree financial security. For Alma most of this held true, but she faced a major adjustment with which she had to come to grips: the gradual loss of her voice. Pride shaped the facade she presented, that her graceful withdrawal from the concert stage was choice rather than necessity. Marcia Davenport thought that, while her mother may have convinced others, she failed to convince herself. Alma buried her pain. Whether or not she confided in her husband, he intuitively sensed her feelings. The Zimbalists were often favorably cited when the question 'Can marriage be combined with a career?' arose in the daily pulps. But in 1923 Alma, still struggling with retirement, wrote to the *Philadelphia Public Ledger*: 'My career was unfair to my husband. My home life was not happy. How could it be? It was erratic and unnatural, the artist's life. I have a right to be happy and rebel at that loneliness now, and it is in my power to choose.'

For a woman who not only acted but also looked like a great opera star should (and seldom does except in the movies), it must have been an agonizing choice. Alma threw herself wholeheartedly into family life, entertaining, and various charitable and fundraising activities. A founder, later vice president, of the American Guild of Musical Artists, she was also a chief supporter of the Musicians' Emergency Fund, the Actors' Fund, the

Society of the Friends of Music and the Red Cross (in 1917 she gave $25,000 of her concert earnings to the latter.)

On 21 December 1921 Alma played her part in helping composer Moritz Moszkowski out of the dire straits to which the war and ill-health had relegated him. An affair had been planned by Ernest Schelling at which Moszkowski's 'Spanish Dances' would be played by as many celebrated pianists as could be crammed onto Carnegie Hall's stage. Josef Lhevinne, Leopold Godowsky, Ossip Gabrilowitsch, Percy Grainger, Harold Bauer, Elly Ney, Ignaz Friedman, Rudolph Ganz, Ernest Hutcheson, Alexander Lambert, Yolanda Mero, Germaine Schnitzer and Sigismund Stojowski were rounded up to join Schelling. The day before the concert Schelling put out an S.O.S. to Walter Damrosch: 'We need a conductor!'

In his autobiography Damrosch reported: 'When I arrived at the rehearsal hall the confusion was indeed indescribable. I rapped on my stand for silence...at least five or six continued their infernal improvising, playing of scales, and pianistic fireworks. By using heroic measures I gradually produced a semblance of order, and gave the signal for the beginning of the music.' Carnegie Hall was jammed for the event. The stage was so crowded with the fourteen concert grands that, after threading his way through them to introduce Alma, who was to auction off one of the programs, Damrosch joked that what the concert needed was not a conductor but a traffic cop.

On a West Coast tour Zimbalist ran into William de Mille, an acquaintance from Berlin days. De Mille was directing *The Sheik*, starring Rudolph Valentino, and extended an invitation to visit the set. 'I always thought William a better director than his more ambitious brother Cecil,' Zimbalist said later. Viewing the day's work in the screening room he found himself seated beside the movie's female lead, whom he decided was the most beautiful woman he had ever laid eyes on. 'How wonderful that you are a musician,' Agnes Ayres twittered brightly. 'I have always loved music, especially opera. My favorite is—oh, now what is it called? You know, the one by Massenet—ah, yes: *Mennin*.'

Ayres was then at the height of her popularity. But her violinist admirer was pointedly to discover the vagaries of Hollywood stardom when he returned to Los Angeles for a recital a few years later. A note was delivered to his dressing room after the concert—Ayres wanted him to call on her at home. He was traveling that night and in a rush, so he phoned instead.

The actress beseeched him to stop by; she sounded so desperate that Zimbalist felt he had no choice. He jumped into a taxi and gave the address she had given him, only to arrive at a wretched tenement house. The former heroine to millions of fans was the very personification of 'down and out,' and it was with a heavy heart that Zimbalist gave her an eagerly accepted $200 before speeding on to catch his train.

An exquisite cross section from all the higher walks of life passed across the threshold of the Zimbalists' home, such people as Edna St. Vincent Millay, Willa Cather, Ogden Nash, Henry and Clare Boothe Luce, John D. Rockefeller, Alexander Woollcott, Dorothy Parker and Oscar Levant. These personalities blended into a rich tapestry that infused the rarified atmosphere at Alma Gluck and Efrem Zimbalist's. Their home took on the aura of a '10 Cornwall Terrace West.'

'Quartet parties' were an integral fiber of that tapestry. Among the musicians on hand to weave the embroidery were violinists Sascha Jacobsen and Louis Kaufman (both students of Franz Kneisel) and cellist Marie Roemat Rosanoff. Sometimes Heifetz sat in, and often Zimbalist. On occasion, Albert Einstein timidly (and dreadfully) played second violin. Samuel Chotzinoff, always trying to beg off on grounds of not having practiced the difficult quintet parts, had to be forcefully cajoled into participating. Alma dismissed his excuses. 'You lazy so-and-so, shut up and play!' she'd exhort, and Chotzi would jump to the piano bench. Theodore Roosevelt's son-in-law Nicholas Longworth, Speaker of the House of Representatives and avid amateur violinist, was a regular. Zimbalist nicknamed him 'Nick the Fiddler' and always offered him the first violin chair. 'All right, I'll try it up to the Allegro,' Longworth would caution, 'but then you'd better be ready to switch.'

Nick and his wife, Alice, were close friends. Zimbalist stayed with them in Georgetown whenever he had a Washington concert. 'Once I arrived just as they were leaving. "We're going to dinner with some stuffy senators. Would you like to come?" Alice asked. Well, I did, and it was the deadliest, dullest dinner I have ever experienced. "Let's get out of here," Alice whispered in my ear, after dessert. We went back to the house and played poker till dawn.' (When Longworth died Zimbalist and Harold Bauer played Brahms's d minor sonata at a memorial program at the Library of Congress on 3 May 1931).

In 1919 Chotzinoff had played some concerts with Heifetz. He was then still Zimbalist's accompanist, often played for Alma Gluck and was also acting as Abigail's piano teacher. But a year or two later he succeeded André Benoist as Heifetz's regular pianist and courted Jascha's older sister Pauline (they married in 1926). It was Zimbalist who had introduced him to the Heifetzes. 'After Chotzi met Pauline it was only natural for him to want to be with Heifetz,' was the mild way Zimbalist categorized what on the surface appeared to be thankless desertion. He started using several accompanists, among them Eugene Lutsky and Emanuel Balaban. Occasionally Chotzinoff was still available—it was some years before Heifetz started including an exclusivity clause in his accompanists' contracts.

By means of the Guild of Musical Artists, through which Alma siphoned money from the John Work Garretts of Baltimore, she made financially possible the founding of the Musical Art Quartet, consisting of Sascha Jacobsen, Paul Bernard, Louis Kaufman and Marie Roemat Rosanoff. Mrs. Garrett had Russian designer Leon Bakst decorate a small theater in the Garrett mansion in which the quartet could privately entertain her friends. The group's impetus to become a permanent ensemble was triggered by those quartet parties at the Zimbalists. During this incubating process Zimbalist was occasionally pressured into deposing Jacobsen for a movement or two. There were never any hard feelings— and even if there had been Zimbalist's modesty could smooth the most ruffled feathers. In his endearing way he would frequently ask, without dropping a note, 'I did it right, you think, Sascha?'

The Musical Art started out among the top quartets and enjoyed an excellent, if relatively short-lived, career. A grateful Louis Kaufman credited the Zimbalists with making it all possible. 'Zimbalist even lent me the little Deconet viola he had bought from Damrosch.' Kaufman, a brilliant violinist, had happily consented to play viola in the quartet. Zimbalist had been a formative influence in Kaufman's career, having heard him in his hometown of Portland, Oregon, when he was eleven and advising his father to send the lad to New York to study with Franz Kneisel (not Auer!). 'Zimbalist was a chamber music fanatic,' Kaufman recalled. 'One summer chamber music party at Fishers Island started in the afternoon. We played till we were dizzy then had a magnificent clambake on the beach—lobster, chicken and fresh corn broiled under seaweed on heated rocks. After stuffing ourselves we started right back in playing. It's too bad the public so seldom had the opportunity of hearing Zimbalist play chamber music.'

Once Einstein sat in the Zimbalists' music room listening to the Musical Art Quartet. They played an early Beethoven then a Mozart. Zimbalist asked him if he had enjoyed the performance. 'Mozart is wonderful,' answered Einstein.

'What about Beethoven, Professor Einstein?' Zimbalist ventured.

'Too complicated.'

Zimbalist enjoyed telling how Einstein came to the United States: 'I had a friend, Abraham Flexner, who was head of the Rockefeller Foundation. One day, after his retirement, a man came to see him and said, "Mr. Flexner, you shouldn't have retired, you should be doing something." Perhaps he didn't realize that Flexner had gone back to school, in his sixties, to study many different subjects. The man told him that he represented a client with a great deal of money, who wished Flexner to spend it. Abraham told him, "I had Rockefeller's money. Now money doesn't interest me—I have enough to live on." "Well, *do* think about it," the man urged. "If you come up with any ideas just let me know." Some weeks or months passed. They met again.

"'I did think of something that might interest me," Flexner said, "but it will take a great deal of money."

"'Oh, what is it?"

"'A super university. It would probably take a couple of million."

"'I can get twelve million for you," the man told him. The client he represented was Bamberger of the department store chain. He admired Flexner and wanted him to do something decent with all the money he had made. Well, Abraham took on the task of organizing the Institute for Advanced Study. His first action was to persuade Einstein to teach physics. He offered him anything he wanted, and Einstein came to the United States with his wife. The three of them had a conference. Flexner asked, "Dr. Einstein, what are your ideas about teaching and financial arrangements?" Einstein answered, "I would like just one student, who can feel free to come to me anytime, night and day. And I hear that life in the United States is very expensive. I will have to ask $5,000 a year." Flexner was about to say something when Mrs. Einstein caught his eye. They met privately later. Abraham told her he was willing to pay her husband $25,000. She agreed to the figure, and suggested that Flexner never discuss business matters with Einstein. "He doesn't understand them," she said. He never even carried any money. It was Abraham who introduced me to Einstein.'

Soon after the famous scientist's emigration, Pennsylvania's Lincoln University held a symposium on various subjects and invited Zimbalist to represent music. The participants, seated at a long table, awaited their turn to address the student body. Zimbalist was flanked by Einstein and Thomas Mann. Both spoke eloquently, at some length. When Zimbalist's turn came he candidly told the audience how inadequate he felt: 'I am at a distinct disadvantage pitted against such great minds and articulate men of words. I express my thoughts in a different idiom, and if you will allow me I will return sometime with my violin.' As he sat down Mann handed him a cigar. 'Congratulations,' he said, 'you made the best speech of all,' then continued, as they both lit up: 'To sit in front of a fire and puff on a Maria Mancini is the acme of human pleasure.' (The University took Zimbalist up on his offer, and he presented a memorable lecture recital.)

He saw much of Einstein and recounted one meeting in Princeton: 'I was lunching with Flexner, Einstein and Oppenheimer, head of the Atomic Commission. I sat between them while they talked physics. After putting forth a theory, Einstein turned to me and said, "That's clear to you, isn't it?" Now, a book could be written on what I *don't* know about physics! "Professor Einstein, it's clear as mud. I don't understand a word of it," I answered. He was surprised: "I don't believe you. Music and physics are so closely allied that you should have been able to follow." "I beg to differ," I said to him. "Mathematics in music and mathematics in your field are two entirely different things. Among musicians Bach was probably the greatest mathematician, but without realizing it. It was intuitive. With you it's not intuition, but step by step." "You're absolutely wrong," he answered, "in studying relativity the answer came first. Then I had to prove its possibility by theorizing. And that involved intuition, which proves that the theories governing music and physics are one and the same."'

Sergei Rachmaninoff was another regular of Efrem and Alma's inner circle, having settled in the United States on 10 November 1918, just in time to watch the entire population of New York go raving mad in their celebration of the Armistice. Zimbalist was one of the first callers at Rachmaninoff's hotel, bearing flowers. Having admired him since boyhood he wanted to meet the great man. Rachmaninoff received him warmly and gave him a signed photograph. He never forgot his young colleague's gesture.

Rachmaninoff had hated his initial visit to America in 1909, and nine years later he turned down directorship offers from both the Boston Symphony and Cincinnati Orchestra. Ysaÿe then took over in Cincinnati. After his U.S. debut in 1894 Ysaÿe had been heard sporadically in the New World. His only recordings, made in America for Columbia, consist of twelve single sides still demonstrating (in 1912) a comprehensive command of the instrument and the tenets of what must have been one of the grandest of styles. Zimbalist didn't hear these records. But he still retained the vivid impression Ysaÿe had made on him in St. Petersburg and was very excited when, in 1922, before returning to Europe for good, the master announced a series of concerts in New York. Zimbalist immediately bought tickets. Leaving the box office, he encountered Sascha Jacobsen, who had heard Ysaÿe recently. On Jacobsen's advice Zimbalist gave his tickets away, preserving intact the cherished memory of Ysaÿe at the height of his powers.

Rachmaninoff never felt comfortable in the United States and thrived on the camaraderie of Old World friends. 'I asked him what he wanted to do, play or conduct,' Zimbalist remembered. 'He said he wanted to play. "Well, I'm with the best management in America," I told him, "I'll talk to them. What fee will you ask for concerts?" "$750," Rachmaninoff answered. When I mentioned this figure to Adams he just laughed.'

Kreisler, another supporter, tried *his* manager, Charles Ellis in Boston. Ellis had just lost Paderewski, whose political efforts leading to the Prime Ministership of Poland left little time for concerts. But Ellis, too, was hard to persuade. 'I agree with you that Rachmaninoff is a great musician,' he told Kreisler, 'but I need a famous pianist—no one here knows him as a pianist!' He did take Rachmaninoff on, but the taciturn Russian had, that first season, to be satisfied with a lower fee than the one he had originally asked. 'Eventually, of course, he ended up getting four times the amount,' Zimbalist said with relish.

When Rachmaninoff visited he often carried the manuscript of an orchestral score in progress. He sought Zimbalist's advice on the playability of his string parts and welcomed suggestions, such as the fingerings and bowings provided for the 'Paganini Variations' and the 'Symphonic Dances.' 'Despite the emotional music he wrote, Rachmaninoff was not an openly warm person,' Zimbalist recollected. 'Time upon time I saw him close up like a clam and not say a single word all evening.'

One, at least, of the new things Rachmaninoff was exposed to in

America appealed greatly to him—the Paul Whiteman Orchestra. His enthusiasm was shared by Zimbalist, whose collection of Whiteman records Rachmaninoff frequently stopped by to hear. Readers acquainted only with the pianist's dour facade will find it hard to picture him sitting for hours in front of the Victrola listening to 'Parade of the Wooden Soldiers' with a blissful expression on his craggy face. 'Play it again, Zimmie,' he would beg. They also enjoyed Harry Lauder singing 'I Love a Lassie' and 'Stop Your Tickling, Jock.' (Incidentally, while it was Alma who coined the nickname Zimmie, it was Rachmaninoff and John McCormack who made it stick.)

Zimbalist, Kreisler and McCormack were Rachmaninoff's best new friends. But they didn't replace Chaliapin, with whom ties went back a long way. The two were particularly close. Neither ever learned to speak lucid English—Rachmaninoff gave up and relied on his wife's prowess. (Commendably, Leopold Auer learned enough to write books in English, his third adopted language.) Sometimes Rachmaninoff arrived at the Zimbalists' with Chaliapin, who seemed the only person capable of making him laugh. On such occasions many a tall tale was spun around the fireplace, punctuated by uproarious guffaws. Zimbalist once relayed a request from a socialite for Chaliapin to sing at one of her fashionable Waldorf-Astoria musicales. The suggested hour was ten. 'Ten in the evening?' the basso asked. 'Ten in the morning,' Zimbalist smiled. Chaliapin thundered his answer. 'Tell Mrs. Bagby that Chaliapin does not *spit* before noon!'

Chaliapin and the Zimbalists were once dinner guests at the McCormacks'. Another guest was Joseph Achron's younger pianist brother Isadore, who had accompanied both Zimbalist and Heifetz. 'We sat around the table having coffee,' Zimbalist reminisced. 'Isadore began talking. He talked and talked and talked. Chaliapin gave him a look—had he been more sensitive Isadore would have sensed his displeasure. But he kept on talking. Chaliapin sat silently, glaring. Finally, when there was a brief pause he stood up and roared his opinion in one word: "Gavno!"' (Shit!) It shut Izzie up fast.'

Another Russian expatriate to appear on the East 72nd Street scene was Sergei Prokofiev, with whom Alma liked to play bridge. Zimbalist remembered him as a sarcastic, unlovable character and always distrusted what he felt to be a corresponding cynicism in his compositions. 'Besides, he was a sore loser. We had much more fun when Harpo Marx came over to play poker.'

Josef Hofmann was a frequent visitor. Once when Rachmaninoff was present Hofmann and Zimbalist began discussing a mutually respected figure, Leopold Godowsky. 'Rachmaninoff had never heard him play,' Zimbalist recalled. 'We told him, "Oh, but you *must!*" Godowsky lived at the Hotel Alamac on upper Broadway. We went over to his suite, and he played for us for hours. Rachmaninoff was amazed by what he could do with his little hands, yet he didn't like his Chopin arrangements and, outside of his technique, wasn't very impressed. But I was.' Zimbalist always considered Godowsky 'one of the most profound musicians I ever knew, a sweet and unhappy man. When I heard him in Berlin in the early years Philharmonic Hall was invariably packed. In New York he sat twiddling his thumbs, with no concerts. He suffered so at the end. He came backstage after one of my concerts shortly before his death. "I'm not afraid to die," he said, "I'm just afraid of the pain."' Zimbalist later paid him tribute by orchestrating his 'Metamorphosis on Themes of Johann Strauss.'

Godowsky much admired Bronislaw Huberman, touted as an equally underrated genius. When in 1921 this controversial violinist made his reappearance in New York after an absence of twenty-five years, Godowsky and Harold Bauer bought a box and persuaded Zimbalist to accompany them. 'They told me that sometimes he played marvelously,' Zimbalist commented. 'It so happened that that evening he did not.'

Lucrezia Bori was in the Zimbalists' inner circle, a 'darling woman who retired at the zenith of her career to learn more about music,' according to Zimbalist. George Gershwin, another regular, also invited Alma and Efrem to his parties, where most guests were Hollywood people. Gershwin entertained from the keyboard, and in this way Zimbalist was introduced to the melodies he later used in his 'Homage to Gershwin' (1951), for violin and piano. There were also parties at Walter and Margaret Damroschs', John and Lilly McCormacks' and the Ernest Hutchesons', where Alma and Efrem mingled with the wealth of New York's artistic world in the '20s. Zimbalist claimed that Kreisler was always the life of the party. But others recalled that he himself could be counted on to provide a spark of fun. Lilly McCormack in *I Hear You Calling Me* describes one dinner given by the Ernest Schellings: 'That night they had an entertainer who did wonderful things with coins. Toscanini and Kreisler were like small boys trying to figure out the tricks. Then Ernest and Zimbalist did their party stunt, a piano duet with a hairbrush and an orange, handling themselves with the utmost gravity in spite of the hilarity of their audience.' (Zimbalist thumped out a bass with the hairbrush while Schelling approximated a melody by rolling the orange over the keys.)

Lilly McCormack speaks of other parties at which Paul Kochanski did magic tricks, Rachmaninoff played jazz and Heifetz in cap and apron cooked bacon and eggs at 4 a.m. At one party Zimbalist found himself sitting beside the great Houdini and posed a question: 'It seems to me that all magic tricks are too carefully prearranged. Don't you ever improvise?' Houdini answered by requesting needles and thread. He performed his famous needle trick in which, after 'swallowing' them, he withdrew them from his mouth all neatly threaded. Improvisatory or not, it astounded all present.

One of Zimbalist's closest unmusical friends (term used advisedly) was the urbane Frank Crowninshield, editor of *Vogue* and *Vanity Fair* magazines. Dubbed 'the last gentleman,' Crowninshield was among the earliest American collectors of French Impressionist paintings, but missing from his otherwise cultivated makeup was even the slightest appreciation of music: along with Dr. Talley, the Zimbalist family physician, he shared a virtual allergy to melody. Music haters both, they nonetheless invariably attended Zimbalist's New York concerts. Zimbalist once dined with Crownie and Condé Nast, the publisher of *Vogue* and *Vanity Fair*. Sharing their table was a fetching young actress, introduced as Miss Goldwyn. Zimbalist had just started to converse with her when a man came over and invited her to dance. The man's name was Mayer. They subsequently married, forming an immortal merger: Metro-Goldwyn-Mayer.

Zimbalist was back in Europe not long after the war ended for concerts in England, Holland, Scandinavia, Hungary, Czechoslovakia, Estonia and the Balkans. He saw little destruction, except in Brussels and in Berlin, where he eschewed the Sans Souci in favor of the once elite Hotel Adlon. Fritz and Harriet Kreisler and Reinhold von Warlich joined him there for a dinner that included caviar and fine wines — cost for the entire meal was the equivalent of $4.00. On more extended subsequent European trips Zimbalist's family was likely to rendezvous with him at some point. Although Alma sang very little publicly after 1921 there were still occasional joint concerts with her husband; their final tour took them across the country, culminating in a performance in Salt Lake City's Mormon Tabernacle.

In spring 1923 Zimbalist joined Heifetz in a vacation trip to London. 'We traveled in one room and were as close as is possible with Jascha — which means we were about as close as two strangers!' Zimbalist later quipped. Actually, the pair kicked up their heels and enjoyed the break, making theater rounds in silk top hats, white tie and tails and treating themselves to choice fare in London's finest restaurants. Paul Whiteman was in town appearing at the Hippodrome, the beginning of a highly publicized trip carrying live American jazz for the first time to many European fans. 'Jascha and I were both crazy about him,' said Zimbalist. They were admitted to an exclusive private club where Whiteman's orchestra was playing. After two and a half weeks, the truant violinists returned to New York and their packed schedules.

Zimbalist continued to champion new works that he found appealing. To the Powell and Stock concertos he now added those by Ernest Schelling and Michel Gusikoff. On a fall 1923 Carnegie Hall recital of music by American composers he introduced Schelling's concerto and a new sonata by Powell; the composers themselves accompanied him. Although the Schelling work was well received, Zimbalist's personal favorite was the Stock Concerto, which became something of a mission for him. He crusaded not only for opportunities to perform it but also, later, recommended the piece to his students. In neither arena were his efforts well rewarded.

Zimbalist's friendship with Gershwin and his admiration for Paul Whiteman's orchestra coalesced in a curious way in 1924. Encouraged by his trip abroad and convinced that Americans didn't take jazz seriously enough, Whiteman set into motion the most important venture of his career: he rented New York's Aeolian Hall for a 'Jazz Concert' because, 'only in the concert hall can I show that jazz is the beginning of a new movement in the world art of music and that it has come to stay and deserves recognition.' Whiteman approached Gershwin, well in advance, commissioning a work for solo piano and orchestra. Gershwin, flattered by the invitation, was to be the soloist. But he was also very busy earning his living writing Broadway tunes, and the commission slipped his mind. He was dramatically reminded during a game at an all-night pool hall on Broadway, when his brother Ira rushed in to show him an article in the

morning's *New York Tribune* headlined 'Whiteman Judges Named /
Committee Will Decide / "What Is American Music?"' The article
announced that the expert judges at the Paul Whiteman concert on the
afternoon of 12 February 1924 would be Sergei Rachmaninoff, Jascha
Heifetz, Efrem Zimbalist and Alma Gluck—not one of whom was
American-born!

Gershwin, catapulted into action, completed 'Rhapsody in Blue' (his
first title was 'American Rhapsody,' one later used by Zimbalist) in barely
three weeks. Ferde Grofé orchestrated it, stopping by Gershwin's 110th
Street apartment daily to pick up page after page. The distinguished
panel's verdict was that this was not only fine American music, but fine
music period. Of course, 'Rhapsody in Blue' became a popular Whiteman
standard. In 1929 Zimbalist admirer Joe Venuti joined Whiteman's
orchestra. Joe became legendary not only as a great jazz violinist but also
as a devilish practical joker. For a particularly important performance
Whiteman's men had been outfitted with royal blue velvet tuxedos. The
theme was further developed by a blue bandstand and deep turquoise
stage lighting. It was Venuti's first 'Rhapsody' with the band. Up to his old
tricks, he dumped flour in the tuba. With the first oompah, half the stage
was coated in white.

Before the '20s the finest music school in the United States was New York's
Institute of Musical Art established by Frank Damrosch in 1905 (which
merged with the Juilliard Foundation in 1936 to become the Juilliard
School of Music). But from the mid '20s it was dominated by another
institution which bore the name of newspaper magnate Cyrus Curtis. It
was in 1923 that rumblings throughout the music world were first felt
relating to a school for advanced musical studies that would accept only
the crème de la crème and would engage the world's greatest musical
celebrities to teach them and guide their careers. This was all the brainchild of Mary Louise Curtis Bok, Cyrus Curtis's daughter and wife of
Edward Bok, editor of *Ladies' Home Journal* and the Pulitzer Prize–
winning author of *The Americanization of Edward Bok*. Mrs. Bok had
founded the Settlement School in a poor section of Philadelphia in 1917
and felt that there was enough talent around to warrant more concen-
trated cultivation. She was a great supporter of the Philadelphia Orchestra

and a friend of Leopold Stokowski's. She confided her idea in him, and in another friend, Josef Hofmann. With their encouragement suitable facilities were sought. Edward Bok purchased the Sibley Mansion on Rittenhouse Square, and some surrounding property.

In September 1924 the Curtis Institute of Music opened its doors, offering the finest musical education in the world, free of charge, to those talented enough to gain admission. Its first director was Johann Grolle (a former Philadelphia Orchestra member who had become head of the Settlement Music School), replaced after a year by William Walter (previously Detroit Symphony manager) then in 1927 by Josef Hofmann, who requested and received an annual salary of $72,500. Hofmann had been head of the piano faculty since the Institute's beginning. The other faculty, as promised, included some of the top names in music, among them Stokowski, Marcella Sembrich and Moritz Rosenthal, at salaries of between $24,000 and $40,000.

Carl Flesch, who had established a formidable reputation as a teacher in Berlin, was appointed head of the violin department; he did not, albeit, make an auspicious entrance on the Philadelphia scene. At an introductory performance with Stokowski and the Philadelphia Orchestra in December 1923, he suffered a memory lapse in the Beethoven Concerto and had to consult the conductor's score before being able to continue. He developed a reputation as a didactic tyrant whose professorial manner extended beyond the violin. His U.S. manager found him to be a purist who hated everybody. But he was fond of himself: when his wife gave birth to twins he reckoned he had received a double fee for a fine performance. Considering his reputation and his declared intention to upgrade 'kultur' in what he considered an uncultured land, his Curtis years (1924–28) produced few important results.

Flesch's haughty assessment of what he found violinistically in the United States in 1923 is of historic interest. From his memoirs:

> Before the war, eastern Jewry had only been represented by Elman and Zimbalist [but after the war,] a number of outstanding virtuosos had taken out American naturalization papers. [The] considerable proportion [that came] from Poland and Russia [were] the staple elements of [symphony] string sections [which] were led by some of the most distinguished of

those fiddlers, such as [Richard] Burgin, [Mishel] Piastro, and
[Mischa] Mischakoff. We owe it [to] these three excellent violinists that an orchestral career is no longer felt to be humiliating
[to] a fiddler who started out as a soloist. Far more numerous
than this *elite*, however, was the class of mediocrities whose
natural, in fact racial, talent could not be denied, but whose
general cultural make-up was distinctly modest. They fiddled
well...but of an ultimate artistic purpose they knew nothing
[and] showed no interest in anything that was not...connected
with the four strings.

Flesch was appalled by this state of affairs, especially since in Berlin he and
his colleagues Artur Schnabel, Ferruccio Busoni and Wilhelm Furtwängler
had come to regard themselves as artistic leaders of the broad mass, rather
than mere musicians.

For all Flesch's pompousness, Leopold Auer's presence in the United
States was acknowledged to be far more exciting. But Zimbalist and Alma
Gluck worried about Auer's decline. Forced to lighten his student load, he
tried to make up the depletion of income by raising his fee. In failing
health and with no prospects of retirement benefits, he faced a future of
unremitting labor in order to provide for himself and Mme. Auer as living
costs rose. The Zimbalists, knowing the proud old gentleman's distaste for
charity, came up with an idea to net a lump sum: why not present an eight-
ieth birthday benefit concert, similar to the Moszkowski fundraiser? Alma
persuaded Mrs. Charles Guggenheim to head a committee that included
Heifetz, Rachmaninoff, Hofmann, Gabrilowitsch, Zimbalist, and Paul
Stasseivich. When apprized of their plans Auer suggested programming
the Vivaldi three-violin concerto, to be played by his most famous students, Heifetz, Zimbalist and Elman. Elman declined, giving as an excuse
his own Carnegie Hall recital scheduled two days before the Auer benefit.
When Zimbalist was dispatched to change his mind, Elman shocked him
by responding, 'Why should I? *I* made Auer, he didn't make *me*!' This was
their last conversation. (Some years later Elman played the Mendelssohn
Concerto with the Philadelphia Orchestra; Zimbalist attended but didn't
go backstage.)

Zimbalist reported back to his teacher, being careful to spare his feelings.
'Well,' Auer shrugged, 'then I'll have to play with you and Jascha.' Zimbalist

took the bait, persuading him (without any difficulty) to play some solo selections as well. However, the Professor had one condition: 'You must put me at the beginning of the program — by the end I'll be asleep.'

Tickets sold out weeks in advance, and standing room was at a premium. At Carnegie Hall on 28 April 1925 the program opened with the Vivaldi Concerto accompanied on the piano by Stasseivich (also an Auer pupil), which brought the house to its feet. Next came the Brahms d minor sonata with Zimbalist and Gabrilowitsch. 'He played the piano part more beautifully than I had ever heard it,' Zimbalist said later. 'He was not only one of the greatest pianists, but also a musician from A to Z.' Then came Auer's favorite solos, Tchaikovsky's 'Melodie' and Brahms's first Hungarian Dance, with an affectionate Rachmaninoff at the keyboard.

After intermission followed a group of pieces played by Heifetz, including two by Auer and one written especially for the occasion by Zimbalist's old St. Petersburg classmate Joseph Achron, entitled 'Pensée de Leopold Auer.' Zimbalist had agreed to accompany him but was tempted to retract his offer when he saw how difficult Achron's piano accompaniment was. Despite diligent practicing he felt apprehensive stepping on stage with Heifetz. As he nervously adjusted the piano stool a lanky shadow ambled over and sat down in a chair to his left. The anxious accompanist turned and with surprise looked into the inscrutable dark pools of Rachmaninoff's eyes. 'What are you doing here?' asked Zimbalist. 'Perevorachevau stranece' (I'm going to turn your pages), replied the prankster. 'What a dirty trick!' Zimbalist muttered, yet he had to laugh. 'I was never more nervous in my life. But Rachmaninoff was a great page-turner.'

Hofmann played some Chopin, Tchaikovsky and Lizst. To close the program Heifetz and Zimbalist teamed up in the Bach 'Double,' with Stasseivich at the piano. 'What a wonderful spirit there was throughout that concert,' Zimbalist reminisced.

Auer evidently stayed awake long enough to make an appearance at the post-concert dinner organized by Alma Gluck. Master of ceremonies Zimbalist, whose strong point was not making speeches, wrote some introductory remarks on a small card to introduce his old teacher. Alma tapped her spoon against a goblet to silence the diners as he rose to address them. Stage fright struck. He cleared his throat, ignored his notes and, gesturing appropriately, announced: 'Ladies and gentlemen, Professor Leopold Auer!' After dinner the gala participants adjourned to the exhausted but happy Professor's apartment for a nightcap. Auer used the $40,000 raised that night to buy a house on the Upper West Side.

Before long Auer had to undergo a gallbladder operation. Suffering, he told Zimbalist that he simply wished to die. But there was still enough paprika in his veins to pull him through and, having recovered and established himself in his new house, he invited Zimbalist over for dinner. The end of an evening meal always signaled, for Zimbalist, a fine Havana cigar. He reached for one in his vest pocket and, settling back in his chair, he lit up and was contentedly puffing away when he noticed the pained expression on Auer's face. All at once he remembered and felt like kicking himself—since the operation Auer was struggling to abide by his physician's censures: no tobacco or alcohol. He looked longingly at Zimbalist's cigar and sniffed the air appreciatively. 'Professor,' Zimbalist said with tenderness, 'we have spent such a nice evening together. Do you think one cigar to celebrate the occasion would really hurt you?' In seconds, Auer was puffing away, his face glowing like that of a child given carte blanche in a candy store. A port decanter rested on the sideboard only inches away. Auer eyed it. His former student fetched two glasses. 'A little port, Professor?' he asked mildly. 'I never saw him happier,' Zimbalist recounted later, 'and he survived another five years happily enjoying port and cigars daily.'

Zimbalist around this time told Auer that Efrem Jr. had expressed an interest in playing the violin. The Professor was excited. 'You must let me have the honor of giving him his first lesson,' he said. So little Efrem was brought before the intimidating old man to be shown the basics of posture and bow-hold. Auer, satisfied that the youngster had been started on the right foot, then allowed Zimbalist to engage another reputable teacher, Ruvin Heifetz, to take over. Time came for the lesson, much to the puzzlement of Efrem Jr.: 'But Daddy,' he protested, 'Professor Auer already showed me how to play!' (Ruvin Heifetz accompanied the Zimbalists to Fishers Island so that Efrem Jr.'s violin lessons could continue uninterrupted during the summer.) Efrem Jr.'s violin playing came along; eventually he and his father performed the Bach 'Double' for the unruffled lad's classmates. 'I was more nervous than he was,' Efrem Sr. readily admitted.

In fall 1926 Efrem Jr. was sent to board at Fay School in Southboro, Massachusetts. 'It was a very difficult decision, but it seemed the only thing to do,' Zimbalist said, 'even if my poor wife was constantly torn between going to the school in Massachusetts or going to the concert hall.' Years later Efrem Jr.'s daughter Nancy unearthed letters that her grandmother had saved, in which her father, aged ten, had made the most heartrending pleas to be allowed home for the weekend. During one such visit Efrem Jr. went to Carnegie Hall with his parents and Heifetz to hear Rachmaninoff. As he leafed through the program, he came across a testimonial Heifetz had given Steinway and tugged on his father's arm to show him. Little Efrem began to read the endorsement ('I have used the Steinway piano exclusively and with genuine pleasure at all my concerts. It is in my opinion a piece of superb craftsmanship that demonstrates the finest musical possibilities' — and so forth) but screwed his nose up halfway through. He sighed and, to Heifetz's discomfort, blurted out, 'But Uncle Jascha doesn't know big words like these!'

Alma had been dreaming of her ideal house for some time. That same year, 1926, she bought a plot in Manhattan's Turtle Bay section almost the size of a full city block. The brownstones standing on it were partially torn down, to be replaced by a pair of grand adjoining five-story townhouses with Tudor-style brick facades and an enormous enclosed garden adorned with Italian fountains. The *New York Times* did a feature on the town-houses in the 1950s, describing a total of thirty-three rooms, many with mirrored walls; there were a dozen bathrooms, and a huge musicale room the length of both houses overlooked the garden. This room was the main reason for the purchase of so large a plot — it was more spacious than many small recital halls. Two beautiful Steinways created an ambience enhanced by antique furnishings and rosewood paneling. There was a Grosvenor Atterbury plaque above the entrance, at 227 East 49th Street. It pictured a singing angel and a violin entwined around the five opening notes of 'O, Rest in the Lord' from Mendelssohn's *Elijah*, Alma's favorite oratorio. The townhouse beside it, 234 East 49th, originally intended for Marcia and her family, was instead rented to *Time* magazine's Henry Luce and his first wife, Lila. Alma waited to sell their property on East 72nd until she could demand her price from a group of businessmen who intended to construct an apartment building on the land.

Concurrent with the East 49th Street purchase was the acquisition of another property that became especially dear to the family. Alma had fallen in love with the delights of rural Connecticut during a visit to Earl and Anna Barneses' countryside getaway in Litchfield. When an adjoining house was put up for sale she lost no time in buying it. The actual structure had already grown from a glorified barn into a fairly comfortable manor and, under her supervision, further evolved into the elegant yet cozy entity known as The Rafters. The property continues to provide solace and restorative seclusion to an ever-expanding clan of Zimbalists. Neither the cacophonous chorus of crickets and 'peepers' (tiny tree frogs) emanating from the verdant summer foliage nor the buzzing hordes of no-see-ums can disturb its timeless serenity.

Alma supervised alterations on East 49th Street from The Rafters, which became a two-week stopping-off point early each summer on their way to Fishers Island. At summer's end they again spent a fortnight there, while their New York house was readied for winter occupancy. What picturesque migrations these must have been, complete with full staff and their trappings, Ladd in the Rolls Landaulet heading the pageantry. But, according to Marcia Davenport in *Too Strong for Fantasy*, there came a time when Alma thought the Rolls too exhibitionistic for the simple life at Fishers Island, which created a transportation problem. She solved it by going to New London and buying a horse for the economical sum, she said smugly, of $36. What she didn't mention was the $350 she spent next on a dapper yellow gig and made-to-order harness, studded with what looked suspiciously like silver.

Many of the years spent at 227 East 49th Street were Prohibition years. Although Alma never drank anything but mineral water or hot milk with a touch of coffee, she thought Prohibition barbarous. Efrem liked nice wines and amassed them for the entertaining they did. He insisted there be a good wine-safe at the new house, and, while he was about it, had a safe built for his wife's jewels, in her dressing room. Alma was furious that she was expected to memorize a combination to open it. She impatiently tapped her foot while the York Safe people told her the number, then promptly wrote it out and pasted it on the door. When it came to the wine cellar, when Efrem was out of town she would have her daughter come over and open it. Marcia was also in charge of mixing 'gin' for her mother's parties, a homemade concoction of grain alcohol (from a bootlegger), distilled water, glycerine and juniper extract.

Several brilliant virtuoso pieces were added to Zimbalists' repertoire during this period, notably the 'Coq d'Or Fantasy,' written on themes from Rimsky-Korsakov's opera. Operatic fantasias were every virtuoso's grist in those days—Sarasate's 'Carmen Fantasy,' Ernst's on *Othello* themes, Wieniawski's on *Faust*, etc. In addition Zimbalist was always coming up with brilliant tidbits that he used as encores, such as his ingenious arrangements from *The Nutcracker* and the elegant solo from Glazunov's ballet *Raimonda* (Glazunov had given him the original manuscript from which to work), or Albert Spalding's arrangement of the Chopin E-flat waltz, which showed off Zimbalist's doorbell trill. He also played a lot of Kreisler, and was one of the very first to be let into his little secret concerning those 'early masterpiece' transcriptions, long before Olin Downes forced Kreisler's scandalized confession.

Then there were the moto perpetuos—Paganini's trend-setting classic, Suk's 'Burleska,' and Tor Aulin's sizzling 'Impromptu.' Zimbalist's recording of the Aulin has become a prized collector's item. He claimed not to have always possessed so spectacular a moto perpetuo technique but decided to develop it after a party held at the home of RCA chief executive David Sarnoff, to which he, Heifetz and other prominent violinists had been invited. One fiddler suggested an endurance marathon: they would all keep repeating Paganini's 'Moto Perpetuo' to determine which of them could outlast the rest. The contestants lined up at the starting gate and took off at a good clip, Chotzinoff keeping the tempo equitable from his post at the keyboard. Not surprisingly Heifetz cantered to the winners' circle with ease, testimony to his faultless mechanism and the relaxation with which he employed it. 'I was one of the first to drop out,' Zimbalist admitted, 'so I started practicing spiccato. My arm must have corrected itself because later I could go on and on.'

And faster and faster, as demonstrated in his recording of Sarasate's 'Carmen Fantasy.' His final tempo is actually speedier than Heifetz's. Zimbalist always referred to his spiccato as 'létaché,' light detaché. He used his forearm in the stroke, thereby increasing the lyrical content of each note. (The group playing of 'Moto Perpetuo' is reminiscent of Josef Gingold's affectionately organized birthday tribute to Ivan Galamian at the latter's summer school, Meadowmount, where Gingold would amass as many Galamian pupils as possible to play the last movement of the Mendelssohn Concerto, in unison, just as Mr. G came out of his studio for lunch.) To demonstrate his astounding control at the other end of the bowing spectrum Zimbalist played pieces like Schubert's 'Ave Maria,' or the Wagner-Wilhelmj 'Albumblatt,' in an exaggerated sostenuto—'I played so slowly that any sense of a melodic progression was lost,' he shook his head in the 1970s.

Not surprisingly, his admirers bragged that he could play both faster and slower than any other violinist. Michael Tree says that he could draw a bow that lasted from Monday to Wednesday; Oscar Shumsky jokingly called it 'the slowest draw in the West — he had the uncanny knack of latching onto the string at just the right angle and speed.' Vladimir Sokoloff, Zimbalist's accompanist during the last twenty-seven years of his career, once lost a bet because of it. Shortly after starting to work with Zimbalist they performed that most popular of encores, Saint-Saëns's 'Le Cygne.' Zimbalist liked to hold the final G of the solo part to the very end, in one bow, while the piano brings the piece to a close with a long series of cascading arpeggiated figures that eventually come to rest on the tonic. After Sokoloff's initial performance Zimbalist, in his gentle way, admonished him for playing the concluding arpeggios too quickly, explaining that he liked to hold the last note very long. His pianist confessed to a fear of stretching his bow beyond its limit. 'Billy,' Zimbalist smiled, 'I'll bet you $5 you can't play the ending slowly enough to make me run out of bow.' The next evening violinist and pianist exchanged glances before 'Le Cygne.' When Zimbalist embarked on his last note Sokoloff jammed on the brakes, seeming to grind almost to a tortuous halt on each note he played. Very pleased with himself, after what seemed an eternity he finally reached the cadence. Looking up, to his astonishment he saw Zimbalist, a scarcely concealed smirk on his face, comfortably sustaining at mid-bow. Sokoloff was $5 poorer.

Family pressures notwithstanding, Zimbalist was also practicing more than he had ever done in the past. His warm-up routine had been published in 1918 (*One Hour's Daily Exercises*), and he stuck to it faithfully. He explained the logic behind it in the foreword (probably realized for him by Marcia Davenport):

> It is my belief that an hour, or at most an hour-and-a-half, of practice on daily exercises carefully selected to meet the difficulties of violin-playing, is sufficient preparation for the actual study of one's repertoire. Since the mechanical side of all playing is but the starting-point for the performer, it is evident that this should consume a minor portion of the time devoted to the instrument. Therefore, of four hours a day spent in practice —

and more than that could hardly be beneficial—from one to one-and-a-half hours would seem to be about the correct proportion for the purely technical preparation. We now have only to invent and arrange such exercises as will, in that space of time, drill the hands in all the essentials of technique.

In arranging and selecting the materials for this book I have proceeded on the assumption that most of the problems to be met in violin-literature are combinations or variations of the usual equipment of the well-schooled violinist, consisting of scales, thirds, tenths, octaves, flageolets, and the like; and that a daily drilling in these would be an adequate preparation for any technical problem likely to arise. Of course, there are any amount of etudes, excellent in their way, and dealing with just these problems; but they are generally discursive and consume altogether too much time. They may have a legitimate place in acquiring a technique during childhood, when any amount of amplification of a principle is necessary to make a lasting impression. When the problem, however, is how to retain the technique already acquired, the Etude is not sufficiently compact to be of service.

To vary the inevitable monotony of all mechanical work I would suggest that the following exercises be played in the different keys, both major and minor.

Eight years later Carl Flesch's *Das Skalensystem*, considered by many violinists to be the 'scale bible,' was published. Ivan Galamian's own system didn't come out till the 1960s. Both espoused ideas similar to Zimbalist's.

During the 1927–28 Carnegie Hall season Zimbalist premièred Joseph Achron's eight-movement 'Suite Bizarre.' Just three years before, Achron had introduced himself and his compositions to the United States by playing his violin concerto in New York; he dedicated many pieces to Zimbalist before being lured to Hollywood, where he spent the last decade of his life writing film music. Maintaining his interest in new music, Zimbalist was among the earliest (with Paul Kochanski) to play Karol Szymanowski's atmospheric violin pieces. The attention he paid to his three 'Mythes' and the 'Notturna e Tarantella,' to pieces like the Powell, Stock, Schelling and Gusikoff concertos and to assorted smaller 'gems'

added the sparkle of diversification to his very substantial standard repertoire. It was this large and intriguing repertoire with which Zimbalist in
the 1920s and '30s enchanted audiences worldwide.

It was also during this period that Zimbalist played his greatest number
of concerts, averaging 110 annually ('It meant spending a great deal of time
getting from one place to another'). Everywhere he was accorded the accla-
mation befitting his artistic stature, but he always felt he received his
sincerest compliment after a concert played in one of the world's less scintillating corners. He prefaced the story by stating a conviction: 'Reception
rooms after concerts are the most insincere places on earth, where nothing
said means much—marvelous!—wonderful!—delightful! Even when
you know you were at your worst!' Once he played a concert in a dreary
Midwestern town. Afterward, while the customary line of socialites filed
through his dressing room, he noticed a tall man with round spectacles
and the air of someone who felt very out of place standing off to one side.
Not until the last in line had left did the man approach, awkwardly, to
pump the violinist's hand, nearly crushing it. 'Mr. Zimbalist, that was very
satisfactory,' he barked, then disappeared abruptly. His demeanor suggested that of a clerk in a drugstore who, having neatly stacked the shelves
with boxes of tissue, had received a similar commendation from his boss.
Zimbalist beamed.

This period was not devoid of interesting chamber music collabora-
tions. Zimbalist joined Paderewski, cellist Felix Salmond and New York
Philharmonic first horn Bruno Jaenicke at Carnegie Hall in the 'Archduke'
and Brahms's horn trio. There was also an auspicious partnership with
Harold Bauer, which should be prefaced: Darryl Zanuck had persuaded his
financially pressed bosses at Warner Bros. to avert bankruptcy by gambling
on a movie made with Vitaphone sound-on-disc equipment. It was *The
Jazz Singer*, starring Al Jolson, released in October 1927. When, in the movie,
Jolson exclaimed, 'Wait a minute, wait a minute, you ain't heard nothing
yet!' he wasn't just whistlin' Dixie, for, although it was not the first sound
movie, after this watershed film the cinema would never be silent again.

In June 1926 Zimbalist and Bauer had been approached to do one of
Vitaphone's pioneering shorts. Combining their talents for the first time,
they recorded in New York the variation movement from the 'Kreutzer'
Sonata. Along with eight other shorts it was presented at the Warner

Theater, New York, on 6 August, with an introduction by the president of the Motion Picture Producers and Distributors of America, Will Hays.

By the mid-1920s Zimbalist's collection of violins had grown to include a fine J. B. Guadagnini and the magnificent 'Lamoureux' Strad, acquired through J. C. Freeman of the Rudolph Wurlitzer Company in New York. This reputable firm then sold pianos and organs as well as violins; twenty years later Rembert Wurlitzer established a separate branch specializing in string instruments. With the exception of W. E. Hill and Sons in London, it was the most recognized violin shop in the world.

On tour Zimbalist frequently used another instrument of which he was very fond — a 1743 Lorenzo Guadagnini, also bought through Freeman, that reminded him of his original 1745 Lorenzo from Hammig. During a Los Angeles recital in 1927 on the 'Lamoureux,' Zimbalist left the Guadagnini resting backstage in its half of his double case. Someone entered the artists' room while he was playing on stage and made off with it, disappearing without a trace. His shock was compounded by the fact that the instrument was uninsured, as was everything he and Alma owned. (Zimbalist was categorically opposed to any kind of insurance, and Alma too had the bizarre obsession of refusing either to lock anything up or to insure it.)

Strangely, the famous 'Lamoureux' too was eventually stolen. In the late '50s Zimbalist had traded it in on a Guarneri del Gesu at the Philadelphia shop of William Moennig (the del Gesu had as much dignity and aristocracy but more brilliance); the 'Lamoureux' was stolen from the person who subsequently bought it and hasn't turned up since. And Zimbalist's strikingly beautiful J. B. Guadagnini also encountered misfortune. Its sale in the early '60s (for $80,000) abruptly raised the price index affecting all future sales of J. B.'s works. The purchaser of this mint-condition instrument slipped on an icy sidewalk while carrying it; serious cracks resulted, lowering its value and permanently scarring its formerly pristine face.

Zimbalist also had several fine bows. He once said, 'A violin is only as good as its bow. . . . To a great violinist the bow is nearly as important as the violin itself. Without a good bow a violinist is helpless in a tonal way and greatly handicapped in a technical way, no matter how good his violin is.' His two favorites were a gold-mounted Charles Peccatte (1850–1920) and a pristine Joseph ('Jacques') Henry (1823–1870); these he bequeathed to the author.

Zimbalist had had to miss, on 27 October 1917, Heifetz's U.S. debut, and a decade later, away on a world tour, he missed another red-letter day in the history of violin playing—the New York Symphony debut on 25 November 1927 of eleven-year-old Yehudi Menuhin playing the Beethoven Concerto (it was his performance of this piece two years later in Berlin that elicited Einstein's comment: 'Now I know there is a God in Heaven'). Menuhin's career soared. 'Heifetz told me that he felt thoroughly humiliated by Menuhin's success,' said Zimbalist.

A few years earlier Zimbalist had heard Yehudi in San Francisco. The September 1924 issue of *Musical America* quoted Louis Persinger, concertmaster and assistant conductor of the San Francisco Symphony, and Menuhin's teacher: 'Zimbalist came to my studio and heard him play a couple of concertos. He was amazed by the boy's brilliancy and said that he had everything necessary to become one of the great ones, the nearest approach to anything of the sort being Heifetz when he heard him at [eight] years of age.'

Persinger, partly on the strength of his success with Yehudi, was appointed to the faculty of the Institute of Musical Art, and in 1928 Persinger and the Menuhins moved to New York. Banker Henry Goldman offered to buy the twelve-year-old Yehudi the violin of his choice, and he and the Menuhins turned to Zimbalist for advice. Moshe Menuhin, Yehudi's father, fully describes events in *The Menuhin Saga*: '[For] ten days Yehudi examined a dozen of the finest [Strads] in America [and] we asked Efrem Zimbalist to help Yehudi make the final choice. We had reduced the field to four. Yehudi, playing them each in turn, deliberately set aside one, the "Prinz Khevenhüller" [dated 1733]. He asked Zimbalist to try them. Finally Yehudi played Handel's "Prayer" on the "Khevenhüller," then on the others, and then on the "Prinz" again. "This is it!" he cried joyfully. "I love it!" Zimbalist could not contain himself. He wiped the tears from his eyes and said: "Yehudi's right! It's the most marvelous Strad in the world. But then Yehudi is the most marvelous violinist of the age: they deserve each other!"'

In 1982 Menuhin recalled the occasion: 'Zimbalist showed me his prize, the "Swan" [Stradivarius's last instrument], made only two years after the "Prinz." He was tremendously gracious. I well remember too my teacher Louis Persinger taking me to the Civic Auditorium in San Francisco when I was six or seven to hear this great violinist.'

Persinger admired Zimbalist wholeheartedly and always spoke of him to his students with awe. Their friendship dated from Zimbalist's first appearance with the San Francisco Symphony in 1911. Shortly after the 'Prinz Khevenhüller' episode Persinger brought his other budding star, Ruggiero Ricci, for a hearing. 'Another wonderful young boy,' Zimbalist remembered.

At one point Zimbalist caught the 'golf virus,' which game he considered a pleasant way of exercising. In her *New Yorker* profile of him, Marcia Davenport described how he half-sheepishly (because he had to avoid anything that might hurt or harden his hands) slipped off to the clubhouse one day and started in with nothing but 'a brassie and a putter—he used no other club, [calling] all irons "dose t'ings."' It wasn't long before he came home with a brown canvas bag complete with every known club, and an umbrella. In succeeding summers he could be seen moving solemnly up the ninth fairway with his characteristic springy step, adding up a neat, truthful score. Although competition took the pleasure out of golf for Zimbalist, he did once invite Heifetz to play with him at Fishers Island. They left for the golf course at the crack of dawn, causing consternation when they returned very late for supper. They had completed only nine holes.

Zimbalist had two serious and long-lasting habits: gambling and collecting. The gambling bug probably bit him in 1915, during the fifty-concert Damrosch tour. In *My Many Years* Artur Rubinstein described an early episode: 'One night at the Biltmore, Zimbalist proposed to take me to a private room for a little gambling. There I found Kreisler, Franz Kneisel, Andre de Segurola, a Catalan singer with a large monocle in his eye, a few other less known musicians, and the editor of the *Musical Courier*, Leonard Liebling. I felt safe in such company and we sat down to a little game of chemin de fer. [That] night I was lucky. I won the nice sum of $600 or $700 mainly from de Segurola, who reminded me of it for the rest of my life.' Zimbalist fared decently but Kneisel was a loser that evening. Mischa Elman heard about it and happened to bump into Mrs. Kneisel a few days later. 'So sorry about all that money Franz lost,' he sympathized. Frau Kneisel gave her husband blazes—Elman had blown the whistle on Kneisel's secret flurries at the gambling table.

Both Rubinstein and Zimbalist were inveterate cigar smokers. Zimbalist tells how it all came about: 'In the '20s I played in Havana. I wanted to meet the most celebrated cigar maker, Fonseca. So I spoke to my manager and he introduced me to a rather small but elegant man with flowing tie

and velvet beret. One had to commission his custom-made cigars—
I asked him to make me twenty-five hundred. For a number of months I
heard nothing from him. Then I received a letter: "Dear Mr. Zimbalist, I am
very sorry to say that I have not yet found suitable leaves." He was a per-
fectionist and used to travel all over Cuba inspecting the tobacco crops.
Some time later the cigars arrived. Each was a work of art. On their bands
was printed "Made by Fonseca, Havana, for Efrem Zimbalist." He made
cigars for J. P. Morgan too, but considerably larger than the ones I ordered.
Once Morgan was traveling through Switzerland. He was sitting in his
coupé smoking a Double Corona when the train entered St. Bernard's
tunnel. A woman came in. "How much is your reputation worth to you?"
she asked. "What do you mean?" "Unless you hand over all your money I'll
make a scandal." "Go ahead," said Morgan. The woman began tearing her
clothes and screaming. Gendarmes came running. "This man attacked
me," she told them. Morgan sat quietly. At the end of his cigar there was a
very long ash. He pointed to it and asked, "How could I have?"'

The collecting bug predated Zimbalist's gambling, beginning in
London with autographs. He later switched to violins, then to Orientalia,
and in Australia in 1927 he started to collect first editions. No wonder he
was so understanding of a predicament his stepdaughter got into when
first away at college. Marcia, it seems, had gone to a bookshop in Boston
and paid $75 for a complete Burton translation of *The Arabian Nights*, in
seventeen volumes. She was thrilled with her purchase, but it had blown a
large hole in her budget and she was terrified of telling her mother. Instead
she made a tearful clean breast of the mess to her Papouchka. (Zimbalist
had taught her to call him this.) 'The angel gave me $200 and swore me to
secrecy, for we would equally have caught hell had my mother ever found
out,' Marcia later told me.

Zimbalist's wistful gyrations in the stock market were considered by his
family more funny than tragic, until the crash of 1929. 'I lost everything—
and I had made quite a lot!' he recalled. 'But I didn't lose as much as
Kreisler did.' On the whole he and Alma fared better than most people, and
the catastrophe served to bring out Zimbalist's philosophic side. As he said
to her, 'Well, I can always make money playing the violin.'

Alma spearheaded a group to help her husband's old mentor Alexander
Glazunov, who had just left his position as director of the (then)
Leningrad Conservatory to accept Sol Hurok's offer of several conducting

engagements in the United States. All except one concert—secured not by Hurok but by Glazunov's ex-student Ossip Gabrilowitsch, then the conductor of the Detroit Symphony—failed to materialize because of the crash. The concert Gabrilowitsch organized for Glazunov was full of emotion. It was Glazunov's birthday, and Ossip knew that the composer had once written a birthday fanfare for Rimsky-Korsakov; he managed to find the piece and, as Glazunov stepped up to the podium, he conducted the fanfare from a box. Glazunov was moved to tears and couldn't start the concert for several minutes. In a strange, newly troubled land he was eventually reduced to near destitution, but with some connections and financial help, he was able finally to settle in Paris.

The '20s had been years of high stimulus for Zimbalist's creative output, always bound by the following strict parameter: 'to achieve simplicity of melodic line within the complexity of a larger form.' His first major work, a violin sonata in g minor (revised in 1968), was premièred at Carnegie Hall on 5 March 1927. Before its 1927 publication Zimbalist showed it to Rachmaninoff: 'He liked the first movement, but I think that's all.' Perhaps it was Rachmaninoff's supposed disapproval that made Zimbalist declare the finale 'of less quality than the rest.' Nonetheless its second theme is among the loveliest he ever wrote. In the slow movement he used the folk theme widely popularized by Tchaikovsky in his Fourth Symphony, adding two eighth notes at the end of each line to make a 4/4 pattern. 'I saw it as a theme of infinite sadness.' He developed it this way, thereby achieving some of the sonata's most poignant moments. 'I destroyed more pieces than I saved,' Zimbalist remembered about this creative period. 'When I was writing something I couldn't put it down, like a drunken sailor with his rum. It wasn't fair to my family.'

Zimbalist's own creativity was stimulated by the great creative minds that surrounded him. Tangible evidence of Edna St. Vincent Millay's influence was the group of songs he wrote to three of her poems: 'Rain comes down,' 'Mariposa' and 'One, two, three.' Edna and her husband Eugene Boissevain were dear friends, and when the Zimbalists came to their home in Austerlitz, New York, Alma would sing for them while Efrem accompanied her on the piano. After one of these impromptu recitals Millay wrote them a thank-you note: 'The very rafters of this room are honored by the guests it had.' 'Edna was such a lovely, soft spoken person,' Zimbalist recalled fondly. 'Every evening ended with Eugene opening a bottle of

champagne. Once I sat improvising at the piano. Edna said, "What a marvelous gift to be able to improvise something right out of the sky." So I
said, "Why don't you try it?" She put her head down for a couple of
minutes then came up with the following:

> Said little Jesus to little Buddha,
> 'The world is getting ruder and ruder.'
> Said little Buddha to little Jesus,
> 'They're just doing this to tease us.'

'She said that she often connected words with music in her mind, and
sang some of her songs for me. I took a piece of paper and wrote down the
melodies. I asked her if she would mind my developing them. She seemed
very happy about the idea. The results were the three songs, which she
loved.' They were published in 1940.

Zimbalist was always visibly moved when telling an ironic story about
Millay. It seems she was walking in London and spotted an idol of hers,
Thomas Hardy (1840–1928), strolling on the opposite side of the street.
While she recognized him at sight, Millay was certain he had never heard
of her, so she went on her way, recalling to mind favorite fragments from
his works as she walked. On his deathbed a year or two later, Hardy was
asked if he had any regrets. 'Only one,' he answered. 'I never had the
pleasure of meeting Edna St. Vincent Millay.'

This anecdote always reminded Zimbalist of another yarn, the reverse
face of the coin, concerning the misapprehensions of Lynn Fontanne. Miss
Fontanne, a friend of Alma Gluck's, heard a Rachmaninoff recording and
became an instant fan. One day she mentioned to Alma her infatuation
with 'that fascinating man.' She told of having once followed him for three
blocks in a vain effort to summon up enough courage to approach and
engage him in conversation. 'Oh, you needn't have fretted,' Alma laughed.
'He is very close to Efrem and is coming to dinner on Wednesday evening.
Why don't you come too and meet him?' Lynn was thrilled and promised
that she and her husband would drop by after the curtain of a West End
play in which they were starring.

In addition to Rachmaninoff, the expected dinner guests included
Professor Auer, the Gabrilowitschs and Josef Hofmann and his new boss,
Mary Louise Curtis Bok (it was the first time Zimbalist met her). Ossip

Gabrilowitsch telephoned just before dinner to excuse his wife on grounds of illness, but he had just spent the afternoon with Vladimir de Pachmann and suggested bringing him along instead. Gabrilowitsch and de Pachmann arrived late. The butler showed them into the entrance hall, where they were welcomed by Zimbalist. As de Pachmann divested himself of coat and gloves, he demanded water. He held the glass he received up to the light and handed it back dramatically: 'This glass is dirty!' Faux pas no. 1.

Zimbalist calmly asked the butler for a replacement. After careful inspection, the eccentric guest downed the second glass in a single gulp and marched into the music room, where other guests were chatting over cocktails. After a pause for introductions, de Pachmann made straight for the Steinway. On the way he passed a small man with neatly trimmed white whiskers and sad coal-black eyes. The old gentleman held out his hand as the pianist approached and said in a pleasant voice, 'How do you do? I'm Leopold Auer.' De Pachmann stopped short. 'Professor Auer? Really?' He seemed incredulous. 'I thought you died years ago!' Faux pas no. 2.

The irrepressible 'Chopinzee' then sat himself down at the keyboard and, unbidden, began to play. Why should the presence only a few yards away of giants like Hofmann and Rachmaninoff or Gabrilowitsch daunt de Pachmann, the self-proclaimed genius who, when asked to name the five greatest pianists in the world, answered, 'Second, Godowsky; third, Rosenthal; fourth, Paderewski; fifth, Busoni'? His face immediately showed disapproval. Turning to a man who sat quietly on his right he began to lecture loudly while playing, as he was wont to do. 'What a terrible instrument the Steinway is. I can't understand why people pay so much money for such rubbish. The *only* piano to play is the Baldwin.' The man he was addressing was Frederick Steinway, head of the New York firm (and, as might be guessed, de Pachmann was paid to endorse Baldwins). With no. 3 de Pachmann had come close to the biggest faux pas of this comical evening. But not quite. His efforts were topped when, at about 11:15, Lynn Fontanne and Sir Alfred Lunt arrived after the theater. Zimbalist chuckled gleefully whenever he told the tale: 'I took Lynn right over to Rachmaninoff, who was sitting in an easy chair. I said, "Lynn, it's my great pleasure to introduce you to Sergei Rachmaninoff." She looked at him with wide eyes and said, "But Efrem, this is not Rachmaninoff!"'

For three blocks, Lynn Fontanne had followed the wrong man.

CHAPTER 17

Discovering the Orient

(1922–1928)

By far the most significant concert tours of his career were the six
Zimbalist made to the Far East between 1922 and 1935. In fall 1921 he was
visited in New York by his old friend from the St. Petersburg opera pit,
Artur Strok. The man was by any account a colorful character. A Russian
Jew who spoke ten languages and was barely understood in any of them,
he had decided in 1914 to give up a secure but tedious job and become an
entrepreneur. From the headquarters he established in Shanghai he
planned to tap the vast, largely unexplored Oriental market for Western
culture. He started out with a bang, engaging the entire Isadora Duncan
troupe on spec for a tour of the Orient. Subsequent ventures were less successful but before long, given his gambler's instincts and with the growing
clamor in the East for exposure to Western arts, Strok became a powerful
impresario. He offered Zimbalist an extended tour of several Far Eastern
countries, adding, as a measure of inducement, that Mishel Piastro (one of
the 'later batch' of Auer students Efrem had heard in 1909) much enjoyed
the tour Strok had arranged for him. Since he had always been captivated
by tales of the Orient, Zimbalist accepted. (Kreisler did the same in 1923
and John McCormack in 1926.) Strok said he could provide an excellent
accompanist. This suited Zimbalist, since Chotzinoff's schedule playing
for Heifetz didn't allow for any long tours with his former boss. Strok
proposed Gregory Ashman, a young Russian war refugee, and was profuse
with assurances that Ashman was well versed in the violin repertoire. The
trip began after a national tour that terminated in San Francisco, where
Zimbalist embarked on an American liner.

On 31 March 1922 he wrote his friend Fred Steinway: 'This is just a short note of farewell before I leave for the Orient, where I go to make another debut. Under ordinary circumstances I should be a bit apprehensive, but as I hear I am to have the Steinway piano for my accompaniments, my uneasiness is removed.' It returned full force, however, when, on board ship, he met Gregory Ashman. They sat down to get acquainted. 'Tell me about yourself,' Zimbalist began amiably.

'I am a graduate of the Kiev Conservatory.'

'I understand you have plenty of experience working as an accompanist?'

'Oh yes. Once on a fellow student's recital I accompanied the first movement of the Mendelssohn Concerto.' So much for Strok's understanding of being well-versed in the violin repertoire. Ashman later reported to Josef Gingold that Zimbalist went rehearsal crazy. Saddled with a green accompanist, Zimbalist apparently had no choice and had an upright installed in his cabin so that they could set to work immediately. He and Ashman were inclined to be unsociable, speaking in Russian and taking most meals in the rehearsal cabin.

But on this voyage, the first of many long ones, Zimbalist, when he wasn't rehearsing, also seized the opportunity to read or reread (he did so every few years) classics like *War and Peace*, some Chekhov and Pushkin — in Russian — and *Gulliver's Travels*, in English. Zimbalist invariably refused to play for the passengers — 'I would say I was out of shape. The whole trip took about three months, and I missed my family so badly — it was the longest time I had ever been away from them.'

Their first concert was in Honolulu. When they arrived in Japan some two weeks later Strok was part of the large welcoming group at Yokohama harbor; he escorted them wherever they played and provided interpreters, in the main newspaper correspondents. 'I had to have a big repertoire. In Tokyo I played six concerts in a week, with one day off to rest. That meant six different programs,' recalled Zimbalist.

At that time there was no European hotel in Tokyo, so they stayed in a very adequate and spotless Japanese one. Also listed in the registry was Frank Lloyd Wright; he attended one of Zimbalist's recitals and offered to give him a guided tour of the hotel *he* was building. Wright was justifiably proud of the newly completed Imperial Hotel. It was not only the most striking building in Tokyo's skyline when it was finished in late 1922 but also achieved added cachet as the only one left standing intact after the

Great Kanto Earthquake of September 1923. Wright's earthquake-proof design had proved it was just that. (Needless to say, when Zimbalist visited Japan a year later he stayed at the Imperial.)

Following a Tokyo performance Zimbalist was introduced to Yorisada Tokugawa and his wife, and Prince Asaakira Kuni, brother-in-law of then Crown Prince Hirohito. Marquis Tokugawa was among the last descendants of the Shoguns; while carrying the mantle of this ancient heritage he and his wife had also cultivated a gracious European style of living. They spoke perfect English and French and were ardent devotees of Western music, literature and art. Zimbalist found them unpretentious and wholly lovable.

Concerts were held in the Imperial Theater. Its director, Kyusaburo Yamamoto, took Zimbalist to meet the man who had pioneered the artificial culturing of pearls, then considered the next wonder of the world. Zimbalist admired their beauty, and Yamamoto presented him with a choice sample.

After Tokyo there were concerts, two each, in Kyoto, Osaka, Kobe, Nagoya and Nagasaki—all sold out within days of their announcement. The twelve-week itinerary also included concerts throughout China and Java, one in Singapore and one in Hong Kong. 'China affected me very deeply,' Zimbalist recalled. 'In Japan [audiences] were mostly Japanese, whereas in China they were almost entirely European. The few Chinese I met were all of a very high caliber. But the country was still under Russian, German, English and French control. So I had the misfortune of seeing greater native intellects subjected to the indignities of minor British or European officials.' All the concerts were recitals, except for one: in Shanghai he played the Beethoven Concerto with an undistinguished orchestra of some twenty-five European musicians.

Exotic Shanghai captivated Zimbalist. Festive weddings were everywhere, and at night the streets were ablaze with neon, the signs shedding their colorful glow on the strolling citizens, many of whom carried pet canaries in cages. The cuisine was an experience too: 'In Tsientsin a rubber plantation baron gave a dinner for about fifty people in my honor. When we arrived at his house we entered a huge hall filled with drinks and hors d'oeuvres. I recognized none of them—one, I was told, was the famous "hundred-year-old egg" delicacy. [In] the dining room [they] must have served us twenty-five courses, from bird's nest soup to sharks' fins and snakes—I was afraid to ask what some of them were. We lightly sampled each. Between courses they served roasted sunflower seeds. Ashman and I carefully put the shells on the table, but we were doing the wrong thing. "Oh, no!" our host said, "they should be thrown on the floor for servants to pick up."

'The 100-plus-degree Fahrenheit temperature in Shanghai, combined with high humidity, was unbearable. The proprietor of the hotel where I was staying, a Belgian, suffered too from the heat. He used a special method of cooling off, which I agreed to try, and we sat together in the ice room where the meats were stored, cooling off almost to the point of pneumonia. I traveled like mad, playing almost every day.' Ad hoc supplementary performances often had to be arranged. What little free time there was he spent sightseeing with Ashman and Strok, who took excellent care of them. 'It was bread and butter to him,' Zimbalist noted.

At home in New York Alma, largely retired, showed the children on a map where their father's adventures were taking him. She also wrote daily—many letters awaited him at predetermined points on the tour. He corresponded less regularly, usually favoring telegrams.

'I was lucky to make so many warm acquaintances with the native people wherever I went,' Zimbalist commented. It was doubtless his gentle nature that so endeared him to them. But he also made a special effort: Zimbalist craved as wide and undiluted a taste of the ancient Orient as still remained possible. In Singapore, where he left Strok to continue on to Java (concerts there were under other aegis), they discussed a return trip in 1924. Zimbalist stipulated that he wanted to be booked in any village, no matter how insignificant, that expressed a desire to hear him play. 'But how will I make any money?' the impresario protested. 'I'll play for nothing.'

Zimbalist's initial impression of Java was of excruciating heat and endless rain—the monsoon season had just begun. Other impressions soon followed. 'Huge bats at dusk and constant mosquitos. In the restaurants and dining rooms they would spray all around—at night we slept under nets.'

Concert halls seated several hundred people, entirely European, ninety percent of them Dutch. 'I had always felt that Holland was the most music-loving country in Europe,' Zimbalist recounted. He and Ashman gave ten recitals to enthusiastic crowds. The pianos were mostly out-of-tune uprights, but in such a climate even the best Steinways would have been unreliable. So were Stradivari. 'My poor violin. It was like leaving it under a hot shower all day—it immediately opened up at the seams.' He was relieved to discover a fine local repairman named, by coincidence, Hill—a Javanese native unconnected to the major London firm of the same name.

Dissolving glue was not the only problem Zimbalist encountered: 'During a performance of the Bach Chaconne I broke two E strings, one after the other, then an A.' This experience made him perhaps the earliest convert to metal strings. Before Java 1922 he had used (as Heifetz did to the end of his career) a plain gut D and A. Like most violinists during the first decade of the century he had switched to an unwound steel E, and silver-wound Gs were becoming standard. But he went one step further and ended up using an aluminum-wound steel A string as well. On his next trip to the tropics he brought along an aluminum violin as well, for prac-ticing (Heifetz also had one).

Other expedient measures were taken for survival in Java. Zimbalist had a set of light silk tails made for him. 'They were not light enough—when I got back to my hotel room I would immediately take off all my clothes. I used to practice naked, stopping every once in a while for a cold shower. Even the cold water was lukewarm! And I sometimes broke a long-standing taboo by taking a little brandy before concerts.' What Zimbalist enjoyed most was contact with native musicians. When he attended the Sultan of Solo's wedding reception an orchestra of gamelans provided the music.

Four concerts were played in Soerabaja, on Java's eastern end. Zimbalist also played in Jogjakarta, on the Indian Ocean side, where he got his chance to see local life 'as it had probably been lived for thousands of years—practically no difference—same chickens,' he laughed. He was referring to the scrawny domestic fowl that planted themselves on roads approaching the villages. Their chauffeur was forced to run right over several that wouldn't budge on their way to an evening concert: 'Someone told me about a magnificent temple at nearby Bahrabatua and I decided to visit it before the performance. I got there and climbed countless stairs. It was just getting dark when I reached the top. All of a sudden I felt some-thing move under my foot—I had stepped on a python! I can tell you that I arrived at the concert breathless.'

The basic Javanese dish was what the Dutch called 'Rijsapfel.' A plate of rice was served. Then came 'a sea of waiters bearing platters of spices and vegetables with which they surrounded the rice. We had plenty of ice-cold Heineken to wash it down with, and afterwards fine Dutch cigars.' His joyful return home was celebrated at Fishers Island amid a mountain of presents he had brought the family.

Meanwhile in Leningrad a young Polish-born pianist by the name of Emanuel Bay was encountering difficulties. He badly wanted to follow the lead of his brother Victor who, earlier, had emigrated to the United States. But Emanuel was denied permission to leave the country until 1922, when he convinced the authorities that his health problems would respond only at a Berlin sanatorium. Zimbalist had been very impressed by him in St. Petersburg in 1909, and his Russian contacts had kept him informed of Bay's struggles. The pianist was already widely regarded as an outstanding accompanist, having graduated with a Grand Prize in 1913. Zimbalist was in Berlin to play with the Philharmonic the same week Bay arrived for his treatment.

Berlin's resident Russian character was Raskov, a former pianist from Petrograd who had shown a genius for business wartime speculation. In Germany, post-war inflation gave him added scope for profiteering. He loved nothing better than throwing extravagant parties for artists, especially Russian refugees. Emanuel Bay quickly made his acquaintance, and it was at Roskov's home that Zimbalist tracked him down to offer the new expatriate a job as his regular accompanist. The terms were generous: $500 weekly whether or not they played concerts. Bay accepted gladly, eager to help his father support the family.

At Raskov's party Bay introduced Zimbalist to Dimitri Tiomkin, another recent emigré. Tiomkin was interested in American folk music and was already composing piano pieces imbued with jazz and cakewalk influences. He played a few for Zimbalist, who assured him he could make large sums of money writing commercial music in the United States. To prove his point Zimbalist sat down at the keyboard and offered a rendition of the latest rage in America, 'Yes, We Have No Bananas.' Tiomkin wasn't interested and opted instead to stay in Berlin to audition for Busoni. But Zimbalist's words were prophetic — Tiomkin later became one of Hollywood's greatest Academy Award–winning score writers. If 'Yes, We Have No Bananas' made little impression on him, the rest of the crowd at Raskov's was charmed. It was immediately taken up and sung by Russian refugee musicians, with a slight modification: 'Yes, We Have No Money.'

Bay, too shy to ask Zimbalist for an advance, borrowed $200 from his brother to get to New York. Shortly after he arrived the young pianist and his new boss were concertizing all over the United States and making their first recordings together. Bay was gifted enough to have been a soloist in his own right, had his unassuming nature permitted; instead, through Zimbalist he gained a reputation as the country's top accompanist. He stayed with Zimbalist for six years, and they were to experience fascinating adventures circling the globe together.

Bay's introduction to Asia was on the 1924 Asian tour, of almost eight months, one of the longest Zimbalist ever undertook. The itinerary included concerts in Korea, the Philippines and Borneo. In Japan alone they spent three months and played more than sixty concerts, many of them, as Zimbalist had stipulated, for novice audiences in outlying villages. 'I opened thirty-five towns in Japan,' Zimbalist liked to say. 'Fascinated as I was with Japanese traditions, it was in these smaller towns that I could get glimpses of the ancient East.' The majority had no hotels — the traveling musicians were put up by European missionaries doubling as interpreters. Zimbalist recollected these concerts with much sentiment. 'At that time, outside of missionaries, small towns had no European or American influences, which were becoming so strong in the big cities. I played in tiny villages where they had never before heard Western music. It was wonderfully rewarding. And it never mattered how much I was paid—I always gave Bay more than I got. We played in traditional Japanese theaters where the audience sat on the floor and we had to take our shoes off before entering. These concerts were some of the most touching of experiences—women would bring their babies with them and, while we played would nurse them quite openly, something that one wouldn't see in Tokyo or Osaka. It was the sweetest thing. Only once did I hear as much as a whimper out of the infants, so well-trained were they right from birth. It's difficult to put into words the great effect the Japanese had on me. I loved the people and I loved playing there.'

The feeling was mutual. Not many Americans realize the importance of Zimbalist's pilgrimages to those Far Eastern areas. Such persistent efforts to expose Asia to his art contributed to the influx of Asian musicians onto the world's platforms. For many Japanese hearing Zimbalist play was an isolated, soul-altering influence. The magical beauty he revealed to them inspired efforts to emulate his example, usually vicariously through their children. Several of these offspring later came to study with Zimbalist in the United States, beginning in 1948 with Toshiya Eto. Conversations with them trace their musical start to parents or grandparents who had heard the violin played for the first time by Zimbalist. He was a modest man, but he was proud of this accomplishment, and the musical world is indebted to him for it.

By 1924 the name Zimbalist was a household word in the big Japanese cities. Six recitals in Tokyo on consecutive evenings (concerts began at 9:15, in accordance with local tradition) all sold out. 'The hardest work was after performances, when the entire audience would come backstage and want autographs. I couldn't insult a single one of them by refusing.' People also brought his recordings to have them signed. Gramophone stores played them constantly. He heard the sound of his playing through open windows, and rickshaw men brought their rigs to a stop to get an autograph. Emanuel Bay proved a perfect traveling companion and colleague. 'A marvelous pianist, easygoing and not very talkative,' in Zimbalist's words.

Zimbalist began his Tokyo stay at Frank Lloyd Wright's proven-safe hotel, but after a few days the Tokugawas insisted that he move into their home. 'They had this extraordinary Japanese estate in the center of the city, surrounded by sculptured gardens and carp ponds. The only thing that wasn't ideal was that, to accommodate me, they moved from their traditional Japanese house to a European-style one on the same grounds — they thought I would be more comfortable.' The house, called Temple de Soleil, was constructed largely out of glass. 'I stayed there whenever I was in Tokyo and became very friendly with their nephew, Prince Asaakira Kuni. One day his sister, a most beautiful young lady, arrived to visit the Marchioness. This girl was engaged to then Crown Prince Hirohito, who succeeded his father, the Mikado Hoshihito, in 1926. In this way I was invited to the palace to hear the Emperor's private orchestra, which was a privilege not accorded the general public, and never before a Western visitor. It had started out, some seven hundred years before, as an orchestra of fifteen or sixteen players imported from China by the Imperial court. Their skills had been passed down from generation to generation so that the players and music were nominally unchanged throughout all those years. The sound was unforgettable — always subdued, washes of musical color that occasionally hinted at what one might hear from Debussy or Ravel. The musicians sat in an alcove at one end of the room. Some played ancient flute- and oboe-like instruments. On either side of the group stood a man holding what looked like a glorified orange into which he would blow when some harmony was desired, each on a different chord—perhaps akin to our tonic and dominant. They made free use of microtones and there was no tonality as I knew it. This all took place in the throne room, with half a dozen extravagantly costumed male dancers swaying to the music.'

Electrical sound recording had been a matter of conjecture for some time. The first workable microphone was used on Armistice Day 1920 to record by remote pickup the Unknown Warrior burial ceremony in Westminster Abbey, and by early 1924, using an exponential horn developed by the Bell Laboratories, Victor had produced a prototype of the first Orthophonic Victrola for the reproduction of electrically recorded discs. Meanwhile covert recording experiments were underway, conducted by both European and American companies. They kept these experiments secret from each other, for obvious reasons, as well as from the general public, in order to assure liquidation of remaining acoustic record stockpiles. Western Electric demanded high royalties for the new process and even after agreements were finally reached and Columbia and Victor signed contracts (Columbia a few weeks ahead of Victor), the companies decided to keep mum about developments for at least a year.

In Tokyo Zimbalist was approached 'with a new thing: recording through a microphone.' He and Bay stepped into the studio of Columbia's Japanese subsidiary to make some historic discs, Zimbalist's first electrical releases and some of his finest recorded achievements, giving a far better representation of his silken tone than any previous recordings; the pieces include 'Zephyr' (Hubay); 'Persian Song' (Glinka-Auer); 'Liebesfreud' and 'Liebesleid' (Kreisler); 'Zapateado' (Sarasate); 'Ave Maria' (Schubert-Wilhelmj); and 'Prize Song' from *Die Meistersinger* (Wagner-Wilhelmj). Some were rerecorded in the United States for Victor. Zimbalist added to his Columbia recordings on each succeeding Japanese visit; among these, not unsuitably, was César Cui's 'Orientale.'

From an early point in his Asian tours Zimbalist had liked to play, as encores, familiar indigenous tunes. In 1924 Prince Asaakira Kuni gave him a Japanese folk melody that was only eighteen notes long. The tune appealed to Zimbalist, and he developed it into one of his loveliest shorter compositions, 'Improvisation on a Japanese Theme,' which he published in the United States that same year and electrically recorded both there and in Japan in 1927. In 1931 he published the Japanese melody 'Kuruka, Kuruka,' taught him by Koscak Yamada.

Of particular note is his sublime recording of Beethoven's romance in G, with the Japanese Broadcasting Symphony under maestro Shiferblatt. One gathers from the record that the Japanese people's appreciation of Western music and their proficiency in performing it were not yet on a par. The serenity with which the soloist transcends blatty brass and painfully sour wind and string chords is indeed a tribute to his powers of concentration. Notwithstanding such encumbrances, Zimbalist's lyricism is at its peak, making the effort of searching out this scarce disc well worthwhile.

It was on his 1924 tour that Zimbalist began to collect Orientalia. 'I knew nothing about the subject till friends showed me their collections. It all started when I fell in love with a few pieces in Marquis Tokugawa's collection. He offered them to me as gifts, but I insisted on paying for them and brought an appraiser to determine their value. I found out afterwards that he was told not to quote me actual market prices. And so, my first priceless pieces were in effect given to me.'

Zimbalist developed a special passion for Japanese inros. An inro is a small box attached to a cord and divided into compartments for items of everyday use, such as seals and medicines. The Japanese had no pockets and wore inros instead. Delicate miniature landscapes and other scenes were applied to the boxes by masters of the lacquer craft, primarily during the eighteenth and nineteenth centuries. 'Of all the important masters and schools of different branches of art,' Zimbalist explained, 'the least known on the European and American continents were those that created the inro. Emphasis must be laid on the extreme accuracy with which the separate compartments were fitted together, making the divisions almost invisible.... Nowadays one finds intelligent collectors here and there, but then the general public was quite unaware of their existence and beauty, and of the imagination and extraordinary skill involved in their creation.'

In 1924 Zimbalist played his first concert in Korea, in Kyongsong (later Seoul), where he was amused by the spectacle of the city's aged taking their leisure on the sidewalks in half-reclining positions, decked out in vivid traditional costume with pointed high-hats. From Kyongsong he and Bay went to Shanghai. 'Lord Lee invited me to dine at his house and asked if I would like to hear some ancient Chinese music,' Zimbalist recounted. 'When I was enthusiastic, he engaged a man to play for me. But he told me that this man would perform only if I would play for him in exchange. After dinner Lord Lee introduced me to an elderly gentleman, blind, as many traditional Chinese musicians seemed to be, holding one of those long one-stringed instruments. He would pluck the string, wait a while, then murmur something that sounded as if he were gargling, then pluck again, then wait another minute or so. And this went on interminably. When my turn did come I said to Bay, "What shall we play that won't scare him? How about a slow piece?" He shrugged and said, "The slowest thing I brought along is the G major romance of Beethoven." So we played it. Afterwards Lord Lee brought the Chinese artist over to tell me something. What he said was, "I was amazed how quickly your fingers moved.'"

From Shanghai they took a steamship to Tsingtao, where a recital was scheduled. For years China had been suffering the disunity of weak leadership; marauding bandits flourished in the countryside, robbing and often killing travelers between cities. Public outrage was heightened when in 1923 Mrs. John D. Rockefeller Jr.'s sister was removed from her train while traversing the notorious forty-five-mile stretch between Peking and Tsientsin and held for ransom. When Kreisler toured China just months later General Chang Tso-lin forced the Kreisler party off their train from Manchuria to commandeer it for military purposes, and only sharing a cramped cattle car with machine-gun-armed police ensured their safe arrival in Peking. By 1924 trains north from Shantung to the Tsientsin-Peking area had stopped running altogether, and the remaining concerts of Zimbalist's tour, slated for both of these cities, were threatened. Nor could they reach Peking by continuing on a coastal steamer around the Shantung peninsula to the port city Tongku — the rail stretch between Tsientsin and Tongku was not operating either.

Zimbalist consulted maps at the Thomas Cook agency in Tsingtao and concluded that the only way of getting to Peking was by car, via Shantung's capital Tsinan, skirting the desert north of the sacred mountain Tai Shan. He takes up the story: 'I loved Peking, had many friends there, and just couldn't stand the thought of not seeing the city and playing the two or three concerts that had been announced. I asked Cook's to get me a car. They said the situation was much too dangerous for my plan and that I shouldn't even try it. I insisted, and they eventually found a driver willing to take Bay and myself. We were told that we could expect to encounter so-called soldiers along the way and to take a case of whisky, offering a bottle as a gesture of peace whenever we were stopped. We set out in a dilapidated vehicle and had gone quite a long way before the car broke down, crossing a deep gully—two flat tires and no spare. The driver, who didn't speak a word of English, started to walk back. Bay and I decided to keep going, guessing that we were at least halfway to Tsinan. So, leaving behind the remaining bottles of whisky we set out on foot, looking for the railroad tracks that would lead us to the capital. We walked and walked. Towards evening we came to a hut. Inside there were about a dozen armed men in uniform. When we entered, we did not know what would happen to us. I took out my violin and plucked the strings to show them that I was neither banker nor bandit. They seemed interested. As a matter of fact they even offered us water and some tough cakes they were baking on a little stove. We struggled to get the inedible things down, but couldn't drink the water for fear of cholera. Without interference we fell asleep on the wooden platforms they used as cots (there was a long row of them). When they let us leave the next morning we were desperate, not knowing how to proceed. I told Bay our only chance was to continue to look for the railroad tracks. We walked that whole day. The ground began turning into fine red sand— our feet made deep imprints and had to be removed quickly before they became stuck. We were about ready to give up. As it grew dark we dropped to the ground. I was sure we wouldn't live through the night—Bay seemed practically gone already. In despair I raised my head to look around. About a hundred yards from where I had collapsed I thought I saw a flag. So I said to myself, "Now look here, you're seeing things." But when I looked again it was still there. I called out, "Bay, if you are not too weak, turn around and tell me if you see anything over there." He turned, squinted and said, "Looks to me like an American flag." We were on our feet in a second and stumbled over to what turned out to be an American missionary school in Weihsien, and the only place between Tsingtao and Tsinan that had a telephone. The people who were expecting us in Peking knew we had not arrived in Tsinan and were sure we must have been killed. At the missionary school we were given food and clean water and after a good night's rest the proprietors took us by car to Peking.'

The concert in Tsientsin had been canceled, but Zimbalist and Bay, a little the worse for wear and four days late, played at the Hôtel de Peking on 22 November 1924. At the hotel they met a St. Petersburg graduate, Joseph Oroop, who had been appointed director of Peking's Far East Conservatory after fleeing Russia that spring. Oroop also headed the small European café orchestra employed by the hotel. He reported: 'At that time even in the capital there was very little Western music — only three or four foreign music teachers at the local university and conservatory. So it was a great pleasure for me to hear and meet Zimbalist. He wanted to sightsee, and so I took him to the palace, the museum and many wonderful temples. Also to Jade, Cloissoné and Ivory Streets, the narrow thoroughfares where craftsmen worked.' Zimbalist was impressed, but seemed most pleased when Oroop's wife prepared a Russian dinner for him. Some months later Oroop received a thank-you note from Zimbalist, with a signed photograph. 'I took many visiting artists on similar sightseeing trips, including Heifetz, Szigeti and Artur Rubinstein,' Oroop said, 'but only Zimbalist expressed gratitude in such a nice way, proving to me that he was not only a great musician but also a considerate human being.'

Barely recovered from their Chinese adventures, Zimbalist and Bay proceeded to the Dutch East Indies, where further excitement awaited them. In Java Zimbalist rapidly became a cause célèbre: 'One day in Batavia I was sitting in the Hotel Byzenes when a man, literally covered with medals, came to see me. He introduced himself as the head of the local orchestra (it turned out to be more of a military band with strings) and asked if I would play with them. They had been learning the Beethoven Concerto, hoping I would consent to play. I did, and we began to rehearse. He told me to start right out with my solo entrance since they had already rehearsed the opening tutti. Before I got to the top of the octaves he stopped and said, "Would you mind doing that again?" Well, we started four or five times and spent two hours on the first page: he just couldn't follow me. Somehow we got through the first movement, very unsatisfactorily. So I said to Bay, "Wait in the wings. It won't be too long before I'll have to finish with piano." It was a full house. At the performance the conductor became extremely nervous and after a few lines things fell apart. I said to him quietly, "It just won't go. Let me finish the concerto with piano." Bay came out from his station in the wings. The hoopla began the next day. I had taken a morning train to Soerabaja, at the other end of the island. A review appeared in the Batavia paper saying that the conductor should have known his limitations and not attempted the Beethoven. The commander-in-chief of the Dutch forces immediately published a haughty rebuttal. He said that, as the conductor's superior officer, *he* would have been the first to recognize any wrongdoing on his part. He had noticed none, so therefore the critic was entirely wrong and the soloist must have been at fault. It was a perfect example of military mentality. I played a few concerts in Soerabaja and returned to Batavia, only to find that events had raised such a clamor for me (the music-lovers who knew what had really happened were indignant) that I had to play two more concerts, delaying my departure for the Philippines. Overnight I had become a national hero!'

A postscript to Zimbalist's hair-raising misadventures in China was delivered 'halfway around the world in my own living room,' as he loved to retell. He and Alma had invited their new neighbors the Luces to dinner; conversation veered in the direction of Zimbalist's planned 1927 world tour, and the near-catastrophic Chinese episode came up. 'At the end of the tale, Henry blinked in disbelief. "Why," he said, "that school was started by my father. I was educated there!"' After dinner Luce's younger brother Sheldon dropped in to visit. On being introduced to Zimbalist, Sheldon exclaimed, 'I've seen you before. When I was at school in China you were one of the men they brought in from the desert. I watched through the keyhole while they were tending to you.' Zimbalist was completely floored. (Sheldon had followed in Henry's footsteps, attending their father's mission school in Weihsien. He joined the staff of *Time* in 1933.)

The tour planned for 1927 was even longer than 1924's. So long, in fact, that Zimbalist's Carnegie Hall concert on 28 March 1927 was advertised as his 'Farewell New York Recital for two years.' The tour would start in Sydney, proceed to the Philippines and Japan, return to Australia via China, Malaya, India and Java and continue from New Zealand to Europe, for a string of winter 1928 engagements. After his trials in China, Emanuel Bay was unwilling to make the trip, so Zimbalist engaged a promising young graduate of the Institute of Musical Art, Louis Greenwald.

Alma Gluck, already beginning to show signs of frail health, had by now sung her last public performance, and she fancied joining her husband to share Australasian adventures. So in early July 1927 she brought Maria and Efrem Jr. to The Rafters and put them in the custody of their neighbors, the Barneses. Alma planned to take a cross-country Pullman to San Francisco, where she would board ship for Melbourne.

Zimbalist had started out many weeks earlier. The tour became the backdrop to an ongoing drama. On the high seas he had received a radiogram from John R. Dobbs of the Chicago Lyon and Healy firm informing him that his Lorenzo Guadagnini, stolen seven weeks before in Los Angeles, had been recovered. Dobbs was getting a few violins out of the vault, when a young man was ushered in; he asked for an appraisal of a violin he might wish to sell. On opening the case, to Dobbs's amazement there lay Zimbalist's marvelous Lorenzo Guadagnini, which he had seen just once before. He checked its 1743 date which, along with sap and iron stains on the instrument's back, confirmed his identification. He left the young man in the office with his assistant and two house detectives on guard, with instructions that under no circumstances should he be allowed to leave.

As the violin had been purchased from the Wurlitzer company's New York shop, Dobbs extended them the courtesy of making the arrest through their Chicago branch. Curiously, Herman Scheiville, the young man detained, had already brought the violin to Wurlitzer's and three other downtown shops where the violin had been recognized, but he had somehow slipped through their fingers. Rembert Wurlitzer was sent for and arrived with two policemen. They waited outside Lyon and Healy's doors.

With the stage set Dobbs asked Scheiville to name his price, and he quoted a sum in the vicinity of $2,000. Dobbs told him he would have to talk it over with his directors, and asked Scheiville to call back in an hour or two. They walked over to the elevator where the house detectives were standing. One of them entered the car with him. On reaching the first floor they were met by Wurlitzer and the police officers, and the arrest was made. Scheiville admitted having stolen the instrument from Zimbalist— a love theft pure and simple. He said that he couldn't help it: Zimbalist's tone was so beautiful it intoxicated him. He had gone backstage during the concert, grabbed it and ran.

Zimbalist cabled his delight at the recovery from Suva, Fiji. He managed to catch Alma in New York just before her departure and asked her to pick up the Guadagnini on her way to the West Coast. But the California courts needed it for evidence, and when Alma reached Chicago the violin was already in Los Angeles. She suggested it be shipped to Sydney as soon as the authorities were through with it.

When her husband and Louis Greenwald arrived in Australia, they immediately proceeded to various cities for concerts. By the time they arrived back in Sydney the Guadagnini had still not arrived. Zimbalist had no choice but to leave on the next leg of the tour. The violin finally arrived in Sydney just as he was arriving in Japan. After much cable consultation and customs red tape, it was packed off to Tokyo.

In Tokyo he had to give nearly a dozen programs. Up to that point things had been going well with Greenwald. But with mounting fatigue, the amount of music he had to keep in his head and aggravation over the Guadagnini (he had missed its arrival in Japan and ordered it shipped back to Australia—where he would miss it yet again), Zimbalist gave a rare display of artistic temperament. Many encores were demanded of him, and once, after the familiar favorites, Zimbalist decided on one they had done less frequently, the Kreisler arrangement of Rameau's 'Tambourin.' In the midst of the piece's many curlicues his memory failed, and he simply couldn't get back on track. The youthful Greenwald, instead of prompting his colleague, burst into uncontrollable giggles. Zimbalist was mortified and left the platform at once. Backstage all was ice, and barely a word passed between them for the remainder of the tour. Zimbalist felt he had been humiliated in public. Greenwald thought that Zimbalist was overly touchy. This unhappy incident explains the omission of an accompanist's name on the recordings Zimbalist made during the tour. Strangely, Zimbalist was to have another memory slip in Tokyo in 1935, while playing the Mendelssohn Concerto with the National Broadcasting Orchestra. His only other was in Bermuda, halfway through the last page of Ravel's 'Tzigane'—a mighty good average in sixty-five-odd years of concerts.

On one occasion on that 1927 tour Strok's efficient arrangements didn't turn out as planned. Zimbalist recollected: 'I arrived in a Malayan city to find the hotel manager very apologetic: "I am terribly sorry. Your rooms were all arranged, but the King of Siam decided to visit and requisitioned the entire hotel." "Is there another hotel in the city?" "I'm afraid not." It was only a few hours before the concert. Greenwald and I had to dress and shave. A man stood listening nearby. As we talked he went over to the manager. In minutes we received word that His Majesty had ordered two rooms vacated for us.'

Zimbalist sailed around the Mekong Delta and played in Phnom Penh, Hanoi and other Indo-Chinese cities before finally arriving in India, where he gave six different programs at the Excelsior Hotel in Bombay. 'I played lots of Paganini.' He was in top form, according to violinist-conductor Mehli Mehta—father of Zubin—who heard all these concerts as a youth: 'Though Heifetz came about the same time, Zimbalist was considered technically and musically easily on a par with him.' (Mehta later settled in the United States and played second violin in the Curtis String Quartet.)

Audiences were made up almost entirely of British and Europeans, along with some Parsees, 'the most Westernized of the Indians. The vast Hindu masses had little opportunity to come into contact with Western music. This disappointed me,' said Zimbalist. Whenever possible he made a point of getting himself invited into Hindu homes for Indian music and curries.

There were also visits to homes of the highly cultivated Parsees. In Bombay he met Dina Mehta (no relation to Mehli), a top society lady and great beauty. She owned a magnificent mansion on the hilly coast just outside town and invited him to a garden party. Tables were set up on the meticulously manicured, deep green lawns. Giant banyan limbs and out-sized ochre umbrellas over the tables sheltered guests from the searing sun. The Union Jack drooped motionless against the white-washed walls. In the background wooded hills stretched into the horizon's shimmering haze. The jungle echoed to the rifle shots of a tiger hunt. Ornate iridescent butterflies flitted by. Zimbalist joined British majors with bushy mutton-chops, gleaming in their white suits, and their wives in gorgeous silk frocks, conversing as they sipped Pimm's cups and enjoyed a traditional English high tea. Zimbalist commented to Dina on the many British and European guests. 'Yes,' she replied, 'we have many foreign friends. They always accept invitations to our home but somehow never reciprocate by inviting us into theirs.'

None of the guests seemed to notice what to Zimbalist was an obvious blight on the otherwise serene picture. Mere yards away stood a tall marble platform over which huge vultures flapped and hovered grotesquely, their guttural cawing at times deafening. These ugly birds were feasting on what appeared to be a mass of bones. Dina lightly informed him that he was observing the legendary Malabar Hill, with its 'Towers of Silence,' and that the bones were human ones. In a holdover of ancient Iranian tradition, Bombay's Parsee dead are placed in slots in these towers. After the vultures have their meal the gnawed bones slide into lime pits, which are period-ically rinsed into the Arabian Sea by Bombay's heavy rains. This information took the edge off Zimbalist's appetite for the mustard-cress and potted tongue savories on his plate.

On to Java, then Melbourne, where Alma awaited him. Alma was filled with a sense of exploration. 'We had a lot of fun on that trip,' Zimbalist recalled. He didn't allow his accompanist and violin problems to affect their spirit of adventure. They caught a transcontinental train to Perth, then traveled east to Brisbane. From there they crossed the Tasman Sea and landed in Auckland. New Zealand was a first for both of them, and after the concert Zimbalist insisted on hearing some native Maori musicians.

The Zimbalists' Australian travels did have their downside—the pleasure of new acquaintances and enthralling sights was marred by poor audiences. In Melbourne the discouraged violinist received a telegram: 'Flesch has resigned [stop] Would you accept position as head of Curtis Institute violin department [stop] Josef Hofmann.' Zimbalist thought it over then cabled Hofmann, stressing his busy concert schedule. 'I could give you only very little time,' he cautioned. Hofmann's reply was succinct: 'Teach whenever you can.' How could Zimbalist have any inkling of the importance these exchanges harbored for his future?

A few days later came a lucky chance that was at once a musical thrill and the beginning of a friendship Zimbalist treasured for the rest of his days. Dame Nellie Melba had recently returned to Australia to spearhead a national touring opera company and retire in style in the house she had built there. She was displeased to hear reports of the small numbers attending Zimbalist's performances in Sydney and expressed herself with characteristic straightforwardness to a *Melbourne Herald* reporter: 'It hurts me, it shames me, for my fellow Australians to see a man like Zimbalist... come here, [a man] who never plays but to packed, enthusiastic houses, and to have [him] realize that our musical appreciation is only a myth.'

She did not take long to act—when Zimbalist played the Mendelssohn Concerto with the orchestra in Melbourne Dame Nellie herself attended. During intermission, very moved, she came to see him backstage. 'We *must* give a joint concert,' she urged. An announcement was made from the stage ('Dame Nellie Melba has asked Mr. Zimbalist to allow her to sing at one of his concerts, because she wishes to show her intense admiration for so great an artist, by paying him the greatest compliment within her power'), and several papers next day carried headlines about the event. Melba was quoted as saying that Zimbalist's genius had taken her breath away. She took the Zimbalists under her wing, insisting they stay at her beautiful country estate, Coombe Cottage.

Five hundred people were turned away on the night of the duo concert, and newspapers ran frothy reports on 3 August 1927. The *Sun News-Pictorial*: 'Over and over again [the artists] came on to take their bows, each time hand in hand, like a pair of happy children, amid huzzas and excitement—Zimbalist some of the time a wee bit embarrassed, maybe.' In addition to his solos, Zimbalist had both provided piano accompaniment and violin obbligatos for Melba. According to another paper: 'After Mozart's *Il Re Pastore* [Melba] went instantly over to Zimbalist, the wonderful player of her obbligato, and stood there gripping his hand, almost forcing the modest man into the picture.' To end in a gala spirit Zimbalist played Dvořák's 'Humoresque' while Melba sang 'Swanee River,' to her own piano accompaniment.

And how did the great Melba sing, a year after her Covent Garden farewell and just four years before her death? 'The high notes were no longer there, but from E to G she was still unique,' was the memory Zimbalist retained. A friend who saw Melba in her dressing room after the concert thought she looked exhausted. She was slumped in an armchair with lines of stress etched deep on her face. If Zimbalist was a 'wee bit embarrassed' by all the fuss, his spirits were considerably lifted, though temporarily. John Hetherington reports in his Melba biography, 'Zimbalist without Melba on the program played to meager houses for the rest of his tour.'

Melba was hospitality itself, and the Zimbalists' stay at Coombe Cottage was joyful. During their visit Pamela Vestay, Melba's granddaughter, came to afternoon tea and still remembers the jolly celebration they all had in the rose garden; when, in 1976, she sent Zimbalist one of Melba's Coombe Cottage greeting cards, he remembered vividly, too. Nor could he forget the grand farewell dinner party Melba threw for him and Alma the night before their departure. While coffee was being poured and dinner plates cleared, she announced a very special dessert. A small covered bowl was placed before Alma. When the cover was lifted a tiny, furry face peered out. Alma shrieked with delight and cradled the miniature ball of black and tan fluff to her face. Melba laughed, 'She's just as small as her mother once was.' She was referring to her own toy Manchester terrier, with which Alma had fallen in love. The pup could comfortably fit into a teacup. It was named So-So and became the most pampered member of the family. Efrem Jr. described his mother's arrival back at The Rafters (his father had continued on to Europe): '"Look what I brought!" she cried gleefully as I ran up to her. I looked, but saw nothing—So-So had completely blended into the shade of her fur coat. On the kitchen floor, the pup fitted within the borders of a single tile. There was uproarious laughter. When the

Barneses asked if the pup came with a pedigree, mother replied that she had torn it up since it looked so much better than her own.'

Josef Gingold was studying with his beloved master Eugène Ysaÿe when Zimbalist played in Brussels on the 1927–28 tour's homeward stretch. Ysaÿe, as Auer had so often done with young Efrem, took Josef to hear the visiting virtuoso. Backstage Ysaÿe gave Zimbalist his recently published solo sonatas, inscribed 'To the young master, Zimbalist, from the old master Eugène Ysaÿe.' On his return home Zimbalist played the first of the sonatas for Rachmaninoff and Hofmann. They were enchanted, and he subsequently recorded it. It is his only Victor Red Seal listing and possibly his most impressive recording.

Alma threw a big homecoming party on East 49th Street with music provided by the Musical Art Quartet, followed by a buffet supper. A shipment of Chinese items Zimbalist had purchased arrived, including an ancient twelve-stringed instrument; his prowess on it a few years later led to the appearance of his picture in *Ripley's Believe It or Not!* with the caption 'Efrem Zimbalist can play any stringed musical instrument.' And what of the errant Lorenzo Guadagnini? A few weeks after Zimbalist's return Ernest Doring of the New York Wurlitzer shop delivered the ill-fated violin into his unbelieving hands; its case was covered with labels and stickers, but the instrument was none the worse for its many voyages.

Zimbalist made an appointment to meet with Hofmann in Philadelphia. Mrs. Bok invited them to dinner at her Delancey Place home. Mr. Bok, very ill, sat silently in his chair. Zimbalist got the distinct impression he and his wife hadn't spoken a word to each other in years, and felt uncomfortable. An agreement was reached with Mrs. Bok and Hofmann — Zimbalist would join the Curtis Institute as head of the violin department that fall.

Leopold Auer came calling in New York to offer congratulations on Zimbalist's new position. 'How I would love to teach at the Curtis Institute,' he said wistfully. His former pupil considered Auer's words tantamount to a royal request. Zimbalist returned to Philadelphia and to Hofmann. 'Professor Auer would like to teach at Curtis,' he told him. 'Can it be arranged?' 'Of course,' Hofmann obliged.

Zimbalist made it clear that, with his old professor on the faculty, there was no way he could accept the title of department head. So Auer was given the title, along with the few extra thousand a year that went with it.

Zimbalist joined the regular faculty, thereby opening a new chapter in his career and giving his latent talents as an educator the chance to flower. Despite the departing Flesch's misgivings about Zimbalist's inexperience, he was to prove one of the century's great teachers.

CHAPTER 18

A New Career: Globetrotting Professor

(1928–1933)

Zimbalist didn't really begin to practice seriously until he started to teach. With typical modesty he remarked, 'All the students in my class played well. I thought, "What can I teach them knowing so little myself about violin technique?" So I started practicing.' In spite of being away a lot on tour those early Curtis years, he was from the outset a devoted teacher. According to Louis Kaufman, who had the opportunity to observe him at close quarters, he 'had the ability to analyze his playing, which not every intuitive violinist could do.' This proved of great help to the novice teacher. He developed his students' ability to listen to their own playing objectively. Closely allied to this self-scrutiny was his recommended practice method, made up ninety percent of repeating different passages very slowly ('like a tonal microscope,' as he explained it to Kaufman). The remaining ten percent, held in abeyance till shortly before a performance deadline, involved practicing much faster than the actual tempo, 'for the discipline' and to prepare one for any eventuality. Practicality was the key word in his method. Julius Schulman studied with him a few years later and remembered taking his final lesson before any important school recital onstage in full formal dress, simulating performance conditions. (Sarasate reportedly always practiced in concert attire.)

Zimbalist later made light of his first teaching experiences: 'It didn't take me very long to realize that I could learn a great deal from my students.' He came to deplore elaborate theories, strongly believing that one 'shouldn't get too clever about playing the violin.' For instance, he never 'corrected' a student's hand positions, unless a problem was clear. From the start he impressed on each student how privileged they were to be immersed in a life of music. At seventeen-year-old Rafael Druian's first lesson Zimbalist advised, 'If you don't find music completely rewarding you shouldn't be in it,' and he gave short shrift to anyone who bellyached about the musicians' lot.

The first lessons he gave preceded the school year: in summer 1928, the Curtis Institute sent selected students to Fishers Island. Not all were violinists—there were some singers and a few pianists studying accompanying, tended by faculty members Harriet Van Emden and Harry Kaufman. They stayed in dormitories at a mainland college and ferried to Fishers Island for lessons. Afterward they might join Zimbalist on the court for a game of tennis.

At school he tried hard to see that students received lessons regularly. Unlike Auer, he didn't adopt the master class method, save for one experimental season and the few occasions when in his nineties he visited the Institute to hear its latest progeny. But he did follow Auer's words from *Violin Playing As I Teach It*: 'The teacher should never confine his teaching to word-of-mouth. In spite of all the verbal eloquence he can call to his service, he will never be able to inculcate properly, to compel the pupil to grasp all the delicacies of execution, if he is unable to illustrate, by means of the violin itself, whatever he asks the pupil to do.' Zimbalist accordingly demonstrated often, going to great pains to master every piece of repertoire he taught. (In later years he played for his students less frequently.)

His 1928–29 class was comprised of eight pupils between the ages of twelve and twenty. Some had been Flesch students. Zimbalist would travel from New York, teach half of them and stay overnight at the nearby Warwick Hotel. Then, beginning bright and early in the morning, he worked with the remainder before returning home.

Interestingly, the formative experiences of one of Zimbalist's ex-Flesch students loosely paralleled his own. When Flesch arrived in the United States he had brought with him a poor Jewish boy named Isaak Briselli. The lad was originally from Odessa, but they had met in Berlin. Flesch went to bat for him at Ellis Island, then established him at the Curtis Institute, where he considered Iso one of the outstanding members of his class. Briselli was taken into the home of Samuel Fels, Joseph's brother, where his day-to-day needs were provided. When the shuffling of students occurred following Flesch's departure, Briselli was slated for Auer's class.

But Mrs. Samuel Fels wanted him with Zimbalist and pressured Hofmann to switch him to Zimbalist's class. This lack of confidence in his old master, now his colleague, affected Zimbalist deeply, but it became increasingly evident that the great Professor Auer was not what he once was. Apart from his general physical debilitation, he had become very hard of hearing. Stories about Auer's teaching during his last years abounded. Student plays for a dozing Auer; after a few minutes, Auer: 'Don't scratch.' Student resumes for several minutes. Auer: 'I said, *don't scratch!*' Student starts playing again to Auer's resigned shrugging: 'Okay, scratch.'

Professor Auer was still capable of a few flashes of his old vitriolic style. Louis Kaufman recollected that, on the death of Franz Kneisel, Auer was brought in to take over his post at the Institute of Musical Art in New York. Kaufman, in his senior year, took a few lessons from him but was loath to relinquish the principles of Kneisel's completely different approach. He was studying the Brahms Concerto. When for the third lesson in a row he chose to ignore a suggestion Auer had made, the eminent Professor stopped him. His dark eyes bored into the cocky youth and his voice was sharp: 'Mr. Kaufman, are you stubborn or just plain stupid?'

Auer's unfortunate situation caused Zimbalist more pain in the case of Oscar Shumsky, arguably the greatest violin talent ever to enter Curtis. After a few months Josef Hofmann relayed to Zimbalist Shumsky Sr.'s wish that his son be removed from Auer's class and placed in his. At that point Auer had only two students. Zimbalist reminisced: 'I told Josef that I wouldn't consider accepting him unless Auer himself asked me to. It just broke my heart when a short time later Auer *did* come to me. He said he could do nothing with Oscar and asked me to take him.' Zimbalist obliged, and with spectacular results. Nevertheless, Auer cannot be gainsaid a few fine successes from his American period, notably Benno Rabinof, Samuel Dushkin and Joseph Knitzer.

The 1930s ushered in Zimbalist's last global tours. The question of whom to take along as accompanist posed a problem. Emanuel Bay still played many domestic concerts with Zimbalist; but Bay was also playing extensively with Heifetz, and within a few years signed an exclusive contract with him. 'Jascha could offer him more money,' Zimbalist smiled (three of Zimbalist's pianists were lured away by Heifetz: Benoist in 1917, Chotzinoff in the '20s, Bay in 1930). The last time he and Bay played together was in winter 1930, on a short cross-country tour. A review of a

Los Angeles recital confirmed Zimbalist's drawing power as he approached middle age: 'Efrem Zimbalist continues to hold his popularity and even deepens the affection of an enthusiastic musical public by the human quality of his performance—a quality that finds an emotional response in his auditors.' On that tour he introduced Frederick Stock's concerto and Joseph Achron's 'Suite Bizarre' to West Coast audiences.

Another big world tour, beginning in spring 1929, would make a wide swing through Europe before continuing on to Asia. Zimbalist's Curtis class accompanist, Theodore Saidenberg, had demonstrated much talent and an agreeable personality and seemed a logical replacement for Bay. Saidenberg was studying with Harry Kaufman, an excellent teacher and pianist with whom Zimbalist had played faculty recitals and recorded. Kaufman was a comical personality, completely dominated by his wife, Lillian, both physically and psychologically. A forceful, conniving woman and a bosom friend of Hofmann's equally domineering wife, Lillian had come to exert considerable influence in the turning of the Institute's wheels. Kaufman, whose insecurity was deepened by the fact that his wife was fully a head taller than he was, lived torn between worship and hatred of her. When, in fall 1929, Zimbalist approached Kaufman for permission to hire Saidenberg, he drew himself up (always trying to look taller than he was) and put his cards on the table: 'Teddy Saidenberg is a nice boy, and it would be a great opportunity for him to accompany you, but I beseech you to take *me* along to play on the tour. You see,' he said, looking just about at his wits' end, 'I have to get away from my wife. The day before yesterday she broke a plate over my head, and I can no longer stand the sight of her!' Zimbalist was taken aback. 'I simply couldn't refuse his plea,' he admitted. Over lunch, they told Saidenberg he would become Zimbalist's regular accompanist, but only after the tour.

It wasn't long after departure that Zimbalist knew he had made a mistake. Kaufman, moody from the start, wasn't a pleasant traveling companion. They sailed on a British liner, and at dinner the first evening he was more than a little irritated that there was no ketchup on the table. The obliging waiter finally located a bottle. Kaufman took one look at it and turned up his nose. 'What, it isn't Heinz?' Zimbalist, normally the essence of even-temperedness, was a bit short with him. 'What on earth is the matter with you, Harry?' Kaufman's head dropped into his hands and between sighs he muttered that he missed his wife desperately. The entire next day Zimbalist watched him scrawling on one sheet of paper after another, then crumpling and tossing them into a wastebasket. 'I'm trying to tell her how much I love her,' Kaufman whined, 'but I never could express myself well enough for her—she always criticizes my writing.' The hint of amusement in Zimbalist's eyes quickly changed to consternation with the pitiful fellow's next words: 'When we reach Southampton I'm taking the next boat home—I just can't be away from her.' 'Be sensible, Harry!' Zimbalist frowned, 'how can I get anyone else at this point?'

He managed to mollify Kaufman. While they fulfilled their concert obligations in England, Belgium, Holland, Germany and Italy, Alma, accompanied by Maria, Efrem Jr. and Sheldon Luce (as tutor), sailed to meet them in Genoa. Efrem Jr. and Maria were then old enough to really appreciate the trip; he recalls a very happy journey from Genoa to Java aboard the Dutch liner SS *Jan Peterzoon Coon*. What delighted him and his sister most was Harry Kaufman's expertise as a jazz pianist. He sat for hours at the out-of-tune upright on B deck, mesmerizing the youngsters with his ability 'to make two hands sound like four.'

From Batavia they steamed northeast on the SS *Tjisondari*. Eleven-year-old Efrem Jr. noted in his diary, 'We sailed up to China, but didn't meet any pirates.' Then on to Japan. After seeing the sights in Tokyo Alma left with the children on the long homeward journey. Zimbalist and Kaufman stayed for further concerts throughout Japan and Korea; in Tokyo they recorded the Brahms d minor sonata, which became a popular seller. Another concrete reminder of the tour: Kaufman wrote an ingenious piano accompaniment to Kreutzer's Etude No. 9 in E, which they played as an encore; Zimbalist was so fond of the arrangement that he was still using it in his farewell concert season.

Zimbalist was still on tour when he received news that Auer had died on 15 July 1930, aged eighty-five, while summering at Loschwitz. The Professor left a substantial sum to his widow, testimony to a fine business acumen that had surmounted the adverse conditions of a foreign environment. Heifetz performed at the memorial service, attended by many of the world's musical celebrities. Auer was buried in New York.

Aside from problems with Kaufman, Zimbalist's sense of guilt at being away from his increasing Curtis obligations had made this trip overall an uneasy one. 'If I hadn't promised Strok, I wouldn't have gone,' he said later. Not a week after Harry and Lillian Kaufman's reunion they were at each other's throats again. Harry appeared in class with a particularly colorful black eye. His students weren't fooled when he explained that he had walked into a door. *They* knew the true cause, even if they tsk-tsked sympathetically.

Zimbalist and Theodore Saidenberg went on a short tour in fall 1930 before their first recital together in New York. 'I was just twenty-one and thrilled,' Saidenberg recalled, going on to recount a dramatic event: 'We ended the Midwestern part of our tour in Indianapolis, then on the way home played in Buffalo. We arrived back in New York early in the morning. That night we were to play a concert at Carnegie Hall, which had been sold out. We walked onstage to a filled hall with an overflow on the platform and started with the Bach Concerto in E. Suddenly, during the last movement, I heard no sound from Zimbalist's violin. I looked up and saw him standing with the violin down at his side and his left hand on his forehead. The interruption was a short one, but it seemed an eternity. Backstage, I asked him what had happened. He said that somehow his mind had refused to work—as if something had happened, or was about to happen. After the concert Mrs. Zimbalist told him that his father had passed away the night before. She and his manager had decided not to tell him the sad news before this important Carnegie Hall concert. He was extremely upset, and furious that he had not been told right away.'

The *Times* review of the concert was headed 'Concert Ended, Zimbalist Told Father Is Dead.' Three sons and four daughters were listed as survivors, Maria having died several years before. The greater degree of closeness sometimes seen between siblings following the death of the second parent didn't happen in this case. Zimbalist never could overcome his feeling that his brothers and sisters were basically strangers. In his last years he was even prone to deny that any of the family had left Russia, and claimed that in spite of being the oldest child, he had outlived all the others by decades. The reason Zimbalist later gave for his reticence in discussing his family's flight to the United States was the fear of reprisal against family members remaining in Soviet Russia. Then, when he was evading my attempts to get him to talk about his parents, he evinced pain that I couldn't help attributing, at least partly, to self-reproach.

Zimbalist succeeded Auer as head of the violin department, which at that time included Lea Luboshutz (he had first met her while a student, when the St. Petersburg and Moscow Conservatory orchestras combined for an event in Moscow — they had shared the concertmaster chair), Albert Meiff (a 'queer fellow who wrote cadenzas to everything in the repertoire'), Vera Fonaroff (a friend of Betty Hofmann's, she had taught beginners before being engaged at Curtis for ten times her former fee) and Edwin Bachman (who had played second violin in the short-lived Elman String Quartet). There were also various assistants in every department, many of whom Zimbalist considered less than first-rate. He showed Rachmaninoff around the Institute. The great pianist was curious about its running. 'How many students are there?' he asked. 'About 130,' Zimbalist replied. 'How many on the faculty?' 'Around forty.' 'Too many!' Rachmaninoff growled.

Zimbalist nonetheless persuaded Hofmann to add Ruvin Heifetz to the faculty on the strength of his yeoman work with Efrem Jr. Papa Heifetz remained at Curtis for a year or two as Zimbalist's assistant but eventually proved 'too difficult.' Once he brought one of his students to play for Zimbalist, who questioned the boy on a point. Ruvin jumped up: 'It's perfectly fine. Jascha does it like that.'

'Who is Jascha?'

'*Jascha!*'

'We don't know him here.'

'What I meant to convey,' Zimbalist later explained, 'was my belief that students should never be taught to do things just because other violinists — even Heifetz — do them in a certain way. Ruvin took my remark the wrong way and quit.'

For two weeks in November–December 1930 one of the most famous musical exchanges of all time took place: Arturo Toscanini conducted the Philadelphia Orchestra on its home turf while colleague Leopold Stokowski took over Toscanini's New York Philharmonic in Carnegie Hall. The exchange led to fireworks for Stokie in New York, where the orchestra was clearly out to prove the superiority of their Maestro. It also led to one of Zimbalist's most remembered performances, when he joined his old friend and the Philharmonic in the Sibelius Concerto.

'Stokowski understood the piece in a way no other conductor did,' Zimbalist recollected. Stokowski's mastery of the unusual texture and drama of Sibelius's score was what so impressed Zimbalist. Stokowski was not given to the indiscriminate praise of soloists, but he much admired Zimbalist's acute awareness of orchestral sonority and color as so vital a part of the whole, and his complete musical involvement. These qualities

were not always found among violinists of that generation: many wanted
to hold the orchestral level down in order to shine above it. Zimbalist's
Sibelius was 'unique in its breadth and excitement,' according to Louis
Kaufman. Olin Downes stated flatly (*New York Times*): 'Mr. Zimbalist gave
not only the best performance of this remarkable and solitary work but
also the first adequate performance that the writer has heard, seeing
deeper into the composition than any interpreter who has previously performed it in this city.' And in the *New York Sun* W. J. Henderson confirmed
that Zimbalist's performance was far and away the leading violin performance of the season.

Eudice Shapiro, who entered Zimbalist's class in 1931, remembers his
being on tour most of that fall. Until he arrived back she had lessons with
Edwin Bachmann. She was always a 'complete natural,' in her own words,
and a close rapport developed between her and Zimbalist. Not so between
him and Iso Briselli. Zimbalist felt the boy couldn't stand any peer pressure, but it was evidently a case of mismatched chemistry from the
beginning. He found it sobering to have to admit that he had 'tried everything and nothing worked.' Briselli eventually studied with Meiff and
graduated, but after a few concerts he moved into the Fels business empire,
playing the violin only for pleasure. Zimbalist kept up a cordial connection
with Iso and the Samuel Felses, often playing chess in their home; he never
saw Mary Fels there, owing to some rift that had developed between her
and her in-laws. After Joseph's death she had taken an apartment in New
York, where she lived until her own death in 1953.

Zimbalist played at least once each season in Carnegie Hall. His class
traveled en masse to New York and occupied a special box to hear these
programs, which were always interesting from both a musical and violinistic standpoint. The first Carnegie Hall recital of the 1931–32 season, for
instance, was comprised solely of Bach and Paganini, the Scylla and
Charybdis of violin playing. He concluded with the infamous 'Moto
Perpetuo,' and his attentive class grinned when he took the repeat. Another
particularly stunning Carnegie program included the Ernst Concerto with
piano accompaniment, as in days of yore.

Zimbalist was an imposing teacher: tallish and of sturdy build, impec-
cably groomed in custom-tailored three-piece suits, he dazzled his
wide-eyed students with brilliant demonstrations of the works they were
studying. The ambience around this impressive figure—whether the

antique furnishings or vintage works of art that lent an air of refined opulence to the Institute's rooms, or the priceless Tokugawa cabinet in
Zimbalist's studio that housed his Orientalia — was equally alluring. When
one bears in mind the modest background shared by most students who
roamed those hallowed halls, it is not difficult to gauge the measure of
their enchantment.

October 1931 marked the twentieth anniversary of Zimbalist's U.S.
debut. A group of distinguished artists gathered at the Zimbalist home in
the afternoon to greet him and present a large anniversary cake. One New
York paper commented, 'Walter Damrosch, paternal and bland of look,
unctuous of speech, acted as master of ceremonies and . . . led the singing
of "For He's a Jolly Good Fellow."' Another reiterated Zimbalist's reputation 'as one of the foremost violinists of the world, a position which he has
won by sheer merit and without the employment of any claptrap methods
of publicity or shopworn tricks of the virtuoso's trade.'

On the subject of claptrap publicity, in the early 1930s Zimbalist was
approached by some TV ad men. They wanted him to sign a thirteen-
episode contract to appear at the beginning of a weekly show and sell
Castoria, a laxative for children. The fee they offered, $3,000 per spot, was
persuasive, especially during the Depression. Simple music was desired.
Zimbalist suggested various short pieces he thought suitable, like Thais's
'Meditation' and Bach's 'Air on the G String.' The ad men didn't know them
but went to confer with their sponsors. They returned to report that the
pieces just wouldn't do. 'You see,' they explained, 'we need music that will
put mothers in the right mood to give their children Castoria.' When
Zimbalist asked for their ideas, they showed him unacceptable material.
'So they went to Albert Spalding, who agreed to play the trash they
wanted,' he recalled. 'It was ironic: I could have used the money, Spalding
didn't need it — and it certainly did nothing to advance his career.'

Zimbalist continued to compose in a serious way. In a note replying to
an inquiry about the progress of his first effort at full-scale symphonic
orchestration, 'Daphnis and Chloe,' he wrote his manager from Fishers
Island on 31 August 1931: 'I am so sorry to say that I will have no news for
publication about my symphonic poem till the second week in October.
Mr. Stokowsky is going to play it for me at one of his rehearsals before I
head for the West, and then we will decide on the date for the performance. That is if I think the work is worthy of a performance.' It evidently

proved worthy enough for Stokowski to première it in Philadelphia. Then, on 5 January 1932, he took it to New York, where he presented it on the same program with the American première of Stravinsky's violin concerto, Samuel Dushkin as soloist. One critic called the concerto 'the apotheosis of nothing' but found Zimbalist's tone poem 'a graceful work.' Zimbalist himself was very disappointed and destroyed it.

A work that did find favor with him was 'American Rhapsody,' another orchestral piece, whose Chicago Symphony première ('Stock advised me to add more percussion') he himself conducted in 1935. The enthusiastic press responses were the only reviews Zimbalist ever saved, and Stokowski programmed it several times subsequently.

In February 1932, the Musical Art Quartet introduced Zimbalist's string quartet at Town Hall. It left *New York Sun* critic W. J. Henderson with 'the impression of a refined, scholarly and generous mind working in a sympathetic medium with musicianly skill and judgement and exquisite taste.' He noted too that some of its harmonies went far beyond anything recognized by pre-Debussy masters, almost touching hands with Stravinsky. The concert was nearly called off: arriving at Sascha Jacobsen's apartment late at night after their dress rehearsal, the quartet discovered their music missing. They searched high and low to no avail. The parts were handwritten by the composer and the only ones extant. The performance was in less than eighteen hours. Zimbalist hired two copyists to work through the night preparing new parts from the score; the quartet then rehearsed frantically, trying to reconstruct fingerings and bowings. The Jacques Gordon Quartet subsequently recorded the work.

In spring 1932 the *Times* announced, 'Efrem Zimbalist, noted violinist, will leave the Newark Airport on May 20 [for a] tour entirely by airplane through Mexico, Salvador, Nicaragua, Costa Rica, Panama, Colombia, Venezuela, Trinidad, Puerto Rico and Haiti.' What with all the planning for a big Asian tour that coming fall, travel details for the Central and South American trip seem to have been sidelined, as Zimbalist realized when he tried to contact his young accompanist in Philadelphia. He learned that Saidenberg had taken off for a long weekend, just when he himself was packing. He reached him by phone at his parents' home in New York. They were having late dinner. The conversation was one for the books: 'Hello Teddy, this is Efrem Zimbalist. How *are* you?'

'Very well, thank you Mr. Zimbalist. How are *you*?'

'Very well, thank you. Tell me, Teddy, do you still intend going on tour with me?'

'Of course. When do we leave?'

'Tomorrow morning.'

Saidenberg met Zimbalist at 5:30 a.m. in Newark. Traveling with them was Samuel Piza, an impresario associated with the New York Philharmonic and a gentleman of distinguished Latin bearing; throughout the trip he addressed the nitty-gritty with style. They boarded a DC-3, getting a spectacular view of the newly completed Empire State building on take-off for Fort Worth, where they would change planes for Mexico City; from Mexico they traveled on various smaller planes. It was the first international air tour undertaken by a violinist, although Zimbalist, like Heifetz, had for some years flown routinely to fulfill his domestic concert schedule.

There were several concerts in Mexico City, including one with orchestra. On a free night they went to a movie; films of Spanish musicals were very popular, and Zimbalist was fond of anything that smacked of operetta. What they enjoyed most was the mood of the audience—such wild applause followed each song that the projectionist was obliged to stop the film and rewind for an encore.

They had an amusing landing in Guatemala City. While taxiing to the terminal Zimbalist noted an unusually large crowd at the gate which, he believed, was composed of welcoming fans. But his satisfaction turned to puzzlement when the cheering throng paid no attention whatsoever as he and Saidenberg deplaned. Only inside the terminal building did they find out that the sports-crazy Guatemalans had been awaiting the arrival, on the same plane, of their favorite soccer player. Another landing proved terrifying. As they crossed the Nicaraguan border the ground below disappeared in a blanket of coastal clouds; but the pilot knew that the San Jose airfield was directly below and dropped two thousand feet with a jolt that alerted his nervous passengers. Spotting a clearing, he touched down safely on the tiny strip. At a recital in Cartegena, Colombia, an infestation of gnats made it difficult for Saidenberg to see his music. Forty years later he came across the score of the Mendelssohn Concerto he had used that night; when he opened it the pages were encrusted with the desiccated remains of thousands of the minuscule pests.

They boarded a German seaplane in Cartegena and traveled south, stopping at several Indian villages before arriving in Bogota, and then on to

Venezuela. 'After the concert in Caracas we had dinner at the home of Ambassador Daniels,' Zimbalist recounted. 'While we dined a government official arrived. He presented me with a medal from the president, General Gomez, and a magnificent solid gold cane. I had never seen anything like it. He said the president had been so impressed by my playing that he wanted to give me something he found difficult to part with. The only thing he could think of was this cane, once presented to him by his subjects.' They left Caracas by seaplane and flew over the spectacular Orinoco Basin to Port-au-Spain, Trinidad. The tour ended with performances there, in Haiti, and in Puerto Rico. From San Juan an enormous Pan Am Clipper with six engines took almost as many hours to fly them back to Miami. Douglas Fairbanks Sr. was a fellow passenger on the next leg, from Miami to New York, a confirmation of the celebrity status of most pioneer air travelers.

Zimbalist and Saidenberg had covered a total of about six thousand miles during the five-week tour, a journey that would have required five months by land and sea. In honor of his plucky trip Zimbalist was dubbed the 'Flying Fiddler, who never steps into a train when there is an airplane within striking distance,' and was one of the first to receive an award from United Air Lines for racking up 100,000 air miles.

In August 1932 Zimbalist and Saidenberg were airborne again, this time to San Francisco. There they boarded the SS *Tatsuta Maru* and whiled away their voyage to Japan by playing chess for a quarter a game. In Tokyo they visited a marvelous bundaki puppet theater, and Zimbalist once again entered the Japanese Columbia Studios, where he and his young pianist recorded Brahms's Hungarian Dance No. 17 (Kreisler arrangement), Drdla's 'Souvenir,' Schumann's 'Träumerei,' Tchaikovsky's 'Andante Cantabile' (Kreisler arrangement), Sarasate's 'Zigeunerweisen' and an outstanding 'Carmen Fantasy.'

On their way back to the United States Zimbalist crossed paths with Joseph Szigeti in Hawaii. It was rather awkward, because the artists' rival impresarios had set up recitals in Honolulu on the same night. Reported Saidenberg, 'The one killed the other. Neither could boast of any kind of a house, although we did a little better than he did.'

A year later Zimbalist and Saidenberg flew again to Mexico City for a recital. Unfortunately Montezuma took such a measure of revenge on Teddy that Zimbalist had to send him home and hire a local substitute.

CHAPTER 19

Soviet Invitation — and Personal Tragedy

(1933–1938)

During this period it often seemed to Zimbalist (and his family) that he was touring more than ever. With teaching duties now added to family responsibilities and worries, he felt the burden. 'He was gone a lot,' Eudice Shapiro says, 'but still managed to give us enough lessons, making up the time by coming from New York an extra day or two when he was home.' By 1933 his class included several first-rate violinists; one, Frederick Vogelgesang, was unusually talented in that he was equally proficient on the violin, piano and French horn (years later he recorded the Brahms horn trio, playing all three parts himself). While Zimbalist's outwardly serious manner sometimes almost approached aloofness, on a one-to-one basis with students he was warm and encouraging. He often employed body language to get his points across without interrupting their playing, pacing around them, gesturing strongly when phrases needed more contour or indicating with his right arm a speedier or slower bow stroke. Shapiro remembers entering his class with a 'nice, fat, unvarying vibrato.' Zimbalist came up to her while she played and put his hand over hers when he considered the vibrato too active. Even from early years he knew it best to chide students in well-chosen, understated terms — knowledge that he later refined to an art. Not having practiced for one of her lessons, Shapiro went in and 'read' the Brahms A major sonata with class pianist Vladimir Sokoloff (Theodore Saidenberg's first cousin, also a Harry Kaufman pupil). Zimbalist didn't stop her once. But when she had finished he said gently, 'Fits you like a glove. What will you bring next week?' 'I went out and wept,' Shapiro told me.

Sokoloff noted, 'He never reprimanded students at lessons. If he was displeased he would withdraw instead, becoming uncommunicative, even disinterested to the point of ignoring the student. They learned to recognize that kind of disapproval.' One student greeted Zimbalist and began to play, with Sokoloff at the piano. The boy, who was obviously unprepared, wondered why Zimbalist was making no comments but continued playing until Sokoloff stopped him and led him to the window. It was a beautiful day out. A distinguished-looking man in a three-piece suit was strolling in Rittenhouse Square, enjoying the sights and sounds. It was Efrem Zimbalist.

Florence Frantz Snyder, another class accompanist during that period, said the most disparaging she ever saw Zimbalist during a lesson was when he once stopped a boy's playing with the query, 'Why so much schmaltz?' In the rare instances when he thought it necessary, his words could be pointed, especially when a student seemed to be trying to pull the wool over his eyes. Once Bernie Eichen, with questionable taste, played the romance from Wieniawski's d minor concerto connecting the second and third notes with a heavy glissando. Zimbalist jumped up. 'Bernard,' he said sharply, 'I told you *two years ago* not to do that slide!' Bernie resumed playing. He was then using a Curtis instrument made by William Moennig. Its large-pattern Strad design invited nicking of its right bout with the bow frog; its bright orange-red varnish seemed to showcase the chipped edge. Zimbalist rose from his chair and slowly came over. Eichen stopped playing but still his teacher advanced, until his face was almost touching the violin. 'What do you do,' Zimbalist asked in wonderment, 'chew on your violin?' Zimbalist facetiously nicknamed another student who was totally lacking in imagination 'the poet from New York,' and after a lesson commented to Sokoloff, 'He has all the makings of a successful president of Sears Roebuck.'

Sokoloff recalled Zimbalist as 'a master improvisor': 'He loved to improvise countermelodies or accompaniments on the violin while the students played. It used to get some of them all fouled up. But he did it for a specific reason—he felt they should be able to integrate what they were doing with whatever was going on around them, as they would have to do as soloists with orchestras.'

Despite Zimbalist's sometimes stern appearance, the twinkle in his eye told one that he knew what was going on. And he was always ready to laugh. When he heard that Jascha Brodsky had perfected an imitation of what many students considered a certain sterility in their teacher's style, he insisted he show him the gag. Jascha, embarrassed, demonstrated the opening to Handel's E major sonata, strictly senza vibrato except for one oscillation, up and down, as indicated by ~:

Zimbalist guffawed, knowing full well how much Jascha adored him. Plenty of fun took its official form in costume balls and hilarious annual Christmas parties, where high jinks ruled and students and faculty staged ludicrous farces and skits.

But partly because of his European upbringing, tied in with memories of the awe in which Auer's students held their master, and partly because etiquette at the Curtis Institute required it, he expected and generally got great respect from his class. Except for a few intimates, he was always 'Mr. Zimbalist' to both faculty and students, and Florence Frantz Snyder, then a teenager, was charmed when he smilingly commended her, 'My dear Miss Frantz, you played with such passion.' Felix Slatkin was once seated with several other class members in the school common room and failed to stand when his teacher entered the room. Zimbalist saw to it that the Institute's top brass heard about what he considered a show of disrespect, and Slatkin was reprimanded.

Zimbalist never failed to come up with fresh ideas for his recitals. Around this time he shared the Philadelphia Academy of Music's stage with critic Olin Downes to present a lecture recital under the title 'The Violin's Coming of Age.' Downes spoke on the history of the instrument and its literature from the early Italian school to the era of nineteenth-century virtuosity. The *Philadelphia Inquirer* stated that Downes 'skipped adroitly and landed successfully on the high spots, which were illuminated by Zimbalist's solos,' which included the same Handel sonata in E some of his class had poked fun at, Bach's unaccompanied Prelude and Fugue in g, the Adagio from Spohr's Ninth Concerto, Auer's arrangement of the finale from Haydn's G major string quartet and three Paganini caprices.

Early in 1934 Zimbalist accepted an offer to return to the land of his birth for a concert tour. While he had never shown his colleague Rachmaninoff's intense interest in the course of Russian events, and American patriotism aside, it was Russian blood that flowed in his veins to the end of his days —

during the last years the expression in his eyes as he spoke of his motherland told all. The full extent of the changes that had occurred since he last set foot there in 1912, overt and subtle, he felt very deeply. Artistically the course of Russian culture after 1917 had veered wildly, struggling through its many vicissitudes like a rudderless ship on a foggy night. In the great conservatories the initial fallout had been faculty loss due to emigration. Auer's departure set the St. Petersburg (later Petrograd, then Leningrad, now St. Petersburg again) Conservatory's violin department flat on its back. The Moscow Conservatory, whose violin faculty at its best had never held the glamour enjoyed by its sister organization, lost all it did have. Among those who escaped was Mikhail (Michael) Press, who eventually taught at the Curtis Institute. The piano faculty fared somewhat better; such stellar figures as Felix Blumenfeld remained and attempted to carry on the glorious Russian star tradition, only to find himself increasingly hampered under Sovietization. To resurrect the violin faculty several of Auer's remaining students were offered full professorships, the best of them such people as Zimbalist's old friend Lev Zeitlin and Abram Yampolski, who, although able craftsmen, could not be considered great artists. Still, their appointment to the faculty in Moscow signaled that the compass for aspiring violin students now pointed there rather than to Leningrad.

Two potentially important contributors to Russian violinism met contrasting fates. Karl Grigorovich (b. 1867), a student of Wieniawski and Joachim, was caught trying to cross the border illegally in 1920; some say he was executed, some he was thrown into jail, where he died of typhoid. Miron Poliakin (1895–1941), one of Auer's greatest students, fled in 1918. Unlike the unfortunate Grigorovich he was welcomed back to Soviet Russia in 1927 thanks to a temporarily more favorable political climate, and appointed to the Leningrad Conservatory. Later he was shifted to Moscow.

An already reputable name who rose to greater prominence during the post-revolutionary period was Konstantin Mostras, teacher of Ivan Galamian, and a slowly emerging new name was almost to approach the magic of Auer's, although he was never associated with either of the larger conservatories: Piotr Stoliarsky (1871–1944). His reputation as a teacher was first centered in Odessa, where from 1911 he had run a private violin school for children, later dubbed 'The Talent Factory.' Following the revolution this school was incorporated into the Odessa Conservatory, and Stoliarsky was named a professor. Among the violinists who began their studies under his direction were Nathan Milstein, David Oistrakh, Elisaveta Gilels, Busia Goldstein and Mischa Fichtenholz. They admired Stoliarsky's teaching but spoke candidly of the defects in his violin playing.

Conditions were hardly favorable for these shapers of the new performance ideals, or for any involved in the various branches of artistic life in Russia. The institutions of higher learning started the policy of admitting students on the basis of proletarian ancestry rather than ability, and since music was not thought a worthy occupation for builders of a communist society, the number of freshmen entering the conservatories dwindled. A more positive consequence was that there was less class discrimination to be found among music students. In the early '20s all 'worker' elements coalesced into the Russian Association of Proletarian Musicians. Over the years better trained new members, especially composers, strengthened the Association's power. It came into its own in 1928, with Stalin's attack on 'class enemies.' Already by 1919 the proletarian associations, consisting mostly of party members, started to regulate musical policies and put ideological pressure on all artists.

Unsympathetic heads of institutions were toppled and replaced by men such as Pszibyzsewsky, appointed director of the Moscow Conservatory. His inaugural speech was a distillation of the newly formulated official beliefs: 'We have no use for soloists; we need mass musicians, we need socially minded musicians. We must do away with the useless system of musical education which arouses in the student the unhealthy desire to compete, an unconscious urge for personal advancement at the expense of the collective effort. As of today I am doing away with all examinations and grades which are nothing but stupid, outmoded bourgeoisie fetishes. From now on in the course of the educational process you will confine yourselves to the composers whose music is close to the proletarian spirit, and you will discontinue the intolerable practice of studying composers who are foreign and hostile to our ideals.' The list of composers to be discarded as degenerates included Bach, Schumann, Chopin, Tchaikovsky, Rimsky-Korsakov, Scriabin and Rachmaninoff. Beethoven was acceptable since his music embodied the spirit of the French Revolution, as was Mussorgsky, who represented the best example of a popular revolutionary trend in Russian music.

After the poor showing Soviet pianists put up in Warsaw at the 1932 Second International Piano Festival the government made a sharp about-face and abolished all the proletarian art groups. Top artistic heads once again rolled, and restoration of older values was begun. Seeing the inherent boost to the national prestige of which contest-winning Soviet musicians were capable, Stalin began to take a direct interest in improving the musicians' lot. Special scholarships were created for the more gifted, and beautiful Cremonese violins, once in the Imperial collection and at that time in State museums, were put at the disposal of outstanding Soviet performers. This change in policy produced brilliant results at international competitions in the next few years—in the 1937 Ysaÿe Concours in Brussels five of the six winners were Soviet competitors. There was even an explosion of enthusiasm for American jazz.

A comparison of salaries in 1934 is illustrative. The average worker's salary was less than 200 rubles a month, and while a staff doctor in a Moscow hospital received approximately 350 rubles a month, a professor at a conservatory got 400 rubles, and a member of a good symphony 400 to 500 rubles a month. Artists in Russia, as always, earned well.

It turned out to be a short-lived progressive period, the lid being clamped down again with the official censure of Dmitri Shostakovich's opera *Lady Macbeth of Mtsenk* in 1936. But in 1934 Stalin's slogan 'Life is better; life is gayer' seemed, on the surface, to be holding true. It was this atmosphere that paved the way for Zimbalist's tour.

In April 1934 Zimbalist and Saidenberg sailed from New York to Stockholm on a Swedish ship. Then they crossed a narrow arm of the Baltic, docking in Helsinki, where Zimbalist was to play the Sibelius Concerto with the local orchestra. It was one of the concertos that he had continued to 'doctor' throughout his career. At that point he was making a sizeable cut in the development section of the last movement. Later he restored those 'meandering triplets' (eight measures before number five) but made double stops out of them. 'Much fuller,' he decided. And he sometimes played the concerto's final run an octave higher ('more brilliant'). Sibelius had not written a note of music since 1926; despite this he was still considered the most influential voice in Scandinavian music. When Zimbalist was told that he would attend the performance, he was a bit nervous: what about the changes? Sibelius had never been consulted about them. He was greatly relieved when just before the concert word was received that the master was indisposed and wouldn't be present after all. But further information disclosed that a telephone connection from the hall to Sibelius's sickbed had been rigged up. Since the performance elicited no immediate reaction from the composer, Zimbalist assumed the worst. He needn't have fretted. Some years later a festival of Sibelius's music was being planned. A letter the composer wrote to its organizer, the conductor Taulovw, was passed along to Zimbalist: 'I hesitate to suggest anything, but if the violin concerto is being played I would personally be very glad if Efrem Zimbalist plays it. A better interpretation than his would be hard, if not impossible, to find.'

From Helsinki Zimbalist and Saidenberg traveled by rail to Leningrad. It was a lovely spring, and they arrived under blue skies. The first concert was a recital in the Conservatory Hall. Zimbalist was awash in memories. A doorman greeted him on entrance: 'I've been waiting for you,' he said. 'I remember you as a student. I was the piano tuner in those days.' The man was 105 years old. Zimbalist opened the program (as he had in 1909) with Bach's d minor partita and ended with the Wilhelmj version of Paganini's D major concerto, with Sauret's cadenza. (The only other violinist performing this fiendishly difficult cadenza at the time was the equally intrepid Jan Kubelik.) 'Coming onstage was one of the most affecting experiences I ever had,' Zimbalist remembered. 'Rimsky-Korsakov's children Volodya and Nadia were sitting in the front row.' As an encore he played his 'Coq d'Or Fantasy,' which added extra meaning. It was a misty-eyed reunion.

Nadia invited Zimbalist to visit with her and Volodya at home. They were now living in Auer's former house on the English Prospect. Like all the older spacious homes, it had been broken up into tiny apartments. Volodya shared one downstairs. Nadia lived upstairs with her husband, composer Maximilian Steinberg, the newly appointed director of the Conservatory. Old times were relived that evening, and cautious comparisons drawn with the new. 'The country was in a terrible way,' was the conclusion Zimbalist drew.

Those weeks spent in Soviet Russia were filled with travel and activity. His next concert was in Leningrad, as part of the 'First Music Festival in Soviet Russia.' The New York Times declared that the highlight was the Glazunov Concerto, which he presented 'in fine form and style.' In Rostov he made a sentimental pilgrimage to the house that Alex had built ('It still looked pretty good,' he commented lightly), and after the concert there more than five hundred people escorted him from the stage door to his hotel.

Just months before, Heifetz had made his return trip to Russia. Despite

this triumph's being fresh in the public's mind, Zimbalist made an enormous impression. Everywhere his playing was compared with Heifetz's,
and hailed in its own right. The Great Hall of the Moscow Conservatory
was filled, and the audience responded with a storm of applause and a
standing ovation. Twenty-six-year-old David Oistrakh, having just graduated and been appointed to a junior teaching position at the Conservatory,
was captivated by him; Lev Zeitlin, then a conservatory professor and concertmaster of Moscow's 'Conductorless Symphony,' introduced them, and
they became permanent friends.

Backstage he met a handsome old man with a huge beard that almost
covered the medals and decorations crowding every inch of his chest:
Mikhail Ippolitov-Ivanov, recently retired director of the Conservatory. He
had been decorated by Lenin on the strength of his sole claim to fame, the
'Caucasian Sketches,' written at the turn of the century. Since then he had
clanked amiably about, displaying his medals and enjoying his status as a
national hero. Also backstage Zimbalist met a composer of far greater significance—Dmitri Shostakovich, already widely admired. 'I was struck by
the pallor of his complexion and that curious haunted look in his eyes,'
Zimbalist recalled.

During his stay in Moscow he was invited to the marvelous Arts Theater
to see Stanislavsky's production of *The Cherry Orchard*, starring Chekhov's
widow. The invitation carried a proviso to which he happily agreed: 'The
company had been unable to come to my concert because of the show, so
they asked me to play for them after their curtain fell. They wheeled a
piano onstage, and the entire company sat in the house to listen.'

Saidenberg made a conquest of his own in Moscow—he became
engaged to Eleanor Levin, an American girl living there with her mother.
They had met earlier, once, in New York, and Saidenberg had looked
Eleanor up when he arrived in Russia. He took very reluctant leave of her
when the 1934 tour came to an end, but already there was talk of return
concerts the following season.

Back in the United States Zimbalist received a letter from Alexander
Glazunov, who was spending his twilight years quietly in Paris and whose
absence was still felt in Russian musical circles:

Dear Revered Efrem Ilitch,
I would like you to do me a huge favor. My very good friend, a

free-lance artist from the Conservatoire, violinist Lev
Jacoblevich Szgelnick would like to go to the United States and
he would like to take a master class with you. He's an absolutely
wonderful musician and a good worker. I would be so happy if
you could find it possible to help him.

Trusting your health is good and with a thousand best wishes,

Always with you,

A. Glazunov

Zimbalist saved this letter and determined to visit his old mentor when he
was next in Europe.

One might think that, with several of the world's finest violins in his
possession, Zimbalist would have been satisfied. But the possible discovery
of a hitherto overlooked masterpiece lurked in the back of his mind. This
led to a little trouble. While on a West Coast tour he met eighty-six-year-
old violin collector George Smith and asked to see his instruments. Among
them were what Zimbalist believed to be an early Strad and a Guarneri del
Gesu. Smith told him that he hadn't thought of selling them, but that he
might consider changing his mind. Zimbalist inquired about prices and
was quoted $5,000 for each violin or $8,000 for the pair, figures that struck
him as surprisingly low. Smith explained that, on account of his advanced
age, he didn't feel he should charge dealers' prices. Zimbalist, wary, had
Smith agree to $2,000 down, the balance to be paid in monthly install-
ments of $1,000. A contract was drawn up and signed by both.

When Zimbalist found the instruments to be fakes, not worth more
than $300, he refused to pay Smith another dime, and Smith sued him for
the remaining $6,000 due. The lawsuit was started in the lowest California
court. Zimbalist's counsel put the well-known violin expert A. Koodlach
on the stand. 'It requires no expert to see that these violins are cheap
German copies,' Koodlach testified. 'I didn't tell Zimbalist that they were
genuine Stradivarius and Guarnerius violins,' responded Smith, by then
ninety-two years old. The Superior Court decided that Smith was not entitled to recover the $6,000. After Smith's death his son, unhappy with the
decision, appealed.

The Appelate Court went over the evidence and found that an exception
to the *caveat emptor* ('buyer beware') rule should be applied because both
Smith and Zimbalist were mistaken about the true identity of the violins.

They had made a contract regarding a Stradivarius and a Guarnerius; since the actual violins were not authentic, the court decided that there really was not a contract. The case proved an absence of deception on both sides, and the Smith v. Zimbalist decision was published, immortalizing Zimbalist's name in the annals of the law. A textbook case regarding contract law, it established a precedent on which lawyers and judges rely.

In 1935 Fritz Kreisler was forced to admit to a spot of deception concerning his famous transcriptions of 'classic masters.' Zimbalist, one of the earliest to know the truth, was interviewed by the press: 'The violin repertoire has been wonderfully enriched by these compositions, and as Kreisler did not think it advisable to say they were his when he wrote them, it was not my place to divulge anything; he had a perfect right to attribute them to anyone he pleased.' That same year Zimbalist added a new facet to his career. As a New York paper announced: 'Efrem Zimbalist, the famous violinist, makes his debut tomorrow night as a conductor of opera, Peter Tchaikovsky's *Eugene Onegin*, the first of a series of Russian operas at the Mecca Temple, presented by the Art of Musical Russia, Inc.' According to the *Boston Globe*, 'Efrem Zimbalist has been bitten by the bug of conducting, and finds the virus not unpleasant.' Zimbalist thoroughly enjoyed the whole thing.

No amount of activity in his career, nor responsibility for the guidance of his students' careers, could distract Zimbalist for long from what had been his main preoccupation for years—the deteriorating state of his wife's health. Already in the early 1930s (when only in her mid-forties) uncharacteristic fatigue plagued Alma, and she began having trouble keeping up her weight. Her delicate stomach became ever more finicky, and she found her tastes leaning more and more toward liquids, principally milk. A battery of tests revealed a liver disorder. For years her strength wavered, but she decided to go on her husband's last extensive tour. Early in 1935 he had told one newspaper, 'I am now forty-four—by the time I am fifty I want to retire.'

Although his heart was no longer in it, he had signed yet again with Strok for an Asian tour that spring (the term 'signed' is used figuratively: all six tours organized by Strok were strictly verbal agreements). Zimbalist and Saidenberg worked their way across the United States; the *San Francisco Chronicle* caught him before his concert there and found him in a 'quiet mood.' He said that his sole ambition when he retired was to open a bookstore specializing in English and American first editions, but that he would refuse to sell any of them. Alma linked up with them in Los Angeles, where they boarded a Japanese ship. She took along a supply of powdered milk for the crossing; Marcia, living in Salzburg with her husband, had arranged for further supplies to be waiting at various points throughout the months ahead. During the ocean voyage Alma displayed her usual cheerfulness and sense of fun. Three-handed bridge games were frequent. Saidenberg reported benefitting greatly from the overbidding that followed the Zimbalists' constant arguments on good bidding procedure. They docked in Yokohama and proceeded, with Strok, through Japan and Korea. Next they headed for Manchuria, where they traveled on the Chinese Eastern Railroad from Harbin to the Soviet border at Manchouli. Aware that there were no dining cars on the Trans-Siberian — an unnecessary luxury — and that it would take fully nine days to reach Moscow, Strok, an old hand, made provision for baskets of food and drink to be taken along.

The journey turned into a party, and they sat up most of the night, eating, talking and playing cards. Top speed for the wood-burning loco-motive with its all-woman crew was about twenty-five miles an hour, with frequent stops at wood piles spaced at intervals along the tracks. They stopped one dusk at Irkutsk. Refueling at the next track was a train from Birobidzhan, a town in a corner of Manchuria. While stretching their legs on the platform the Zimbalist party watched the passengers alighting. All were elderly men with long beards. Strok knew that a plan was underway to establish a Jewish settlement in Birobidzhan, and he strolled over to engage one of the men in conversation. Back on board Zimbalist asked him what he had found out ('Nu?'). By Strok's sober response ('Nu? Nu?'), Zimbalist knew just how bad things were.

They arrived in Moscow on 15 July 1935; Saidenberg's fiancée, Eleanor, was waiting for him, and they were married the same day. There was also a happy reunion with Efrem Jr. and Maria, who had been summering in Europe chaperoned by family friend Ruth Dodge. Ruth's financial condition was very strained when Alma befriended her (she and her son Washington had survived the sinking of the *Titanic*); the chaperoning idea had been Alma's way of bestowing kindnesses. She later appointed Washington a trustee of her estate (at the time of his death in 1975 he was one of the very few remaining *Titanic* survivors).

At this point Soviet inefficiency showed its hand. Strok was informed that through some miscommunication no concerts had been arranged. With profuse apologies in their wake, the whole Zimbalist group was parceled off to the Black Sea resort town of Sochi to rest up and await further word, which suited the newlyweds just fine. Zimbalist played one concert there, with the local orchestra under Oscar Fried, but his memories of the stay, which lasted until September and included watching Stalin drive by in an open-topped limousine, were less than euphoric.

Eleanor Saidenberg's mother had come to Moscow with her daughter to study the great communist experiment. Eleanor and Alma had ample opportunity to discuss it. Alma herself had earlier 'succumbed to the communist intellectual game' and was friendly with Troyanovsky, Russian ambassador to the United States. She had always felt that she lacked true intellectuality, which made her admire it all the more in others. Many of these intellectually inclined friends had leftist leanings. A prime reason Alma had insisted on making this trip with her husband was to observe the communist regime first-hand. While he remained unimpressed, she saw much in it to commend and decided that Maria and Efrem Jr. would benefit from a winter in Soviet schools.

The weeks of rest and ideological pondering in Sochi did nothing to bolster Alma's flagging strength. When Zimbalist finally began his tour, it was thought best for her to stay at the resort with Ruth Dodge. The children left with their father for the first Moscow concert. Saidenberg's bride went along too, and with typical consideration Zimbalist gave up his preferred lower berth to make her more comfortable on the trip. She remained in Moscow while they toured.

Saidenberg remembered their first performance: 'It was an afternoon concert at the Moscow Conservatory. I started the piano introduction of whatever we were playing. When I came to the violin entry, there was no entry forthcoming. I stopped and looked around. In the front row, right under Zimbalist's nose, was an old man reading a copy of *Pravda*. Zimbalist stared at him for a moment. Finally, the man looked up from the paper, and Zimbalist said, kindly, "Nye chitaite, pajallstuh" ("Please stop reading"). The old man, completely unflustered, folded up the paper and the concert went on.'

Maria was enrolled in a school in Moscow; Merfe (Efrem Jr.'s new nickname) was taken to one in Kiev. There Zimbalist was asked to hear a very talented brother and sister, Emil and Elisaveta Gilels (his suggestion that they come to the Curtis Institute to study with him and Hofmann came to nothing).

While her husband toured, Alma had to be checked into a hospital in Moscow. They met there at tour's end and formulated plans. Zimbalist had concerts in Kaunas, Vilna and Riga; from there he would continue on to Poland. Alma would travel with Ruth Dodge to take the cure at the Czech spa Karlovy Vary. Eleanor Saidenberg headed for Paris to meet her mother and presently sail on the French liner SS *Champlain* to Southampton, where Zimbalist and Saidenberg would join them for the voyage home. Ruth would bring Alma back to the United States; Marcia persuaded them to stop off in Salzburg on the way and spoke of the piercing shock she had when she saw her mother on the platform. Alma was emaciated — Marcia doubted she weighed much over a hundred pounds. Nor when Marcia took her mother to hear Arturo Toscanini conduct *Fidelio* did Alma's old mentor recognize her backstage, her physical deterioration was so great. Yet, weak and tired as she was, Alma was full of enthusiasm about the Soviet Union. Marcia found out later that she had been a patient in the diagnostic clinic in Moscow reserved for the Russian top brass, where she and her husband were told, for the first time, that she had cirrhosis of the liver.

Meanwhile Zimbalist, struggling under the brunt of Alma's mortal diagnosis, was on the way to an engagement in Lodz. Two additional concerts had been scheduled in Poland — a recital in Krakow and a concerto with the Warsaw Philharmonic. Aware that Zimbalist and Saidenberg were coming from Russia, the Nazis made their crossing of eastern Prussia as difficult as possible. The harassed travelers were landed on the wrong train in Warsaw, taking them hours out of their way. They finally arrived, dead tired, in Lodz, where no sooner had they checked into their hotel than the local impresario came by. He said that the performance had been canceled because he had been unable to obtain a required work permit from the local police. He wasn't sure about the status of the Krakow and Warsaw concerts. He left.

Zimbalist sat on his bed, dazed and worried sick about Alma. At this point they had been on the road nearly six months. He turned to Saidenberg. 'What should we do, Teddy — go on to Krakow?' 'You know what I'd like to do,' came Saidenberg's answer. 'I'd like to do the same.' Zimbalist's vote clinched it.

In the hotel lobby was a Thomas Cook branch. Saidenberg went down to change their train tickets, and they left quietly without even unpacking, heading west instead. In Berlin they separated with plans to meet in Holland. Zimbalist was to play a concerto in Paris, and Kreisler had invited him to rest up in the interim at his home in Berlin's quiet Grunewald section. The property was on several acres and included, in addition to the main mansion, a comfortable house for the caretaker and his wife, a conservatory, and a rose garden, which was Harriet's special pride. All this was reduced to smoldering rubble by the Allies' 1943–44 'curtain of fire.'

Harriet was out of town, and Kreisler tried to lift his old friend's mood with wine-tasting, a passion they had always shared. 'Fritz could tell a vintage just by sniffing,' Zimbalist marveled. There was also plenty of good food and poker.

In Paris Zimbalist honored his promise to Rachmaninoff to visit the Russian Conservatory, where Rachmaninoff was an honorary director. 'If you would be so kind, Zimmie,' he had written, 'when you come please bring your violin and play specially for the professors and students for at least half an hour. You would give us a great deal of pleasure.' Zimbalist also kept his promise, to himself, to visit Glazunov. When the composer died only months later, Zimbalist lost the last of the formative figures from his boyhood.

Paris responded to Zimbalist's playing with overwhelming enthusiasm. According to *Le Figaro*: 'This great artist has everything—an amazing technique and a rich and beautiful tone, with the whole vivified by an imaginative and human musicianship.' One member in a corner of the gallery in the Champs Élysées Theater was a young Frenchman who became a friend, Zino Francescatti. Zimbalist told an amusing anecdote about that concert: 'The Champs Élysées Theatre was owned by Gana Walska, a fabulously wealthy beauty who had been married and divorced half a dozen times. Long after I returned to New York my manager mentioned that he still hadn't received a bill for the rental of the theater. Gana came to our house for dinner, and I asked her about it. "But Efrem, you're a friend," she answered. "I don't charge my friends. It's my husbands who have to pay up!"'

Zimbalist hooked up with Saidenberg for a recital in The Hague. They also did an RCA broadcast to the United States from Hilversum, ferried to England for a Queen's Hall concert (it too was destroyed a few seasons later in an air raid), then boarded the *Champlain* to rejoin Eleanor and her mother for the homeward voyage. The first evening their attention was drawn to four young men sitting to one side in the dining-room. Nursing black eyes and bruises, they 'looked like thugs,' Saidenberg recalled. 'As we passed by one of them called my name. I turned round and recognized a cellist friend, Bedrich Vaska. The four men were the New York String Quartet. They had been touring Europe and had just come from Italy, where they had a terrible experience. In Rome there had been a Fascist parade honoring Mussolini. As they stood by the road watching, some soldiers got out of line and started beating them up. When they reported it to the U.S. Embassy they were advised to go back to the United States as soon as possible. Every attempt was made on diplomatic levels to hush up the incident.'

Saidenberg resigned after the tour: his new bride had greater ambitions for him than that of mere accompanist. Back at The Rafters, Alma spent most of her time resting but was able to marshal her energies sufficiently to allow for a return to semi-normal social life. The remorseless grip of her disease was worsened by a catastrophe in summer 1936: Alma struck and killed a thirteen-year-old girl while driving in nearby Torrington. The child had run out from between parked cars. Civil action was taken against her, resulting in payment of damages. Although she was completely exonerated of negligence, the experience was nevertheless devastating to Alma.

Alma began her visits to the Rockefeller Institute, a research facility at which only the Rockefellers themselves and very close friends were actually treated. The institute was run by Simon Flexner, brother of family friend Abraham Flexner. Friendship aside, there was a more significant reason for her admittance: an eminent research pathologist at the institute was engaged in the study of cirrhosis. Well aware of the hopelessness of her case, Alma felt that she could contribute to a bank of scientific knowledge useful in saving other lives and elected to be a guinea pig for any, and every, experimental treatment. However badly she felt, she was courageous enough to hide her suffering, always presenting a cheerful picture when friends dropped in for a quiet card game or chat. Meanwhile, although it was an unimaginable pressure to continue his concert activities at such a time, Zimbalist's schedule was unremitting.

Back in the Soviet Union Maria and Merfe were bored. 'We didn't even try to get anything out of school,' Efrem Jr. says. 'School was hardly the word for it; about the only things I learned were some wonderful vodka recipes. We went through thousands of rubles, buying everything from diamonds to a grand piano. We would wake up at 4 p.m., take a Russian lesson at five, dinner at six and then toddle off to the theater at seven. Afterwards we would spend hours in the Hotel Metropole bar and take the 3 a.m. sleigh home.' Their jollity was hampered only by the weather. The light clothing that had sufficed in Sochi didn't equip them against the advent of winter 1935–36, and more suitable attire was not readily available for purchase. After much effort they were able to find a couple of thick fur coats to bundle over their summer togs. Having exhausted theater prospects in Moscow and Kiev, they conspired to leave school and meet in Leningrad. Efrem Jr. went ahead to scout out the territory. He checked into a hotel and entered the dining room. After an interminable wait a hefty, disobliging waiter approached his table and kicked off the following testy repartee: 'You Amerikanski?'

'Yes.'

'What are you doing in glorious Union of Soviet Socialist Republics?'

'My sister and I came with our father, who just left.'

'And who is your father?'

'A musician, Efrem Zimbalist.'

'What was he doing here?'

'He was giving concerts.'

'Does he play with the Leningrad Philharmonic?'

'Sometimes. And sometimes he plays alone.'

'Does he give many concerts?'

'He plays concerts all the time.'

'Do many people attend these concerts?'

'A great many people do.'

The waiter eyed the youngster in obvious disbelief and sneered, 'He must be very good for people to come to hear a cymbal player.' Shades of Budapest 1909!

Although his days of round-the-globe concertizing tours were over, Zimbalist was in constant demand within the United States and in Europe. Bookings were now done by George Engles at NBC. Saidenberg's place was taken by his cousin, Vladimir Sokoloff, who had been acting as Zimbalist's class accompanist. On early U.S. tours Zimbalist had performed with Sokoloff's uncle Nikolai, founder and first conductor of the Cleveland Orchestra. Vladimir (or Billy, as Zimbalist called him) remained with him for the rest of his concert career — some thirty years — excepting the period Sokoloff spent in Special Services during World War II.

Sokoloff remembered how things started: 'It was so casual. I was just playing my regular schedule in the studio when he said, "Would you like to be my accompanist?" I was flabbergasted — never in my wildest dreams did I think I would be asked to fill so important a post. I was a young kid and had had no experience except playing in school and a few outside concerts that had been arranged for me. The end of August I went up to The Rafters, and we rehearsed solidly for two weeks.'

On 6 September 1936 they sailed aboard the USS *Scanpenn* from Hoboken, New Jersey, to Helsinki, on the first leg of a tour that would span the length and breadth of Europe. As Sokoloff told it:

> Zimbalist took two programs: 'La Folia' or Vitali's 'Chaconne' as an opener, followed by either the Mendelssohn or Glazunov Concerto; next we would play the Chausson 'Poème' and Ravel's 'Tzigane' as a pair, or the Strauss Sonata; on both programs he would do Ysaÿe's 'Ballade,' and we would end with either 'Zigeunerweisen' or his 'Coq d'Or Fantasy.' Then would come the encores: Chopin's Mazurka in a, some Hartmann arrangements or his particular favorites, Tor Aulin's 'Berceuse' and the 'Impromptu,' which he played so brilliantly. Right from the start he liked me to be able to play these short pieces without the music and made a habit, at performances, of selecting the encores he knew I had not brought along. Once the season started Zimbalist never saw any need to rehearse further. He was not a persistent 'grinder' in the sense that interpretation or ensemble had to be molded into a concrete pattern, never to be altered. In fact, I can truthfully say that every performance was a new experience. I learned a great deal from him, not only about accompanying but also about piano playing — it is a well-known fact that he was a fine pianist and could sit down at the keyboard and play anything by memory.
>
>   Once at Curtis vocal auditions a huge brute (he must have been six foot eleven) walked into the room and handed me the accompaniments to his selections. One was in very poor manuscript and transposed down to the key of d-sharp minor to

accommodate his deep bass. The part was covered with double sharps and smudged ink—absolutely illegible. When we got to it I announced to the examining judges: 'Sorry, I can't make head or tail out of this.' Zimbalist came over to have a look and recognized it as an aria from Anton Rubinstein's obscure opera *The Demon*. Having heard it as a kid, and certainly never in the fifty-odd years since, he sat down at the piano and accompanied the singer faultlessly from memory. We were all awestruck.

The *Scanpenn* was a twenty-five-passenger freighter. 'Much cheaper than the fashionable liners—also much slower,' Sokoloff laughed. They spent the eighteen days aboard in a time-honored fashion: playing poker or gin rummy. They were just finishing a round downstairs in their cabin when the *Scanpenn* docked. Sokoloff, anxious not to miss a single new experience on his first trip abroad, wanted to disembark at once. Zimbalist, sadly, sounded world-weary. 'Sit down and deal the cards, Billy—all cities look alike after a while.'

Sokoloff gave these impressions of Zimbalist on the road:

> Every morning I would hear him practicing, very slowly, with a mute, for about an hour. He never 'sawed away' at passages the way I had heard many players do. For concerts the procedure was either to meet downstairs in the hotel lobby, or if I was ready a little earlier, I would go to his room. He taught me to use a code knock, and told me this story as explanation: 'Shortly after I began teaching at the Curtis Institute I was staying at the Warwick Hotel. There was a knock at my door. When I opened it a woman pushed me aside and entered my room, threatening to make a scandal unless I gave her money. I was afraid and told her that, while I had very little cash, I could give her a check. Foolishly she agreed and I made the check out for $700. She took it and left. I immediately phoned the police, they sent some men to my bank, and when she came in they arrested her.' After that experience he was very careful about opening his hotel door unless the 'signal' was used.

Leopold Auer thought enough about concert nerves to devote a chapter to the subject in his book on violin playing. He quotes Zimbalist, age twenty, admitting to him that he was generally 'greatly agitated before coming onto the stage.' But Sokoloff had an opposite impression of the seasoned Zimbalist:

> He was completely calm before concerts and would sit quietly, often joking. There were only two places we played where he was sufficiently concerned to want to go over a few spots right beforehand: the Curtis Institute and Carnegie Hall. Otherwise he was very placid and amiable. Onstage his demeanor was the same. He tuned quietly and started, without any of the histrionics one so often sees. While playing he held his violin very high, adding to an overall sense of nobility. His acknowledgment of the applause, with a gentle smile, was modest and dignified. He had a wonderful stage presence and always left the audience feeling ingratiated. On the European tour he played on his Strad, but there were periods later when he would switch between it and his Guadagnini — he never seemed fussy, unlike many other violinists. And, when we went to places where the accommodations were not the best, or the food or traveling conditions were bad, he always took things in such good humor. After the European concerts there would be many colleagues and old friends backstage — he invariably suggested dinner and would spend money lavishly.

They concertized through Scandinavia. In Bergen Zimbalist collaborated with his Russian conductor-friend Issai Dobrowen in the Brahms Concerto — he recalled that during rehearsals King Haakon listened with the score perched conspicuously on his lap. From Norway he and Sokoloff traveled south via Estonia and Latvia, playing in such places as Riga and Dvinsk (Daugavpils). They passed through eastern Prussia, where Zimbalist and Saidenberg had so much trouble the year before. The contrast within relatively so few miles was striking: everywhere on the streets of Dvinsk were Orthodox Jews with their yarmulkas and braided hair, and throughout the Baltic countries, billboards announced concerts by 'Ephraim' Zimbalist. (This spelling didn't please him.)

In Lodz Zimbalist met Emanuel Bay's father, who proudly reported that his son was now traveling the world with Heifetz. There was an amusing incident before the concert there. Zimbalist and Sokoloff were waiting backstage about seven-thirty when the local manager arrived. 'Maestro, is everything all right?' he asked Zimbalist. 'Just fine.' 'How are the lights?' 'Fine.' 'How is the temperature?' 'Everything is fine, thank you,' Zimbalist assured him. The manager went on: 'Maestro, this is a very poor community, and we have many people in outlying areas who can't afford concert tickets. Would you mind if we broadcast your performance for them?' Again, 'Fine.' The manager breathed a sigh of relief and felt free to explain to Zimbalist:

> You know, Mischa Elman was here recently, and we went through a terrible time with him because *nothing* was fine. The lights were all wrong, the piano was no good, and when he walked onstage to see some empty seats in the front rows he made an announcement: 'I want everyone to move forward, because Elman does not play to empty chairs.' When I requested permission to broadcast the concert he asked, 'How much will you pay?' I answered, 'This is a poor town. How much do you want?' He thought for a minute and said, 'Well, when I play in New York and the concert is broadcast I get $2,000. I'll give you permission to do it for $1,500.' I was astounded. 'Fifteen hundred? Maestro, that's 35,000 zlotys—there aren't that many zlotys in Lodz!'

On this tour Zimbalist appeared for the first time in Vienna, with the Mendelssohn Concerto and the Vienna Symphony under Oswald Kabasta. He also gave a recital. Afterward, backstage, a man presented him with a card that read 'Franz Drdla, composer.' Zimbalist was tickled. There must have been few violinists alive who were not acquainted with his syrupy 'Souvenir.' (To date it has been recorded over two hundred times, twice by Zimbalist himself.)

From Switzerland they did an RCA 'Magic Key' broadcast, the network's weekly Sunday afternoon showcase featuring popular concert artists. There was a side trip to play with the Concertgebouw in Amsterdam. Within days of the concert Bronislaw Huberman was giving a recital in town, and Zimbalist, remembering his unfavorable impression in New York in 1921, stayed to hear him again. Huberman had been stirring intense feelings throughout Europe since his refusal to play in Germany after the Nazis had taken power, stated in a letter to Furtwängler. In spring 1936 interest was heightened when, in an open letter published by the *Manchester Guardian*, he condemned the growth of Nazism and announced plans to form an orchestra for refugee Jewish musicians in Palestine. (Toscanini conducted the first concert, with Huberman as soloist.)

Also creating a stir in Europe that year was the Curtis String Quartet— Jascha Brodsky, Charles Jaffe (both Zimbalist students), Max Aronoff and Orlando Cole. The group's original name was the Swastika Quartet, one they quickly dropped with the Nazis' advent. Zimbalist heard them in Holland— 'They were like a breath of fresh air.' They talked of home and touring experiences, then the conversation turned to Huberman. Zimbalist mentioned having gone to hear him. Evidently his initial poor impression had not been erased, and Zimbalist's comment to the quartet became a classic example of his cutting wit: 'They say he thinks. I think he stinks!'

His remark was not aimed as much at Huberman as against an entire school of thought that he (and others of his background) predictably found unappealing. During the turbulent transition years signaling the end of the golden era of violin virtuosos and resounding even today, war waged between the advocates of 'sheer virtuosity' and those who espoused 'serious musicianship.' The gap was gradually bridged, often resulting in performances that led to Harold Schonberg's 1985 remark, in the preface to his *The Glorious Ones*: 'By and large, artists are literal-minded and careful, and there is a dreadful unanimity of approach. Performers seem much too worried about the text and not enough about its message.' How objective. Most modern critics, with their purportedly privileged insight into the true intent of a composer's score, have only themselves to thank for stamping out the individuality inherent in the old-style virtuoso.

By current critical standards Zimbalist may be judged old-fashioned. In historical context, however, he was among the first to expound musical principles above mere 'violinistic gratification' (Oscar Shumsky's term). At the same time, Zimbalist was one of violinism's supreme virtuosos, complete with all the entitling qualifications. Such elite virtuosos, then as now, are equipped with an unfailingly beautiful tone, faultless intonation and technical facility, plus a certain intrinsic interpretive 'sizzle,' to quote Itzhak Perlman. Virtuosos of this caliber for the most part use these qualities to serve the end of sincere musical expression. So did Zimbalist. But, like other performers of his schooling, he was loath to condone performers of purportedly lofty artistic ideals who lacked technical refinement. It was the age-old question of medium-versus-message. In the playing of Huberman, Zimbalist disliked a certain roughness of detail, even when the architectural outline was inspired. Huberman's style fell short in the areas of finesse and elegance, two indispensable words in the Auer vocabulary.

Belgrade and Budapest were the next ports of call. When Zimbalist applied for visas at the Yugoslav consulate in Vienna he was questioned sharply: 'How much money will you get for your concert?'

'10,000 dinars [around $100]'

'What are you going to do with that money?'

'Probably spend it.'

'I'm afraid you may try to take that money out, so I must refuse you a visa.'

Zimbalist pressed his case: 'That amount of money is much less than I pay my accompanist. The only reason I accepted the concert was to visit Belgrade.'

Officialdom relented—he and Sokoloff got their visas. The hall was less than half full at the concert. At intermission the applause had scarcely ceased when Zimbalist's manager burst in, beaming. 'What can he be so happy about? The hall is empty and the applause meager,' Zimbalist wondered aloud to Sokoloff. 'Good news,' boomed the manager, 'I have just had word that Huberman is coming next month!' ('Huberman was extremely popular in the Balkans,' Zimbalist drily commented.)

There was a recital in Budapest and an appearance with orchestra. The concerto was the Mendelssohn, and Tibor Zelig, later a student of Lea Luboschutz's at Curtis, remembered Zimbalist playing the last movement so fast that the orchestra had a hard time keeping up. Perhaps Zimbalist had a train to catch: once in South Carolina, Sokoloff recalled, there was concern that, with the recital scheduled for 8:15, they wouldn't make a 10:30 train, the only one that could get them to the next engagement on time. During intermission Zimbalist calmly took a pencil to the second half of the program, sketching in numerous lengthy cuts. 'It ended up a complicated road map,' Sokoloff told, 'but we made our train. It always amazed me that, playing as he invariably did by memory, he never forgot any of the last-minute cuts he marked in my part.' The Budapest recital elicited the *Buda-Pester Lloyd*'s highest approval: 'One of the very great violinists. Under the magic of his tone the souls of his listeners are overpowered.'

Traveling west on the Orient Express they had a lengthy stop in Berlin. Zimbalist refused to leave the train and spent three or four hours quietly in his seat. Sokoloff, who did step off to look around, remembered seeing troops everywhere, a disturbing sight.

From England Zimbalist took the *Queen Mary* to New York for a Carnegie Hall recital marking the twenty-fifth anniversary of his U.S. debut. Samuel Chotzinoff was the accompanist; Zimbalist temporarily relinquished Sokoloff to Oscar Shumsky, who arrived in London to embark on his first European tour, sponsored by the Curtis Institute. Ironically, this time because of a pogrom, Shumsky too was prevented from playing in Lodz. When the *Queen Mary* docked in New York Zimbalist told reporters: 'In the Central European countries people just go through the motions of carrying on their regular lives, but their minds seem to be on only one thing—the threat of war.' He also noted that his arrival, 18 November 1936, coincided with the eighteenth birthday of his son, who, having put aside his violin, was now a freshman at Yale.

Zimbalist hadn't worked with Chotzinoff for many years but for sentimental reasons had engaged him for the Carnegie anniversary. After Heifetz had replaced him with Emanuel Bay, Chotzi had been more involved in writing books and musical criticism than in daily piano practice. His performance reflected this, and observers reported him nervous and not up to the task. Nonetheless there was considerable nostalgia to fall back on. And reviews were positive, as in the *New York Sun*: 'A great and brilliant audience received the violinist with prolonged applause, and there was a spirit of joy in the air from beginning to end of the recital, for Zimbalist is not merely popular; he is profoundly admired and held in singular affection by a very large public.' Olin Downes wrote, 'Zimbalist is a musician first, a virtuoso and box office figure second, and it is significant that in the years which have passed since he came here as a young man of twenty-one he has steadily risen and developed as he was certain to do, and that his immense following today is as substantial as his accomplishments and as genuine as his selfless devotion to his art.'

A big anniversary season followed, with Sokoloff once again at his post. Before leaving on tour Zimbalist was fêted at a jamboree thrown by the

New York Beethoven Society (Harold Bauer, president) on 9 December 1936. It was the first time anyone had been thus honored, and a dinner attended by two hundred notables was followed by 'The Life of Zimmie,' a skit in twenty scenes. The sketch was written by Chotzinoff and featured Jascha Heifetz in the leading role; Marc Connelly narrated.

In the opening scene Heifetz, in swaddling clothes, portrayed the infant Zimbalist with his parents, played by Pierre Luboshutz and Mrs. Thomas Finletter (daughter of Walter Damrosch), who thought it time for their son to choose a career. The father placed before the young genius a triangle, a salami and a violin and said, 'If he chooses the triangle he will be a conductor, if he grabs at the salami he will be a tenor, but if he stretches his little hand toward the violin he will be the greatest of violin players.' The infant immediately reached for the salami, though when the violin was forced into his arms, commenced a sonata. His troubles began when his teacher learned that his name was Efrem. 'What! Your name doesn't end with "scha"?' he exclaimed. 'No violin virtuoso ever had any name but Jascha, Mischa, or Toscha!' The sketch ended with Zimmie celebrating his anniversary at home, where he receives telegrams from many colleagues, all mentioning their own triumphs and forgetting about his own commemorative.

Zimbalist was obviously much in the public's eye and heart. But for all this he was denied the satisfaction he might otherwise have enjoyed at this juncture of his career. There was constant worry about Alma, and by 1937 Efrem Jr. was having problems at Yale. He later elaborated: 'I was kicked out of college at nineteen because, frankly, I was behaving like a silly ass. I had run up a mountain of bills, dashing around buying things and living very high. I was too afraid to go home and face the situation. Finally, chasing a showgirl across the country, I was jailed for the night for speeding through a small town and trying to bribe the officer who arrested me. My father very quietly went there and cleaned up the mess.' (Forty-odd years later, when everyone mistakenly thought that Zimbalist was on his deathbed, Efrem Jr. sat at his side. 'Is there anything you want to tell me?' he asked. His father smiled. 'You know, darling, when you were nineteen at Yale you caused me some worry.' It was the first and only mention Zimbalist ever made of the incident.)

Alma's condition seemed slightly improved in summer 1937, and, knowing what allure Arizona and New Mexico held for her husband, she suggested that he and Efrem Jr. take a trip together. 'Daddy loved the West, it was one of the real fantasies of his life,' Efrem Jr. says. They drove to the Southwest in a brand new Plymouth. Somewhere in New Mexico they pulled over and asked a hayseed sitting by the road how to get to Albuquerque. The man slowly stood, pushed back his hat, took out a bandanna and mopped his brow. Chewing on a wad of tobacco, he scratched his head and thought hard. Finally he spat, rubbed his nose, then drawled, 'Albuquerque, huh?' Another chew and a spit. 'You did say Albuquerque?' Zimbalist nodded. A chew and a spit. 'Let's see—Albuquerque?'

'You have been so very kind,' Zimbalist smiled, putting the car into gear, 'but it sounds like too long a story.'

The Grand Canyon was a very special experience for them both. On the homeward journey they were stopped by a highway patrolman just outside Chicago. 'Are you Efrem Zimbalist?' the officer asked. Zimbalist nodded and received the news that his wife's condition had worsened and that he should return home without delay. Taking turns driving nonstop, he and Efrem Jr. made it to The Rafters in twenty-one hours. They arrived to find that Alma, once again, had rallied.

Merfe decided to take a stab at an acting career. Diana Steiner, a Curtis student at the time, remembers her parents giving Zimbalist a ride to New York. Mr. Steiner drove, she sat beside him on her mother's lap, and Zimbalist was in the back leaning forward in earnest conversation with her parents: 'Can you believe it?' Zimbalist moaned. 'My son wants to be an actor! What can I do?'

On 16 August 1937, Zimbalist battled the heat and poor acoustics at New York's Lewisohn Stadium to play for the largest audience of his career. 'The eminent violinist,' reported the *Herald Tribune*, 'whose presence drew an audience of nearly ten thousand persons, assigned himself a substantial evening's work, playing both the Glazunov and Brahms concertos, and received the prolonged applause of genuine warmth reserved for those few artists whose long careers are remembered gratefully.' Zimbalist also participated in a benefit concert at Carnegie Hall for victims of the colossal January 1937 Ohio–Mississippi Valley flood; $30,000 was raised.

The *New York Times* (21 February 1938) noted, 'An innovation was introduced in the playing of the second movement of the Bach Concerto for two violins by Mr. Zimbalist and Jascha Heifetz, but only Mr. Zimbalist was present.' Heifetz, who was playing a concerto in Philadelphia the same evening, had just enough time to broadcast his part from station KYW,

Philadelphia, over a special radio transmission wire to Carnegie Hall. Loudspeakers in the hall picked up his playing, and Zimbalist joined him. The season ended with a whirlwind tour through Scandinavia, France and England.

Arturo Toscanini and the Zimbalists had remained close friends. Before the NBC Symphony was created for Toscanini, they sat with the Maestro listening to Bruno Walter conducting the Philharmonic in a Brahms symphony. At its conclusion, before Zimbalist had a chance to ask him what he thought of it, Toscanini, pocket watch in hand, snapped, 'Half a minute too long.' In March 1938 Alma was strong enough to help Chotzinoff organize a surprise party for the Maestro to celebrate the end of his first season with the new NBC Symphony. Toscanini hated surprises. At the party he sat in a corner next to Alma and spoke only to her all evening, completely ignoring the entertainment—a burlesque show whose cast included Zimbalist, Heifetz and Vladimir Horowitz. Toscanini was about to leave for an extended stay in Italy and, when he said goodbye, wondered if he'd ever see her again.

As always brave, Alma didn't try to hide her jaundiced emaciation from the public and with indomitable will summoned enough energy to accompany her husband to important events. One such was when her friend Troyanovsky, the Russian ambassador, invited Zimbalist to be the entertaining artist at a state dinner at the Russian embassy in Washington. With the advent of the Bolsheviks in 1918 America had severed diplomatic relations with Russia. Only within the last five years, under FDR's administration, had the United States recognized the Soviet set-up. Because of this recent restoration of amicability, the dinner was a big event. Nellie Lee Bok, one of Zimbalist's future in-laws, remembered Alma's courage at that Washington affair: 'She was exceedingly gracious, but obviously desperately ill.' Eudice Shapiro remembers that courage, too, when the Zimbalists attended a concert by her Trio Classique at the home of President Roosevelt's mother; despite the yellow hue of her skin, in shocking contrast to the white dress she wore, Alma still looked beautiful.

She spent fall 1938 at The Rafters, distracting herself with needlepoint. Her husband was often away playing concerts. Vladimir Sokoloff: 'On tour his concern for Alma was so great that he never stopped talking about her. But he felt he had to keep busy.' Maria had recently married and was away with her husband. Efrem Jr. was very involved in attending the

Neighborhood Playhouse in New York, where his fellow students were Gregory Peck, Eli Wallach and Tony Randall.

On 21 September the Eastern seaboard was devastated by the country's worst hurricane on record. Six hundred died, and property damage was estimated at more than $1 billion. Phone and electric lines were down and Marcia, returned from Salzburg and frantically concerned for her mother's safety, had a hectic drive next morning from New York on roads that were sometimes under feet of water and obstructed by fallen trees. The Rafters had survived without major damage, and when Zimbalist arrived days later he found his wife and stepdaughter safe, if frustrated because the battery-powered radio, their sole source of information from the outside world, gave only intermittent transmission.

Zimbalist remembered the hurricane for another reason: 'I was very surprised when the son of a minister friend in Winsted (about ten miles away) knocked at the door, bringing a telegram from Cecil B. DeMille offering me $5,000 to fly out to Hollywood and play Rimsky's "Flight of the Bumblebee" on the Lux Radio Theater.' DeMille and Jack Benny were scheduled to appear together as guests on the show. Benny had been bragging to DeMille that, at just under ninety seconds, he could perform the 'Bumblebee' faster than any other violinist. William de Mille persuaded Cecil to put up the money to bring Zimbalist out to challenge Benny's smug claim, as a gag. Zimbalist takes up the story: 'Somehow I got to an airport and caught a night plane, arriving in Los Angeles the next morning. I was met at the airport. "What time do the music stores open?" I asked. "Probably not for a while. Why?" "Oh," I said, "I must buy the Bumblebee." He had never played the piece.

Between the second and third acts of the show, which aired on 26 September 1938, Zimbalist got behind the mike with Cecil DeMille. It was a brief interview. DeMille: 'What do you think of the show so far?' Zimbalist: 'Not too much.' DeMille then informed listeners of a bet between him and Jack Benny that a violinist couldn't be found who could play the 'Bumblebee' in less than Jack's eighty-six seconds. The stopwatch rolled. 'I finished in fifty-eight seconds, packed up and flew home,' Zimbalist laughingly recalled. 'They must have been the highest paid fifty-eight seconds in musical history. Poor Rimsky didn't earn a fifth of that for writing the entire opera [*Tsar of the Sultan*].'

Helen Mobert, Zimbalist's representative at NBC Artists, launched publicity for his 1938–39 season with the announcement of a series of five Monday evening concerts at Town Hall devoted to all the violin and keyboard sonatas of Bach, Beethoven and Brahms. It was the first time such a cycle was to be heard in New York, and judging from the attention it received in the press and the large audiences that were drawn, the idea was a good one. Of the opening concert on 10 October 1938, *The New Yorker* opined, 'Mr. Zimbalist as usual gave beautiful performances, making fine music without any professorial overtones.'

The remaining concerts were scheduled for 17, 24 and 31 October and 7 November. Alma attended the first three in the series, returning after each to the serenity of The Rafters. She was clearly sinking but vowed to reach the needlepointing goal she had set herself: completion of eight seat-cushion covers for Marcia. A few lines in the *New York Times* indicated that the end was approaching: 'Due to unforeseen circumstances Efrem Zimbalist's last two Town Hall concerts have been postponed to December 10 and 17 — tickets already purchased will be honored on those dates.'

Alma spoke matter-of-factly to Marcia about her funeral arrangements. In *Too Strong for Fantasy* Marcia gave the full exchange: 'I was not as strong as she; suddenly I said, "Oh, must you put us through this?" She pulled herself upright in her bed. Her huge sunken eyes widened as they used to do when I had been naughty as a child. "Look here," she said. "Who's doing this dying, anyway? If I can have the guts to do it well, you can have the guts to listen to me now!"'

Marcia accompanied her mother on the last trip to the hospital. By the time Zimbalist arrived with the other children, Alma had slipped into a coma, yet her strong constitution held out. Zimbalist talked softly about the ghastly memory: 'The poor darling suffered so terribly, but she just *couldn't* die.' He and Marcia sat by the bedside; Maria and Efrem Jr. waited outside.

The end finally came on 27 October 1938. Alma was fifty-four. Just three days before, she had finished the last needlepoint chair cover.

ABOVE: With Edna St. Vincent Millay at The Rafters, 1940.

UPPER RIGHT: Zimbalist and Feuermann resting in Rittenhouse Square, en route to Philadelphia Orchestra rehearsal, 1942.

RIGHT: Wedding portrait, Lyndenwood, 6 July 1943.

UPPER RIGHT: The Zimbalist residences, 10 Cornwall Terrace, London ... (Courtesy Zelda Malan)

LOWER RIGHT: ... and 227 East 49th Street, New York.

UPPER LEFT: The Rafters, Connecticut (1926 Plymouth outside).

CENTER LEFT: 1816 and 1818 Delancey Place, Philadelphia. (Courtesy Irving Ludwig)

LOWER LEFT: Party circa 1943. Left to right, Eugene Ormandy, Mary Zimbalist, Zimbalist, Edith Braun. Efrem Jr., in uniform, stands behind her.

UPPER LEFT: Rehearsing the Brahms 'Double' with Piatigorsky and Hilsberg for Curtis Institute twenty-fifth anniversary performance, 1949.

CENTER LEFT: Rehearsing Menotti's concerto with the Philadelphia Orchestra, 9 December 1952. Jacob Krachmalnick is concertmaster.

BELOW: Zimbalist with pupils John Dalley, Michael Tree and Toshiya Eto in Rockport, Maine.

ABOVE: With Efrem Jr. on the set of *The Deep Six*, 1958.

RIGHT: Soviet violinist David Oistrakh and Leonid Kogan greet their American colleague at Moscow's Vnukovo airport, 1958.

ABOVE: Three generations of Efrem Zimbalists, 1959.

UPPER RIGHT: Contestants and jury about to enter the Great Hall of Moscow's Tchaikovsky Conservatory for the official beginning of the competition, 1958. Van Cliburn, who would win first piano prize, can be seen in the crowd just to Zimbalist's left.

LOWER RIGHT: The jury voting, 1958. Oistrakh is on Zimbalist's right. Khachaturian is on his left.

ABOVE: Demonstrating at a lesson, Curtis, 1968.

RIGHT: Zimbalist's last formal portrait with violin, Reno, 1978.

BELOW: Preparations at Zimbalist's home in Reno for the author's 1976 recordings of sonatas by Zimbalist Sr. and Jr.

Upper left: Guest of honor at Curtis Institute celebration, 30 April 1978. Next to Zimbalist are 'Little' Stephanie, Efrem Jr. and Menotti. Eleanor Sokoloff is directly behind Stephanie, and Jacob Krachmalnick can be seen standing at the back of the hall. (Photo by Henry Grossman)

Lower left: Zimbalist's last visit to The Rafters, his favorite home, with the Sokoloffs and granddaughter Nancy, August 1984. He died six months later.

Below: Zimbalist's final posed portrait, 27 April 1982, intended for his biography. He wore a black suit and tie to match Leopold Auer's attire in the photo the Professor gave him in 1909.

CHAPTER 20

Mary Louise Curtis Bok and the C.I.M.

(1938–1947)

Zimbalist asked the Musical Art Quartet to play the slow movement from Beethoven's Op. 18 No. 1 at Alma's funeral. She was buried near The Rafters, in New Hartford's Town Hill Cemetery, and had chosen her own epitaph: 'From All My Masters Have I Learned.' Soon after, Zimbalist resumed touring, and Sokoloff recalled that many nights, after they had retired to their Pullman, Zimbalist would draw the curtain to his lower bunk, and Sokoloff, opposite, heard him sobbing the night away.

The last 'Three Bs' concerts took place in December 1938. A friend paid Zimbalist tribute in his memory of the series:

> One went into Town Hall harried by the metropolitan day to escape whatever may be one's industry. Musicians would go in to escape the industry of their music. Of course, the officiant at these vespers had to be above and beyond the herd, else you would not obtain what you came for, confession and absolution at the hands of art raised to the absolvatory power. I felt that Zimbalist was the perfect officiant. He had passed through all the stages of technical and mental growth and had put the course behind him. One might have said that he was on the last lap; a little spent, cooled off before the finish and able to coast in with style. And he had adaptability, almost unheard of among the virtuosos of his rank. He could, when required, 'accompany' his pianist, with both men utterly subservient to a third man unseen on the stage, the composer.

The bleakness of that Christmas and the thought of living alone in the big
New York house was unbearable. Zimbalist put it on the market, auctioned
off most of its contents and moved with Efrem Jr. and a few belongings into
a Park Avenue apartment. In a beautifully inlaid wooden box Zimbalist
saved some two hundred notes and telegrams of condolence; these were
moved to The Rafters, along with other keepsakes (the Fishers Island property, severely damaged in the hurricane of '38, he sold to the Coast Guard).
And he assumed with great reverence, in accordance with her wishes,
administration of the large inheritance Alma had left her children.

On the surface Zimbalist was tending to his obligations quite normally:
when not on tour, he went as usual to Philadelphia to teach his students.
But as time passed deep changes in his personality became evident. He
developed a distaste for material things and sought to dispose of all physical aspects of his past. Along with the furniture and trimmings of 227 East
49th Street, a lot of first editions and a good percentage of his Orientalia
were auctioned off too. The collection was so large that Parke-Bernet's
catalog of the items resembled a hefty paperback. Sokoloff overheard
Zimbalist on the phone to the gallery. 'Prices were uneven but he was disinterested, even bored, and just wanted to get rid of everything.' A first
edition of Keats's poems in the original boards, uncut, went for $950. A
copy of the Kelmscott Press edition of the works of Chaucer, bound in
white pigskin, fetched $900, while $825 was paid for a fourth folio of the
works of Shakespeare with the earliest imprint of Joseph Knight and
Francis Saunders. The collection yielded a total of $22,059, considerably
less than what it could have brought if sold by dealers.

However, judging from a January 1940 piece in the *Philadelphia Record*,
Zimbalist did retain an interest in collecting:

> 'I had too much,' says the gentle, grey-haired musician with the
> boyish blue eyes, courtly manners and soft, still somewhat gut-
> tural Russian voice. 'The scope of my collection—English and
> American things from Shakespeare down—was too wide. Now
> my collection is smaller and how shall I put it?—more intimate.
> I have an almost complete Shaw that is probably unique, a com-
> plete Edna St. Vincent Millay and a complete Sinclair Lewis. I
> only buy the authors I really like. I'm a great admirer of the work
> of Henry Handel Richardson, the Australian woman novelist,

and I have first editions of all her books. For years I tried to get something more personal, but it seemed impossible. Then a few months ago in London I came across a collected set of her works inscribed by her to her publisher.' From the gleam in his eye and the manner in which he rubbed his hands as he said this, it was evident that Zimbalist's case is a hopeless one.... 'I also play a pretty wicked hand of bridge and poker,' he says, 'and I'm [very] fond of meat balls and noodles, though you'd hardly call that a hobby.'

Despite the upbeat tone of this interview, with the loss of Alma's luminescence, Zimbalist also lost a degree of his own natural sparkle, some thought never to regain it. His demeanor became more somber and, approaching fifty, his face all at once showed traces of the years of stressful travel and concert pressures, and bereavement.

In the 1939–40 season Zimbalist and Sokoloff gave a second series of five violin and piano sonata recitals in Town Hall. After the first program the *Tribune* reported: 'When a public performer temporarily renounces the triumphs of virtuosity for the field of chamber music he is taking a great risk, for the demands of musicianship might expose a barrenness that had been safely hidden behind the black pages of running sixty-fourth notes, [but] Mr. Zimbalist reminded us again — if that were necessary — that he has nothing to fear on that score.' The series was successful both in terms of attendance and critical response, and at his manager's suggestion he took it on the road to colleges and conservatories, where the concerts were followed by open forums for faculty and students.

As early as 1934 Zimbalist had turned over the proceeds of a Carnegie Hall recital to the Anti-Nazi Fund, and at the outbreak of World War II he contributed more money, time and talent to the Allied cause. He tried to exert his influence, too. As a sponsor and vice chairman of the American-Russian Committee for Medical Aid to the U.S.S.R., he tried unsuccessfully to get Koussevitsky to join. He was also a sponsor (Pablo Casals was chairman) of the Musicians' Committee to Aid Spanish Democracy and persuaded Rachmaninoff to add his name to those of Amy Beach, John Alden Carpenter, Elizabeth Sprague Coolidge, Aaron Copland and Olin Downes, among others, to a letter urging President Roosevelt to lift the U.S. embargo against the 'legitimate' government of Spain, claiming that it served not the interests of neutrality, but of Hitler and Mussolini. In January 1941 Zimbalist gave a concert in aid of British War Relief. From 1941 to 1945, during Sokoloff's stint in the armed forces, Jacob Lateiner or Seymour Lipkin accompanied him.

Zimbalist received a note from Mary Louise Curtis Bok in the late summer of 1940 asking him to come to her summer home in Rockport, Maine, to talk about an important Curtis Institute matter. He was glad to oblige, although, considering the handful of times they had met since he joined the violin faculty, she was 'little more than a complete stranger. Her words to me were "Mr. Zimbalist, we're on the rocks. Things have been mismanaged, and in less than two years we'll have to close the Institute. Would you take the responsibility of seeing whether or not it can be saved?"'

He was stunned. During his comings and goings at Curtis he had made an effort to steer clear of politics. Forces regulating the functioning of the school were of little interest to him. All he knew was that Hofmann's resignation had been under less than spotless circumstances, ostensibly to free him for more concert work. And Zimbalist had had an indication of financial problems in 1938: 'Josef confided in me — "Our financial condition is not so good. I am opposed to it, but the board has suggested cutbacks. I know you're well fixed. Would you, just for a year or two, accept half salary?" "Josef," I answered, "of course I will, if everyone will do the same." Hofmann smiled. "I don't know how I can ask it of Salmond — he has two ex-wives to support!"' Zimbalist later laughed, 'I consented to the salary cut anyway.'

For an interim period, Hofmann's post was filled by Randall Thompson, who felt that the Institute's original goal of producing nothing but concert stars was neither realistic nor valid and that more emphasis should be placed on ensemble players and teachers. Although Hofmann had always run the school according to the spirit of the letter as it was seen by Mrs. Bok, it would be disingenuous to describe every student who had graduated from the Institute as a celebrity. Still, among students and alumni were such stellar names as Leonard Bernstein, Samuel Barber, Gian Carlo Menotti, Shura Cherkassky, Jorge Bolet, Abbey Simon, Oscar Shumsky, Boris Goldovsky and Rose Bampton. Mrs. Bok believed the original ideals of the Institute worth preserving and considered such talent justification enough for her conviction. She also believed that Zimbalist knew the school's daily workings inside out, which he didn't. But she was correct in seeing in him an ally in favor of the original premise of her brainchild. To her he seemed the logical choice to succeed Thompson.

Zimbalist described his reaction: '"Mrs. Bok, I'm flattered, but I have had no experience whatever in the running of a school. I don't know what to say." "Think it over," she suggested. I asked for two weeks to examine the books before deciding. In Philadelphia Mr. Mattis gave them to me, and I went back to New York to go over them. [Jay Mattis was the Institute's financial adviser; initially he had been engaged by Mrs. Bok's sons Curtis and Cary to put some restraints on what they considered runaway philanthropic spending by their mother.] When Mrs. Bok came back to Philadelphia I went to see her. I told her I would like to try. She was pleased, and asked what sort of salary would be acceptable. I was not sure I could succeed so I answered, "For the first year, or longer, until I prove that I can do anything, I would like to take only my usual violin teacher's salary."'

Mrs. Bok, the Curtis Board and Zimbalist reached an agreement, and his appointment was announced in 1941. He soon proved that he could, indeed, do something about the situation: his shrewdness in financial matters emerged as the salvaging factor. Zimbalist reminisced: 'When I entered the picture as director we had a few hundred thousand operating dollars left which, with a loan from a bank, was just enough for two more years. The twelve or thirteen million Mrs. Bok originally gave had been so badly handled. The school under me had to be run on less than half the budget that Hofmann had at his disposal. Well, we did it, making it a better school. On the advice of a stockbroker friend I took the money and reinvested it, eventually bringing the value of the endowment back to its original amount. It was quite a feat!' Zimbalist chuckled. 'But it seems that I had a certain gift for that sort of thing. Experience taught me. You know, in my first marriage my wife and I had a great deal of money, much of which we lost in 1929. But we were still able to earn a lot, and when she died she left nearly half a million dollars, which I put in trust for Efrem and Maria. I kept ten thousand myself, which I invested. I learned fast and with the help of an innate gift, today I am a wealthy man.' (Twenty-five years later, following the Serkin era, he was again able, by suggesting reinvestments, to improve the Institute's monetary situation.)

Zimbalist's righting of the Institute's listing financial ship involved some sacrifices and corner-cutting. Wasting of the Institute's money took many forms; the head of the chamber music department, Louis Bailly, was in Zimbalist's opinion responsible for a certain amount of it. At some point Bailly had been put in charge of assembling and maintaining a collection of instruments and bows for the Institute. It was Mrs. Bok's idea to place the collection at the disposal of students whose own instruments were inadequate. From the outset the Institute's coffers were presumed bottomless. Among those seizing the chance of dipping into the gold mine were certain instrument dealers. When Bailly made selections they charged the Institute top dollar, which included a handsome commission for Bailly. It worked well until Zimbalist happened on a violin he thought suitable for the school's collection. After consulting Mrs. Bok he ordered it and a few days later received a commission check from the dealer. Understanding at once, he turned the check over to the Institute, thereby putting an end to the system. When he took over as director, one of his first actions was to sell a large percentage of the collection. He considered it excessive: those students who were not acutely in need of a better instrument would do well to keep working on what they had, as he had had to do during his school years. He himself, at market value, bought from the collection a bow that he fancied.

One of Zimbalist's first directorial acts was to attend to his recordings, housed downstairs in the Institute's library. Since he hated listening to them and didn't intend to put students through the same displeasure, he had them thrown out, which was certainly a mistake. In later days at Curtis, most students had no concept of his artistic stature, basing their assessment on some of his latter-day post-peak performances; at that point few of his 78s had become readily available on LP.

As Zimbalist had suspected, during the Hofmann era several faculty members were hired on grounds other than those of competence: some were rumored to be Hofmann's former female companions, others society friends of his wife's. A kaffeeklatsch headed by Betty Hofmann and Lillian Kaufman (aka 'the Curtis Gazette') was privy to internal Institute policy and saw fit to influence the school's day-to-day operations. This venomous group thrived on intrigue and gossip. Zimbalist determined to end such counter-productivity, later explaining: 'I always felt we had the advantage of being a well-mannered school created by a woman with elegant manners. As director I wanted to keep backstabbing to a minimum.' With Betty Hofmann's departure Lillian's manipulative powers were constrained, and by the time a third ringleader retired, the klatsch had run out of steam.

Some thought that Zimbalist tended to take his position, and himself, too seriously. One detractor was severe: 'He developed a reputation about as democratic as the Tsar under whose aegis he studied.' Mary Bok's son Curtis put it even more bluntly: 'There's something damned imperious about Zimmie.'

Around this time a piece appeared in the *Musical Journal* in which Zimbalist's old accompanist Samuel Chotzinoff discussed the relative qualities of Kreisler, Zimbalist and Heifetz. His evaluation sheds clearer light on Zimbalist's way of doing things: 'Efrem Zimbalist is classical, remote, Olympian. [He] does not astound with super mastery like Heifetz, nor does he take one into his confidence like Kreisler. This Olympian approach is Zimbalist's individuality. If he can be compared with any other living violinist, it may be with Heifetz, whose artistic integrity and detachment he shares.' Olympian nobility, patrician intellectuality, classical reticence, orderliness—all describe not only Zimbalist's approach to music-making but also his view of directorship, which was from time to time misconstrued as an overly serious aloofness.

Cutting financial corners at Curtis proved much easier than trimming the faculty. 'My duty was to reduce in quantity, but not in quality,' Zimbalist put it. Having cleared the way he was able to rehire on a different level. Naturally he was besieged with letters from hopefuls seeking jobs. Wherever a vacancy was created he tried to get the finest replacement available. His first appointees were Barber, Menotti, Emanuel Feuermann and baritone Richard Bonelli, followed shortly by William Primrose. Zimbalist did make a few mistakes. In his own words: 'It wasn't difficult to weed out the weaklings who by hook or by crook somehow got into the Institute. But to tell a person whom you and everyone knew to be worth something that, for whatever reason, they were being dismissed?—that was probably the most painful thing I ever had to do. Elisabeth Schumann was a supreme artist and wonderful person—everyone loved her. She was one of the great lieder singers of all time, on a par with Sembrich, Frieda Hempel and Julia Culp. But it turned out that she couldn't teach. Students didn't want to study with her. Her dismissal just broke my heart, especially since I had engaged her. "Elisabeth," I told her, "you have no students." And the dear woman took it so well.' The brilliant pianist David Saperton, Hofmann's protégé, was a dismissal Zimbalist found very tough. 'It was my sad duty to tell him there was no place for him. It was particularly difficult because I admired his playing so much and he was a good teacher. But there just weren't enough students.' Richard Bonelli, because of differences with Zimbalist, was shortly asked to leave as well.

Some critics viewed Saperton's firing as part of a general sweeping out of all the Hofmann cronies. And some were against Zimbalist's appointments: 'We had an excellent man teaching cello, Felix Salmond, but I wanted to add Feuermann to the faculty. It created quite a stir. I felt strongly that there should be more than one influence in each department, to avoid any one teacher controlling a monopoly. Just like in the violin department when I later engaged Ivan Galamian, a teacher I fully believed to be a much better one than I was.' But there was no opposition from the most important quarter. 'Never in all the years I was associated with the school did Mary question my judgment. There wasn't a single argument.'

It was very important to Zimbalist to create 'an atmosphere of imagination' at Curtis. He believed that musical imagination was the most important attribute of a great performer and liked to quote German playwright Ludwig Fulder: 'If one lacks imagination one becomes a critic.' Considering his views on the field as a whole, perhaps his only odd appointment was Chotzinoff, to teach a course in music criticism.

Nellie Lee Bok, Zimbalist's stepdaughter-in-law and a member of the Curtis board for many years, told the author: 'In some ways his was a rather loose administration composed of little islands in the sense of great teachers each surrounded by their cluster of students. He felt that the teacher should be in charge of his or her own students, and he gave the faculty completely free rein.' Free rein except for one imposed detail: no classes could be held until after lunch. 'How can any student become a serious pianist or string player if they start the day with theory classes?' he asked. So he reserved mornings for practicing and individual lessons.

On 26 April 1941, Kreisler met with a serious accident just blocks from his home. Louis Lochner described the event in his biography: 'Deep in thought, he was crossing Madison Avenue [against the light and] was struck by a delivery truck. For a while he lay there bleeding, unnoticed and unrecognized. Melvin Spitalnik, a messenger boy, happened to come by, took the $16 camera he always carried with him and photographed the elderly man without the faintest idea that this snapshot would [be named] "Picture of the Week."' Dr. Aldo Santiccioli also passed by and searched the unconscious traffic casualty's pockets. There he found letters identifying

Kreisler and had him taken to Roosevelt Hospital. There were frantic calls to locate Harriet, who, like her husband, was on her way home for lunch. Head surgeon James I. Russell issued a statement: 'Mr. Kreisler has a severe head injury. It is probably a skull fracture.' For weeks Kreisler remained in a coma, and it wasn't until 23 May that the medical authorities pronounced him out of danger.

Kreisler's first public performance following the accident was on 28 January 1942 in Albany's Palace Theater. Nine months later, on Halloween, he gave a recital in Carnegie Hall. Around that time Zimbalist was having lunch in a New York hotel with Edna St. Vincent Millay and her husband. At a table nearby sat Harriet; she was surrounded by a group of women, enjoying a hearty meal and engaged in loud conversation. 'I just didn't have the heart to go over and break in,' Zimbalist remembered.

Zimbalist gave a memorable recital of his own on 20 January 1942, beginning with the Strauss Sonata and ending with a group of Paganini's most daunting pieces, including the unaccompanied 'Nel cor più non mi sento.' In the *New York World* Chotzinoff wrote, 'The characteristics of [Zimbalist's] lofty art have remained unimpaired from the time he first played in Carnegie Hall.' The *New York Herald Tribune*'s redoubtable Virgil Thomson started out by confessing his general distaste for violin recitals but went on to say: 'The evening's great success seemed to me to be due to fine technical work and genuine musicianship, and it was pleasant to observe a large musical public being completely responsive to these qualities without the artist's having recourse to the sentimental, the violent or the meretricious.' In another paper, Henry Simon wrote, 'One of the remarks attributed to Efrem Zimbalist is that a fiddler is at his best at the age of twelve; for the rest of his life he tries to hang on. [More] than forty years later [Zimbalist is] still busily belying his witticism.' The most descriptive review was John Brigg's, in the *New York Post*: 'In the realm of violin playing there is nothing quite comparable to a Zimbalist recital; Mr. Zimbalist's [of last evening was] the caviar of a profession which often shows a lamentable tendency toward Swiss on rye.'

Rafael Druian was the page-turner. He and Zimbalist were at Pennsylvania Station together after the recital when Druian noticed that his teacher was empty-handed. 'Where is your violin?' he asked anxiously. Zimbalist laughed. 'The porter, a friend of mine, watches the paper for announcements of my New York concerts and waits for me so that he can

look after my violin for me.' (It was the 'Lamoureux' Strad!) They went off
to have a bite to eat before the train's departure, Zimbalist not showing the
slightest concern.

By this time he had moved to an apartment in Philadelphia's Belgravia
Hotel on Chestnut Street; William Primrose also lived there. Having permanently settled in Philadelphia, Zimbalist quickly proceeded to ferret out
its chief delights, among them Harry Tint's cigar shop and Charles
Sessler's antiquarian bookstore on Walnut Street. From Sessler he acquired
one of his greatest treasures: four manuscript chapters from George
Bernard Shaw's early play *Love Among Artists*. Shaw generally destroyed his
manuscripts after publication — these chapters were a rare exception.

Early in May 1942, Zimbalist ran into Feuermann in Rittenhouse Square
on the way to rehearse the Boccherini Concerto with the Philadelphia
Orchestra. Feuermann wasn't feeling very well and asked Zimbalist to help
him carry his cello to the Academy of Music. Zimbalist was glad to oblige
and sat through the rehearsal in awe of Feuermann's art. 'Never had I seen
such effortless playing. He played "violin" on the cello.' Feuermann died on
25 May 1942, victim of a simple hemorrhoidectomy gone wrong, aged
thirty-nine. Zimbalist hired Gregor Piatigorsky to fill his post.

On 28 March 1943, Rachmaninoff died. At a Carnegie Hall recital just
days later his friend Zimmie played Schubert's 'Ave Maria' as a moving
encore tribute.

Zimbalist started to appear on Philadelphia's social scene. Occasionally,
then more frequently, he was seen in the company of Mrs. Bok and Edith
Evans Braun, bosom friends since childhood and both now widowed.
(Some saw in this trio a parallel to his courtship of Alma Gluck, costarring
Althea Jewell.) Courtship, according to Zimbalist, was the furthest thing
from his mind. Nevertheless the trio was much in evidence summers in
Rockport, where for years Mrs. Bok had supported a unique seaside
gathering of teachers from the Institute and their broods. Ludwig von
Lunt, in the *Camden-Rockport Bicentennial Commemorative Book* (1969),
gives a sense of it:

> Near the end of the fabulous twenties Rockport became a sort of
> Summer Mecca and meeting place for some of the greatest
> concert artists in the world. The famous Curtis Institute had
> chosen it as a summer studio for its more gifted pupils and its

illustrious faculty. Mary Louise Bok saw to it that special housing was prepared, and a place for boating, sunning and swimming was amply provided on the Eastern shore of Rockport harbor. This was not only some years before the days of a Tanglewood, a Marlboro or a Saratoga music center, but also of quite a different atmosphere. It was what one might call an informal musical colony. There were no set routines. From the student's standpoint, his very presence depended upon his teacher, who would map out a special work program. Many students boarded in a community house along Mechanic Street in Rockport, where certain liberal rules had to be observed, and someone from the Curtis Institute staff provided [food] on a home-cooking type basis.

From early June until Labor Day music was in the air.... Englishman Felix Salmond, after musicmaking at one of the houses, would belt out a bawdy British barroom ballad. [An] act most often clamored for was Pierre Luboshutz and his Russian Choir [with] the Curtis Quartet as [choir] members. He would stand in front of his chorus, a broom in hand upside down, facing the audience, all the while furiously beating the broom handle on the floor. A few sad but risqué choruses would be sung, then Pierre would point a finger at Jascha Brodsky, which meant it was his chance for a solo. But Jascha would have a bandage around his chin pretending that he had a toothache. An evening might end with Pierre doing an impersonation of the dying swan as done by Pavlova, with Gregor Piatigorsky providing the famous music. One memorable evening he and Piatigorsky did an Apache dance together. Piatigorsky, as the girl, was almost two heads taller than his partner.

Vladimir Sokoloff could usually be heard across Rockport Harbor coaching [students of Elisabeth Schumann], while his wife Eleanor was teaching piano in another room. Irra Petina might go out sailing with composers Gian Carlo Menotti and Sam Barber; if they got becalmed a version of the Habanera from *Carmen* might be heard and seen by passing boatmen.

Zimbalist's old protégé Alexander Hilsberg had been concertmaster of the Philadelphia Orchestra since 1931. After his graduation from the St. Petersburg Conservatory the 1917 revolution drove him to China, where he spent the intervening years. With Zimbalist's move to Philadelphia, a warm friendship developed. Hilsberg, like many a concertmaster, harbored the desire to ascend to the podium. After much prodding he persuaded the orchestra's management to give him a chance to make his conducting debut during the summer Robin Hood Dell season, but they did so with a condition: 'You must find a soloist who can draw a good crowd.' 'I think I can get a world-famous violinist who would be happy to play a concerto with me,' Hilsberg countered. He asked Zimbalist, who agreed at once.

On a swelteringly hot Saturday afternoon in summer 1943 Zimbalist traveled from The Rafters to give Hilsberg his 'first podium.' After an overture came the Glazunov Concerto. But at intermission a thunderous cloudburst sent everyone scurrying home. In such cases the concert was to be repeated intact the following afternoon, depending on soloist availability and barring continued foul weather. With considerable trepidation Hilsberg approached his soloist to ask him to repeat the Glazunov. 'Of course,' was Zimbalist's answer. He stayed an extra day and drew crowds again. Nearly twenty years later Hilsberg repaid his friend's kindness by conducting the première of Zimbalist's piano concerto.

Zimbalist and Mary Bok were having tea at Lyndonwood, her summer home. He remembered the scene very well. She looked at him and asked matter-of-factly, 'Efrem, why don't we marry?' On 6 July 1943, at Lyndonwood, they did. Many had claimed a premonition of something romantic brewing but couldn't decide whether the lucky lady was going to be Mrs. Bok or Mrs. Braun. Some assumed he had arbitrarily chosen the lady with the money, and they were quick to point out the age difference: Mrs. Bok was thirteen years older than Zimbalist. The truth is that Zimbalist's admiration for Mary Bok's vision and character had with time matured into something deeper. He always considered her a thoroughly enigmatic woman, and the marriage proved very successful. He liked to say that he had spent fifty years of his life happily married to two remarkable but completely different women.

Those who looked at Zimbalist's position enviously and read opportunism into it didn't know that the couple, each wealthy in their own right, kept their personal finances separate. Besides, years had passed since his free-spending days. His marriage to Mary Bok made him even more con-servative financially and politically—up till then he had been a liberal and Roosevelt supporter. (When she died he inherited $100,000, a small frac-tion of her estate; the bulk was equally divided between the descendants of her two sons.)

This may be a good point at which to take stock.

Zimbalist's career was definitely lightening, which seemed a natural corollary of having put former times behind him—times filled with struggle, triumphs, the height of joy and the depths of despondency. He led the life of an artist yet had taken a path totally divergent from those of his colleagues, although all had had a similar point of departure. The last time he had seen Heifetz, for instance, was many years before, when the first Mrs. Heifetz, silent movie star Florence Vidor, invited the Zimbalists to visit them in Balboa Island, California. Heifetz had struck up an argu-ment with Florence that soon turned ugly. His language, Zimbalist said, 'became vile.' Florence shrank. 'You shouldn't talk that way, Jascha,' Zimbalist chided. When they returned to the dock, he and Alma packed their bags. Now, as then, Heifetz was the undisputed king of violinists. But, adulated though he was, Heifetz led a driven, disciplined, unhappy life.

Mischa Elman's once-magic name had lost a good deal of its luster; its diminishing impact hurt both his career and his ego, and his ongoing battles with managers, recording companies and critics were legendary. Kreisler was also under great pressure, which ran completely against his nature. He had to maintain a ferocious concert schedule partly because of financial need and partly to get away from his equally ferocious wife. Zimbalist's words were pointed: 'Towards the end of his career Kreisler played an afternoon recital at Carnegie Hall, which I attended. People were hanging from the rafters. Afterwards I went backstage. "Fritz, how good to see you," was the only thing I could say. Exhausted, he stared for a while before he recognized me, then he smiled. "For God's sake, Efrem," he said, "don't leave me. Wait and we'll have a drink at my hotel." After all those years, with all the money he earned (his fee at that time was $2,000 or $3,000 a concert), he still lived in a couple of small rooms on the sixth floor of the Wellington—he had gambled and given away a lot. Well, after all the felicitations were over, we walked to the hotel in silence. He said to me: "Was it that bad?" I said nothing. He went on. "I know it, of course, but what can I do?" "Fritz," I said, "the only thing I could suggest is practice."

"How can I practice?" he asked. "They book me every day. I have no time for anything." Fritz was miserable the last years of his career. Naturally for the listeners there were still those moments of heavenly beauty that only he could provide. But he was struck by the irony of it all. "You know," he said to me, "when I was young and played well they would have to remove rows of chairs so that the halls where I played wouldn't look so empty. Now that I can no longer play they turn crowds away at every concert."

Zimbalist's musings must have brought him tranquility. It was music that always counted to him, not the blind pursuit of ambition. And yet, here he was, director of one of the world's most prestigious learning institutions (Olga Samaroff once stated that the Curtis Institute did for musical education what Johns Hopkins did for medicine); he was able to look back with satisfaction on his years of worldwide concert activities and was free to accept whatever amount of activity still appealed to him, while enjoying a security envied by many. He put his thoughts into words thirty years later: 'First and last I am a musician. Good or bad has nothing to do with it—it is simply my life's profession. My luck was that I was so sheltered. I had a decent career in 1928. Then I came to Curtis. When I was made director my position became unassailable—I was protected both musically and financially and in the happy position of not having to ask any favors. I was terribly lucky. I have often asked myself: what if I hadn't been in such a position? Now, I can truthfully tell you that I would have been just as happy being in an orchestra, playing great music. Many orchestral players are miserable because they never wanted to play in an orchestra. But a person interested in inner satisfaction, as I was, rather than outward display, can learn so much about great music that way. I would much rather have earned $100 a week in a good symphony orchestra than $1,000 by playing the sort of trash that many "commercial" musicians do today. You know, we musicians are extremely fortunate in our calling. Not only have we the satisfaction of the work itself, but through it we constantly come into contact with the minds of supreme beings like Beethoven or Mozart; these extraordinary humans reveal to us their deepest thoughts and inspirations if we are willing and able to receive them. How lucky we are!'

Zimbalist settled contentedly into his situation. He and his new wife lived in her three-story mansion at 1816 Delancey Place. Mrs. Zimbalist owned 1818 too, in which Edith Braun lived. Both houses contained extensive oak woodwork and furniture (worth a small fortune today) that were custom-installed by the Rose Valley Community, an arts and crafts endeavor supported by the late Mr. Bok. A connecting door assured the neighbors easy access, and scarcely an evening went by that didn't find the three of them together over a genteel dinner, followed by three-handed rummy. Life was considerably quieter than on East 49th Street, although some elite social gatherings did take place. There were noticeable parallels—the beige Bentley driven by Patrick McAuley (counterpart of George Ladd of yore), the fanatic balletomane of a butler (counterpart of 'out of this world' Ross) and Frieda Schenk, a super-efficient German maid of bluff countenance.

The Zimbalists' circle was drawn from all civilized strata of society. One member was Grace Kelly's father, a Philadelphia bigwig who presented State Supreme Justice Curtis Bok (Zimbalist's new stepson) with his appointment. Curtis was only six years younger than Zimbalist, which caused the latter a little uneasiness at first. Then they got along famously. Curtis was an amateur bassoonist and threw weekly chamber music parties at which Philadelphia Orchestra members played. Curtis Bok's widow, Nellie Lee, reminisced:

> Efrem became a wonderful member of the Bok family. We were all aware of his musicianship but, in the family, we knew him best by his many kindnesses. He was always doing countless little thoughtful things. The day before my daughter turned sixteen he said to her, 'Rachel, you know I am your only grandfather.' [Both her biological grandfathers were dead.] 'So you'll just have to have your sixteenth birthday lunch with me!' He took her to the Barclay and gave her a lunch she never forgot. When her first marriage ended in divorce, he called her and said, 'I've known you since you were seven. Is there anything about this divorce you'd like to tell your grandfather?' She just melted, of course, and said, 'Yes—*everything*.' By the time my other daughter got married Mary was too ill to attend the wedding, but he came. It was these caring touches that made him a great human being.

1816 Delancey Place was an easy two-and-a-half-block walk, down 18th Street, to the Institute's doors on Locust and Rittenhouse Square. Although there was an occasional arrival in the Bentley, Zimbalist usually strolled to school. In later years he was seen more than once enjoying a chocolate malted at Harvey House (a popular hamburger joint), en route. Most of the faculty and students lunched here and across the road, at Papa Day's delicatessen.

How did Zimbalist manage to combine the responsibilities of husband, parent, stepparent, grandparent, director, teacher, composer and concert virtuoso? 'My energy seemed to increase with age. But then I had always managed to take everything easily,' he said in answer to my question.

Zimbalist was still active on the concert front. Although he turned down longer tours because of his teaching commitments, the short ones took no more than three weeks each. He and Sokoloff rehearsed a largely standard repertoire before heading off, first trying out their programs at Curtis. Sokoloff talked about that period:

> Each month Zimbalist would give me a personal check for X number of concerts. My schoolmate Ralph Berkowitz was Piatigorsky's accompanist. After our tours we would compare notes. Ralph would ask, 'What's Zimmie like?' and I would ask, 'What's Piat like?' Then we got down to the nitty-gritty of salaries. Piatigorsky, married to Jacqueline Rothschild, was overly generous, and when I told Ralph what I got he was horrified. He told Piatigorsky, who talked to Zimbalist: 'You know, Efrem, things have gone up.' Next month I got a big raise.
>
> Zimbalist loved to eat in cheap dives. He always picked up the tab, but the lavish spending days were over. After concerts in small towns few if any restaurants would be open, but in every one of them he knew a 'little place' that kept late hours. They served the food he liked best — stews, chili or anything with a thick spicy sauce, which often disagreed with his stomach.

Judging by the size of his audiences, Zimbalist's Carnegie Hall recitals were still eagerly anticipated, and the reviews glowed. In addition to his recitals, Zimbalist continued to play concertos on the major symphonic circuit. The Sibelius Concerto, a favorite of his, was often requested, as in 1942 when he played in Toronto with the Philadelphia Orchestra. After his profound reading of the second movement the audience broke into applause, delaying resumption of the performance by several minutes. On a private tape of a 1944 Sibelius performance with the Cleveland Orchestra and Leinsdorf, Zimbalist again drew warm applause at the same point. Zimbalist's 1946 Brahms Concerto with the Boston Symphony under Koussevitsky ('he had the funniest beat I ever saw') was broadcast live and fortuitously recorded (Zimbalist employed his own cadenza, of characteristic old-style length and virtuosity).

A revision and performance in 1943 of 'American Rhapsody' attracted lively interest. Stokowski, recovering from a painful sprain, arrived late to the first rehearsal and was impatient with Zimbalist's suggestions. At a certain point he asked Zimbalist to mount the podium to demonstrate his intentions. Afterward Stokowski wrote Zimbalist a letter apologizing for keeping him waiting, assuring him that he was looking forward to the next rehearsal and hoping that he would be happy with his interpretation. He signed it 'Always with affection and friendship.' But Zimbalist didn't like the results at succeeding rehearsals: 'When I made suggestions [Stokowski] would politely agree with my ideas—in performance he would invariably do what he wanted.'

The final outcome, on 5 February 1944, was written up in the *Philadelphia Inquirer*: 'Efrem Zimbalist, world-famous violinist, stepped to the podium this week to conduct the Philadelphia Orchestra in a première of his "American Rhapsody."' The review noted that seldom had a new work scored so instant, emphatic and well-earned a success. It lauded Zimbalist's resourcefulness in his tasteful inclusion of such melodies as 'O Susanna' and 'Turkey in the Straw,' and praised his unaffected, batonless conducting. ('I conducted without baton because the orchestra was used to Stokowski doing that,' Zimbalist said.)

He always considered 'American Rhapsody' one of his best pieces and was pleased when people admired its orchestration, 'even if, knowing nothing of "modern" orchestration, I still used the old kind Rimsky-Korsakov used.' Two works that he found disappointing enough to destroy were a tone poem, 'Portrait of an Artist' (based on the life of James Joyce, introduced by the Philadelphia Orchestra on 7 December 1945), and the concerto in c-sharp minor (which he performed with Ormandy and the Philadelphia Orchestra on 28 November 1947.) 'They made good firewood,' he commented later. Published at William Primrose's urging was a viola transcription of a work Zimbalist did like, 'Sarasateana,' an arrangement of six Spanish dances by Sarasate he had originally published for violin in 1942: 'I wrote "Sarasateana" just for fun, because I so much loved Sarasate's own playing of his Spanish dances.' Primrose played and recorded the suite, and Zimbalist reworked it once again, for piano quintet, in 1985.

Zimbalist also attended concerts. Among them was Milstein's perform-ance of the Goldmark Concerto, which wowed him. Zino Francescatti was a special favorite of Zimbalist's. The admiration was mutual; when they met in 1944 Francescatti spoke of the thrill he had experienced hearing his colleague in Paris. Zimbalist was on the lookout for 'the very best' violin teacher he could find to provide Curtis students with fresh input. Francescatti mentioned 'un homme très intéressant' by the name of Ivan Galamian, whom he had met in Paris and who was presently teaching at the Henry Street Settlement School in New York. Zimbalist sat in on one of Galamian's lessons and drew an instant conclusion: 'That's the man I want.' It was a decision that always brought him much satisfaction, although many didn't share his high opinion of Galamian: George Szell, for one, considered Galamian the worst thing that had ever happened to music.

Shortly after Galamian was installed at Curtis in 1944 (two years later, rival Juilliard also hired him), Zimbalist visited his third-floor studio to observe him at work. 'I was astounded by [his] ability to "make" a violinist,' he modestly commented. 'He could teach a table to play the violin. I myself couldn't "make" a violinist—I wouldn't know what to do. All I could do was improve a violinist.' To illustrate his point Zimbalist liked to tell a story: 'In Hartford, Connecticut, I once went to visit a friend who taught at the college there. He asked me to listen to a young violinist, hoping I might teach him. I didn't think he showed much gift. "Well, what do you recommend?" my friend asked. "The very best teacher is Galamian. Perhaps he can make something of him."' Here Zimbalist chuckled. 'He made him concertmaster of the New York Philharmonic.' The young boy's name was David Nadien.

Zimbalist called Galamian 'the greatest teacher in my experience' and openly recognized the extent of his influence on the direction of twen-tieth-century violin playing. When one listens to the playing of any typical contemporary violin star, their brilliant articulate sound is directly attrib-utable to the imprint of two people: Jascha Heifetz and Ivan Galamian. While Heifetz lit the blazing beacon of perfection, Galamian was able, by an acute understanding of the mechanics behind the radiance, to put it within reach of ordinary mortals. He was born in 1903 in Tabriz, Iran, to Armenian parents and brought to Russia as an infant. He studied with Konstantin Mostras in Moscow (1916–22) and with Capet in Paris (1922–23), whose bowing theories intrigued him. According to Boris Schwarz in *Great Masters of the Violin*, Galamian's early career was 'not marked by particular distinction. [He opened a studio in New York in 1937, where he taught] from eight in the morning until six at night. He had the razor-sharp ability to analyze and correct his students' violinistic ailments. "His lessons were always intense work," said a former student. After a few scales in an adjoining room the intimidated student would face the stern professor at exactly the appointed time while the previous "victim" was dismissed. Those who could not endure the strict discipline were better off with another teacher.'

Zimbalist's recognition of Galamian's work didn't deter him from following his own teaching convictions or blind him to both the pluses and minuses of their respective methods. In later years, when laurels had been stacked up on each side and a rough tally was possible, Zimbalist wasn't far from the truth in observing: 'The great violinists of the past all played differently. However, one could always recognize Galamian's students: they all spoke the same "language," which was not the case with mine or Auer's. So, while Galamian was a greater teacher than either of us, yet he was more limited. We had entirely opposite approaches. Galamian showed one how to do things. I preferred to let students find their own way, following behind to help them up if they fell. In the final analysis, all I wanted from my students was a little beauty.' And according to Sokoloff, 'By the sheer magic of osmosis Zimbalist's supreme qualities were absorbed by his better pupils. It was only a callous and indifferent student who, after four years of study under his tutelage, didn't come away showing evidence of something precious.'

Zimbalist consciously tried to preserve the individuality of each student. And he encouraged them to express what they felt. 'Do something,' he'd gently urge, 'good or bad, *do* something.' While a less impressed student likened this approach to 'constantly trying to put a mustache on the Mona Lisa,' it produced the sort of imagination Zimbalist liked to see. He summed up: 'Although Galamian produced more good violinists than I did, I probably produced more artists.' Among the better known are Oscar Shumsky, Shmuel Ashkenasi, Toshiya Eto, Joseph Silverstein, Aaron

Rosand, Michael Tree, John Dalley and Rafael Druian; prizewinners in important international competitions include Ashkenasi (Queen Elisabeth, Tchaikovsky); Silverstein (Naumberg, Queen Elisabeth); Nicolas Chumachenco (Tchaikovsky); Hidetaro Suzuki (Queen Elisabeth, Tchaikovsky); Daniel Heifetz (Tchaikovsky). And Zimbalist definitely produced the most concertmasters: Norman Carol (Minneapolis Symphony, Philadelphia Orchestra); Jesse Ceci (Denver Symphony); Eliot Chapo (New York Philharmonic, Dallas Symphony); Chumachenco (Zurich Chamber Orchestra); Druian (Cleveland Orchestra); Bernie Eichen (Denver Symphony); Jacob Krachmalnick (Philadelphia Orchestra, Concertgebouw, San Francisco Symphony, Dallas Symphony, San Francisco Opera); Helen Kwalwasser (Bach Aria Group, Pennsylvania Ballet); Roy Malan (San Francisco Ballet); Mi-Young Park (Mostovoy Soloists); Julius Schulman (St. Louis Symphony, San Antonio Symphony); Silverstein (Boston Symphony); Suzuki (Quebec National Orchestra, Indianapolis Symphony).

Maria Zimbalist's daughter Jane was born on 29 April 1944. Just months later Efrem Jr.'s wife, Emily, gave birth to Nancy. Within a couple of years Maria had a second child, Susan, and Emily brought Efrem III into the world. Zimbalist doted on them and spoiled them shamelessly, just as he had his own children. Nevertheless, one precious grandchild reduced him to the most intense display of rage Nancy ever saw from him. It seems that, while her parents were away, she and Skipper (Efrem III) were under Grandpa's supervision one weekend at The Rafters. Skipper was at a mischievous age. He and a friend decided, with the aid of some kerosene, to burn their initials into the floor of the Barneses' barn. Things got out of hand, and the building was set ablaze. After the fire brigade had left Zimbalist, livid, called Skipper over. While the lad awaited sentencing his grandfather, trembling with rage, mentally struggled to come up with a punishment dire enough for such terrible misbehavior. There was a long silence and then, in barely audible choked tones, Zimbalist said, 'You go upstairs right now, put on your pajamas and go to bed!' It was ten o'clock in the morning.

Marcia Davenport, in her *New Yorker* profile of her stepfather, described him as an 'uncompromisingly strict' teacher—one lapse condemned a student for good. The author, as a Zimbalist student, formed a different impression. In my experience Zimbalist's mien as teacher was always kindly. I grant that as director the case may have been different, and there is an instance on record where his actions were viewed in certain quarters as draconian. It involved a time, only a dim memory in the climate of today's scepticism, when instrumentalists were captivated by self-styled specialists who claimed the ability to solve any and all problems through the 'secret' of their unique methods. The prevailing such mystical figure was D. C. Dounis, who enjoyed much success just before the twentieth century's midpoint. Players of every instrument (he himself had reputedly played the guitar) flocked to his New York studio seeking the truth and willing to pay large sums for it.

To spare professionals who consulted him the embarrassment of running into their colleagues at the front door, Dounis had them leave through another. This arrangement was also appreciated by students of other teachers, whose consultations needed to be kept strictly confidential. Two violin students from Curtis were in the latter category during the summer of 1949. But when school resumed in the fall enthusiasm overrode discretion, and the boys were full of Dounis's ideas. Galamian came to see Zimbalist. 'Students at Curtis are given, free of charge, the finest teaching available,' he fumed. 'I happen to know that one of your students, and one of mine, spent the summer paying for lessons with Dounis. Now they are distributing his exercises here. I don't know what you intend doing, but I want my student expelled from the Institute.' (Galamian's student was Michael Serber, a fine talent who later entered the psychiatric field; Galamian was particularly angry because two of his best Juilliard students, David Nadien and Berl Senofsky, had also fallen under Dounis's spell.) 'Who is my student?' Zimbalist asked. 'Joseph Silverstein.' Distressed, Zimbalist pondered deeply before deciding to uphold Galamian's decision: he called Silverstein in and softly said, 'Joseph, you are dismissed.' Silverstein's accomplishments following his dismissal are too well known to enumerate. In an attempt to ease his lingering lack of conviction about the decision, twenty-eight years later Zimbalist had the Institute award Silverstein his diploma.

Although Zimbalist once dismissed another student for what he considered disrespectful conduct, it was his lenient side that was most often seen. During a winter storm a group of Curtis boys were merrily working off steam in Rittenhouse Square with a snowball fight. An oboe student, taking the worst beating, ran to take refuge. Pursued by his determined adversaries, he flung himself through the school's doors and, to ensure escape, turned the latch. He stood in the entrance lobby shaking himself free of snow particles, gleefully anticipating the satisfaction of taunting his pursuers when they began banging at the door. But outside all was silence. From the safe distance of the square a group of boys apprehensively watched a familiar figure in boots and heavy coat approach the Institute's portals. It was the director. He turned the doorknob only to find himself barred admission to his own school. He was visibly bemused, but those expecting repercussions never saw any—when told the full story, Zimbalist howled with laughter.

CHAPTER 21

Winding Down

(1947–1968)

In an effort to broaden the scope of his programming Zimbalist fairly early in his career developed an interest in ancient essays for his instrument. He was foreshadowing a trend that is now *the* thing, although his approach was completely different from the stuffy pedantry of many of today's self-proclaimed early music specialists. In his editing he tried, above all, to maintain a sense of flowing melodic line, employing any violinistic and harmonic means to do so. (This had always been his way with unaccompanied Bach.) The results of his scholarship were published by Theodore Presser in 1951. He wrote about them in the foreword: 'I realized some time ago that very little is known about the beginnings of literature for the violin. My subsequent research in this field proved highly rewarding. I discovered compositions of the earliest period of real merit, some of them of great beauty. Among them were the first composition ever written for solo violin, with figured bass ("La Romanesca" by Biagio Marini [1590–1660] and the first piece for violin alone ("Capriccio Stravagante" by Carlo Farina [b. 1595]). I hope the publication of this group of compositions will give others as much satisfaction as it has given me. I arranged the piano parts from the figured basses.'

As he investigated the roots of violin composition an idea came to him: why not give a series of recitals tracing the development of compositional techniques for the instrument from the beginning up to the present? Although some years earlier Elman had played several concerts under the heading 'The Development of Violin Literature,' its scope wasn't nearly as broad.

Zimbalist's series, billed by his manager as 'A Rare Opportunity for Students and Lovers of Violin Music,' was held at Town Hall in the 1947–48 season: 'Zimbalist, one of the world's truly great violinists, will be heard in the first presentation of the entire history of violin literature, in five concerts. Chronologically, the concerts will embrace the outstanding composers who have influenced violin development from the sixteenth century through the present day.' A list of the thirty-nine featured composers—baroque, classical, romantic and virtuoso—followed. Zimbalist concluded the series with the Sibelius Concerto, which he said was 'the greatest violin concerto written in the twentieth century.'

All the concerts were at 5:30 on Saturdays ('the cheapest time to book Town Hall,' smiled Sokoloff). Patrick, the chauffeur, transported them to New York in style, in the Bentley. Each historical program first underwent a dry run at Curtis, where students referred to them as the 'Hysterical Series.' Although one critic dismissed the entire thing as a publicity stunt, audience response and reviews were generally favorable. Many critics no longer condoned performing concertos with piano accompaniment; others found their attention span taxed, and blamed overkill for the noticeable dwindling in attendance as the series ran its course. It was an idea ahead of its time. Today a presentation of this kind would be given to sold-out houses of pointy-headed musicologists (or music 'criminologists,' as Heifetz liked to call them).

Excessive work over long months of preparation, added to Zimbalist's disappointment in the general response, took their toll. At the end of the final concert he quieted the applause to address his audience, something he had never done before, in a rambling, incoherent speech. Afterward, the concerned Zimbalist family rushed backstage. Efrem Jr. reports: 'He had worked so hard his mind just cracked. When he got to his dressing room he was his own sweet self, but his memory had gone. He couldn't remember where his violin was, or where we were going for dinner.' Isabelle Vengerova was throwing a party for them; while there the fifty-eight-year-old Zimbalist collapsed from fatigue. It took weeks for his memory to return to normal.

Nellie Lee Bok was at the Town Hall concerts. Her insight was keen: 'Efrem was aging a little faster than he would admit. People grow older imperceptibly, then all of a sudden something happens, perhaps an exertion of some kind, from which they never fully recover. There is no doubt in my mind that the turning point for Efrem was that Town Hall series.'

Mary Zimbalist was worried when he had to go off on tour again. She made Sokoloff promise to keep a watchful eye on him. Fortunately there were fewer concerts each year. 'His farewell year we played no more than ten concerts,' Sokoloff recalled.

Zimbalist's students, always important to him, assumed an even greater role in his advancing years. As youngsters Toshiya Eto, Michael Tree and John Dalley spent several summers with the Zimbalists in Maine. Edith Braun, the accompanist for summer lessons, joined them at dinner every evening. John Dalley once prepared Lalo's 'Symphonie Espagnole' for a lesson. He attempted, evidently unsuccessfully, to imbue the piece with every bit of color possible. Zimbalist approached him very closely (as he was wont to do) and looked him straight in the eye. 'John,' he said in a fatherly manner, 'you play it just like a piece of toast—very crisp and square.' Another time John joined Zimbalist for lunch. 'What did you do this morning?' his teacher inquired amiably. John proudly announced: 'I learned the entire first movement of the Mendelssohn Concerto.' Zimbalist's tongue-in-cheek comeback put the youngster in his place. 'Hmm...I spent the entire morning practicing the first three lines of the Beethoven Concerto.'

Michael Tree remembers those days: 'We felt we were witnessing one of the last great "hero" violinists. During the later years I studied with Zimbalist there was an element of sadness about him, as he watched the musical world turn upside down. That "golden era of the virtuoso" had simply disappeared: while there remained a few stand-out fiddle players, the day of the violin recital the way he had known it was gone.'

Zimbalist's relationship with some of his former colleagues was also a source of pain, which became evident to the bewildered fifteen-year-old Tree, unaware of the rift that had developed between his teacher and Heifetz: 'I remember asking Zimbalist naively at a lesson if he was going to hear Heifetz, who was playing in town the next night. He looked at me quizzically for a moment, in his customary way, not saying anything while he let me think. Then he answered, "I don't think so." When I persisted, mentioning the program Heifetz was to play, he said: "No, Michael. Except for the pleasure of hearing that lovely silvery tone again I really don't have much interest in Heifetz anymore."'

Conversation once veered in the direction of Pablo Casals, at the time enjoying boundless adulation at the Marlboro Festival. Someone present lauded Casals to the skies and ended with a reference to his great modesty. Zimbalist piped up, 'It's very easy to be modest when everyone addresses you as "your godship."'

Tree, whose middle name is Efrem, continues: 'He was more than generous with me. He personally sponsored my Carnegie Hall debut [as he did for Toshiya Eto], which was naturally the most exciting event of my life at that time. A couple of months before the event he lent me his Guarneri to use. Since I was so young when I came to study with him, he really took a fatherly interest in me. It was he who suggested that I change my name to Tree. He felt that the name Applebaum was neither here nor there since my forebears had already changed it after leaving Russia. Then too, he thought that my father Samuel Applebaum's renown may be a confusing issue in the furtherance of my own career. He was always extremely practically minded. We abided by his wishes, although it was not an easy decision, one that took much thought and adjustment. But after all, what's in a name?'

The story goes that Samuel Applebaum journeyed from his New Jersey home to meet with Zimbalist at Curtis 'about a matter concerning Michael's career.' In Zimbalist's studio they sat facing each other, Applebaum greeting his host's suggestion of a name change with incredulous silence. Zimbalist began mulling over the possibilities: 'Now, Applebaum, Apple. Apple. Michael Apple? No. Well, "baum" is "tree." Perhaps Michael Appletree? No. Tree—Michael Tree. Nice and simple. How about Michael Tree?" Papa Applebaum's response was quick: 'The only member of the family who would be happy about that is our dog!' Other Zimbalist students who changed their names for stage purposes were Bernie Eichenbaum, who dropped the last four letters of his surname, Aaron Rosen, who expanded his to Rosand, and a pupil who came to Zimbalist right from a World War II concentration camp, Haim Arbeitman—he became David Arben, former associate concertmaster of the Philadelphia Orchestra.

Zimbalist's farewell Carnegie Hall recital, on 14 November 1948, 'attracted more than ordinary attention,' as *Musical America* reported:

> A large and affectionate audience gathered to pay tribute to him.
> He accepted the applause with the modest dignity which has

always been one of his most endearing traits on the concert platform.... Mr. Zimbalist still produced a tone of extraordinary
beauty. In the Glazunov Concerto the refinement and ease of his
performance freed the music from the slightest taste of vulgarity. He opened the program with Beethoven's violin sonata in
c minor and the Romance in G. So heartfelt was his interpretation of the Romance that it aroused a prolonged ovation, despite
the introspective and completely unsensational character of the
music. After intermission came the fireworks Mr. Zimbalist has
always done so delightfully—Kreisler's Recitative and Scherzo
for violin alone; the Saint-Saëns–Ysaÿe Caprice; and five songs
by George Gershwin, arranged by Mr. Zimbalist.

If the occasion gave rise to any special pangs in Zimbalist's heart, he
didn't show it. 'He wasn't ambitious in the usual sense and was always so
casual about concertizing,' Sokoloff, the recital's 'expert accompanist' reminisced. 'Playing concerts was something that he did because he had done
it from infancy and was trained to do well. On the whole, I *think* he
enjoyed playing them.'

Zimbalist, in fact, had quite a few concerts ahead. He figured promi-
nently at the Curtis Institute's twenty-fifth anniversary observance in 1949.
Afternoon and evening events were scheduled: at the Academy of Music he
conducted Menotti's *Amelia Goes to the Ball* and at Curtis he played the
Brahms 'Double' with Piatigorsky. (Alexander Hilsberg was on the podium.
He was then—thanks partly to the boost Zimbalist had given him—associate conductor as well as concertmaster of the Philadelphia Orchestra, a
Curtis violin faculty member and conductor of the student orchestra. He
later became director of the New Orleans Symphony.)

Nellie Lee Bok described the soloists' entrance onstage: 'They were
different kinds of Russians. Piatigorsky moved briskly with his cello held
high. Efrem, appearing much smaller, moved more slowly. During the performance he stood quietly, dignified and relaxed. His acknowledgment of
the applause was rather solemn, although if one knew his smile one could
recognize a trace of it.' The performance was preserved, thanks to the anti-
quated recording system (on large acetate discs that ran inside-out) then
employed for the Institute's archives. It is a mellifluous rendition, despite
some stylistic differences between the soloists.

Efrem's 'farewell' concert with the Philadelphia Orchestra was a performance of the Tchaikovsky Concerto at a pension concert on 15 February
1950 that attracted such prominent audience members as Piatigorsky and
Isaac Stern. For sentimental reasons, Hilsberg conducted. Zimbalist
declined to speak but, according to one reviewer, played with 'a magic,
wonderfully cultivated style,' and he cherished the large autographed
photo of the orchestra that was presented to him. Since Ormandy was able
to prevail on him to come out of 'retirement' a few times during succeeding
seasons, this actually was not his last appearance with the orchestra.

On 9 December 1952 Zimbalist joined it in the première of Gian Carlo
Menotti's concerto. Menotti had consulted him while at work. There was
some deadline heat. 'I received the last movement only two weeks before
the performance,' Zimbalist recalled. He very much liked the work and
reveled in its lyricism. The only other violinist to take it up was Tossy
Spivakovsky, despite Zimbalist's untiring efforts to interest his students in
the piece.

By this time Zimbalist pupil Jacob Krachmalnick had been appointed
concertmaster (the youngest ever at twenty-eight) of the orchestra. He
replaced Hilsberg, and no love was lost between them. The first two years
of Krachmalnick's violin studies at Curtis had been under Hilsberg, who
in his string orchestra classes was detested for his cold, sarcastic manner
and appearance—students nicknamed him Dracula. At lessons
Krachmalnick was surprised that Hilsberg never demonstrated on the
violin, illustrating his points instead by whistling. Soon, never lacking
gumption, he told his teacher that he had come to study violin playing, not
whistling, which didn't improve the teacher-student relationship. Finally
Hilsberg refused to admit him to orchestra class. Krachmalnick aired his
grievances to the head of the violin department. 'That's fine, Jacob,'
Zimbalist answered tongue-in-cheek, 'it will give you more time to practice.' And he took Jake into his own class. Zimbalist too disliked whistlers.

Hilsberg was dismayed by Ormandy's choice for his replacement as
concertmaster. Krachmalnick's maiden voyage included Strauss's 'Ein
Heldenleben'—by any standards a trial by fire. Before the performance
Hilsberg came backstage to taunt his nemesis. 'Do you remember all those
times you sat in the front row and laughed when my bow trembled?' he
spat. 'Well, tonight *I'll* be in the front row laughing.' Not one to back down,
Krachmalnick countered, 'If my bow trembles you can watch me eat it. If

it doesn't, I'll do something else with it!' There was no trembling, and Hilsberg wasn't to be seen after the concert.

Several months into his new job Krachmalnick decided to upgrade his violin, and Zimbalist helped him choose an exquisite Guarneri del Gesu. Ormandy had been complaining about his old violin but didn't seem very enthralled with the replacement. Krachmalnick mentioned this to Zimbalist. One Friday at noon (the orchestra had as usual rehearsed all morning in preparation for a 2 p.m. performance), Zimbalist showed up at the Academy of Music. He disappeared into Ormandy's room. 'From that day on,' Jake guffawed, 'Ormandy considered my del Gesu the greatest violin he ever heard.'

Zimbalist gave performances with the orchestra of the Brahms Concerto and, at Carnegie Hall on 15 March 1955, the Beethoven, which was repeated in Washington, D.C. *Musical America*'s warm review side-stepped a growing problem: for the past few seasons an unsteadiness of Zimbalist's pitch had drawn hushed comment. Zimbalist was irked that his oldest American colleague, Chotzinoff, was the first to draw attention to it in print. It was a sad situation for two reasons—firstly because this un-reliability was the result of hearing loss, and secondly because, at its peak, his was a particularly satisfying sense of pitch.

Many attempts have been made over the years to formulate laws governing intonation. One result was the standardizing of the pitch A at 440 kilohertz. Today's early music performance practice specialists tune considerably lower, to A 410. In *Intonation on the Violin*, Konstantin Mostras presented the various viewpoints in a comparative, critical light. He discussed the experiments that led N. A. Garbusow to his 'pitch zone' theory. According to it, people hear a note within a zone of three or four hertz on either side of the scientifically 'correct' pitch. The more acute a person's sense of 'perfect pitch,' the more subtle the variations they could discern within this 'zone.' Other factors affecting pitch judgment include the timbre, volume and register of a sound, a person's physical condition and the key or melody in which the note occurs.

One of Garbusow's experiments was an attempt to tabulate finitely the intonation frequency used by Zimbalist as opposed to Elman. He listened to the first twelve bars of their respective recordings of Bach's 'Air on the G string' and measured intervals, trying to analyze them scientifically, using the four recognized systems, Pythagoras's formula, absolute intonation, even-tempered intonation and the twelve-tone system. What he discovered was that while neither violinist's intonation fell strictly under any of these classifications, both demonstrated tendencies more akin to Pythagoras, in that their chromatic half-tones were larger than their diatonic half-tones and their augmented fourths larger than their diminished fifths. Each of the violinists had his own unique 'system,' Garbusow concluded, and each was attempting to bring out the individual character of successive intervals, to avoid 'neutralizing' them. His findings explain why Zimbalist's students never seemed able to play the second note (B-flat) of the Tchaikovsky Concerto low enough to satisfy his ear. One student reported success only when eventually playing what to their ear sounded like A–G-sharp–A (first three notes).

Soon began the succession of farewell recitals at Curtis—strung out over the next fourteen years. There are many stories about these 'presidential' recitals, as one admirer termed them. Krachmalnick reported that he turned pages at one on which Zimbalist was to begin with a stock show-stopper, Sinding's 'Suite.' He came out and tuned very carefully as usual. From his station behind the keyboard Sokoloff awaited a sign to begin. Instead Zimbalist asked for another A. While tuning again he sidled over toward Sokoloff. 'Billy,' he said calmly, 'I've been trying to remember. What is it we are going to play?'

On another occasion Norman Carol was turning for Sokoloff. Carol looked the part—in neatly pressed suit and deadpan expression, he became very popular as a page-turner, to the point that some observers were surprised to learn that he could also play the violin. In Bazzini's 'Ronde des Lutins,' Zimbalist fluffed the left-hand pizzicato scales. When he finished the piece, students unleashed their usual display of noisy approval, augmented by foot stomping. They had to wait what seemed an eternity for Zimbalist's reappearance onstage for bows and, perhaps, encores. Since the Curtis Hall stage was then only about ten feet deep, and the area behind the glass doors entering onto it even smaller, no one knew why it took so long, until Carol filled them in. Chagrined at having missed the pizzicato runs, Zimbalist had cornered him and Sokoloff backstage and insisted on demonstrating, half a dozen times, the fact that he *could* play the runs perfectly.

In 1948 Donald Brook interviewed Zimbalist for a British publication, *Violinists of Today*. Brook's opening lines refer to him as 'a celebrated artist who in this country is rather less known today than most of the other world-famous violinists.' Zimbalist's last appearance in England was in 1936, and his recordings had not been well distributed in Europe. In the early '50s he was invited to play with several orchestras in Italy. It was not a happy experience. Barely managing to extricate himself from unrelenting administrative duties at Curtis, he arrived in Florence in the middle of winter and felt unprepared. He stayed up all night to practice for the first rehearsal and came down with a bad cold that developed into pneumonia before the trip was over. On top of this, for the first time in his long career, he found the orchestra players less than cooperative. And he didn't like the communistic currents he saw in industrial Florence. This was his farewell to Europe, whose countries and peoples had once been so dear to his heart.

Efrem Jr. served as his father's assistant at Curtis from 1950 to 1953. During World War II he had been seriously injured crossing a minefield and was treated in a British hospital. His anxious father received no news until old friends Lynn Fontanne and Sir Alfred Lunt visited the patient and sent an encouraging report. Efrem Jr. spent months recovering in England, only to learn when he returned that his beloved wife, Emily, had cancer. Her death in 1950 was shattering. Zimbalist offered his son the position to provide structure for the years he spent putting his life back together.

During that dark period Efrem Jr. was drawn once again to his old love, music. He took some lessons with Rosario Scalero and started work on a violin sonata; like his father, he took active interest in the work of Gian Carlo Menotti, co-producing Menotti's Pulitzer Prize–winning opera *The Consul*. Efrem Jr.'s years at Curtis produced not only compositions but also quickened heartbeats. A contemporary source affirms he was so handsome that female students rerouted between classes to catch a glimpse of him in his office. In 1954 he turned again to an acting career, although his interest in composition lingered. In 1955, at Town Hall, the John Harms Chorus presented Efrem Jr.'s new opus, 'Laudate Dominum,' which the press called 'a short work of agreeable if not original nature.' It was an added accomplishment for an actor who was scoring major successes in Hollywood. By 1958 he was touring his father around the set of *The Deep Six*, showing him the advances motion picture technology had made since the 1926 Zimbalist-Bauer Vitaphone short; October of that year saw the debut of the TV series *77 Sunset Strip*, in which Efrem Jr. played the part of detective Stu Bailey, establishing himself as a household name.

At 5:30 on 20 November 1955 the Soviets' leading violinist, David Oistrakh, was introduced to the American public at Carnegie Hall. Primed by the press's anticipation of Oistrakh's arrival and heightened by rumors of cancellation due to illness, audiences exploded in their enthusiasm. Reviews glittered. Mischa Elman had played a recital at Carnegie Hall earlier that day, at 2:30. (It was an unparalleled day in the annals of violinism, for that evening at 8:30 Nathan Milstein also played a recital there.) When Elman arrived at the hall after lunch he was greeted by the spectacle of a blocks-long line at the box office, which he took as a sign of his fans' devotion. One can sympathize with his disgruntlement when he discovered that the line was for standing room at Oistrakh's performance. Although he stayed to hear the newcomer his critique, loudly delivered afterward to a group of Elman fans in the foyer, was far from complimentary—a clear sign that he had been impressed.

Of course Oistrakh's audience bristled with violinists. 'It was the presence of Fritz Kreisler that excited me more than anything else,' Oistrakh later reminisced. 'When I saw him deep in thought listening to my playing, and then rising to applaud, I was so overcome I thought I was dreaming.' Zimbalist heard Oistrakh several days later, playing the Sibelius Concerto with the Philadelphia Orchestra. He was deeply moved. Backstage he was delighted when Oistrakh reminded him of their 1934 Moscow meeting and told him of the great effect Zimbalist's playing had had on *him*.

However, disapproving as ever of publicity, Zimbalist found all the hoopla surrounding Oistrakh's arrival distasteful. When a colleague brought it up Zimbalist quipped, 'Oh, he's a great violinist, but he's no Oistrakh.' These words have been misconstrued. In the first place he was echoing Leopold Godowsky's famous comment to Josef Hofmann on first hearing Paderewski: 'He's good, but he's no Paderewski.' Beyond that his comment was aimed at the propaganda machine behind Oistrakh's appearance, not at the artist himself, whom he adored. After the concert Lea Luboshutz gave a dinner in Oistrakh's honor. Zimbalist managed to persuade Ormandy to join them, which was a considerable feat—a teetotaler and nonsmoker, he hated parties and was usually in bed by ten. The time Zimbalist and Oistrakh spent together in Philadelphia cemented a warm, enduring friendship. They corresponded regularly until Oistrakh's death.

Emil Gilels also first appeared in the United States in 1955. When he made his debut with the Philadelphia Orchestra Zimbalist got a call from

Ormandy. 'Efrem, you *have* to come over and meet Gilels. You've never heard anything like him,' he enthused. 'Yes, I have,' Zimbalist laughed, 'I heard him in Russia twenty years ago.'

Zimbalist's compositional creativity had, it seemed, slowed down in the early '50s—only some songs and a suite of piano pieces, 'Impressions,' surfaced. The latter, dedicated to the Zimbalists' friend Edie Braun, was a set of musical portraits of some of his favorite composers, among them Chopin, Rachmaninoff and Rimsky-Korsakov. But meanwhile something big was percolating. It was a full-scale opera, his first, dedicated to Mary. Zimbalist not only wrote the music but also undertook to coach the singers, drill the orchestra (composed of Curtis students) and lend a hand in the staging. During rehearsals Zimbalist had a difficult time maintaining orchestral discipline. This had never been the case with the professional groups he had conducted. But his undemonstrative manner, which proved so productive in the teaching studio, evidently lacked sufficient assertiveness to secure the undivided attention of a student orchestra. He took the youngsters' wandering attention as a personal affront. 'I just can't understand it,' he said to a friend. 'When I was in school we lived in mortal fear of teachers and conductors. We would never have dreamed of talking during rehearsals.'

'For the first time in his long musical career,' *Musical America* reported, '[Zimbalist] emerged as a composer of opera with the première of a three-act dramatic piece called *Landara* at the Academy of Music on April 6, 1956.' Bernice Kenyon's libretto concerned two American seamen who land on an eastern island ruled by a king who has a beautiful daughter; the princess falls in love with one of the sailors, but the opera concludes tragically, with her death. From the *Philadelphia Inquirer*: 'Zimbalist...has a flair for felicitous melody of a highly romantic order.'

A letter Zimbalist received in 1957 added a whole new aspect to the last decades of his life:

> In March–April 1958 in Moscow the first Tchaikovsky Competition will be held. This competition will be a showcase for young and very talented musicians. We are inviting young players of every nationality. We hope the competition will provide a lot of exposure and publicity for [them]. We are aware, esteemed Zimbalist, that you have done a lot for talented

young musicians, and your artistic name stands very high in our
country and the whole world.

We would like to invite you to be on the jury of the competition, and we will pay all expenses while in our country, and fly
you to Moscow and back to the United States. We will do anything possible to make your trip comfortable, and would be very
happy to receive a positive reply.

D. Shostakovich
Director
Committee of Tchaikovsky Competition for
Pianists and Violinists

Zimbalist accepted, becoming a regular on the jury for the Tchaikovsky
Competitions, held at four-year intervals. For the first competition all
jurors received an honorarium of $100 a week, plus living expenses. As in his
visits to the Soviet Union in the 1930s Zimbalist found the political climate
disquieting. During the weeks he was there, Bulganin was toppled but for
appearances officiated at the competition's closing ceremony, as he had
done at the opening dinner in the Kremlin. Khrushchev stood at his side.

At a cocktail party at the American embassy, *Time* correspondent Paul
Moor was approached by U.S. ambassador Llewellyn Thomson. Since the
closing of the Moscow *Time* office, Moor had been on secret assignment,
and he noticed that Thomson was subtly grilling him about any communistic leanings on Zimbalist's part. He wouldn't have given any
information, even had he had it. In the Cold War that followed McCarthy-
ism—and decades before 'cultural exchanges'—any display of interest in
the Soviet Union other than militaristic was viewed by the U.S. government with suspicion. The CIA had probably run down Zimbalist's
involvement in Russia's 1905 student strike, his exposure (through Joseph
Fels) to Henry George and above all, Alma Gluck's avid interest in the
'communist experiment.' Actually, Zimbalist's feelings about the Soviet
regime were strongly negative. He told Michael Tree after his return: 'In the
United States we squander so much energy in politicking and deciding on
policy that we are rendered virtually ineffectual in dealing with the Soviets.
On the contrary, they are so single-minded in their malevolent pursuits
that they feel they have no one to answer to but themselves.'

The Tchaikovsky Competition became a yardstick of virtuosity, on a par with the Queen Elisabeth in Brussels, but with its own very special significance. The prestige of being a Tchaikovsky contest winner automatically opens doors to the best concert halls in the world. By 1974, the first time each of the five continents was represented, there were 281 competitors. Applications were received years in advance.

In the Great Hall of the Moscow Conservatory, where the contests are still held, the judges' table, about 30 feet from the stage, runs the width of the hall. Zimbalist was treated with utmost respect from the start, always being seated at the center, next to chairman Oistrakh. (He brought Oistrakh a present: the signed copy of Ysaÿe's sonatas that Ysaÿe had presented to him in 1928. 'I thought he should have it because he had won the Queen Elisabeth prize.') Whenever Zimbalist entered the hall to make his way to his seat, the audience applauded. 'I guess they knew my name,' he joked drily. He and Oistrakh passed notes back and forth during sessions, and they spent a good deal of their free time together. Oistrakh was very proud of his car, being one of very few Soviet musicians to own one. He drove Zimbalist all over the city. They usually wound up at Oistrakh's home for dinner and more conversation. There Zimbalist met Konstantin Mostras, with whom Galamian had studied. Someone had recently given Oistrakh some of Joachim's recordings. They all listened to them with much curiosity but were disappointed by what they heard.

Entrants from the Soviet countries naturally predominated at the first Tchaikovsky Competition; indeed Valery Klimov, who won first violin prize, was a Russian and an Oistrakh student. Zimbalist found the Soviet school 'on a par with the American school.' Already by the second competition, in 1962, American-trained violinists were moving up in the running; in preparation for it Zimbalist had drilled three of his star pupils, Shmuel Ashkenasi, Hidetaro Suzuki and John Dalley. 'We had a great number of extra lessons,' Ashkenasi remembers. The proceedings took on added meaning for both him and his teacher when his second round fell on 9 April 1962, Zimbalist's seventy-second birthday. Ashkenasi was runner-up to Russia's Boris Gutnikov; Suzuki and Dalley also received high honors. In later competitions Zimbalist did well by his students Nicolas Chumachenco and Geoffrey Michaels. Michaels's program included Zimbalist's 'Coq d'Or Fantasy,' which had been added to the 'official list.' (Oistrakh frequently played it on his recitals and suggested to Zimbalist an improved fingering for its signature descending chromatic run.)

The uniformity of so many of the musicians Zimbalist heard at these competitions only reaffirmed his belief that 'to kill a pupil's individuality is the worst thing a teacher can do. A teacher may have greater experience, but nevertheless, if he has a talented student he should go *their* way, not his own. If I saw something special a student was trying to do, even if it didn't conform with my thinking, "Fine," I told myself "let them do it."'

He found the jury schedule convenient: 'The afternoon session ended just in time for dinner and the theater.' Of course there were also numerous social obligations. Leonid Kogan hosted a party for jury members. Throughout the entire affair the guests ate, drank and made merry to background sounds of violin concertos on the record player. 'Whose recordings are you playing?' Zimbalist inquired of Kogan. 'Mine,' he answered, without batting an eye. Although he had no need for one, Zimbalist was provided with an interpreter, a Russian woman of whom he became fond.

There was a nostalgic excursion to Leningrad to visit Rimsky-Korsakov's children, still living in Auer's former residence. Nadia wept with the observation that it was exactly fifty years since her father had died. Zimbalist brought back memories when he shared with them a letter from the violist of those carefree bygone quartet parties, Vitold Portugaloff. He was now a professor at one of the imperial music schools.

In 1965 Zimbalist took his student Nicolas Chumachenco to a recital given by David Oistrakh and introduced them. They decided that the youngster should compete in the next Tchaikovsky Competition. Chumachenco, a Russian by heritage and in the United States by way of Poland and Argentina, had come to Zimbalist from Heifetz's class in 1963. 'What I was most grateful for was the help Zimbalist gave me to simply live quietly and have time for my practicing,' he remarks. 'And his financial help removed all economic worries.' On the competition agenda were some Paganini caprices. 'Prepare all twenty-four for the next lesson, and we'll choose three,' Zimbalist told him. Chumachenco remembers their 1966 trip to Russia, where he came in fourth: 'He stood the trip very well, and we had fun. The flight from Copenhagen was loaded with jury members [including] Szigeti and Pierre Fournier. Zimbalist took me over to meet them. [I went to Zimbalist's] hotel to play for him before the second round. About a month before the competition Zimbalist had lent me his del Gesu — it was such a kind gesture and the first time I had a great violin in my hands. He borrowed my fiddle, a Lupot, for his own practice, which he did every day.'

Between the '62 and '66 contests Oistrakh had suffered a severe heart attack. When Zimbalist saw him he looked older, with tired, sagging features. He occupied a unique position in the Soviet Union, receiving 6,000 rubles a concert. In addition he had achieved almost ambassador status outside Soviet borders. As a result there were those on the lookout for a chance to topple him. Some who jockeyed for power tried to do so by courting government connections. Khrennikov, head of the Artists' Union, for instance, was a good friend of Leonid Kogan, generally considered the second-most important Soviet violinist and an active Party member. He was even suspected of KGB ties. Oistrakh somehow managed to sail over sticky political issues. But the inner tension had obviously taken its toll. And despite his condition the Soviet government continued to overwork him mercilessly.

For Zimbalist, associating with Oistrakh was the high point of each of the competitions. He also enjoyed Shostakovich and Khachaturian. He heard much of their music, Shostakovich's symphonies making a particular impression on him. However, he was honest in admitting that his understanding of them was limited. 'I was sure he was a very great composer,' Zimbalist said, 'but his musical language was so different from the one I grew up with.' Shostakovich was often unwell. Zimbalist told a touching story about the composer's strong will and loyalty to friends: 'Towards the end of the [1966] competition I was sitting quietly during a break [when] Shostakovich entered the hall and came over to me. I had been told he was very ill and confined to bed. But he didn't want to miss the chance to say goodbye to me before I left.'

He also had a fair dose of Prokofiev's music, which he didn't like. Prokofiev had returned to Soviet Russia, where he spent his later productive period, dying there in 1953 on the same day as Stalin. Zimbalist saw a lavish staging of his *War and Peace*. He confided later, 'Being an old-fashioned musician, I always judge a composition by its melodic line. Prokofiev's melodies sounded artificial, manufactured, unnatural and disjointed.'

Zimbalist admired his Soviet colleagues' stoic attitude toward government policies that regulated their artistic lives. 'They undoubtedly love their country,' he mused over a cigar after his return, 'and Russia is a country one can love. Why, even now I — ' and his thoughts trailed off into the swirls of smoke.

One of Zimbalist's greatest satisfactions was that his piano concerto was finally to be premièred, in New Orleans. The work was completed in 1953 and dedicated to Olga Samaroff's brilliant student William Kapell, who was to have introduced it with the Philadelphia Orchestra the following season. It bristles with difficulties, and Kapell, anxious to get a head start, took the only full score with him that fall to study while on tour in Australia. On the way back, on 29 October 1953, his plane crashed into King's Mountain, just south of San Francisco. There were no survivors. Zimbalist, shocked with the entire musical world by Kapell's death, set about the daunting task of rescoring his piano concerto. All he had to go on was a manuscript copy of the solo piano part.

A new pianist too had to be sought. Serkin was approached; but his repertoire had long been narrowed down to the specialized area of the German classical masters in which he had no peers, and he confessed with profound apologies that the Zimbalist work no longer fitted his style. Eugene Istomin liked it but didn't think he could spare enough time to master its intricacies. Lee Luvisi finally took on the project; he tried to interest Leonard Bernstein, reading the concerto through with Bernstein at a second keyboard, but Lenny threw the score across the room with an expletive-laden dismissal. The San Francisco Symphony came close to programming it but didn't because it was 'too similar' to Rachmaninoff.

Musical America ended its complimentary review of the concerto's eventual première in March 1959, which both Zimbalist and Serkin attended, by noting that the applause 'indicated that the concerto could become a useful addition to the standard repertory through its ability to be evolutionary without being too revolutionary for audience appreciation.' Audience reaction notwithstanding, the concerto has not had many performances. Luvisi considers it the most difficult he ever had to learn, which could be a factor.

This New Orleans concert was Zimbalist's final collaboration with Hilsberg, who died in 1961. A year later, in 1962, days before his eighty-seventh birthday, Fritz Kreisler died. Although during recent years he and Zimbalist had seen each other only rarely, they had kept in touch by phone and Zimbalist was deeply affected by his passing: 'In my professional life there were two men, in all those years, who were closest to me — Rimsky-Korsakov and Kreisler.'

His Curtis Institute recitals continued. The 1963 one included Ysaÿe's g minor solo sonata and his arrangement of the Saint-Saëns 'Valse Caprice.' At about this time *The World of Carnegie Hall* was published. Sokoloff showed Zimbalist the book, and as he flipped through the pages, Zimbalist's mild interest was raised to amused attention when he came to a full-page photograph whose caption began 'Efrem Zimbalist, who made his Carnegie Hall debut in 1911.' But the photograph was of Mischa Elman. 'Anyone but him!' Zimbalist laughed.

On 27 February 1964, Zimbalist stepped on stage to play his last concert. He was seventy-three. This historic event took place in the Institute's recital hall. Poignancy was heightened by Zimbalist's inclusion of his son's sonata. Begun a decade earlier, it had just achieved its final form. It is a striking work, doubtless inspired by the brilliance of Zimbalist's violin, a perpetual sound in Efrem Jr.'s ear. The slow movement, based on a Russian folk song, is handled in an interesting way: a special pedaling effect is heard at the beginning, an octave in the bass that is allowed to vibrate sympathetically throughout the statement, reminiscent of cathedral chimes. The last movement, marked 'Giojosamente,' has a rollicking hornpipe theme. His father thought the piece was 'pretty modern.'

PROGRAM FOR THE LAST PUBLIC PERFORMANCE, 1964

Zimbalist played Paganini's 'Moto Perpetuo' as an encore. He played it as he always had, fast, easily and *with* repeat. Age seemed not to have diminished his facility — there was an abundance of the expected technical brilliance. But age had scored in a spot that it often did with older violinists: 'His vibrato was gone,' Curtis Quartet member Mehli Mehta, always a fan, had to admit.

If his playing in his seventy-fourth year showed minimal deterioration, what of his general physical condition? I had been studying with Ivan Galamian at Juilliard and entered Curtis in 1964 as a Galamian student. Having always admired Zimbalist, I made an appointment to meet him. Outside the door of his studio on the second floor I awaited his arrival. I heard a light step ascending the stairs. 'A student,' I thought, so youthful were the strides. But no, it was Zimbalist who strode over with his characteristic springy, energetic step. He held out his hand. It was the smooth, pliable hand of a young man. As we shook I noticed with fascination that his left thumb was almost twice the width of his right one, the result of seventy years of supporting the violin. I also noticed a copper bracelet around his right wrist, indicating the bouts of arthritis which bothered him in varying degrees for the rest of his life.

During my first year at Curtis I determined that I wanted to study with Zimbalist. When I told him, he wouldn't hear of it: 'I would never take another's student, unless they asked me to. Anyway, you have the greatest teacher in the world right now.' Realizing how the switch must be accomplished, I wrote to Galamian, telling him how much I valued all that he had taught me, but expressing my wish to work with Zimbalist before it was too late. Galamian permanently endeared himself to me by his response, although when I went to my next lesson and found the door open and the studio empty I momentarily panicked. My back to the door, I was putting my music on the stand, when I heard the door being quietly closed. I turned around. Galamian was smiling gently. 'I have just come down from talking with Zimbalist,' he said. 'You will study with him next year. What did you bring today?' At first I was speechless, then volubly thankful. Galamian tossed this off: 'What kind of a teacher would I be if you thought you could learn something from someone else and I wouldn't let you?'

I spent summer 1965 recalling all I knew about the 'Auer bow arm' and the 'old-fashioned' violinists Galamian had discouraged his students from hearing. I also dispensed with the shoulder rest he had recommended I use.

At my first lesson with Zimbalist, he paced around me slowly as I played, studying my bowing. His comment shocked me: 'Very nice, but tell me, did Mr. Galamian teach you to hold your bow that way?' 'Mr. Zimbalist,' I answered, 'would you please show me how *you* hold the bow?' He demonstrated to me a much more 'modern' bowhold than I had expected. He had a further observation: 'Your shoulder looks a little uncomfortable when you play. Have you ever thought of using a shoulder rest?'

At another of my lessons, while I was still enjoying the lifting of restrictions placed on me by Galamian, I arrived in a grey cutaway and striped trousers, rounded out with spats and a gold-topped cane. Zimbalist's comment to Sokoloff after I had left said it all: 'Last week he was Heifetz, this week Sarasate. When will he be himself?'

Zimbalist was an almost invariably patient, diplomatic teacher. It was only with Sokoloff that he vented his true feelings. A boy who later became concertmaster of a major orchestra had just left after a frustrating lesson. Zimbalist turned to Sokoloff: 'Billy, he's a talented boy, but brains we can't give him.' His wit often came to the fore. Once at the Curtis Institute's annual violin auditions, a brash youngster swaggered in, tuned loudly and asked, 'Well, what would you like to hear?' 'How about the C major scale in four octaves?' Zimbalist suggested pleasantly. The boy attacked it with perfect confidence but less-than-perfect intonation. At its conclusion he held his bow high in the air, leered triumphantly at Zimbalist and asked, 'Now would you like to hear C-sharp?' 'Don't bother — you just played it.'

Student Paul Windt once heard Heifetz's recording of the Saint-Saëns Sonata, was enchanted and slaved on it for hours before bringing it to his lesson with Zimbalist. At one of its thickest points, Zimbalist stopped the proceedings and studied the page for a few moments with the genial expression that was an unfailing barometer of impending action. Then he reached for a pencil and in his careful hand opened a cut. He flipped over one page and then another before closing it with a distinct air of satisfaction. Paul was thoroughly crestfallen. 'Mr. Zimbalist,' he moaned, 'had I known, think how much practice time I could have saved.' Zimbalist's eyes twinkled as he offered consolation: 'Just think of the time Saint-Saëns could have saved himself!' Zimbalist found it difficult to countenance longwindedness in compositions, often resorting to cuts; once after a performance of Bach's St. Matthew Passion, he remarked, 'It was very beautiful, but even Jesus had to go to the bathroom!'

Danny Heifetz once accepted an engagement to play solos on a cruise ship. Zimbalist seemed surprised, but I assured him it was all the rage and mentioned several top stars who had done it. 'If I should ever again take a cruise,' he laughed, 'I will first make sure no entertainers have been engaged.'

Rafael Druian hadn't seen Zimbalist for many years when he dropped in to visit in Philadelphia in the late 1960s. Zimbalist asked what he had been up to recently. Druian mentioned several recordings he had made, among them sonatas by Charles Ives and Quincy Porter. Zimbalist said that he didn't know these sonatas and would like to hear them. His former student ran down to Sam Goody's, bought one of his records and immediately sent it to Zimbalist. Some weeks later he received the following note:

> Dear Rafael,
>
> May I *not* thank you for sending me your and John Simm's recordings of the Ives and Porter sonatas. The playing of them I liked very much, I imagine you and John Simms have done all in your power to make things clear. I wish that music of this sort would be more comprehensible to me, but I regret to say, it is not. Please remember me affectionately to Mrs. Druian.
>
> Efrem Zimbalist

Around that time I asked him why the once-so-popular short pieces no longer appeared on concert programs. 'Short pieces are simple things,' he answered. 'In the old days they reflected the simplicity of the times. Later, simple tastes were satisfied by popular musicians such as Bing Crosby and his ilk. Today people's lives reflect more complicated needs, like Charles Ives sonatas.'

But Zimbalist had once written Paul Hindemith a fan letter, telling him how much he liked 'Mathis der Maler.' Zimbalist was hurt that Hindemith never replied. He wrote that letter after hearing 'Mathis' for the first time in the 1950s — the symphony was composed in 1934 and had become a standard repertory item. He didn't realize why his letter hadn't impressed Hindemith.

After Zimbalist took an arthritis treatment at a New York outpatient facility, an amusing incident occurred, of a kind that became more typical as his son occupied the limelight and he moved further from it. Leaving the hospital, he phoned for a taxi, giving his name. The taxi arrived and Zimbalist got in. 'So you're Efrem Zimbalist?' the cabbie asked. 'Yes.' A pause. 'Say, any relation to Efrem Zimbalist Jr.?' 'Yes.' A pause. 'Just what are you to him?' 'He's my son.' Pause. 'Say, haven't you also done something?' 'I'm a musician.' Pause. 'Why sure, now I recognize you. You're the famous pianist!' Zimbalist was amused by his growing recognition as the father of the film star, and he was very proud of Efrem Jr.'s success. He watched him regularly in *77 Sunset Strip*, having patiently sat in front of the Curtis Mathes set until a maid or butler found the channel for him. But he did somehow master the intricacies of the household's top-of-the-line Marantz hi-fi, and he and Mary spent many an evening listening to LP reissues of their favorite Kreisler and Rachmaninoff recordings.

During Zimbalist's tenure at Curtis he was criticized for denying the Institute the public exposure many thought it should have. To quote Sokoloff: 'Some people believed he turned the school into a cloistered ivory tower. Concerts were not open to the public, and students were forbidden to give outside performances except on the rare occasions the Institute saw fit to sponsor them. Zimbalist sincerely felt the school was for the students and that they should be sheltered while studying.'

Some maintained that he allowed the school to be run by a bunch of old ladies. True, he gave few outward indications of power and believed that too much government was a bad thing. He did largely delegate the carrying out of day-to-day school activities. But the secretaries and assistants so assigned were highly efficient. It was the height of futility, for instance, for anyone to try to sneak by the office of registrar Anne Smith after committing some minor infringement of the rules. Moreover, these ladies not only devotedly upheld the spirit of the Institute's firm code of ethics — they seemed to embody it as well.

Zimbalist, understandably, saved his energy for artistic matters. In later years, his schedule began around noon, when he strolled to school to open his mail and dictate replies. He then played a scale or two (always four octaves), or perhaps some runs in thirds and fingered octaves at dizzying speed, or the opening flourishes of his 'Coq d'Or Fantasy.' While doing so he enjoyed a post-lunch pre-Castro Havana. At precisely 12:55 it was extinguished — the one o'clock student could hear him running the faucet over it in his bathroom as they waited outside the studio door. It was time to get down to business, and while teaching Zimbalist never smoked. Sokoloff, without his summer beard, would be waiting too. During the school year he was clean-shaven save for a small mustache—Zimbalist was not fond of beards. Precisely on the hour, the door would open, and there would be cordial greetings and a handshake. Then a brief glance at the music placed on the stand, 'What do we have here?' and Zimbalist would seat himself in a big armchair. The lesson began. With Sokoloff's accompaniment one played through a concerto movement, often the entire piece. At times Sokoloff seemed to lag immovably, at others push. (He once explained: 'I knew his tempi and wanted to save time.') Zimbalist listened, visibly involved. At the end, a brief encouraging comment, then to work, violin in hand.

'Do you know, I used to do this'—'What would you think of…?'—'But this passage is easy, see?'—'May I suggest…?'—'You know, I prefer…' These typical comments were followed by a commanding demonstration. (There was no mistaking the gleam in his eye when he had illustrated a thorny passage with particularly brilliant dispatch.) His suggestions made, Zimbalist might advise reworking the concerto, or going on to another. Sokoloff would leave, and it would be time for the unaccompanied works—an Ernst or Paganini etude, and Bach. Only in the study of Bach's solo works did Zimbalist tend to impose his views on students—here he could be a tiresome stickler. Nicolas Chumachenco remembers having 'two Bach scores—one that I used at the lessons and one for myself.' Ideally Zimbalist expected a different concerto plus a Paganini caprice and a movement of Bach for each lesson. Surely this represented eight hours or more of daily slavery? 'Certainly not. You have to learn what *not* to practice,' he would say. (Heifetz too told his pupils: 'Don't practice the easy parts.')

Once I brought the Goldmark Concerto to a lesson. I played the first movement, which alone takes almost fifteen minutes, and is full of notes. Then I apologized for not having prepared the rest of the concerto. Zimbalist put on his hat. 'Well,' he said, holding out his hand, 'It was a very short lesson.'

Zimbalist's emphasis was on covering the repertoire, not perfecting it, unless working toward a specific performance or contest goal. Technical competence was always taken for granted, and no one unqualified gained admission to his class. In that sense, as he admitted, he didn't 'build' the way Galamian did, but he could expand a student's technique by sharp analysis and demonstration. Above and beyond technique, he never lost sight of its raison d'être. Rafael Druian speaks of his 'loftiness and high regard for music. [He] always tried to raise the human spirit by looking for that special something. Dismissing technical problems and putting music first, he gained his rewards.'

Taking all these inspiring sentiments into consideration, it was often Zimbalist's sense of the pragmatic that was most helpful. The Curtis Institute demanded no further proof of having profited from its curriculum than a senior recital. In order to graduate, however, one also needed to receive the director's blessing. 'My feeling,' said Zimbalist, 'was that a student's area of specialty, the means by which he or she would earn their living, should take precedence. If a talented oboist, for instance, didn't do too well in solfeggio or counterpoint, I would say, "Give him a passing grade." It was his oboe playing that would provide him a livelihood. I graduated many singers who knew very little about music — if they had a voice. I was quite aware that their voices would make careers for them, more than their musical knowledge.' This accommodating attitude should not be misinterpreted. To some it suggested the viewpoint of a dyed-in-the-wool virtuoso, but these critics overlooked the fact that as a student Zimbalist spent more time studying theory than practicing the violin. Experience evidently taught him an appropriate balance, which characterizes the best graduates of the Curtis Institute under his directorship.

He continued spending summers in Maine and teaching a few students there. Chumachenco once drove with him from Philadelphia. Patrick had chauffeured Mrs. Zimbalist and her maid Frieda to The Rafters a week earlier. Mary had made big renovations to the Connecticut stopover where, following time-honored tradition, the Zimbalists spent some time before proceeding to their Rockport summering spot. Zimbalist was an overly cautious driver, and his poor sense of direction directed him to Maine by a different route each time. A passenger in the studiously driven Buick, Chumachenco found himself wondering how his teacher had survived so many trips. Nineteen-year-old Nicolas had just obtained his driving license. 'If you would like any help with the driving, do let me know,' he hinted. His offer was declined the first day — 'No thank you, Nicolas. But if you would like to stop for a hamburger, you let *me* know.' They arrived at The Rafters in time for an elegant dinner, which struck Chumachenco as out of keeping with the simple Connecticut countryside setting. A faux pas relating to his incorrect use of cutlery was lightly redressed by Mrs. Zimbalist. The next morning Zimbalist and Chumachenco left for Maine, this time with the nineteen-year-old behind the wheel. 'He told me to take it easy,' Chumachenco remembers. 'Whenever I thought he wasn't looking I would speed up. But he would look over and say, "Nicolas, I think it's a *little* too fast."'

Lyndonwood is situated in one of the most sublime settings on the eastern seaboard, its long veranda overlooking Curtis Island and magnificent Penobscot Bay. Zimbalist practiced on this veranda, starting at 5 a.m., with a mute. An hour or two of scales and exercises, done to restless pacing, would greet seagulls and lobstermen each summer morning. I once asked if he took any exercise. He answered, 'I walk miles every day while practicing.' Just around the corner was Rosemary Cottage, where Edith Braun stayed. This much-beloved gentlelady could be seen toward dusk each day sitting bolt upright behind the controls of her vintage Plymouth as she negotiated the mile-and-a-half that lay between her cottage and Lyndonwood. Never exceeding ten miles an hour, she arrived in time for dinner and a hand or two of rummy. On the grounds behind Rosemary Cottage stood what had once been a barn, later converted into a music studio with a grand piano. It was here that Zimbalist taught from June to August. To get to the studio, it was necessary to walk down the driveway past the kitchen's Dutch door, from which a clothesline was suspended to a nearby tree. One morning Zimbalist arrived a little earlier than usual to find Mrs. Braun leaning over the bottom half of the door busily reeling in the clothesline. Zimbalist pointed in mock surprise to the half-dozen frilly bloomers pinned to it: 'Edie,' he said with incredulity, 'are those *yours*?'

Zimbalist was the essence of generous hospitality, and dinners and tea parties for the students and other summer residents were regularly given at Lyndonwood. During one buffet dinner Zimbalist was told I was a vegetarian. On top of the constant ministrations of Frieda and her helpers, Zimbalist himself came around periodically with plates of vegetables, just to be sure I wouldn't go hungry. At that point I had met him only once before, briefly at that. Many of his students retain fond memories of this kindly concern even outside the lesson studio. He served as best man at the wedding of both Chumachenco and Hidetaro Suzuki.

Zimbalist remained physically trim until his very last years. Even in his fifties, however, his hearing had started slipping. Specialists all concurred that nothing could be done, and the situation worsened. By the time I met him he was wearing a hearing aid in one ear. It was not that he couldn't hear sounds per se — he just couldn't distinguish between them. In a room full of people, voices fused so that it was impossible for him to tell who was saying what; worst of all, the notes in a melodic progression melded together à la Mantovani, and harmonies were unbearable cacophonies. A violinist playing alone was still tolerable, but with piano accompaniment the effect was painful. His hearing aid was aimed at clarity rather than amplification. When attending performances in his last years he usually turned it off, relying on memory to transmute the movements he saw into sound.

Galamian too suffered eventual hearing loss. Violin students stepping onto the Curtis Hall stage to play a recital would peer nervously at the faculty box to their left, barely yards from the stage and mere feet from the audience. Zimbalist's white head could be spotted at a glance. That was enough to put one on one's best behavior. But recognizing Galamian's bushy mane beside him meant sure butterflies in the stomach, for fear of the embarrassingly loud things the audience might overhear. Galamian always grabbed a taxi from 30th Street Station to get to Curtis. Once, at audition time, the cabbies were on strike and Zimbalist didn't expect him. Just as things started, Galamian slipped in. 'Vanya, how did you get here?' Zimbalist asked. 'The boy plays quite well,' Galamian replied. Zimbalist beamed. 'Where there's a will, there's a way.'

A significant event in 1967 put Zimbalist's low profiling of his ethnic roots to the test: the publication of Marcia Davenport's *Too Strong for Fantasy*. In it she presented a touching portrait of her mother and the Zimbalist-Gluck love affair. She sent Papouchka a copy. After a week he phoned her at her New York home, in tears. She had brought Alma so much to life that he was beyond words. Marcia was equally moved by the call. But she had also made clear reference to their Jewish heritage, considering the world in 1967 changed enough from the one that in 1915 had prompted their conversion. Several weeks later her stepfather returned the book, with no explanation. He had read the rest. Marcia's half sister Maria, accepting her heritage but preferring to ignore it, took her to task for what was nothing more than affirming truths that had been stated before, though not with Davenport's authority as a member of the family. Maria pointed out that grandchildren and great-grandchildren existed who, thinking themselves Gentiles, now for the first time would know otherwise. Since both Alma and Efrem Zimbalist were featured in two well-circulated books by Gdal Saleski that paid tribute to the plethora of Jewish-born musicians throughout recorded history, this is difficult to believe. To quote Saleski: 'Zimbalist is beloved of his fellow Jews and one can often hear him in concerts of a specifically Jewish nature, on which occasions he plays his own transcriptions of traditional Jewish airs.' One such performance on record was at the Manhattan Opera House in 1925 for the ninth memorial of Sholem Aleichem. (Incidentally, when Serge Koussevitsky's biography was published, the conductor sued its author, David Ewen, because he called him Jewish. Ewen won — because he had stated nothing but the truth.)

Zimbalist had long since become entrenched, and accepted, in Philadelphia's high society Episcopalian circles. He would neither speak to Marcia nor countenance mention of her name in his presence. The entire question is a puzzling one — anyone who knew Zimbalist well knows that he was a person of strong principle and that his convictions, once formulated, became inviolate. Many admire him for sticking to his guns, even when the cost was family disunity; others condemn his attitude as inflexible, callous, even sacrilegious.

Zimbalist's last years at Curtis were not happy ones. By the mid '60s Mary Zimbalist was in failing health, although she occasionally presided over Wednesday afternoon teas in the Institute's foyer, sitting next to the tall Russian samovar and serving with great poise. She also developed dementia, which made her jealously turn on faithful friend Edie Braun, adding to the gloom on Delancey Place.

The deterioration of Zimbalist's hearing made him ever more doubtful of his continued usefulness as a teacher, and he couldn't help feeling that he was struggling to keep hold of the administrative reins too. As his wife became less capable of cogent thought, her son Cary became more influential on the Board of Directors. Zimbalist and Cary had never got along. Conflicts between them wore Zimbalist down and prompted his resignation from the board in 1966. Two years later he announced his resignation as director. Cary's second wife, Stormy, provided great solace throughout this discouraging time by her neutrality and unfailing kindness to Zimbalist. She begged him to remain as director, but no one's entreaties had any effect. In March 1968 the *Philadelphia Inquirer* announced that Zimbalist would retire on graduation day, 11 May. 'Well, Billy, that's that,' he said to Sokoloff the morning his decision became public. 'Forty years is a long enough time.'

As the Curtis Institute's founder, Mary was in attendance at the last graduation ceremony over which Zimbalist presided, as she had been at every graduation for forty-three years. She sat onstage in the bosom of her creation, beside her husband and surrounded by family, friends and admirers. Yet it was sadly evident at this point that she existed in a world of her own.

To Zimbalist's discomfort, the order of events was diverted for a special nostalgic observance of the occasion's historical significance. Efrem Jr. was called upon to pay his father tribute and present him with a choice Steuben vase. A few additional words were said marking the concurrent retirement of Jay Mattis, in recognition of his contributions to the Institute's successful functioning. Impatient as ever where speeches were concerned, Zimbalist glanced nervously from the program on his lap to the Steuben, to his watch and back again. When the moment seemed propitious, he handed the vase to Orlando Cole (seated to his left) and stood: 'Now we will all sing "The Star-Spangled Banner,"' he announced with a tone of relief.

On that fateful afternoon Zimbalist passed through the Institute's doors for the last time as director. He descended the few stairs to Locust Street and strolled, with his family, toward Delancey Place. He had just passed his seventy-eighth birthday. Spring was in the air. In Rittenhouse Square the sycamores were displaying signs of renewed green. Was nature hinting at what no one else knew — that sixteen productive years of unchecked creativity lay ahead of him?

CHAPTER 22

Productive Retirement

(1970–1978)

Mary Zimbalist died on 6 January 1970, leaving the musical world a heritage of incalculable value; among the condolences that flooded in were a
letter from Oistrakh and a telegram from Heifetz. On a different note,
a routine letter arrived from Moscow requesting Zimbalist's presence at
the fourth Tchaikovsky Competition, scheduled for the upcoming May.
Meanwhile he had more immediate preoccupations: the settling of the
estate and the dismantling of the household. Edie Braun moved to a comfortable apartment on West Rittenhouse Square overlooking the Curtis
Institute—she too had retired from her duties there. He himself could see
no point in remaining in Philadelphia.

He proposed turning the two Delancey Place houses over to the
Institute—the need for expanded quarters had long since been demonstrated. Cary Bok vetoed the idea. Instead Cary persuaded the Institute to
buy a building adjoining the school that it had once owned but sold to the
Elizabeth Arden Company when Zimbalist became director. Then, the
considerable sum that sale engendered had helped to stabilize Curtis's
financial condition. Now, repurchasing the building at market price contributed to the advent of new financial problems. Since then, outside
donations for the running of an expanded school have been elicited—a
concept as repugnant to Zimbalist as it would have been to his wife.

Zimbalist's children opened their arms to him. 'Efrem so much wanted
me to live with him,' Zimbalist said, 'but I knew he led a very busy life, and
I wasn't sure I wanted to fit in with a great deal of activity. What I wanted
most was an escape from the turmoil that I had been used to all my life.'

The fact that Efrem Jr. and his second wife, Stephanie (mother of television's *Remington Steele* star), were just then reconciling after nine years of divorce, could also have influenced his decision not to move into their home in Encino, a suburb of Los Angeles. Instead he accepted daughter Maria's invitation to join her in Reno, Nevada—an unlikely retirement perch for so sophisticated a world figure.

Sokoloff stopped by Delancey Place to bid Zimbalist farewell: 'I had no reason to think that I would ever get to Nevada to see him. The house was being packed up around him. We sat in the living room and chatted just as casually as when he first asked me to be his accompanist. We reminisced a little about our association and briefly touched on his successor [Serkin]. He told me not to worry about my position. When it was time for good-byes I said, "Mr. Zimbalist, this is a very sad moment." "Oh, it's just the end of a life," he replied.'

It was Reno's out-of-the-wayness that appealed to Zimbalist. 'I've done enough. All I want now is a little peace and quiet.' His presence in the self-proclaimed biggest little city in the West added an immeasurable richness to the town's life and put it on the map musically. But there was another reason for his move to Reno: he wanted to be close to his daughter Maria, who had started having serious bouts with the ugly disease lupus.

Maria had lived in Nevada for many years. She had initially gone there for a quick divorce, then stayed when she met a local man who became her second husband. The wide-open, freewheeling atmosphere of the West suited her spirit, which had been cramped by eastern society's propriety. At the time her father came to stay she had been divorced for a second time and was living alone in a handsome house on Skyline Drive in Reno's exclusive southwest section. Her daughters were married; Susan lived in Reno, Jane in California.

Zimbalist's first order of business in 'retirement' was to put the finishing touches to his cello concerto and resume work on a second opera, *The Two Stories*, which had kept his mind occupied during the grim months of his wife's invalidity in Philadelphia. To keep up his cheer he had chosen a comic theme, based on a libretto by Ludwig Fulder. The action depicts the daily lives of a wealthy landlord on the ground floor and his underprivileged tenants upstairs. The musical score contains some of Zimbalist's more adventurous writing, all set down in a meticulously neat hand that makes the running of one's eye over it a pleasure.

He was just getting into his work when it was time to leave for Moscow—he had agreed to be on the Tchaikovsky jury because he wanted to see Oistrakh again. The trip was beset with difficulties from the start. His flights were exhausting, and he arrived to find Oistrakh far from well—he had suffered another heart attack and developed diabetes. Shostakovich too was ill. Zimbalist immediately went with Oistrakh and Rostropovich to visit him in hospital.

During the contest Moscow was groaning under a heat wave, and musically Zimbalist found the overall level less good than in previous years. He sat beside Oistrakh, who mopped his brow continuously—during breaks attendants brought him bowls of ice cream in an attempt to cool him off. Despite his problems, Oistrakh showed him every consideration; every afternoon he took him to his home where his devoted wife, Tamara, would serve lunch. Afterward he insisted Zimbalist lie down for a rest. 'They lived in a tiny apartment,' Zimbalist recalled, 'which meant that Tamara had to make up a special bunk for me in a corner.'

At the competition's end, not permitted to take his earnings out of the country, Zimbalist wanted to put them to good use and asked to be taken to an earthquake relief donation center. Leaving the building he slipped on the stairs and broke his left hip. 'I don't look back with pleasure on my medical experiences in Russia,' he recounted later. 'At the hospital I found myself surrounded by medical student observers. Oistrakh had me moved to one of the very scarce private rooms. When he brought the entire jury to visit me, he asked if I was being well taken care of. I assured him that I was, joking that the only thing I missed was the American custom of orange juice with breakfast. Some mornings later I was served a glass of freshly squeezed juice—he had phoned all over trying to find oranges. Finally he had some flown in from Mongolia.' Zimbalist was visibly moved when he spoke of this act of kindness.

Oistrakh insisted that his own doctor examine Zimbalist. The prognosis was three months of immobility—they were taking no chances with their renowned eighty-year-old patient. But he found the thought of lying for so long in a Russian hospital untenable and determined to return to Reno. While the State Department looked into travel arrangements, Zimbalist felt bored and wanted company. 'So they put me in with another patient, more ambulatory than I—he could go to the kitchen and bring us back huge wursts for snacks.' After several weeks, travel plans were formulated:

wearing a body cast and tended by a nurse, Zimbalist would fly to Copenhagen, then on to New York, where Maria would meet him.

Before leaving Moscow Zimbalist asked his interpreter friend to deliver the score of his recently completed cello concerto, a work he considered of real merit, to Rostropovich, who had expressed interest in it. There was a final snag—when he was given his hospital bill Zimbalist was told that he couldn't use American Express Travelers Cheques to pay it. He must have been firm: 'In the end they had to take them,' was the way he put it.

At her New York home Marcia Davenport received a call from Maria asking her to meet her at JFK: she didn't know how much help she would need getting their father onto the flight from there to San Francisco. He was wheeled off the plane and into the first aid room. 'I arrived like King Arthur in a suit of armor—but flat on my back!' Marcia was not sure what his reaction to her would be and waited at the door. Maria hugged Zimbalist and told him, 'Marcia is here too. Would you like to see her?' He assented, Marcia came in, they kissed, and he behaved as if the last few years of noncommunication hadn't existed. Maria and Marcia settled him as comfortably as possible onto the westbound plane. Maria traveled at his side.

In Reno a pin was inserted into his femur. The consideration he always showed others endeared him to the entire hospital staff. He was a model patient, joking about aches and pains instead of complaining. His few requests of the nurses—invariably prefaced by 'I wonder, if it is not too much trouble, if you would be kind enough to…'—were followed by profuse expressions of his gratitude. (An instance of this unwillingness to inconvenience others is related by granddaughter Nancy: 'Once at The Rafters, I was awakened at about three in the morning by sounds. I got up to investigate and found Grandpa downstairs trying to phone the hospital—his appendix had ruptured. Despite the terrible pain he didn't want to disturb us.')

Zimbalist's Reno doctors let him leave the hospital fairly soon, although it was weeks before he was allowed to stand up. They gave him a walker and told him he would never walk again without a cane. This was the first of many occasions where he confounded the medics—within months he was walking almost as well as ever and, for nearly a decade more, without the assistance of a stick.

To ensure good circulation while he was convalescing, Maria engaged a masseur. Over the next fourteen years this Mr. Wilson's weekly visits were an important entry in Zimbalist's calendar. He and Wilson, an elderly man himself, developed a pleasant friendship, and they would go gambling together following massage sessions. Zimbalist, concerned as ever for the well-being of those around him, put his masseur on a regular (and generous) salary, which he continued to pay after Wilson's own state of health put an end to his services. In the early years of his stint Wilson came across a copy of *Too Strong for Fantasy* and brought it to his friend in the hope that he might get the author to sign it. Marcia came to visit a few months later. Zimbalist lightly mentioned a book his masseur wished signed, and she was glad to oblige. He placed the volume on the table. When she saw its title, Marcia matter-of-factly opened the cover and picked up a pen. As she wrote Zimbalist put his hand on hers. 'Please forgive me,' he said.

I moved to the West Coast in 1973. I had corresponded with Zimbalist since his retirement, and he urged me to stop by for a visit on my cross-country drive. He and Maria had by this time moved to Lindley Way, a secluded cul-de-sac just off Lakeside Drive—with her daughters gone, a smaller house seemed more practical. My knock at the front door of No. 2255 was answered by Trini, the Mexican live-in maid; she ushered me into a sizable room just off the kitchen, over the garage.

It was this room, isolated from the rest of the house, that Zimbalist now called home. He rose from an easy-chair to greet me. He was puffing on a fine cigar—indeed the room was a pall of smoke, and he was attired in the sort of casual slacks and open-collared sport shirt I had seen him wear only once or twice before, during summers in Maine. He looked and moved well and appeared contented. He was happy to see me but decided that his surroundings needed some explanation. My eye followed his gesturing arm as he spoke. There was a vintage Steinway in the corner by the window. The walls were covered with his priceless collection of photographs, presented to him by the world's celebrities. Countless additional mementos of his life and travels sat on the piano and on a chest of drawers by the door; these included precious Chinese vases, an exquisite Japanese doll, the miniature Strad Hammig had given him as a wedding present and, in a glass case, a model train built by former student Frederick Vogelgesang. (What remained of his collection of Japanese inros and Chinese snuff bottles—he had already given most to his son—was displayed in a wall cabinet in the main house's living room.) On a small

worktable was a sheaf of manuscript paper and a battery of writing imple-
ments. Above the bed a print of Michelangelo's *Moses*, his favorite
sculpture, presided with solemn dignity. Beside it and adjacent to the chair
on which he kept his violin, a music stand held his daily practice selections.
Bookshelves and a closet occupied the room's far corner, leading off to a
full bathroom with photo-studded walls. Opulent Oriental rugs were all
over. It all struck me as very comfortable. Yet the explanation: 'Well, here is
my little room. It's more than I ever thought I'd end up with. All my life I
have loved simple things, but until now I've been unable to live simply.
I lived grandly before because circumstances were such that I couldn't do
anything else—and I always felt a little as if I were on the outside of it all.
How I ever survived all those society types amazes me now,' he laughed.

But Zimbalist's Reno domicile in no way smacked of asceticism.
Wherever Zimbalists live they carry with them a grand aura, a certain
characteristic je ne sais quoi, and in line with Maria's fondness for freer
Western ways, the ambience she maintained in her home was of a casual
elegance. A brilliant linguist, she spent her time translating ancient classical manuscripts, playing bridge with friends and resting when her state
of health required it. She also did the shopping. Trini attended to everything else. During the early years of their setting up house together, Maria
hadn't much need to look after her father. He was relatively self-sufficient
and soon established a general pattern of living that was not too different
from his previous daily routine. He rose at four or five in the morning (as
the years passed it might even be an hour earlier). He would turn on a prepared coffeemaker and, while it percolated, quietly fix the sort of breakfast
he had subsisted on for more than forty years: orange juice then toast with
cheese, usually Stilton. Tori, the household's lovable superannuated Skye
terrier, joined him while he ate. Then he took a cup of coffee back into his
domain and lit up his first morning cigar, a 'tiny' commercial variety.
His revered pre-Castros he saved for after the evening meal, although on
special occasions he might occasionally break one out earlier.

Work began after breakfast: a half-hour of scales (his own warm-up
system), a page of Paganini and one of Bach, then he was ready for excerpts
from whichever concerto might interest him. The session sometimes
lasted as much as three hours. When asked why he still practiced, with
Carnegie Hall no longer in the offing, his answer was logical: 'I did so all
my life. Why should I stop?' He practiced more than he had in the later

Curtis years and continued practicing in retirement simply because it brought him pleasure. He no longer owned his del Gesu. A year after his retirement it had been coveted, then bought, by his student Daniel Heifetz, who wanted a 'famous name' violin to boost his embryonic career. Zimbalist took Danny's instrument, an Andreas Guarneri, in part exchange. He grew very fond of this 'little fiddle,' as he called it. It was wonderfully preserved and, while not a concert vehicle, proved a comfortable practice instrument. (He bequeathed it to Curtis.)

The end of the daily practice session generally coincided with the arrival of the mail and the *Wall Street Journal*. He continued to do well in the market and always read the stock columns first. Maria attributed this business acumen to gambler's luck, an opinion her father didn't share. He claimed he had made successful investments because he had never taken any advice. 'My contention is that stockbrokers are none too clever. To play the violin one needs to be much smarter.' One could believe this when watching him in action. As a rule he never answered the telephone on his desk—Maria would pick up in her bedroom, or Trini in the kitchen. But should either knock on his door to tell him a certain Mr. Dubow was on the line, he quickly reached for the phone. Mr. Dubow was his broker. Eavesdropping on Zimbalist's side of the conversation was amusing. He would listen sympathetically at some length, then speak in tones that left little doubt as to who was giving the advice, always with the utmost charm.

With practice, mail and business affairs out of the way it was time to settle down to his most nourishing daily work: composing. Despite quipping to Serkin 'I ain't Verdi,' during this last period of his life Zimbalist was extremely productive. He completed *The Two Stories* in 1974. Ted Puffer, who single-handedly wrought a respectable opera company in Reno, looked at the score and was impressed. But the staging called for more than the Nevada Opera Company could handle (Puffer: 'How could we afford two tenors?'). Although he would dearly have loved to see his opera bouffe staged, Zimbalist let the idea drop. He was incubating new ones all the time, though he declared each his last. He received constant encouragement from colleagues. William Primrose journeyed from his home in Provo, Utah, to renew friendship. The oldsters quaintly exchanged signed photos, and Primrose got the go-ahead on a reprint of the 'Sarasateana' arrangement he had made for him decades before; Schirmer's rights were cleared for a new edition, published in Los Angeles.

A fortuitous happenstance was the establishment, some thirty miles away in Virginia City, of a summer concert series that provided Zimbalist with a showplace for his works and stimulated his interest in composing more chamber music. The series was held in historic Piper's Opera House, built by John Piper during Virginia City boom days, when the town had more than enough silver to persuade artists such as Wieniawski, Gottschalk, Jenny Lind, Sarah Bernhardt, Edwin Booth and Lillie Langtry to interrupt their stagecoach trips to San Francisco for performances on its opera house stage. Louise Driggs, an East Coast socialite and one-time violin student of Kathleen Parlow, inherited the building and started the chamber music concerts, bringing in many Curtis-associated musicians as participants. Vladimir Sokoloff became a regular, providing the opportunity, to their mutual delight, for him and Zimbalist to keep in touch. Zimbalist's 1979 'Fantasy' for oboe, string quartet and piano was written for the series. Festive receptions always followed the concerts; at one, Zimbalist was introduced to the son of silver magnate Clarence Mackay. The two of them made the connection that Zimbalist had performed in his parents' mansion in New York in 1911, the year of his U.S. debut.

The tackling of each new writing project, despite the high quality of his output, led to increasing self-doubt, because by this time his debilitated hearing made trying things on the piano out of the question. 'What I write today I can't hear—it's all "headwork."' He spoke openly, at times humorously, about his deficient hearing. 'Being deaf has its advantages—one is spared many things one doesn't want to hear. But I can always look at a score and hear it perfectly in my head.' (Three favorite scores were *Meistersinger*, *Rosenkavalier* and *Carmen*.) Still, he sent newly completed works to Sokoloff for his professional once-over: 'Billy knows more music than anyone I have ever met.'

He could hear himself well enough when he played the violin. 'I have a young hand for my age,' he would say, 'and I'm surprised how well my fingers still run.' Once on a visit I noticed Ysaÿe's sixth solo sonata on his practice stand. He asked if I had played it, and I took the bait, claiming unfamiliarity with the piece. His ensuing demonstration, captured on tape, is a remarkable testament to his natural facility and enduring virtuosity. As he tossed off the final chord, he snickered, 'Well, not too bad for my age. I never claimed to be the world's greatest violinist, but I think I am certainly the world's greatest eighty-five-year-old violinist!' As the years passed he updated this line. This would be followed by a cautionary word against getting old. 'Things aren't as easy as they used to be. Pianists can play until they are a hundred—all the keys are served up in front of them on a platter. Violinists can never hope to last as long.'

Zimbalist's family visited often, especially his granddaughter Susan Hardesty, who lived in Reno, and Efrem Jr. or his daughter 'Little' Stephanie (to distinguish her from her mother, 'Big' Stephanie). Many well-meaning local acquaintances pressed him to accept dinner or party invitations, which he always declined. 'He doesn't go anywhere,' Maria told them, but this was not strictly true. He shied away from social functions for two reasons: 'My hearing condition makes being in a room full of people agonizing,' and 'I've done with all that.' But he did travel occasionally, including to Los Angeles once a month to visit his son. There was a trip east to see an ailing Edie Braun in 1973. There were infrequent trips to San Francisco for maintenance work on his violin, and the family customarily convened for Christmas in either Encino or San Rafael, California, granddaughter Jane's home.

On the maid's day off, and often when Zimbalist was entertaining guests, there were outings to restaurants like the Peppermill Inn. Sometimes when I visited and Maria was not feeling well, I took him out to dinner. On such occasions, as soon as he was settled in the car, he looked at me with a gleam in his eye and suggested that we go to his favorite 'little place,' the International House of Pancakes. Here he downed slices of turkey with a large side order of pancakes, drowned in maple syrup, and tried to tempt me with strawberry shortcake. 'You will need it for your long journey home—my dessert will be a cigar back in my room.' He loved IHOP's unsophisticated setting. 'I can only come here with you,' he'd chuckle. 'The others refuse to take me.' The end of dinner invariably signaled the beginning of an argument as to who would pay: 'You can pay next time,' he would insist, opening a bulging wallet. He was always a generous tipper. When, toward the end, his eyesight was too far gone, he asked me to read him the bill's total. He would mentally calculate for a few moments then leave a grossly padded gratuity on the table. At the exit followed the traditional 'Alphonse and Gaston' routine. His aura of oldwordly charm made him a beloved figure in Reno's restaurants.

Dating back to early touring days, when banking and traveling conditions were less certain, Zimbalist always carried large amounts of money on him. Since he made no secret of this, those close to him worried for his safety. As a parting kindness before my trips home to San Francisco he invariably asked, 'Are you *sure* you have enough ready cash?' Once, out of curiosity, he asked me to count the contents of his billfold—it totaled over $2,000.

Friday afternoons were reserved for forays to the Reno gambling tables with Mr. Wilson. 'Sometimes I feel like losing $20,' he joked. Blackjack was his game, and he managed to spin $20 out for a surprisingly long time— obviously he had not lost his touch. On the way back they usually stopped at their barber for a trim.

Zimbalist whiled away his scant free time by watching television; he especially enjoyed game shows (regularly *Hollywood Squares*) and wildlife documentaries ('animal pictures'). He was also interested in televised concerts, watching rather than listening to them. This remained his chief means of keeping abreast of violinistic trends, which he measured against the yardstick of 'the three aces among violinists, Ysaÿe, Kreisler and Heifetz.' 'There seems no reason why modern violinists shouldn't be able to play as well as the greats of my early years. But times have changed. Violinists today subscribe to a different propaganda. There is, for instance, a lack of delicacy in their playing. Tenderness, you know, is an important ingredient in one's musical vocabulary. The violin is after all a coloratura instrument, a lyrical one—a beautiful phrase beautifully done is much more important to me than when the fingers fly. Violinists seem to have lost the technique of playing passagework more gracefully and slowly. [Both Kreisler and Elman spoke similarly at the end of their lives.] There have been very few great violinists—perhaps no more than a dozen. All the great players of my day had sufficient technique to give free rein to their individuality—and they all had something to say beyond just playing the notes. The times are wrong today for individuality; the world is too mechanical—and commercial. Now, I like money as much as anyone, but more as an interest than as proof of accomplishment. We were brought up in a different way. Heifetz, for instance, took his career very seriously in its own right, not simply for the financial success that accompanied it. He took great pride in learning new things just for the sake of learning—in his life he probably learned more works than any other violinist I know. Today a satisfying career is all about making as much money as possible.'

Television coverage of a U.S. visit by Japanese pedagogue Shinichi Suzuki greatly impressed Zimbalist. But he deplored the popular singers he accidentally tuned into: 'They open their mouths till you can see their tonsils and scream endless stupid words. Such vulgarity.'

What with operating the toaster himself each morning, and the twelve-inch television on his working table, Zimbalist for the first time in his life enjoyed utilizing mechanical gadgets to enhance his sense of independence. Still, some mysteries remained. He had years ago mastered the art of the manual pencil sharpener. Then one birthday he received an automatic sharpener from a doting family member. Shortly after, I visited him. At some point he wanted to write out a bit of information for me but found the lead in his pencil broken. Immediately he reached into a drawer for his trusty little sharpener of established habit, then smiled. 'They gave me a fancy new one,' he motioned to the sharpener on the desk, 'but it's beyond me.' 'May I try, Mr. Zimbalist?' I asked. He handed me the pencil. I inserted it into the device and in less than two seconds handed it back, razor-sharp. 'A genius!' he exclaimed.

He was enamored of two other modern developments in office equipment—felt-tipped pens ('easier to write the notes') and correction fluid ('it saves my life—can you believe you just brush it on and write right over it?') Later additions to his worktable included the gift from Efrem III (Skipper) of a large high-intensity-lit magnifying lens. As his eyes grew weaker it was an invaluable aid in the completion of his final compositions.

David Oistrakh wrote to urge Zimbalist's jury membership yet again for the 1974 Tchaikovsky Competition. Much as he would have loved to serve, he realized that so strenuous an undertaking was just no longer physically possible. Oistrakh was himself fully acquainted with the limits of man's mortal constitution and died the fall after the competition; his grieving widow took her own life four years later.

Shmuel Ashkenasi and Nicolas Chumachenco, meeting in Zurich for a performance of Mozart's 'Sinfonia Concertante' (Chumachenco on viola), decided to send their old teacher a joint postcard. It touched him and sent his mind drifting back to his performance of the work with Kreisler. After dinner while enjoying a *good* cigar (in 1975 he still had a stash of five or six hundred pre-Castro Cubans, 'just enough to last me'), his mind usually turned to the past. 'When I think that over seventy years ago I was sitting in a chair talking with Rimsky-Korsakov and Glazunov just as I now am with you, it seems like yesterday. Things like that will remain with me till the end. You see, the old world still means so much to me.' He spoke of Auer. 'When I came to Auer I remember thinking he was ancient. I laugh when I think that here I am thirty years older than he was then!' He often thought of Kreisler, fondly: 'All those years since he died, yet my memories of him are still so dear. To me he was the Chekhov or Maupassant of composers for the violin — what a gift for creating priceless miniatures.' He also thought a lot about Heifetz: 'I wonder if I should see Jascha when I am in Los Angeles,' he mused, taking a long puff. 'If I would see him it would only be for old times' sake. He's lived his life — I've lived mine — today we have nothing in common. It's been thirty-five years since I saw him. We'd just sit and look at each other.'

But the thought of getting the two aging lions together was too enticing to drop. Both Efrem Jr. and I tried to get the ball rolling. I attended Heifetz's penultimate public performance, in 1974 at the University of Southern California, and approached him at the reception afterward. 'Mr. Heifetz, I am a student of Efrem Zimbalist's.' Silent stare. 'He has retired now and lives in Reno.'

'I know,' crisply.

'He often speaks of you. Would you like to see him again?'

Long stare, then, 'Tell him to come and see me.'

End of conversation. Efrem Jr.'s follow-up calls went unanswered. Great pity.

But another of Zimbalist's Russian colleagues made a determined effort to see him. In 1975 Rostropovich was engaged to conduct the San Francisco Opera in Tchaikovsky's *Pique Dame*. During a rehearsal break I asked him if he would like to visit an old friend who lived in the vicinity. When I mentioned Zimbalist's name his face lit up and he vigorously agreed, immediately pulling out his schedule to look for a free day. I made the arrangements. Several days later, airline tickets in hand, I set out by taxi to fetch Rostropovich at Seiji Ozawa's house, where he was staying. Although it was only a distance of half a dozen blocks, the driver got completely lost in the maze of little one-way streets that criss-cross the Twin Peaks area. I anxiously eyed my watch. As we finally swung around a corner onto Mountain Spring Avenue, I spotted a lanky, loping figure walking a minuscule black dog. The taxi screeched to a stop beside him. I flung a door open and, not calmly, urged Rostropovich to jump in. 'Maestro, we are late,'

I apologized, shooting a glare at the driver. Without a word he did as I suggested, while Ozawa's housekeeper ran up to grab the dog. We raced off. I told the unperturbed cellist that we were heading for the airport—this was the first inkling he had that we would be flying anywhere. In retrospect the entire episode strikes me as amusing. The trip took place years before his defection. He had only just met me and didn't know a thing about me. Yet he must certainly have been bucking whatever watchful Soviet eyes were overseeing his stay in San Francisco—proof of the regard in which he held Zimbalist.

The meeting in Reno was a jolly one, with the customary warm Russian embrace and kisses on each cheek. Maria had arranged a delightful lunch, which was served by the new Mexican maid, Margarita (Trini had returned home to marry). Conversation during the visit was entirely in Russian. I could gather only some of the liberal musical references. Maria filled me in on the rest. The sad note of an otherwise joyous occasion was Rostropovich's confirmation that he had never received Zimbalist's cello concerto. This was one of the biggest disappointments of Zimbalist's life; he never was able to determine its fate.

The first time Zimbalist set foot in the Curtis Institute after his retirement was at the commencement ceremonies of 12 May 1975, when he accepted an honorary doctorate. In a short acceptance speech he recalled his forty years of association with the Institute, mentioning Marcella Sembrich and other names from the past. He referred to a coincidence that often crossed his mind during his Curtis years: that of meeting Adolf and Fritz Busch during his 1907 European debut season and then, years later, finding their respective daughters married to faculty members Rudolf Serkin and the great French singer Martial Singher. He closed on a humorous note, complimenting Serkin (who presided and with whom he had become very friendly) on his mastery in pronouncing the graduates' names—a task he claimed had often been too much for him, despite the careful coaching of his secretary, Mrs. Elizabeth Erickson.

Serkin urged him to return in February 1976 to give master classes. Zimbalist said that his teaching days were over. Galamian phoned in fall 1975 and persuaded him. In preparation he lengthened his practice sessions, determined to get in top shape for the students. But the stumbling blocks of advancing age thwarted him. He fell and sprained his left thumb, forcing him to lay off for a month. He had barely started practicing again before he was hospitalized with a severe flu. Dr. John Davis's advice against going east in the middle of winter had to be heeded. The trip was postponed a year. During his recovery he received a heartwarming letter from Japan:

> Dear Sir,
> I'm seventy-five years old and old friend of you. About forty years ago I have a Victor record played Mr. Zimbalist, music L'Alouette transcribed by Leopold Auer. I loved that record very much, but I'm sorry it was broken by the American air forces bomb in second world war with my house at Kochi City, Japan. I was very sad. I cannot forget record because your violin melody was very wonderful. You played music as if lover.
>
> Therefore, several years I searched for your record but I could not get it in Japan.
>
> I would like to buy cassette of L'Alouette. Please write me name and address of cassette shop in USA.
>
> Yours very truly,
Chozo Takahashi

Zimbalist asked me to send Takahashi a cassette of Glinka's 'L'Alouette,' which I gladly did.

I also pulled out other Zimbalist recordings, and to mark his eighty-sixth birthday I put together a two-hour tribute for radio station KPFA in Berkeley. It began with a message from Piatigorsky, who was recuperating from the removal of a lung—which didn't prevent his death from cancer a year later. His words were separated by audible gasps for breath, a factor that added much sentiment to their impact: 'Here is Gregor Piatigorsky. I will take this opportunity to wish a very happy birthday to my old and dear friend, the great master of the violin, Efrem Zimbalist, with whom I worked for a great many years at the Curtis Institute. I miss him now and have missed him for a long time. So, dear Efrem, happy birthday to you.'

The broadcast continued with other birthday wishes and a discussion of his life and career with family, students and colleagues. Included were several of his recordings. Zimbalist professed polite interest and, since KPFA was not on the dial in Reno, asked to hear a tape of the program. Maria served lunch, then the three of us settled into sofas in the living room. I put a cassette player close to Zimbalist's good ear (his left) and turned it on. His facial expressions bespoke far more than casual interest, with a smile or chuckle accompanying each recording.

Some selections were recordings by Alma Gluck with him first at the piano, then playing violin obbligatos. Before they began I pressed the pause button: I knew that since Alma had died in 1938 he had not been able to bear hearing her voice. I leaned over and said softly, 'Mr. Zimbalist, next are some of Alma's recordings. I can easily skip ahead. Or perhaps you would like to hear them?' There was a lengthy silence and then, 'I think so.' As I pressed the play button, Maria tearfully left the room. Her father sat utterly still, scarcely breathing while he listened. He made no comment then or later. None was necessary. The scene was profoundly moving.

Having learned Zimbalist's sonata for the birthday broadcast, I was soon approached to record it; the resulting album, *Sonatas by Efrem Zimbalist, Father and Son*, helped stimulate fresh interest in his compositions upon its release in fall 1976. Former student Philip Frank recorded the same sonatas in Canada. Diana Steiner recorded his arrangement of the 'Carmen Fantasy' and Carl Engel's 'Sea Shell,' a favorite Zimbalist encore. Plans were underway in Richmond, Virginia, for a revival of Zimbalist's opera *Landara*. And in New York collectors were scampering to find a pirate release of his piano concerto, performed by Lee Luvisi and the Philadelphia Orchestra.

As part of the new wave of fascination with the glories of the past, much interest was also shown in recordings of Zimbalist's own playing. Rococo Records in Toronto put out two LPs of remastered 78s and the broadcast of his 1946 Brahms Concerto with the Boston Symphony. These were followed by releases under the aegis of James Creighton's 'Masters of the Bow' series, and by Japanese RCA. For some years a ten-inch album, made up mainly of the Japanese electrical Columbia recordings, had been available in Soviet Russia. Despite Zimbalist's efforts as director to shield Curtis students from hearing them, his recorded achievements were now finally accessible to students everywhere.

All at once, it seemed, the music world was in the midst of reawakened appreciation of 'Romantic violin playing.' Aaron Rosand sent Zimbalist copies of his recordings of concertos by Joachim and Hubay, with the inscription, 'You were my inspiration in reviving these virtuoso masterpieces,' and Oscar Shumsky gave him his recently released first volume of the complete works of Kreisler. (Zimbalist was able to hear these by listening through headphones to cassette copies I made of them.)

The value Zimbalist placed on his independence sometimes made things difficult for Maria. The half-dozen-plus cigars he smoked daily predictably permeated his clothes—and since he tended to wear the same comfortable things every day she had to resort to subterfuge to sneak particularly offensive garments off to the cleaners. At one point, attempting a complete spring cleaning, she packed him off to the Continental Inn for a week in order to make a few changes. One was to throw out his accustomed (and threadbare) chair. Shortly after his return I visited him with Jacob Krachmalnick. Seated gingerly in a bright new chair in front of a new table, Zimbalist explained: 'I came home and found this situation. Women are always changing things. Alma's greatest delight during the early years of our marriage was moving furniture about.' 'Well, do you like the chair?' growled Jake. 'Since you ask, no, I don't, but what can I say?'

He became increasingly worried about Maria's health. She was frequently hospitalized and when she was home almost constantly bedridden. An additional part-time maid was hired to help Margarita.

But Zimbalist's own health, too, had begun to slip. His appetite was sharply on the decline, which he attributed to worry about Maria—and about the Curtis Institute. Serkin's resignation had been announced, and scarcely a day went by without his receiving calls from Institute high-ups requesting advice. 'It used to be a small school—now it's a music factory,' he commented. Although he had claimed a complete washing of his hands of all affairs relating to the school, in fact he ceaselessly pondered its vicissitudes. On his suggestion a triumvirate of interim directors was installed consisting of Vladimir Sokoloff, Max Aronoff and Orlando Cole. He promised to discuss his views with them when he came to give master classes early in 1977. He found that the limitations imposed by his hearing didn't unduly hamper him during these classes: as he confided, 'I stood very close to the students and asked Billy to play very softly.'

At Zimbalist's meeting with Sokoloff, Aronoff and Cole, several names were considered for director. That of John de Lancie interested him the most. He had always admired both his artistry as principal oboist with the Philadelphia Orchestra and his teaching at the Institute. He also approved of his conservative outlook and dignified bearing and was happy to see him appointed the following year. Equally pleasing was Stormy

Bok's appointment as president of the board. (On the death of her husband, ex–vice president Cary, William Carson Bodine moved into his position, and the board was headed by a vice president until Stormy became president in 1976.) 'Stormy has an excellent business head,' Zimbalist commented. Both she and de Lancie were to draw heavily on his years of administrative experience.

Galamian by that time had stopped his exhausting commute to Philadelphia. Instead he taught Curtis students in his New York home on Sundays. The Institute provided them with round-trip train tickets. One Sunday during Zimbalist's Philadelphia visit Jascha Brodsky drove him to New York to visit Galamian. Zimbalist reported: 'I had thought we would only take a few minutes of his time, but we ended up staying for hours. He kept his students waiting and wouldn't let me leave.' (It was their last meeting; Galamian died on 14 April 1981, after teaching a full day.)

A major task facing de Lancie as director was finding a successor to Galamian. Galamian himself wished his former student and assistant David Cerone to succeed him, but Zimbalist wanted to see his own musical progeny passing on traditions at the school. Oscar Shumsky wasn't interested in the job, and Toshiya Eto, living in Japan, couldn't see his way clear to being in Philadelphia for more than half the school year. Several 'outside' names were then bandied about, including those of Arthur Grumiaux (de Lancie sent Zimbalist some of his records for an opinion), Leonid Kogan (who had given some master classes at Curtis and reputedly wished to leave the Soviet Union) and Nathan Milstein. Milstein declined the position and recommended in his stead a friend and former Zimbalist student who in recent years had been making a name for himself in Europe: Aaron Rosand. This suggestion fitted in with Zimbalist's line of thought, though he and Rosand had largely lost touch (he still remembered him by his original name, Rosen), and the appointment was made. Another former pupil, Jascha Brodsky, had already been on the faculty for over forty years. While all this satisfied Zimbalist, he continued to keep his finger on the violin department's pulse by phone consultation and master classes.

Back at home Zimbalist was taking a massage when Wilson remarked on a walnut-sized lump on his back, which Zimbalist himself had noticed more than a month before. His suspicions were borne out — driving me to the airport, Maria told me a biopsy had confirmed lymphoma. 'It's just so unfair,' she wept. 'Why couldn't he live out his remaining years in peace?' Zimbalist himself must have wondered the same thing. When he first talked to me about the cancer, his eyes too filled with tears. In December 1977, on the advice of family doctor Davis, Maria took him to Stanford University Hospital for further testing by specialists and a consultation with Dr. Henry Kaplan, the hospital's top radiologist. She checked into the San Francisco Airport Hilton, where I was invited to dinner. Zimbalist was cheerful and seemed far more worried about the trip's effect on Maria than the outcome of his tests. He underwent extensive four- and five-hour sessions over the next few days to determine the extent of the disease and the best course of treatment (as he put it, 'whether or not to treat it just locally or give me some horrible stuff as a general measure'). The doctors decided on both approaches, starting radiation at once, shortly followed by chemotherapy. The prognosis was guardedly hopeful, thanks partly to his advanced age: slow tumor growth was expected, and by the 1970s good results in lymphoma management had been recorded. The methods of medical orthodoxy were also to be supplemented. Efrem Jr.'s faith in the powers of a doctor who ran a clinic in Tijuana ('Saint Frances,' he called her) was enough to persuade his father to include her suggestions, which involved 'live cell' therapy and a host of German-manufactured pills. Zimbalist's Reno doctors shrugged them off, convinced they couldn't harm him.

The chemotherapy soon produced its side effects, and Zimbalist's full head of snow-white hair thinned. 'It makes me look like an intellectual,' he joked. He took to radiation easily (by this time a second growth had metastasized to the side of his neck) and described it with typical good humor: 'It's all very pleasant—they take me to the hospital where I lie down quietly for a while, then they bring me home.' But he was unhappy not to be able to practice for more than a month while the tumor on the side of his neck was being shrunk. During this hospital stretch, a television production of a Gian Carlo Menotti opera buoyed his sagging spirits, as did a new Soviet biography of Oistrakh, in which a chapter is devoted to their friendship. But despite his brave front, his illness at times made him understandably morose. 'Scarcely a soul I once knew is still living. If I were to go back to Russia now, for instance, think how terrible it would be— Oistrakh dead, Shostakovich dead, and Rostropovich gone. If it weren't for my family...'

Within a few months he was feeling and looking much better, even if his appetite refused to return. Radiation therapy for the tumor on his neck had left his mouth too tender to handle solid food. Beside him at all times was a glass of the most unappetizing-looking liquid—chalklike but evidently nutritious. He was naggingly, and mostly unsuccessfully, reminded to sip it steadily. All that appealed to him was hot cereal like oatmeal or Cream of Wheat, and he subsisted on the minuscule amounts he was able to force down.

Still based on the old fallacy of an 1889 birth date, the Curtis Institute was planning an extravagant celebration to honor him on his 'ninetieth' birthday. With the prospect of his reaching that landmark now seeming questionable, plans were moved a year forward. The date settled on was 30 April 1978, when Zimbalist would be entering his eighty-ninth year. He spoke of the event with a mixture of anticipation and dread. His doctors weren't in favor of his making the journey but, plans having been announced, he insisted on going. And as usual his sense of humor came to the fore. When told of the enthusiastic response and the many former students expected to attend he commented drily, 'Too many in my condition.'

It was around this time that he began to mention severe stomach pains. Just before his birthday on 9 April, a third test of stomach secretions turned up precancerous cells. Eating solid food was still impossible. The iron will the frail Zimbalist demonstrated in calling up enough strength for the trip will never be forgotten by those who witnessed preparations for his departure. Maria was too ill herself to travel, but her daughters Susan and Jane went with him on the plane. There was a family gathering at The Rafters before they all went on to Philadelphia.

The celebration was described by Vladimir Sokoloff in the Curtis Alumni Association newsletter:

> An occasion of historic significance took place the weekend of April 28–30. Mr. Zimbalist traveled from his home in Reno, Nevada, on April 27, accompanied by two of his granddaughters, Mrs. Susan Hardesty and Mrs. Jane Ribbel. A tea honoring him was held at the Institute the following day. There were tea tables in the common room, sandwiches and cakes in the library and excellent music in front of the fireplace. A warm and friendly atmosphere prevailed as time came for the arrival of

Mr. Zimbalist and his entourage, which included Mr. and Mrs. Efrem Zimbalist Jr. and their daughter Stephanie. A natural pathway opened in the crowd of returning students, faculty, current student body and guests as Mr. Zimbalist entered, surrounded by the press of Philadelphia and New York papers as well as *Time* and *Newsweek* magazines.

Other family members in attendance were Efrem Zimbalist III and his wife Nancy, Rachel Seymour and Enid Schoettle (on the Bok side), Mrs. Efrem Zimbalist Jr.'s parents, Mr. and Mrs. Spalding. Also among the illustrious crowd were composers Samuel Barber, Gian Carlo Menotti and George Rochberg, as well as the great grandson of Richard Wagner, Gottfried Wagner. Altogether three hundred were present, including Mr. Zimbalist's students Franklin Siegfried, Frederick Vogelgesang, Philip Frank, Iso Briselli, Charles Jaffe, Bernie Eichen, Hidetaro Suzuki and Takaoki Sugitani, many of whom had not seen him since their student days. The excitement of this reunion was a fitting prelude to the concerts that followed on Sunday.

The afternoon's program opened with the concerto in b minor by Antonio Vivaldi for four solo violins (with Joseph Silverstein, Jacob Krachmalnick, myself and Geoffrey Michaels), accompanied by a string orchestra of current Curtis students. Next Toshiya Eto and his son, Michael, performed the Pugnani-Zimbalist Sonata in E major.

Throughout the event there hovered in the air a respect bordering on the religious. During intermission John de Lancie spoke glowingly about Mr. Zimbalist's contributions to the Institute, and there came a point when a response from the person being honored was appropriate. Zimbalist had declined to speak, and his son had agreed to do so for him. In the silence that accompanied Efrem Jr.'s setting up behind the dais, Zimbalist sat in the front row beside his granddaughter 'Little' Stephanie. Those seated near them clearly heard, much to their amusement, his irreverent aside to her: 'Now, let us all pray.' Efrem Jr.'s words were eloquent:

> Ladies and gentlemen. My father, as you know, has expressed himself all his life, as most of you have, with his instrument. I

am known to have a loose tongue, and this is the only reason why I am here. It is not very loose now, but I would like to tell you briefly what my father feels today. In this extraordinary atmosphere, for me to say that he is grateful only proves my inadequacy. I certainly have no words, nor has he, to express to everybody responsible for this day how full his heart is.

The Curtis Institute, at which he spent almost half his life, like all institutions, schools and everything that is human, has experienced both rough and calm seas. The fact that it is coming out of a rough time under the leadership of John de Lancie gives my father more happiness, joy and comfort than I can tell you. He is thrilled with what is happening with the school.

To his ex-students who have come from so far and wide to honor him, there is nothing I can say to describe adequately the fullness of his heart. You, his wonderful sons and daughters, are so close to him that it is as if you are my own brothers and sisters. I only wish I were worthy of you. But you are his sons and daughters as much as I am. And he loves you.

Finally, I would be remiss if I didn't tell you what is perhaps overriding everything else in his heart. It is this hall and these rooms which are so inseparably linked to the memory of one of the most remarkable women of our time, Mary Louise Curtis Bok Zimbalist. I wish that those of you present, who only know her from her portrait or from what someone said about her, could have known her personally. Mary Louise Curtis, who inherited from her father one of the great fortunes of this century, literally spent her lifetime giving it away; not squandering, but giving it away thoughtfully, carefully and meaningfully. She conceived and endowed this institution and spent her life administering it.

I wish you could have known this marvelously warm, humorous, generous, pixyish, fun-loving woman as we did. I hope that you will carry this description of her in your hearts and minds as you walk through these rooms, rather than just the image of a great lady of the past, which, of course, she was. She created the opportunity for young people to study in an atmosphere of the greatest quality, the greatest idealism, and under the very highest standards possible. She was an institution, but she was more than everything she did.

Well, I have talked enough. Now we are going to hear some Zimbalist recordings—three of my father's favorite encores.

These were 'Burleska' by Josef Suk, Chopin's 'Minute Waltz' and 'Impromptu' by Tor Aulin, from my collection. Many of the Zimbalist students attending the celebration were hearing them for the first time; their brilliance astounded them. The concluding performers were Paul Gershman playing the Rimsky-Korsakov-Zimbalist 'Coq d'Or Fantasy,' Diana Steiner playing the Engel-Zimbalist 'Sea Shell' and the Bizet-Zimbalist 'Carmen Fantasy,' and Oscar Shumsky playing Zimbalist's sonata with Sokoloff.

Between the afternoon and evening concerts, the Zimbalist family and I retired to the Barclay Hotel for dinner. The 'delectable Dover Sole' on the menu appealed to Zimbalist, and he ordered it with pleasant memories of Hans Richter and his favorite fish house in London's Regent Street. He had taken no more than two bites when he turned to me and muttered, 'This sole has never seen Dover.' Conversation turned to the afternoon's performers. One had given an impromptu speech before performing. Afterward this player mentioned having been nervous. 'Not too nervous to make a speech,' said Zimbalist.

The evening program opened with a repeat of the sonata. Jorge Bolet then played Zimbalist's 'Impressions for Piano.' Soprano Ilona Kombrink sang 'Three Songs of Edna St. Vincent Millay' and the concert's brilliant finale was the Guarneri Quartet's exquisite playing of the Zimbalist string quartet. 'The enthusiasm was electrifying,' commented Sokoloff. Zimbalist was particularly moved by the Guarneri's performance ('It was as if I was hearing it for the first time, exactly the way I felt it'), the dignity and beauty of Toshiya Eto's execution, and Oscar Shumsky's rendering of his sonata. Both tribute concerts were broadcast on National Public Radio.

For Zimbalist and all who were around him, 30 April 1978 was a day filled with nostalgia. He sat under his portrait, commissioned during his tenure as director; on the table beside him was a bust of his wife Mary. That sunlit Friday afternoon, despite his family's concern that he might wear himself out, he eagerly received his friends' and students' adulation. John de Lancie dedicated Zimbalist's former second-floor studio, 1A, as the Efrem Zimbalist Room, and Zimbalist fondly watched Jascha Brodsky unveiling the plaque on the door. Tears of pride streamed down Jascha's face.

Daniel Webster summed up events and Zimbalist's exit for the *Philadelphia Inquirer* of 1 May: 'As he moved toward the door, he stopped to think a moment about the day. "It is hard to put into words," he said softly, making a wave with his bow arm. Then with a glint of humor that his students recall, he said, "I guess you could call this a once-in-a-lifetime affair, couldn't you?"'

CHAPTER 23

Coming to Terms with Bach—and Mortality

(1978–1985)

I have saved for special consideration Zimbalist's dominating absorption throughout his Reno years, a project he regarded as of extreme significance: preparation of a new edition of Bach's unaccompanied violin sonatas and partitas. His interest in this had begun years before. He had misgivings from the start. 'It's like taking the Bible and changing the New Testament. How dare I?' But he persevered: 'I have never heard Bach played to my satisfaction. It's all done out of my adulation for him. Bach is a puzzle of the first order to any violinist who ever played him—he must have written the unaccompanied violin works for fun, the theoretical ultimate of what could be done on four strings, because he knew he wouldn't hear them played. The extent of his contemporaries' abilities and of his own practical knowledge on the violin is to be found in his concertos. The "advancements" of violinists and composers who followed him were childish when compared with what he himself imagined possible. However, the fugues were written by an organist, not a violinist. Anything is possible on the organ. Given four strings, he tried to use them simultaneously whenever he could, and his heavenly melodies, both in the fugues and the slow movements, are constantly interrupted by chords that can be made to sound very unmusical. I believe one should be able to sing these melodies as naturally as in a Schubert lied.'

To accomplish this he advocated judicious elimination: 'Harmonies indicated by chords do not suffer from the leaving out of a few notes.' He also considered it harmless to invert the voicing in some of the more finger-wrenching chords—'I'm not really changing anything, just making it more violinistic.' In chord playing he particularly abominated down-ward breaking: 'The way in which most people break chords when the melody is on the bottom sounds so ugly.' His smooth lyrical approach to Bach playing, with its gently rolled chords and unexaggerated dynamic levels, was not dissimilar to the 'correct early music performance practice' currently in vogue.

And for nearly a decade, violin always at the ready, Zimbalist sat daily at his worktable with his old Joachim edition. Although an earlier edition ('full of wrong notes') had been done by Ferdinand David, he credited Joachim with the first real study of the Bach sonatas and thought that Galamian's then recently published version, complete with autograph urtext, 'didn't do much to improve on Joachim.' When Zimbalist's health declined, he asked me to check his work. I was often bewildered by the layers of pencil, pen and correction fluid, the holes worn through the page by countless erasures. Zimbalist was tireless in trying out his changes on the violin, both for his own certainty and for my decidedly modest opinion. At first I was hesitant about some of the changes—I became more convinced the more I immersed myself in his thinking.

It seemed a never-ending undertaking. He had no sooner entered his last marking in the concluding E major gigue than he turned back to the g minor prelude and began all over again. On the third go-around, he started thinking about a publisher. He wanted the job handled by a West Coast firm, to facilitate his overseeing the work. The Highland Music Company in Los Angeles agreed to take it on. Herman Langinger, the company's head, was a former violinist and had a particular interest in the assign-ment. He visited Zimbalist in St. Mary's Hospital to discuss details. In January 1978, between bouts of poor health, Zimbalist personally delivered the final draft to Langinger in Los Angeles. (Efrem Jr. during that trip took his father on a tour of a movie lot where, for the first time, he saw back-ground music, 'trash,' being recorded by studio musicians.)

Highland Music prepared the first proofs while Zimbalist was being fêted at the Curtis Institute in April. Shortly after he returned to the West, his steel will gave way, resulting in alarming deterioration. Injuring his back in a fall didn't help. When the proofs were ready he was in hospital and in no condition to check them himself. He arranged to have one copy sent to Encino for his son to look over and installed me for a fortnight at the Continental Inn to do the same. Efrem Jr. and I compared notes, and I visited Zimbalist daily to report on progress. Some days he showed less interest than others. One event that did spark his interest was 'Little' Stephanie's appearing with her father in a made-for-TV movie. Efrem Jr. and I finished our proofing and sent the results off to Langinger.

In early June 1978, on my way to a seven-week engagement in Colorado, I stopped by to see Zimbalist. He had been moved to intensive care at Washoe General Hospital. With an assortment of multicolored tubes protruding from his withered body, he looked more dead than alive. He slept through most of my visit, periodically murmuring short musical phrases while waving his arm in rhythm. I was sure I would never see him again.

Vladimir and Eleanor Sokoloff arrived in Reno for the Piper's Opera House summer series, bringing with them the diploma that Zimbalist had asked the Curtis Institute to bestow on Joseph Silverstein. With great difficulty, Zimbalist found enough energy to scrawl his signature on it. While he was at Washoe General, Maria's own grave illness had landed her in St. Mary's Hospital, adding to the pervading depression. But she rallied, and her call to me in Boulder three weeks later was chilling: 'Daddy doesn't have much time. I think you should come right away.'

A horrible scene confronted me on arrival. Zimbalist's ghostly white, gaunt features and limbs were in cruel contrast to his stomach, swollen grotesquely by his disease. Hospital personnel hovered around him in masks as a precaution against infection, although I couldn't see what difference it would make. I too wore one to say farewell.

Inexplicably that unhappy summer, Zimbalist began to recover. When I returned to Washoe General in the fall, I found him attentively watching his son on TV. He greeted me with his usual wit: 'Well, I guess I'm not ready to go yet.' His doctors were flabbergasted. 'It must be something in his genes,' Dr. Davis told me. (Strong genes do run in the family — Efrem Jr. and Efrem III have seldom known a sick day in their lives.)

Zimbalist left the hospital on 9 September, almost four months after he had entered it. He had not touched the violin for as long. Gradually he got back into his practicing, starting with half an hour every other day. Sitting upright or standing for protracted spells resulted in severe backache, and most of his time was spent on his bed or in a reclining chair. With the cessation of chemotherapy his hair began to grow back — before long it had almost regained its former bushy splendor. As his strength slowly increased, Maria's, on the contrary, was sapping away.

That fall, after Efrem Jr.'s final proofreading, his father's Bach edition
was published. Marcia Davenport wrote the informative preface:

> A new edition of a work by Johann Sebastian Bach will rightly
> be measured by the stature of its editor. Efrem Zimbalist's
> authority as virtuoso, pedagogue, and composer has been estab-
> lished in the course of more than seven decades of international
> eminence.... Like the body of Bach's works, the manuscript of
> the six Sonatas and Partitas for Unaccompanied Violin included
> few, if any, directions for dynamics, phrasing, articulation, or
> other technical specifics.... It met the vicissitudes of so many
> of his autographs—neglect and even oblivion after his death;
> inexplicable dispersal across great distances; confusion arising
> from copies made by Bach's wife and his pupils. We have
> glimpses, however, of the thrill of [its] discovery: by Mozart in
> 1789, when he visited Johann Doles, Bach's pupil and successor
> [at] the Thomasschule; by Mendelssohn after he became con-
> ductor of the Gewandhaus Concerts in 1835; by Joseph Joachim,
> the great nineteenth-century predecessor of Efrem Zimbalist,
> who in his youth was concertmaster at the Gewandhaus under
> Mendelssohn. Joachim's [edition] of the six Sonatas and Partitas
> remained for most of a century the authoritative version,
> though [he had prepared it] from copies and early editions and
> did not see the autograph score until 1906, the year before he
> died. Subsequently there have been many editings and revisions
> based on [the urtext that have] led my father to prepare this new
> edition of the Sonatas and Partitas. Its importance to per-
> formers, teachers, and students of the violin is self-evident. For
> them and for their students, this reaffirmation of and new access
> to the genius of J. S. Bach will be a lasting inspiration.

Below the preface Zimbalist added a few words of his own, which brought
me immeasurable pride: 'I wish to thank my dear friend Roy Malan for the
time he so generously gave, for his painstaking review of this complex
work, and for his valuable suggestions.'

Soon after his edition came out I stopped by to find him scrutinizing it.
He commented on his efforts: 'It was the hardest job I ever had to do, even

harder than writing operas. Some will swear at me—I hope they do. A work of this kind has to draw criticism. But some of the things Bach wrote just couldn't be done well, until now. I'm not looking for quick acceptance. At first I will be criticized, but in time people will change their minds.'

Instead it was Zimbalist who changed his mind. Less than a year after its publication he withdrew Highland Music's rights to it and paid them to destroy all existing copies. He had become disillusioned with his work. 'Someday I hope to publish another edition, if I am still on this planet of ours,' he laughed.

He began to compose again and to take an interest in Curtis affairs. The sale of the Institute's collection of Wagneriana held his attention. It was the largest outside of Bayreuth. 'My wife's original outlay [was] $250,000 [and] the collection fetched $1,200,000. The sale was a good move for the school.'

He had a lingering anemia problem, and blood transfusions became a monthly ritual. Despite this he finished four songs set to words by James Stephens, sketches for which he had started a year before. He also sent John de Lancie a revision of an earlier work for woodwinds, suitable for use in his Curtis woodwind class.

What of Silverstein's Curtis diploma? Sokoloff had taken it back to the Institute, and John de Lancie called Silverstein, who had taken over the conductorship of the Utah Symphony. When the call came he was on a ladder painting the ceiling of his new Salt Lake City studio. He couldn't help chortling at the news. 'John,' he said, 'do you mean that after twelve years as concertmaster of the Boston Symphony I'm finally qualified enough to graduate?' Concurrently, Zimbalist had me send Silverstein a copy of his Bach edition. Joey replied in a warm letter to Zimbalist, thanking him for his kindness and praising his editing. Several months later he picked up the diploma, when he went to Curtis to play a recital for the benefit of the scholarship fund. Jascha Brodsky, to whom he had sent a copy of the Zimbalist thank-you letter, was at the concert, and they talked about the turn of events but, for some inexplicable reason, the original never reached its intended recipient. (Silverstein found this out years after Zimbalist's death.)

Zimbalist spoke of returning to attend the spring 1979 violin auditions. But in Southern California in January, progressively less steady on his feet, he slipped and refractured his already weakened left hip. Going east was out of the question. He was treated at the Tarzana Medical Center, where

his student Eudice Shapiro got a surprise. Having come to visit her ailing
father, she stepped out of his ward and saw Zimbalist in the room directly
opposite. 'I thought how strange it was to have my first and last teachers
laid up in the same hospital,' she says. They were delighted to see each
other (she had had to miss the big 'ninetieth' celebration), and when she
explained her presence Zimbalist wanted to hop out of bed to meet her
father. In reality he hadn't the strength.

Though his recovery was, again, little short of miraculous, Zimbalist
from then on was obliged to walk with a cane. I told him I had heard that
Heifetz now did so. 'Well, I'm glad we still have something in common,' he
countered with a twinkle.

Maria died on 15 March 1981. Her final stay in the hospital had been a
lengthy and agonizing one, during which Susan Hardesty took Grandpa to
visit her daily. Being responsible for attending to Zimbalist's needs while
Maria was hospitalized proved too much for Margarita, and she had quit.
This meant added responsibility for Susan as well as lonely nights for
Zimbalist on Lindley Way, with only Tori to keep him company. By this
point the faithful old Yorkie was infirm with arthritis. One evening I
visited and was told the vet had advised that Tori be put to sleep the next
morning. When I left to catch the last night flight to San Francisco it was
with a leaden heart. Zimbalist waved goodbye. Never had I seen him look
more alone. Through the window I watched him sit down in front of the
television. Tori nestled against his feet.

Because he had worried so much about Maria I thought that her death
might have brought with it some small sense of relief. His reply when I
visited days later filled me with remorse: 'You haven't known how terrible
it is to lose a child.'

Around that time, in an evaluation of his compositions, he ended up
rating his piano concerto at the top. He spoke so often of this that I knew he
would like to hear it performed again. I managed to interest Ron Daniels,
then music director of the Reno Philharmonic, in a Zimbalist tribute
concert on which the concerto would be programmed. I agreed to serve as
concertmaster. While delighted at the prospect, Zimbalist despaired of
finding a pianist capable of tackling this difficult work. I had no hesitation
in recommending Robin Sutherland, the spectacular San Francisco–
based pianist with whom I had recorded the Zimbalist sonata. Expressing

confidence in my choice Zimbalist next set about ensuring that I should also play a solo at the concert: he orchestrated his 'Coq d'Or Fantasy' for me.

During rehearsals Zimbalist sat onstage beside me and behind Sutherland. He was totally immersed in the music, eyes closed as he leaned forward to rest on his cane, sometimes waving from side to side with the music. At one point the accompaniment came unglued. Zimbalist was all eyes. While the orchestra regrouped Sutherland turned to him and said, 'You know, this passage is extremely difficult.' Zimbalist was nonchalant: 'Oh, I don't have to play it!'

The Reno Chamber of Commerce and Rotary Club gave a lunch for him on the day of the concert, at which Marcia Davenport delivered an address on the current musical climate in the United States and the part her stepfather had played in its development. Her concluding words: 'Today [we are here] to honor a great and most extraordinary figure in the life of music in the United States—who sits quietly here and seems not ever to have shaken a finger at anybody. But, you would be surprised.' Nevada Governor Robert List presented Zimbalist with the keys to the city and proclaimed 9 March 1982, the day of the celebration, Efrem Zimbalist Day. He also presented the guest of honor with a telegram from President Reagan: 'The American people and your friends and admirers of many lands and cultures join us in expressing appreciation for the enrichment you have brought to our lives.' Zimbalist mounted, unaided, the stairs leading up to the stage and to thundering applause received the honors with a soft 'thank you.'

The Philharmonic board went all out with a grand post-concert dinner. At each place setting was a reproduction of the first page of the Piano Concerto score, rolled up in a scroll. Maria's presence was keenly missed, but the rest of the family were there, as were Sokoloff and early students Eudice Shapiro, Philip Frank and Diana Steiner. William Primrose had also planned to attend. Though by that time his health was waning, he nonetheless set out, alone, on the long drive from Provo. Halfway he collapsed. Hiroko Primrose rushed to him and brought her disappointed husband home. He died two months later.

Following Maria's death, Zimbalist had declined the offers from his Southern California family to furnish him with a new home. He felt his new roots were in Reno and didn't want to leave. Granddaughter Susan lived there, but he also resisted her offers, explaining with characteristic candor: 'I've lived with women all my life. I'm now going to live by myself.'

He took an apartment on the sixth floor of a luxury high-rise at 100 North Arlington Avenue; through its windows the majestic Sierra could be seen looming beyond the city and in the foreground the Truckee River wound its picturesque way through a park. Once all his things were around him, he loved this retreat. Susan engaged a maid for an hour a day to attend to his laundry and minimal cleaning requirements but soon had to replace her for pocketing some 'ready cash' he had left out. He continued his normal schedule, which included fixing his own breakfast, often lunch, and sometimes even light supper. Bread, salami, eggs (cooked in an automatic cooker), cheese, canned foods, packaged soups and beer were always on hand—Susan did the shopping and took on day-to-day responsibility for him, showing enormous devotion and thoughtfulness. She and her husband, Donald, took him out for dinner twice weekly at first, every night toward the end. Early on he had decided that it was proper to allow Donald, as her husband, to pay for half of Susan's dinner, which for Zimbalist was a big capitulation. His new favorite place was a coffee shop that served bagels, cream cheese and excellent lox, a culinary 'discovery' he claimed never to have had before.

He still did his own banking and continued his weekly gambling excursions with Mr. Wilson. Sometimes he went out alone for dinner, walking a short diagonal block to the Comstock Hotel, where he particularly fancied their hot turkey and, on Fridays, fresh trout. His awareness and self-sufficiency at ninety-two were mind-boggling. I remember accompanying him one evening to the Comstock. I supported his arm as we walked slowly along following the sidewalk. Halfway there his firm prodding veered me off course. 'I'll show you a short cut,' he said knowingly, steering me between the pumps of a corner gas station. We entered the hotel in moments through a side door, only to be confronted by a blockade of blinking 'one-armed bandits' and the accompanying din of clinking coins and partying crowds. I felt totally intimidated. Unerringly he guided me, as we threaded a path through the throng until we came out clear across the room and directly in front of the entrance to the dining room. How he found his way there and back with his poor eyesight and worse sense of direction still baffles me.

A year later Vladimir Sokoloff walked there with Zimbalist, then ninety-three. By then the Comstock had installed a ramp specifically designed for handicapped access that Sokoloff thought would facilitate matters for Zimbalist. He aimed him toward it. His companion pulled away. 'Billy, that's only for senior citizens!' he smiled, taking the stairs. At dinner Sokoloff inquired after his health. The reply was laconic: 'Ritenuto poco a poco.'

When I next joined Zimbalist for dinner he decided to eschew the customary Friday night meal at the Comstock for a fancier fish dinner at the Sahara Club. As we entered he announced: 'This is considered a first-class place. That just means you lose more money here.'

His family continued to bring him immense satisfaction. 'Little' Stephanie's emergence as a star on the TV series *Remington Steele* made him ache with pride—and he never missed a show. He made a trip to Los Angeles to see Skipper's new baby, Efrem IV. Efrem Jr. seized the opportunity and whisked Zimbalist to Tijuana for some 'cell' shots, but his father was irked when Saint Frances suggested he knock off cigars for a week.

During this period he could often be drawn into soul-searching evaluation: 'All I ever wanted were a few friends and students who liked me, my playing and my teaching. I think I might have had a more brilliant career if I had not so disliked publicity. But the approval of the general public meant nothing at all to me. Life does come to an end, you know, and when it does you have to ask yourself, What did I do? If you ask me what I did I can say that, starting out as a lazy boy, with age I picked up a little here and there and learned a few things about music. I wrote concertos, orchestral pieces and two operas. I can say that I taught myself the mechanics of composition, and all this outside my profession as a violinist and teacher. If I could live my life through again, knowing what I do now, I would change only one thing. I wouldn't spend more time on violin practicing than I did in my youth, but I would spend ten or twelve hours each day studying other subjects: languages, physics, literature and so on. That's what I would have *liked* to do—a life of learning seems to me the most important aspiration. If you were to ask whether or not I have any regrets about my violin playing career, there is just one—I'm sorry that my great-grandchildren never heard me perform. And, perhaps I'm sorry I didn't make more recordings later in my life, when I knew how to play!'

Seldom did a day's mail not bring requests for autographs. He ignored them all—writing replies had become a physically insurmountable obstacle. He was also besieged with requests to serve on the major violin competition juries. These he would answer, usually via Susan or myself, 'Honored, but too old.'

The brilliance of Robin Sutherland's piano playing inspired him to get to work on a piano quintet rewrite of his 'Impressions,' scheduled for performance at Piper's Opera House in summer 1983. This was his most extensive chamber music essay; in the end half of its ten movements were new material. When word of ninety-three-year-old Zimbalist's completed work reached Donald Henahan of the *New York Times*, he wrote: 'Some day the brain doctors may be able to explain to us the final mystery: why certain people are driven to build, or paint, or write, or compose and why they go right on wanting to do so until the lid is snapped shut on them.'

As we discovered while rehearsing it for performance, 'Impressions' is clearly an autobiographical work. The title of each movement suggests Zimbalist's association with past experiences, although he demurred when asked to provide program notes, wanting audience members draw their own conclusions. The ten movements (my notes in parentheses) are (i) Motion-Repose; (ii) Baby at the Piano (Maria as a child); (iii) Chopin; (iv) A Musical Thought; (v) Lest We Forget (Mary Zimbalist); (vi) Picnic; (vii) Rachmaninoff; (viii) Ballet-Scherzo; (ix) Caress (Alma) and (x) Rimsky-Korsakov. Zimbalist pointed out that the movements bearing other composers' names were not written in imitation of their styles, but as his portrayal of their personalities. Several movements were written with specific performers in mind: violist Eric Shumsky (Oscar's son) and the outstanding local cellist John Lenz. The piece made a profound impact. 'Impressions' lasts fifty minutes; listeners seem unaware of this imposing length.

Plans were under way in fall 1983 for the implementation of an Efrem Zimbalist International Violin Competition, to be held in Philadelphia every two years beginning in 1985. The initial impetus was provided by a gift of $10,000 from retired Philadelphia Orchestra violinist-composer Charles Miller (Elman often played Miller's 'Cubanaise' as an encore). In a letter accompanying his check, Miller said he was giving it 'because we're still waiting for another great violinist like Zimbalist, with a ravishing tone, enormous technique, impeccable taste, dignity, elegance and respect for the composer.' A total of $50,000 was deemed necessary to launch the project, and Sokoloff shouldered the task of raising the difference. He unearthed another potential $10,000 donation, contingent on raising the balance by a deadline. It was a bitter disappointment to Sokoloff when, despite his valiant efforts, the deadline couldn't be met. Zimbalist was more relieved than disappointed when the whole idea was scrapped.

The latest pop culture had understandably passed Zimbalist by. But he did remember a few names from the rock 'n' roll hierarchy because of the deleterious effect he believed they'd had on the world's musical young. While driving with family to dinner at Harrah's in 1984, he spotted a gigantic neon sign advertising a current stage show attraction, 'Tribute to the Beatles.' 'Tribute?' he snapped, 'They should put them in jail!'

The revised 'Impressions' was repeated in summer 1984 in Rockport, Maine, and Zimbalist made a sentimental last trip east to hear it. He and the family stayed at Lyndonwood, now the remodeled home of Stormy Bok. Presented by pianist Andrew Wolf as part of his Bay Chamber Series in the Rockport Opera House, the concert was made up entirely of Zimbalist's works, spanning sixty years, also including the String Quartet and the Oboe Fantasy, with John de Lancie. New York, Boston and Portland papers made much of the event. Afterward the Zimbalists made a stop at The Rafters, where Maria's ashes had been interred beside the graves of her mother and stepmother.

On his return home he set to work fulfilling a promise to orchestrate his 'Suite in Alter Form' for strings, which he dedicated to Vahe Khochayan, director of Reno's Chamber Orchestra. In my program notes I aired an inner fear when I wrote: 'It would be distinctly Zimbalistian in balance if, in this new presentation of his "Suite," he were to come full circle, rendering his first published composition also his last.'

My fear proved groundless. He next began work on a piano quintet version of his 'Sarasateana Suite'—to be premièred at the Piper's 1985 summer series—for Robin Sutherland and me. But progress was painfully slow—a renewed malignancy lurked, undetected at the time. He struggled on, declining my offer to write out the parts, which I had done for 'Impressions.'

This goal kept him going, although he spoke of constant pain in his side. To say that he complained would be inaccurate—the most he ever admitted to was being 'uncomfortable.' When he returned to St. Mary's for tests, his doctors decided to check his stomach. The tumor they discovered was large enough to leave little choice for treatment. Only major surgery might have been effective, 'turning him into a mess of tubes,' explained Dr.

Gilbert Lenz, father of cellist John Lenz. All concerned decided to let things take their course. Zimbalist suffered bravely, as always. Family doctor John Davis admired his courage. 'It took a big effort, but he was determined to die with dignity. His only request was to have enough time to finish the composition he was working on.'

With just weeks left him Zimbalist was allowed to go home. Shortly after arriving back in his apartment, he completed the parts of 'Zapateado,' the last movement of the quintet. Efrem Jr. arrived the next day. 'Daddy, I hear you finished "Sarasateana,"' he greeted him brightly. His father still retained his wit. 'Yes,' he replied, 'I thought it would be a good idea.'

He sank fast. An adjustable bed was installed in the living room so that he could see the snow-capped Sierra from where he lay. On the cocktail trolley to his left, unopened boxes and bundles of his once-savored Cuban cigars were piled on a silver tray—he had had no hankering for them for months. Pens and blank manuscript paper still lay under the illuminated magnifying lens on what had doubled as dining-table and workbench. The stand beside it supported open copies of the Mendelssohn Concerto and Paganini Caprices, and a piano score of 'Sarasateana.' His Steinway had been moved aside to make room for the bed. There was a large bouquet on top of it, alongside a photo of Alma. The antique ivory fan he had bought her seventy years ago in Paris rested, framed, on the music rack near her picture.

Family members were in and out constantly. Susan sat for hours feeding him chilled fruit cut into tiny pieces.

One of the two nurses who had been engaged around the clock let me in for a brief visit around 3 p.m. on 21 February 1985. Stroking a white lock over Zimbalist's brow, the nurse informed me in his southern drawl, 'He's been hurtin' pretty bad today.' From the wall above, long-departed friends gazed out through their frames, watching over his gaunt features. He appeared to be asleep and didn't stir.

Susan and Donald arrived at 6:30. Shortly after midnight, when they went home to get some rest, Grandpa entered a coma. The night nurse settled himself in an adjoining room. At a little past 2 a.m. he heard a choking sound. The cover had gently closed on a large volume of musical history.

A private funeral service was held on 30 March at St. John's Episcopal Church in New Hartford, Connecticut. Zimbalist's ashes were taken to Town Hill Cemetery and buried there in the family plot. A violin is carved on the tall gravestone, and beneath it are these words from Psalm 42:8: 'In the night His song shall be with me.'

On 1 April a memorial concert was given at the Curtis Institute.

On 1 September 'Sarasateana' was premièred at Piper's Opera House on schedule, just as Zimbalist would have wished.

Zimbalist's Violin Mastery and Influence

One needs to be a consummate technician (with just the right degree of tasteful virtuoso glitter), enlightened musician and captivating but controlled personality to be a successful performing artist today. Zimbalist was all these in 1907. No other violinist of the period could lay claim to an equivalent balance of attributes. Through the wide range of his influence he had a considerable hand in laying the ground rules that now make it impossible to achieve a career without these ingredients. The niche Efrem Zimbalist occupies in the evolution of violin playing is, therefore, a pivotal one in that he was the first to strive for a happy juxtaposing of high virtuosity and serious musical ideals, taking pains to ensure that neither his physical appearance nor his personality got between the music he was interpreting and his audience. Such goals are as obvious to cultivated present-day musicians as they were totally novel a century ago.

One has only to note the names that followed Paganini's legendary embodiment of everything both commendable and reprehensible in the realm of sheer virtuosity to recognize that their artistic makeups were out of balance: Ernst, Vieuxtemps, Wieniawski, Sarasate, Kubelik — all virtuosi short on musical sympathies, major figures though they were. What about Joachim or Ysaÿe? Joachim certainly regarded the composer's prerogative paramount, but his vociferous eschewing of virtuosic display brought him too to the brink of imbalance. Ysaÿe admittedly was more in 'modern' balance than the rest of the major violinists whose careers began in the nineteenth century; yet even Flesch's sympathetic judgment of him couldn't avoid a reprimand of his rubato and eccentricities. Clearly Ysaÿe's impact derived from his overpowering personality. And what of Kreisler? Here it is more difficult to divine the fine line that leaned his style backward rather than forward. Determining it becomes easier if one listens to his playing during the last years of his career: tendencies toward extremes that in mid-career are held in check often give themselves away when advancing age weakens discipline. With Kreisler, as in the case of Ysaÿe, personality definitely took the upper hand.

We have then to look to Leopold Auer's 'Russian school' to provide us with a tangible link to twentieth-century style. Zimbalist was that first important link. Although he was older than Elman (by one year) and entered Auer's class before him, Elman's big debuts preceded his, placing Elman chronologically before Zimbalist. But this fact had no effect on the progression of violin playing—Elman was a notorious anachronism by his last years. On the contrary, right from the outset Zimbalist's interpretations were considered more 'modern' than Elman's, and with age and experience he demonstrated progressively modernistic tendencies. But here is the pivot and with it Zimbalist's uniqueness—while his style was inherently progressive, it was backed by the authority of tradition to an unparalleled degree. Datewise he preceded Heifetz by a decade, adding to this extra measure of historical continuity a musical span widened by the great age he attained. In his nineties he was a true living link—or fossil, as he liked to joke. He had contributed more important students than Heifetz had, which pointed out the advantage of his being able to balance the authentic touch of tradition with contemporary meticulousness of style and intent. No better example can be mentioned than Oscar Shumsky, considered by critics a violinist's violinist and musician's musician, and by many possibly the greatest violinist of the twentieth century. It is the author's contention that while Zimbalist bent the twig to make new growth possible, Shumsky embodied a blossoming that aspired to and achieved the ultimate in violinistic and musical symmetry, going beyond Heifetz in this respect.

It is strange, since he contributed so substantially to today's musical environment, that toward the end of his career Zimbalist was labeled 'old-fashioned.' His age was often fuel enough for such an allegation. But anyone looking at the facts in light of their historical setting cannot help but arrive at a different conclusion: Zimbalist (i) was a pioneer in exploring and building a 'modern' approach to violin playing; (ii) rubbed shoulders with the important composers of his day and was actively interested in their work; (iii) appointed himself a proponent of the contemporary works of his time; (iv) introduced works which have become standard repertory and (v) produced students who have won prizes in today's major international violin competitions.

Of course Zimbalist retained certain characteristics of his epoch and schooling—his contribution would have meant less without them. He had little sympathy for purely 'cerebral' interpretations: when he heard enthusiastic reports about the formation of a certain sonata partnership, he commented, 'Oh yes, Flesch and Schnabel show considerable knowledge, of a most uninteresting kind.'

The twelve-tone movement and atonalists he confessed as being beyond his ken, although he studied and admired Berg's *Wozzeck*. Highly commendable for a musician of his era, he made an effort to study and understand works written outside the scope of his musical language. He was strongly moved by Shostakovich. But he had no patience with 'contemporary specialists.' He would say, 'Don't the violinists who absorb themselves in the intricacies of Schoenberg realize how difficult it is to play Beethoven?'

In an earlier chapter I stated that the impact of two men was discernible in modern violin sound, that of Heifetz and Galamian. Zimbalist in a sense paved the way for both, first by preparing the public for Heifetz's modernism (think how much 'colder' and more 'unemotional' he would have been considered without Zimbalist's prior audience conditioning), then by giving Galamian's marvelous methods credence and sustenance by engaging him at the Curtis Institute.

What other violinist who in his prime was considered one of the world's top four and who earned his living mainly as a touring virtuoso could lay claim to no fewer than a dozen major creative works, including two full-scale operas? Zimbalist alone could point to a long list of successful performances of his works by the music world's top conductors and organizations.

Lastly, what of touring virtuoso Zimbalist's violin playing? In 1915 his friend Rawlins Cottenet opined that it was of rare and exquisite beauty, elevating and replete with fervor but restrained with the unerring instinct of genius. He considered Zimbalist's art to be particularly conspicuous for the purity of his style and the lofty idealization of his interpretations. He compared hearing him to beholding a Madonna of Botticelli. 'While the sensuous charm of a Boucher or Fragonard is not there,' he said, 'his is a higher plane of expression. It is emotionally uplifting by its inspired simplicity. The perfection of his intonation, the opulence of his tone, and the clarity of his finger technique is such that his execution admits no criticism. He is an artist of the highest order and one who has no superior.'

Composer-critic Virgil Thomson in his nineties described Zimbalist's tone to me with characteristic straightforwardness: 'I still remember the sound — it was never "squeaky," had more substance than "silky" implies, and it always had a rich "matte" finish.'

When Zimbalist turned seventy-five David Oistrakh told Jascha Brodsky, 'Acquaintance with Efrem Zimbalist is for me one of the most glowing and meaningful of musical experiences. I first heard him during his tour in Moscow in 1934. He came, one must say, at a most unpropitious moment: he appeared right after a series of concerts by Jascha Heifetz, who astounded the Moscow public by his generous diversity of programs and the splendor of his talent, then in full bloom (he was thirty-three years old). It seemed that after such a triumphant success no other violinist could possibly again conquer the public. But then we heard Zimbalist, and again triumph, again ecstasy of the audience and endless applause and acclaim. His success, however, was of a different nature: while Heifetz conquered by sheer brilliance, Zimbalist captivated people by appealing to profound mysteries of heart and soul.'

On the purely superficial, human interest side, with the accrued ingredients of age and maturity Zimbalist gained in a certain exoticism associated with his ties to Asia, his adventuresome touring lifestyle and his esoteric concert programming. Even his name, unusual enough to hold allure for the general public, signified to them a kind of mysticism resplendent in colorful silk shirts, steeped in vintage port and perfumed with Chinese incense and the fumes of Havana cigars.

As Zimbalist himself summed it up, with unfailing honesty, 'People always seemed to like me.'

The Zimbalist Students

Compiled by Vladimir Sokoloff; the year of graduation appears in parentheses.

Arben, David (1954)
Archera, Laura (1940)
Ashkenasi, Shmuel (1963)
Bertolami, Viviane (1947)
Bielski, Noah (1940)
Blakeslee, Lynn (1964)
Bolotine, Leonid (1935)
Briselli, Iso (1934)
Brodsky, Jascha (Jacob) (1934)
Campione, Eugene (1940)
Carol, Norman (1947)
Ceci, Jesse (1940)
Chapo, Eliot (1967)
Cheney, Doris (1931)
Chumachenco, Nicolas (1967)
Cusimano, Giuseppe (Jesse) (1949)
Dalley, John (1957)
Druian, Rafael (1942)
Eichen, Bernie (1948)
Eto, Toshiya (1952)
Feldman, Harry (1926)
Fisher, Florence (1927)

Frank, Philip (1934)
Gerhart, Pamela (1955)
Gershman, Paul (1934)
Gronsky, Harry (1930)
Harbert, Nancy (1949)
Heifetz, Daniel (1971)
Ilvonen, Jouko (1951)
Ippolito, Carmela (1934)
Jaffe, Charles (1935)
Kakei, Ryoko (1967)
Krachmalnick, Jacob (1941)
Kuehne, Marguerite (1942)
Kwalwasser, Helen (1939)
Maazel, Saundra (1942)
Malan, Roy (1968)
Malkin, Anita (1930)
Michaels, Geoffrey (1965)
Montrose, Albert (1942)
Ovcharov, Sol (1946)
Park, Alan (1946)
Park, Mi-Young (1971)
Pepper, Joseph (1949)

Putlitz, Lois (1929)
Reed, Elza (1938)
Reynolds, Veda (1942)
Rosand, Aaron (1948)
Schulman, Julius (1938)
Sewell, Frederick (1954)
Shapey, Ronald (1943)
Shapiro, Eudice (1935)
Shefeluk, Marie (1946)
Shumsky, Oscar (1936)
Siegfried, Franklin (1933)
Silverstein, Joseph (1978)
Simpson, Claire (1945)
Sitjar, Felix (1949)
Slatkin, Felix (1933)
Steiner, Diana (1949)
Sugitani, Takaoki (1962)
Suzuki, Hidetaro (1963)
Tree, Michael (1955)
Tsumura, Mari (1971)
Vogelgesang, Frederick (1939)
Wada, Keiko (1967)
Waldo, Elizabeth (1938)
Windt, Paul (1970)
Wippler, Harold (1947)
Woodruff, Marilyn (1951)

Discography

Single-letter abbreviations: v = voice; c = cembalo; s = soprano.

ABT
WHEN THE SWALLOWS HOMEWARD FLY v & pf - arr. v, vln & orch.
   with A. Gluck s & orch.   A 15908   HMV 7-43066
                                           Victor 87236, 87516, 3007

d'AMBROSIO
SERENADE, Op. 4 vln & pf
   with S. Chotzinoff pf   HMV 4-7994, DA407
                                           Victor 64710, 891

ANONYMOUS
HATIKVA (Zionist hymn) - arr. v, vln & orch. Imber
   with A. Gluck s & orch.   A 22232   HMV 2-3333, DA448
                                           Victor 87296, 87522, 3003
SWEDISH CRADLE SONG (folksong) - arr. v, vln & pf
   with A. Gluck s & pf   Victor 87566, 3004

AULIN

(4) AQUARELLES vln & pf
   NO. 2, HUMORESQUE
      with S. Chotzinoff pf   HMV 4-7988, DA405
                                    Victor 64241, 887

(4) PIECES, Op. 16 vln & pf
   NO. 2, IMPROMPTU IN E
      with E. Bay pf   98562   Columbia 50090D, 7275M,
                                      J7356

BACH

CONCERTO IN D, BWV 1043 2 vlns, strs & c
      with F. Kreisler vln & str qt   A 15560/2   HMV 2-07918, 2-07922 &
                                      2-07920
                                      DB587/8
                                      Rococo 2005
                                      Victor 8040/1, (in set LM6099),
                                      76028/30, A430569, RB6525

(4) SUITES, BWV 1066/9 strs & c
   SUITE NO. 3, IN D: AIR (2nd mvt) BWV 1068 2 obs, 3 tpts, drms, strs & c -
   arr. vln & pf as 'Air on the G-string' by Wilhelmj
      with E. Bay pf   Columbia 50289D, 7293M

BARNBY

SWEET & LOW (mixed voices) - arr. v, vln & orch.
      with A. Gluck s & orch.   Victor 87283

BEETHOVEN

(6) MINUETS, G167 pf
   NO. 2, MINUET NO. 2, IN G arr. vln & pf Burmester
      with unknown pianist   A16088   HMV 2-07931, DB461
                                        Victor 74444, 6332
ROMANCE NO. 1, IN G, Op. 40 vln & orch.
                       NE 55004-2 & 55005-3
                                      Columbia 68596D, DX772
      with Japanese Broadcasting Symphony   J7696, W94

BETHIER
PETITE SERENADE vln & pf
   with unknown pianist   Victor 6621, 988

van BIENE
BROKEN MELODY vlc & pf - arr. vln & pf
   with S. Chotzinoff pf   Victor 74445, 6331

BOWEN
SUITE NO. 1, IN D (1909) pf
   No. 1 HUMORESQUE arr. vln & pf Schott-Sohne
   with pf (possibly E. Lutsky or F. Moore)   HMV DB806
                                       Victor 74884, 6451

BRAGA
(7) MELODIES (1867) v & pf
   No. 5 LA SERENATA 'Angel's serenade'
   with A. Gluck s & E. Lutsky pf
                       A12995   HMV 03349, DB574
                                      Victor 88434, 89092, 802

BRAHMS
(21) HUNGARIAN DANCES pf duet
   HUNGARIAN DANCE NO. 17, IN F-SHARP arr. vln & pf Kreisler
   with T. Saidenberg pf   M 55084-3   Columbia 264619, DX785
   HUNGARIAN DANCE NO. 20, IN E arr. vln & pf 'in d' Joachim
   with S. Chotzinoff pf   HMV 3-07908, DB462
                                       Victor 74303, 6333
   HUNGARIAN DANCE NO. 21, IN E arr. vln & pf Joachim
   with S. Chotzinoff pf   HMV 3-07908, DB462
                                       Victor 74303, 6333
SONATA NO. 3, IN D, Op. 108 vln & pf
   with H. Kaufman pf   Columbia 67786/8D, (set M140)
                                       J7655/7

CHOPIN

(3) WALTZES, Op. 64 pf

   No. 1. WALTZ No. 6, IN D-FLAT 'Minute Waltz' arr. vln & pf Zimbalist

   with S. Chotzinoff pf   A 12974   HMV 3-07907, DB461

                                         Victor 74338, 6332

(3) WALTZES, Op. 70 pf

   No. 1. WALTZ No. 11, IN G-FLAT arr. vln & pf Spalding

   with E. Bay pf   HMV DA788

                                         Victor 1154

CORNELIUS

(6) LIEDER, Op. 3 v & pf

   No. 3. EIN TON (The monotone) arr. v, vln & pf

   with A. Gluck s & pf   Victor 87208

CUI

KALEIDOSCOPE, Op. 50 vln & pf

   No. 9. ORIENTALE

   with S. Chotzinoff pf   HMV 4-7991, DA404

                                       Victor 64261, 886

No. 9. ORIENTALE

   with E. Bay pf   Columbia 181M, 2125M, J5041

DRDLA

GUITARERRO, Op. 88 vln & pf

   with E. Bay pf   Victor 1056

SERENADE No. 1, IN A vln & pf

   with unknown pianist   Victor 64561

SOUVENIR vln & pf

   with F. Moore pf   HMV 4-7995, DA406

                                       Victor 64813, 892

SOUVENIR vln & pf

   with T. Saidenberg pf   M 200208-1A

                                       Columbia 17105D, DB1701

                                       DO1740, P10

DRIGO

(2) AIRS DE BALLET orch.
> NO. 2. VALSE BLUETTE arr. vln & pf Auer
> with E. Bay pf   146918   Columbia 5314, 181M,
> 2125M, J5041

(LES) MILLIONS D'ARLEQUIN (1900) - ballet orch.
> SERENADE arr. vln & pf Auer
> with orch.   HMV 2-07965, DB462
> Victor 74467, 6333

> SERENADE arr. vln & pf Auer
> with E. Bay pf   98567-2   Columbia 9674, 50162D,
> 7279M,
> J7348, P93

ELGAR

SALUT D'AMOUR, Op. 12 orch. - arr. vln & pf Elgar
> with H. Kaufman pf   Victor 66101, 890

FOSTER

MASSA'S IN DE COLD, COLD GROUND (1852) v & pf - arr. vln & pf Pasternack
> with string orch. & celeste   A 18933   HMV 4-7927, DA493
> Victor 64638, 888

OLD BLACK JOE (1860) v & pf - arr. vln & orch.
> with string orch.   A 18934   HMV 4-7921, DA493
> Victor 64640, 888

(THE) OLD FOLKS AT HOME 'Swanee River' (1851) v & pf
> with A. Gluck s &   A 12977   HMV 2-3107, DA450
> S. Chotzinoff pf   Victor 87196, 87518, 3006
> (vln obbligato is Dvořák's 'Humoresque')

GLINKA

FAREWELL TO PETERSBURG (1840) - 12 songs v & pf
> NO. 10. THE LARK arr. vln & pf Auer
> with F. Moore pf   A 22235   HMV 3-07909, DB460
> Victor 74582, 6331

RUSLAN & LUDMILA (1842) opera
  PERSIAN SONG arr. vln & pf Zimbalist
  with E. Bay pf   HMV DA788
                                                        Victor 1154

  PERSIAN SONG arr. vln & pf Zimbalist
  with E. Bay pf   149719   Columbia 2191D, 2090M,
                                                        J5118

GOODEVE
FIDDLE AND I v & pf - arr. v, vln & pf
  with A. Gluck s &   A 16079   HMV 03565, DB573
  R. Bourdon pf   Victor 88539, 89093, 8027

GOSSEC
ROSINE (1786) - opera
  GAVOTTE arr. vln & pf Burmester
  with S. Chotzinoff pf   A 16088   HMV 2-07931, DB461
                                                        Victor 74444, 6332

GOUNOD
AVE MARIA (Meditation on Bach's 'Prelude No. 1, in C') v & pf - arr. v, vln & pf
  with A. Gluck s &   A 12975   HMV 03347, DB574
  E. Lutsky pf   Victor 88433, 89091, 8026

GREENE
SING ME TO SLEEP v & pf - arr. v, vln & str qt
  with A. Gluck s & str qt   A 17834   HMV 03555, DB573
                                                        Victor 88573, 89094, 8027

HALVORSEN
(4) MOSAIQUES (Suite des morceaux caractéristiques) vln & pf
  NO. 4. CHANT DE VESLEMOY
  with S. Chotzinoff pf   A 20098   HMV 4-7985, DA402
                                                        Victor 64737, 884

HANDEL
(15) SONATAS, Op. 1 (?1731) fl or vln & c
SONATA NO. 9, IN B: ANDANTE (1st mvt) arr. vln & pf as 'Larghetto' by Hubay
with A. Lambert pf   HMV 4-7989, CA401
                                            Victor 64335, 883

HERBERT
(THE) FORTUNE TELLER (1898) - operetta
GYPSY LOVE SONG arr. vln & pf
with E. Bay pf   Victor 1056

HILDACH
(2) LIEDER, Op. 15 v & pf
NO. 1, DER SPIELMAN arr. v, vln & orch.
with A. Gluck s & orch.   A 18936   HMV 2-043018, DB593
                                            Victor 88583, 89095, 8046

HUBAY
(6) BLUMENLEBEN, Op. 30 vln & pf
NO. 5. DER ZEPHIR
with E. Bay pf   146916   Columbia 5314, 03623,
                                            2123M,
                                            J5042

CONCERTO NO. 3, IN G, Op. 99 vln & orch.
ADAGIO (2nd mvt); SCHERZO (3rd mvt)
with E. Bay pf   Columbia 50297D, 7235M

KRAMER
CHANT NÈGRE, Op. 32, No. 1 vln & pf
with pf (possibly E. Lutsky)   HMV 4-7986, DA402
                                            Victor 64736, 884

ENTR'ACTE, Op. 46, No. 2 vln & pf
with E. Bay pf   Victor 1054

KREISLER
LIEBESFREUD vln & pf
    with E. Bay pf   Columbia 50257D, 7287M,
                                                         J7677

LIEBESLEID vln & pf
    with E. Bay pf   98566-1   Columbia 9650, 7287M,
                                                         J7627

LANE
IN THE HOUR OF TRIAL v & pf - arr. v, vln & org
    with A. Gluck s & organ   A 22230   HMV 2-3399, DA449
                                                         Victor 87300, 87523, 3005

LEROUX
(LE) NIL v & pf - arr. v, vln & pf Renaud
    with A. Gluck s & organ   A 11601   HMV 2-033038, DB572
                                                         Victor 88358, 89090, 8028

MacDOWELL
(4) SONGS, Op. 56 (1898) v & pf
    No. 1. LONG AGO arr. vln & pf
    with S. Chotzinoff pf   HMV 4-7990, DA403
                                                         Victor 64266, 885

MARSHALL
I HEAR YOU CALLING ME (1908) v & pf - arr. vln & pf
    with S. Chotzinoff pf   Victor 64330

MASSENET
ÉLÉGIE v & pf - arr. v, vln & pf
    with A. Gluck s & pf   A 11603   HMV 7-33005, DA449
                                                         Victor 87101, 87513, 3004

MENDELSSOHN
(6) SONGS WITHOUT WORDS, Op. 62 pf
    No. 6. SONG WITHOUT WORDS No. 30, IN A 'Spring song' arr. vln & pf
    with orch.   Victor 66034, 892

MOSZKOWSKI
(6) KLAVIERSTÜCKE, Op. 15 pf - 4 hands
No. 1. SERENATA arr. vln & orch.
with orch.

HMV 4-7993, DA406
Victor 64576, 891

NEVIN
(THE) ROSARY (1898) v & pf - arr. v, vln & orch.
with A. Gluck s & orch.　　A15909　　HMV 2-3225, DA450
Victor 87237, 87517, 3006

PIERNÉ
SERENADE IN A, Op. 7 (1875) pf - arr. vln & pf Haddock
with E. Balaban pf　　　　　　　Victor 64936, 890

RAVEL
(4) CHANTS POPULAIRES (1910) v & pf
No. 4. CHANSON HÉBRAIQUE arr. v, vln & orch. Pasternack
with A. Gluck s & orch.　　　　Belcantodisc BC247
HMV 7-13360, DA448
Victor 87276, 87519, 3003

REGER
(4) SONATAS, Op. 42 solo vln
SONATA No. 2, IN A: ANDANTINO
(unaccompanied)　　　　　　　HMV 3-7996, DA403
Victor 64518

RIMSKY-KORSAKOV
(4) SONGS, Op. 2 (1865/6) v & pf
No. 2, ENSLAVED BY THE ROSE & THE NIGHTINGALE arr. v, vln & pf
with A. Gluck s & pf　　A 20087　　HMV 7-33027, DA519
Victor 87146, 87251, 87287

SAINT-SAËNS

(LE) BONHEUR EST CHOSE LÉGÈRE v & pf - arr. v, vln & pf
with A. Gluck s & pf	A 15387	Belcantodisc BC247
		HMV 7-33011, DA519
		Victor 87209, 87515

(LE) CARNAVAL DES ANIMAUX (1886) small orch.
LE CYGNE arr. vln & pf
with S. Chotzinoff pf	A 12974	HMV 3-07907, DB461
		Victor 74338, 6332

(LE) DÉLUGE, Op. 45 (1876) - oratorio
PRÉLUDE vln & orch. - arr. vln & pf Saint-Saëns
with F. Moore pf	HMV DA404
	Victor 64827, 886

SARASATE

CARMEN FANTASY (on themes from the opera by Bizet) Op. 25 vln & pf
with T. Saidenberg pf	M 55086-2 &	
		Columbia 9095M, DX765, W38
	55087-1	

(8) DANZAS ESPAÑOLAS vln & pf
No. 6. ZAPATEADO, Op. 23, No. 2
with unknown pianist		Victor 74883, 6451

No. 6. ZAPATEADO, Op. 23, No. 2
with E. Bay pf	98561-1	Columbia 9650, 50162D, 7279M
		J7348, W93

No. 7. DANZA ESPAÑOLA No. 7, IN A, Op. 26, No. 1
with pf (possibly F. Moore)	HMV DB806

ZIGEUNERWEISEN, Op. 20 vln & pf or orch.
with T. Saidenberg pf	Columbia 9101M, W95

SCHUBERT

(7) GESÄNGE (set to Scott's 'Lady of the Lake') Op. 52 v & pf
No. 6. AVE MARIA, D839 arr. vln & pf Wilhelmj
with E. Bay pf	98560-3	Columbia 9674, 266058,
		50090D,
		7275M, J7356

SCHUMANN
(13) KINDERSCENEN, Op. 15 pf
    No. 7 TRÄUMEREI arr. vln & pf
        with T. Saidenberg pf   M 200207-2   Columbia 17105D, DB1701,
                                                DO1740, P10

SCOTT
TALLAHASSEE SUITE, Op. 73 (1910) vln & pf
    No. 2. AFTER SUNDOWN
        with E. Bay pf   146197   Columbia 03623, 167M, 2123M,
                                                  J5042

SIMONETTI
MADRIGALE pf - arr. vln & pf
        with unknown pianist   Victor 66220, 988

SPALDING
ALABAMA (plantation melody) vln & pf
        with S. Chotzinoff pf   Victor 74443

SUK
(4) PIECES, Op. 17 vln & pf
    No. 4. BURLESKA
        with E. Bay pf   149721   Columbia 2191D, 2090M,
                                                    J5118

SULLIVAN
(THE) LOST CHORD (1877) v & pf - arr. v, vln & orch.
        with A. Gluck s & orch.   A 20673   HMV 03643, DB572
                                               Victor 88593, 89096, 8028

TCHAIKOVSKY
(THE) MONTHS (12 characteristic pieces) Op. 37b pf
    No. 10. AUTUMN SONG (October) arr. vln & pf Burmester
        with orch.   HMV 4-7905, DA401
                                               Victor 64577, 883

QUARTET NO. 1, IN D, Op. 11 2 vlns, vla & vlc
  ANDANTE CANTABILE (2nd mvt) arr. vln & pf Kreisler
    with T. Saidenberg pf   M 55085-1   Columbia 264619, DX785
(6) SONGS, Op. 6 v & pf
  NO. 6. NONE BUT THE WEARY HEART arr. v, vln & orch.
    with A. Gluck s & orch.   Victor 87244, 87518, 3007
(3) SOUVENIRS DE HAPSAL, Op. 2 pf
  NO. 3. CHANT SANS PAROLES IN F arr. vln & pf Kreisler
    with H. Kaufman pf   Victor 66119, 885

TOMER
GOD BE WITH YOU 'TIL WE MEET AGAIN (1883) v & pf - arr. v, vln & orch.
  Rankin
    with A. Gluck & orch.   Victor 87278, 87520, 3005

WAGNER
(DIE) MEISTERSINGER VON NÜRNBERG (1868) - opera
  MORGENLICH LEUCHTEND 'Prize song' arr. vln & pf Wilhelmj
    with E. Bay pf   Columbia 50289D, 7293M

WIENIAWSKI
LÉGENDE, Op. 17 vln & pf or orch.
    with E. Lutsky pf   HMV 3-07910, DB586
                   Victor 74337, 6369

YSAŸE
(6) SONATAS, Op. 27 solo vln
  SONATA NO. 1, IN G
  (unaccompanied)   HMV ED263/4
                   Victor 16194/5 (set M669)

ZIMBALIST
IMPROVISATION ON A JAPANESE TUNE vln & pf
    with pf (possibly L. Greenwald)   Columbia 2087M, J5113
IMPROVISATION ON A JAPANESE TUNE vln & pf
    with E. Bay pf   Victor 1054

(3) Slavonic Dances vln & pf

No. 1. Russian dance

with E. Balaban pf   Victor 64955, 889

No. 2. Hebrew dance

with S. Chotzinoff pf   HMV 4-7987, DA405

                                         Victor 64550, 887

No. 3. Polish dance

with orch.   HMV 4-7992, DA407

                                         Victor 64562, 889

Suite dans la forme ancienne vln & pf

No. 2. Sicilienne

with S. Chotzinoff pf   HMV DB586

                                         Victor 742880, 6369

No. 3 Minuet

with S. Chotzinoff pf   HMV DB586

                                         Victor 74280, 6369

Bibliography

Auer, Leopold. 1921. *Violin Playing As I Teach It*. New York: Stokes; reprinted Dover 1980.

————. 1923. *My Long Life in Music*. New York: Stokes.

Benoist, André. 1978. *The Accompanist*. Neptune City, New Jersey: Paganiniana.

Bird, John. 1982. *Percy Grainger*. London: Faber & Faber.

Brook, Donald. 1947. *Six Great Russian Composers*. London: Rockliff.

————. 1948. *Violinists of Today*. London: Rockliff.

Campbell, Margaret. 1981. *The Great Violinists*. Garden City, New York: Doubleday.

Chasins, Abram. 1979. *Leopold Stokowski*. New York: Hawthorn.

Chotzinoff, Samuel. 1964. *Day's at the Morn*. New York: Harper & Row.

Creighton, James. 1974. *Discopaedia of the Violin*. Buffalo: University of Toronto.

Damrosch, Walter. 1930. *My Musical Life*. New York: Scribner's Sons.

Davenport, Marcia. 1967. *Too Strong for Fantasy*. New York: Scribner.

Elkin, Robert. 1946. *Royal Philharmonic*. London: Rider & Co.

Erskine, John. 1950. *My Life in Music*. New York: William Morrow.

Flesch, Carl. 1958. *The Memoirs of Carl Flesch*. New York: Macmillan.

French, Maida Parlow. 1967. *Kathleen Parlow*. Toronto: Ryerson Press.

Gaisberg, F. W. 1942. *The Music Goes Round*. New York: Macmillan.

Gorky, Maxim. 1969. *Chaliapin*. New York: Stein & Day.

Hetherington, John. 1967. *Melba*. New York: Farrar, Straus and Giroux.

Jelagin, Juri. 1951. *Taming of the Arts*. New York: Dutton.

Kaufmann, Helen L., and Eva Hansl. 1933. *Artists in Music of Today*. New York: Grosset & Dunlap.

Key, Pierre V. R. 1918. *John McCormack*. Boston: Small, Maynard.

Lochner, Louis. P. 1951. *Fritz Kreisler*. London: Rockliff.

Magidoff, Robert. 1956. *Yehudi Menuhin*. London: Robert Hale.

Masur, Gerhard. 1971. *Imperial Berlin*. London: Routledge & Kegan Paul Ltd.

McCormack, Lily Foly. 1949. *I Hear You Calling Me*. Milwaukee: Bruce.

Menuhin, Yehudi. 1977. *Unfinished Journey*. New York: Knopf.

Moorehead, Alan. 1958. *The Russian Revolution*. New York: Harper.

Prokofiev, Sergei. 1979. *Prokofiev by Prokofiev*. Garden City, New York: Doubleday.

Rimsky-Korsakov, Nikolay. 1936. *My Musical Life*. New York: Tudor.

Robinson, Paul. 1977. *Stokowski*. New York: Vanguard Press.

Roth, Henry. 1987. *Great Violinists in Performance*. Los Angeles: Panjandrum.

Rubinstein, Arthur. 1980. *My Many Years*. New York: Knopf.

Russell, Thomas. 1949. *The Proms*. London: Max Parrish & Co.

Saleski, Gdal. 1927. *Famous Musicians of a Wandering Race*. New York: Bloch.

———. 1949. *Famous Musicians of Jewish Origin*. New York: Bloch.

Schickel, Richard. 1960. *The World of Carnegie Hall*. New York: J. Messner.

Schneider, David. 1983. *The San Francisco Symphony*. Novato, California: Presidio.

Schonberg, Harold C. 1963. *The Great Pianists*. New York: Simon & Schuster.

————. 1967. *The Great Conductors*. New York: Simon & Schuster.

Schwarz, Boris. 1983. *Great Masters of the Violin*. New York: Simon & Schuster.

Steinway & Sons. 1929. *Portraits of Musical Celebrities*. New York: Steinway & Sons.

Strakacz, Aniela. 1949. *Paderewski As I Knew Him*. New Brunswick, N.J.: Rutgers University Press.

Swanberg, W. A. 1972. *Luce and His Empire*. New York: Scribner's.

Szigeti, Joseph. 1947. *With Strings Attached*. New York: Knopf.

Thomson, Virgil. 1945. *The Musical Scene*. New York: Knopf.

Wallechinsky, David, and Wallace Irving. 1975. *The People's Almanac*. Garden City, New York: Doubleday.

Index

Abell, Arthur 93, 122

Achron, Isadore 160

Achron, Joseph 11, 18, 28, 38, 160, 167, 173, 208

Adams, Jack 135

Adams, 'Pop' 92-93, 100, 107, 109, 123, 135, 147, 148, 159

Adolf Friedrich V See Mecklenburg-Strelitz (grand duke)

Aleichem, Sholem 292

Alexander (grand duke) 24

Alexandra (queen) 69, 76, 97

Alexis (tsarevich) 30

Andreiev (conductor) 32

Anselmi (tenor) 18

Applebaum, Samuel 270

Arben, David 270, 337

Archera, Laura 337

Arensky, Anton 18

Arnoldsen, Sigrid 18–19

Aronoff, Max 237, 310

Ashkenasi, Shmuel 263, 264, 279, 305, 337

Ashman, Gregory 183–184, 186

Astor, Nancy 112

Atterbury, Grosvenor 169

Auer, Leopold 5, 8–14, 17, 18, 19–21, 22–25, 28, 29, 30, 31, 32–34, 35–40, 41, 44, 47, 48, 49, 52, 56–58, 59, 65–66, 67, 74, 75, 76, 78, 85, 86–87, 92, 95, 121, 141, 144–146, 147, 148–149, 160, 166–168, 180–181, 183, 191, 202, 206–207, 209, 210, 219, 220, 223, 234–235, 238, 263, 280, 284, 306, 308, 334

Aulin, Tor 87, 118, 126, 171, 233, 316, 335

Ayres, Agnes 154–154

Bach, Johann Sebastian 22, 55, 78–79, 85, 89–90, 92, 110, 158, 167, 168, 187, 210, 212, 213, 219, 221, 223, 241–242, 244, 267, 285, 288, 300, 319–323

Bachman, Edwin 211, 212

Backhaus, Wilhelm 68

Bailly, Louis 249–250

Bakst, Leon 156

Balaban, Emanuel 118, 156

Balakirev, Mily 19

Bampton, Rose 248

Barban (physician) 90

Barber, Samuel 248, 251, 255, 314, 335

Barnes, Anna 169, 202

Barnes, Earl 169, 202

Battestini, Matteo 18–19

Bauer, Harold 79, 115–116, 150, 154, 155, 161, 174–175, 240, 275

Bay, Emanuel 87, 188–190, 191, 192–193, 193–196, 207–208, 235 -236, 239

Bazzini, Antonio 274

Beach, Amy 247

Beethoven, Ludwig van 10, 12, 15, 18, 22, 38, 87, 90 92, 95, 105, 106, 121, 125–126, 136, 157, 165, 185, 192, 193, 195, 221, 240, 244, 245, 269, 271, 273, 335

Benckendorff, Paul (count) 69, 75, 97

Benny, Jack 243

Benoist, André 100–101, 156, 207

Berg, Alban 335

Berger, Francesco 95

Berger, Karl 73

Berkowitz, Ralph 260

Bernard, Paul 156

Bernhardt, Sarah 302

Bernstein, Leonard 248, 282

Bertolami, Viviane 337

Bielski, Noah 337

Bizet, Georges 316

Blakeslee, Lynn 337

Blumenfeld, Felix 32, 35, 220

Boccherini, Luigi 254

Bodine, William Carson 311

Boissevain, Eugene 179–180

Bok, Cary 249, 292, 295, 311

Bok, Curtis (state supreme justice) 249, 251, 259

Bok, Edward 164, 202, 259

Bok, Mary Louise Curtis See Zimbalist, Mary Louise Curtis Bok

Bok, Nellie Lee 242, 252, 259, 268, 271

Bok, Rachel 259

Bok, Stormy 292, 310, 329

Bolet, Jorge 248, 316

Bolotine, Leonid 337

Bonelli, Richard 251–252

Booth, Edwin 302

Bori, Lucrezia 161

Borodin, Alexander 19

Botticelli, Alessandro 335

Boucher, François 336

Bowen, York 73, 85, 110, 126, 335

Braga, Gaetano 135

Brahms, Johannes 12, 15, 23, 37, 39, 40. 48, 54, 55, 56, 59, 64, 66, 67, 70, 80, 90, 92, 95, 110, 122, 125, 146, 155, 167, 174, 207, 209, 216, 217, 235, 241, 242, 244, 261, 271, 273, 309

Brandukov (cellist) 29

Braun, Edith Evans 254, 256, 258–259, 269, 277, 290, 295, 303

Briselli, Isaak (Iso) 206, 212, 314, 337

Brodsky, Adolf 29, 65–66

Brodsky, Jacob (Jascha) 218–219, 237, 255, 311, 317, 323, 336, 337

Brown, Eddy 37, 85, 146

Bruch, Max 12, 51, 76, 77–78, 98, 142, 335

Bruckner, Anton 92

Bulganin, Nikolai 277

Bull, Ole 14, 116

Burgin, Richard 37, 166

Burmester, Willy 50, 94

Burnhardt, August 8, 31–32

Busch, Adolf 66, 307

Busch, Fritz 66, 307

Busoni, Ferruccio 122, 166, 181

Campione, Eugene 337

Capet, Lucien 263

Carol, Norman 264, 274, 337

Carpenter, John Alden 247

Caruso, Enrico 54, 70, 116

Casals, Pablo 247, 270

Cather, Willa 155

Cavalieri, Lina 18

Ceci, Jesse 264, 337

Cerone, David 311

Chabban (professor) 2

Chaliapin, Feodor 19, 30, 160

Chang, Tso-lin 193

Chapo, Eliot 264, 337

Charlton, Loudon 123, 124, 127

Chaucer, Geoffrey 246

Chausson, Ernest 233

Chekhov, Anton 184, 224, 306

Cheney, Doris 337

Cherkassky, Shura 248

Chessin, Alexander 94

Childs, Calvin 116, 135, 137–138

Chopin, Frederic 69, 128, 161, 167, 171, 221, 233, 277, 316, 328

Chotzinoff, Samuel 99–103, 104, 105, 106, 107–109, 111–113, 114–116, 118, 124, 129, 155 -156, 171, 183, 207, 239, 240, 242, 251, 252, 253, 273

Chumachenco, Nicolas 264, 279–281, 288, 289–290, 305, 337

Coates, Walter 65,

Cole, Orlando 237, 293, 310

Connell, Horatio 98, 99

Connelly, Marc 240

Constantine (grand duke) 3

Conus, Jules 22, 136

Coolidge, Elizabeth Sprague 149, 247

Copland, Aaron 247

Cottenet, Rawlins 106, 109, 125, 126–127, 335

Crosby, Bing 286

Crowninshield, Frank 162

Cui, César 18, 19, 118, 191

Culp, Julia 79, 251

Curtis, Cyrus 164

Curtis String Quartet 198, 237, 255

Cusimano, Giuseppe 337

Dalley, John 264, 269, 279, 337

Damrosch, Frank 150, 164

Damrosch, Walter 125, 138, 142–143, 148, 150, 154, 156, 161,177, 213, 240

Daniels (ambassador) 216

Daniels, Ron 324

Dargomisky, Alexander 19

Davenport, Marcia (Abigail) 109, 113, 126, 129, 130, 133, 134–135, 141, 148, 153, 156, 169, 170, 172, 177, 178, 227, 229, 243, 244, 264, 291–292, 298–299, 322, 325

Davenport, Russell 135

David, Ferdinand 320

Davies, Ben 70

Davis, Dr. John 308, 312, 321, 330

de Beriot, Charles 5, 96, 125

Debussy, Claude 51, 190, 214

Deconet, Mishel 156

de Lancie, John 310–311, 314, 314, 316–317, 323, 329

de Maupassant, Guy 306

DeMille, Cecil B. 154, 243

de Mille, William 154, 243

de Pachmann, Vladimir 128, 181

de Plehve, Vyatcheslav 23

de Segurola, Andre 177

Destinn, Emmy 50 -51, 104, 106

Dinicu, Grigorash 80

Dobbs, John 196–197, 199

Dobrowen, Issai 235

Dodge, Ruth 227, 228, 229

Dodge, Washington 227

Dohnányi, Erno von 47

Doles, Johann 322

Doring, Ernest 202

Dostoyevsky, Feodor 45

Dounis, D.C. 265

Downes, Olin 104, 171, 212, 219, 239, 247

Drdla, Franz 110, 118, 216, 236

Driggs, Louise 302

Drigo, Riccardo 20, 52

Druian, Rafael 206, 253–254, 264, 286, 289, 337

Duncan, Isadora 10, 183

Dushkin, Samuel 207, 214

Dvořák, Antonin 91, 135, 201

Eames, Emma 116

Edward (king) 70, 76

Eichen, Bernie 218, 264, 270, 314, 337

Einstein, Albert 155, 157–158, 176

Elgar, Edward 76, 97–98, 121, 335

Ellis, Charles 123, 159

Elman, Mischa 13, 23–25, 30, 37, 38, 48, 55, 56, 60, 64, 87, 93, 97 100, 103–104, 104–105, 115, 116, 121, 122–123, 127, 135, 141, 144, 145, 146, 147, 166, 177, 236, 257, 267, 273–274, 276, 283, 304, 328, 334

Elman String Quartet 211

Elman, Saul 23, 24

Enesco, Georges 48

Engel, Carl 309, 316

Engles, George 232

Erickson, Elizabeth 307

Ernst, Heinrich 12, 171, 212, 288, 333
Essipoff, Annette 17–18, 32
Eto, Toshiya 189, 263, 269–270, 311, 314, 316, 337
Evans, Ethel 141
Ewen, David 292

Fairbanks, Douglas Sr. 216
Farina, Carlo 267
Farrar, Geraldine 116, 123
Fauré, Gabriel 22
Feldman, Harry 337
Feller, Dora 99
Fels, Joseph 63- 65, 66–67, 70–72, 74, 92, 96, 97, 98, 107, 109–110, 111, 123, 129, 140, 212
Fels, Mary 63- 65, 66–67, 70–72, 74, 96, 98, 99, 100, 103, 109, 111, 114, 129, 212
Fels, Samuel 71, 206, 212
Feodorovna, Dagmar 28, 69, 97
Feuermann, Emanuel 251–252, 254
Fichtenholz, Mischa 221
Fiedler, Max 104
Finletter, Thomas, Mrs. 240
Fisher, Florence 337
Flesch, Carl 14, 58, 93–94, 122, 165–166, 173, 200, 202, 206, 333
Flexner, Abraham 157–158, 231

Flexner, Simon 231
Fokine, Michel 20
Fonaroff, Vera 211
Fonseca (cigarmaker) 177–178
Fontanne, Lynn 180–181, 275
Fournier, Pierre 280
Fragonard, Jean-Honoré 336
Francescatti, Zino 230, 262
Franck, César 22
Francke, J. E. 93
Frank, Philip 309, 314, 325, 337
Freeman, J. C. 175
Fresh Air Art Society 73
Frey, Emile 51–52, 54
Fried, Oscar 228
Friedman, Ignaz 154
Frohman, Daniel 127–128
Fulder, Ludwig 252, 296
Furtwängler, Wilhelm 166, 237

Gabrilowitsch, Ossip 133, 134, 150, 154, 166–167, 179 180–181
Galamian, Ivan 13, 58, 171, 173, 220, 252, 262–263, 265, 279, 284–285, 288, 291, 307, 311, 320, 335
Galli-Curci, Amelita 116, 138
Ganz, Rudolph 154
Gapon, George 31
Garbusow, N. A. 273–274
Garcia, Manuel 96

Garden, Mary 100, 112
Garrett, John Work 156
Gatti-Casazza, Giulio 107
Geller, E. M. 64, 65, 66, 67, 70, 94, 96, 98
Geltzer, Ekaterina 20, 85
George (prince of Wales) 69
George, Henry 71, 277
Gerhardt, Elena 47, 94, 96, 121
Gerhart, Pamela 337
Gershman, Paul 316, 337
Gershwin, George 161, 163–164, 271
Gibson, Charles Dana 112
Gilels, Elisaveta 221, 228
Gilels, Emil 228, 276–277
Gingold, Josef 141, 171, 184, 202
Given, Thelma 37, 145
Glazunov, Alexander 17, 30, 32–33, 35–37, 39, 40–41, 43, 44–45, 46, 48, 52, 54, 55, 67, 77, 78, 81, 85, 95, 100, 104, 105, 106, 121, 171, 178–179, 223, 224–225, 230, 233, 241, 256, 271, 305
Glinka, Mikhail 19, 191, 308

Gluck, Alma (née Reba Fierson) 107–109, 113–114, 116, 118, 119, 124, 125, 126, 128–130, 133–136, 139- 142, 144, 148, 149, 151–152, 153–154. 155, 156, 158, 161, 162 - 163, 164, 167, 169–170, 175, 179, 180, 186, 196, 197, 199–200, 201, 202, 209, 210, 226–229, 231, 240, 241, 242, 245, 247, 254, 257, 278, 291–292, 309, 310, 328, 330

Godfrey, Dan 75

Godowsky, Leopold 47, 141, 144, 150, 154, 161, 276

Goldman, Henry 176

Goldmark, Carl 5, 8, 12, 13, 126, 252, 288

Goldovsky, Boris 248

Goldstein, Busia 221

Gomez, Juan Vicente 216

Gordon, Jacques 214

Gottschalk, Louis Moreau 302

Grainger, Percy 138, 154

Granados, Enrique 136

Grechaninov, Alexander 122

Greene, Herbert 135

Greenwald, Louis 196, 197–198

Grigorovich, Karl 220

Grofé, Ferde 164

Grolle, Johann 165

Gronsky, Harry 337

Grumiaux, Arthur 311

Grün, J. M. 94

Guadagnini, J. B. 175

Guadagnini, Lorenzo 49–50, 52, 67, 74, 75, 109, 175, 196–198, 199, 202, 235

Guarneri, Andreas 301

Guarneri, Guiseppe (del Gesu) 175, 225–226, 273, 280, 301

Guarneri Quartet 316

Guggenheim, Charles, Mrs. 166

Gusikoff, Michel 163, 173

Gutnikov, Boris 279

Haakon (king) 235

Hadley, Henry 115

Hambourg, Mark 79, 94

Hammerstein, Oscar 93

Hammig, Walter 49–50, 52, 55, 74, 79, 91, 109, 129–130, 175, 299

Handel, George Frederic 52, 176, 219

Hansen, Cecilia 37, 85, 87

Hanslick, Eduard 29

Harbert, Nancy 337

Hardesty, Donald 326

Hardesty, Susan 141, 264, 296, 303, 313, 324, 325–326, 330

Hardy, Thomas 180

Harrison, Percy 68, 79, 94

Hartmann, Arthur 233

Harty, Hamilton 68, 70

Haydn, Franz Josef 90, 92, 219

Hays, Will 175

Hegedus, Ferenc 79

Heifetz, Daniel 264, 286, 301, 337

Heifetz, Florence Vidor 257

Heifetz, Jascha 13, 14, 57, 86–87, 100, 121–122, 144, 145, 146, 150 -151, 155, 156, 160, 162, 163, 164, 166–167, 169, 171, 176, 177, 187, 195, 198, 207, 209, 211, 215, 223–224, 236, 239, 240, 241–242, 251, 257, 262, 268, 269, 280, 285, 288, 295, 304, 306, 324, 334, 335, 336

Heifetz, Pauline 156

Heifetz, Ruvin 86, 87, 121, 168, 211

Hempel, Frieda 68, 251

Henderson, W. J. 143, 212, 214

Henry, Joseph 175

Hess, Willy 44, 122

Hilsberg, Alexander 84–85, 255–256, 271, 272–273, 282

Hilsberg, Ignace 84

Hindemith, Paul 286

Hirohito (crown prince) 185, 190

Hitler, Adolf 248

Hochstein, David 145

Hofmann, Betty 134, 211, 250

Hofmann, Josef 30, 112, 131, 134, 150, 161, 165, 166–167, 180–181, 200, 202, 207, 229, 248–252, 276

Homer, Louise 139, 149

Horowitz, Vladimir 242

Houdini, Harry 162

Hubay, Jenö 79–80, 91, 148, 191, 309, 335

Huberman, Bronislaw 122, 161, 236–238

Hurok, Sol 124, 126–127, 178–179

Hutcheson, Ernest 154, 161

Ilvonen, Jouko 337

Ippolito, Carmela 337

Ippolitov-Ivanov, Mikhail 224

Istomin, Eugene 282

Ives, Charles 286

Jacobsen, Sascha 155, 156, 159, 214

Jacques Gordon Quartet 214

Jaenicke, Bruno 174

Jaffe, Charles 237, 314, 337

Jewell, Althea (Alfy)107–108, 128, 129, 130, 133, 140, 148, 254

Joachim, Joseph 10, 12, 13–14, 23, 38, 48–49, 56–57, 59, 79, 87, 89, 90, 93, 116, 118, 121, 146, 220, 279, 309, 320, 322, 333

Johnson, Roy Hamlin 73

Jolson, Al 174

Jonas, Samuel 127

Jonas, William 127

Joyce, James 261

Judson, Arthur 135

Junkermann, Karl 55, 61, 64, 74, 75, 77, 80, 127

Kabasta, Oswald 236

Kahn, Otto 113

Kajanus, Robert 18

Kakei, Ryoko 337

Kapell, William 282

Kaplan, Dr. Henry 312

Karsavina, Tamara 20

Kaufman, Harry 206, 208–210, 217

Kaufman, Lillian 208–210, 250

Kaufman, Louis 155, 156, 205, 207, 212

Keats, John 246

Keith, Charlton 62, 65

Kelly, Grace 259

Kenyon, Bernice 277

Khachaturian, Aram 281

Khochayan, Vahe 329

Khrennikov, Tikhon 281

Khrushchev, Nikita 277

Klengel, Julius 84

Klimov, Valery 279

Kneisel, Franz 105, 106, 147, 150, 155, 156, 177, 207

Kneisel Quartet 93, 106, 150

Knitzer, Joseph 207

Kochanski, Paul 85, 162, 173

Kocian, Jaroslav 44

Kogan, Leonid 280, 281, 311

Kombrink, Ilona 316

Koodlach, Abram 225

Korguiev (Auer student) 10

Koussevitzky, Serge 22, 247, 261, 292

Krachmalnick, Jacob 264, 272–273, 274, 310, 314, 337

Kreisler, Fritz 22–23, 45, 57–58, 68, 77, 97, 100, 105, 109, 116, 121–123, 126, 135, 136–138, 139, 141, 143, 144, 147–148, 149–150, 151, 159–160, 161–162, 171, 177, 178, 183, 191, 193, 198, 216, 226, 230, 251, 252–253, 257–258, 271, 276, 282–283, 287, 304, 305–306, 310, 334

Kreisler, Harriet 23, 122, 123, 137, 141, 150–151, 162, 230, 253

Kreutzer, Leonid 90

Kreutzer, Rudolphe 5, 20, 209

Kruse, Johann 67, 72

Kschessinska, Mathilde 20

Kubelik, Jan 21–22, 41, 43–45, 55, 116, 118, 122, 223, 333

Kuehne, Marguerite 337

Kuni, Asaakira (prince) 185, 190, 191

Kunwald, Ernst 48, 54, 55

Kwalwasser, Helen 264, 337

Ladd, George (chauffeur) 152, 259

Lalo, Édouard 18, 30, 58, 62, 269

Lambert, Alexander 106, 118, 154

Lambrino, Telemaque 90, 91

Langinger, Herman 320–321

Langtry, Lillie 302

Lansbury, George 71

Lateiner, Jacob 248

Lauder, Harry 73, 160

LeBlanc, Georgette 112

Leinsdorf, Erich 261

Lenin, Vladimir 224

Lenz, Dr. Gilbert 330

Lenz, John 328, 330

Leschetizky, Theodore 17, 73

Letz Quartet 148

Levant, Oscar 155

Lewis, Sinclair 246

Lewisohn, Adolph 112

Lhevinne, Josef 154

Liadov, Anatoly 17, 30, 32, 38, 83

Liebling, Leonard 177

Lind, Jenny 302

Lipkin, Seymour 248

List, Robert 325

Liszt, Franz 88, 119, 122, 125, 167

Litvinoff, Maria See Zimbalist, Maria

Longworth, Alice 155

Longworth, Nicholas 155

Luboshutz, Lea 210, 238, 276

Luboshutz, Pierre 239, 255

Luce, Clare Boothe 155, 302

Luce, Henry 155, 169, 196

Luce, Lila 169

Luce, Sheldon 196, 209

Lunt, Sir Alfred 181, 275

Lupot, Nicolas 281

Lutsky, Eugene 3, 30, 83, 135, 156

Luvisi, Lee 282, 309

Maazel, Saundra 337

Mackay, Clarence 302

Mackenzie, Alexander 72, 335

Maeterlinck, Maurice 112

Mahler, Gustav 92, 105, 108–109, 143

Malan, Roy 264, 322, 337

Malibran, Maria 96

Malkin, Anita 337

Mann, Thomas 158

Mannes, David 142

Margulies (physician) 90

Marie (tsarina empress) See Feodorovna, Dagmar

Marini, Biagio 267

Marshall, J. P. 118

Marteau, Henri 47, 93–94

Marx, Harpo 161

Masini, Angelo 18

Massenet, Jules 135

Mattis, Jay 249, 293

McAuley, Patrick 259

McCormack, Cyril 138

McCormack, Gwendolyn 138

McCormack, John 70, 116, 126, 138, 160, 161, 183

McCormack, Lily 138, 161–162

Meany, General Edward 107, 108

Mecklenburg-Strelitz (grand duke) 32

Medtner, Nicolai 47

Mehta, Dina 199

Mehta, Mehli 198, 284

Mehta, Zubin 198

Meiff, Albert 211, 212

Melba, Nellie 70, 123, 200–201

Mendelssohn, Felix 12, 22, 86, 92, 95, 121, 122, 142, 150, 166, 169, 171, 184, 198, 200, 215, 233, 236, 238, 269, 322, 330

Mengelberg, Willem 74

Menges, Isolde 14, 37, 85

Menotti, Gian Carlo 248, 251, 255, 271, 272, 275, 312, 314, 335

Menuhin, Moshe 87, 176

Menuhin, Yehudi 122, 176

Mero, Yolanda 154

Meyerbeer, Giacomo 125

Michaels, Geoffrey 279, 314, 337

Michelangelo 300

Millay, Edna St. Vincent 155, 179–180, 246, 253, 316

Miller, Charles 328

Mills, Ogden, Mrs. 112

Milstein, Nathan 144, 221, 262, 276, 311

Mischakoff, Mischa 166

Mobert, Helen 243–244

Moennig, William 175, 218

Moiseiwitsch, Benno 73

Montrose, Albert 337

Moor, Paul 278

Moore, Francis 118

Morgan, J. P. 178

Morini, Erica 44

Moser, Andreas 93

Mostras, Konstantin 220, 263, 273, 279

Moszkowski, Moritz 154, 166

Mottl, Felix 62,

Mozart, Wolfgang Amadeus 12, 90, 92, 129, 138, 143, 157, 201, 305, 322

Muck, Karl 19, 105–106, 125

Musical Art Quartet 156–157, 202, 214, 245

Mussolini, Benito 231, 248

Mussorgsky, Modeste 19, 221

Nadien, David 262, 265

Nalbandian, Ioannes 9, 20, 85, 86

Nash, Ogden 155

Nast, Condé 162

New York String Quartet 231

Ney, Elly 154

Nicholas II (tsar) 10, 11, 19, 31, 32, 69, 97, 141, 144

Nikisch, Artur 40, 47, 62, 79, 87–90, 91, 95–96, 121

Offenbach, Jacques 147

Oistrakh, David 13, 87, 221, 224, 276, 279, 280, 281, 295, 297, 305, 312, 336

Oistrakh, Tamara 297, 305

Oppenheimer, Robert 158

Ormandy, Eugene 261, 272–273, 276–277

Oroop, Joseph 194–195

Ovcharov, Sol 337

Ozawa, Seiji 306

Paderewski, Ignacy 49, 115, 122, 123, 128, 131, 133–134, 159, 174, 181, 276

Paganini, Nicolo 9, 10, 12, 21, 24, 45, 59, 67, 85, 86, 109, 110, 116, 125, 142, 159, 171, 198, 212, 219, 223, 253, 280, 284, 288, 300, 330, 333

Park, Alan 337

Park, Mi-Young 264, 337

Parker, Dorothy 155

Parlow, Kathleen 20, 36–37, 145, 302

Pasternack, Josef 119, 136

Patti, Adelina 28, 94–95

Pavlov, Ivan Petrovich 27

Pavlova, Anna 20, 255

Peccatte, Charles 175

Peck, Gregory 243

Pepper, Joseph 337

Perlman, Itzhak 237

Persinger, Louis 95, 176–177

Petina, Irra 255

Petipa 20

Piastro, Mishel 166,183

Piatigorsky, Gregor 254, 255, 260, 271, 272, 308

Pierné, Gabriel 118

Piper, John 302

Piza, Samuel 215

Poliakin, Miron 87, 220

Popper, David 80

Porter, Quincy 286

Portugaloff (physician) 27, 28

Portugaloff, Vitold 14–15, 27, 28, 43, 280

Powell, John 73, 77, 119, 122, 126, 163, 173, 335

Powell, Maud 116

Press, Mikhail (Michael) 220

Pressman, M. L. 2, 5

Primrose, Hiroko 325

Primrose, William 251, 254, 261–262, 301, 325

Prokofiev, Sergei 30, 36, 83, 160–160, 281

Pszibyzsewsky, Boleslav 221

Puffer, Ted 301

Pugnani, Gaetano 314

Pugno, Raoul 22

Pushkin, Alexander 184

Putlitz, Lois 338

Rabinof, Benno 207

Rachmaninoff, Sergei 158–160, 161, 162, 164, 166, 167, 169, 179, 180–181, 202, 211, 219, 221, 230, 247, 254, 277, 282, 287, 328

Raff, Joachim 142

Rameau, Jean-Phillipe 198

Randall, Tony 243

Raskov, (pianist) 188

Ravel, Maurice 51, 125, 190, 198, 233

Ray, Ruth 37, 145, 146

Reagan, Ronald 325

Reed, Elza 338

Reger, Max 90, 118, 137, 335

Reinhardt, Max 50

Reisenauer, Alfred 46

Reiser, Alois 126

Reynolds, Veda 338

Ricci, Ruggiero 177

Richardson, Henry Handel 246–247

Richter, Hans 29, 62, 65, 66, 76, 77–78, 98, 121, 136, 316

Rimsky-Korsakov, Andrei 14–15, 29, 37

Rimsky-Korsakov, Nadia 14, 223, 280

Rimsky-Korsakov, Nikolai Andreyevich 14–15, 17, 19, 28, 31–34, 37–38, 39, 40, 49, 85, 108, 170, 179, 221, 223, 243, 261, 277, 280, 283, 305, 316, 328

Rimsky-Korsakov, Volodya 14–15, 37, 85, 223

Rochberg, George 314

Rockefeller, John D. 154, 157, 193, 231

Rode, Pierre 5

Ronald, Landon 58, 60, 62,–63, 65, 67, 70, 75

Roosevelt, Franklin Delano 242, 247

Rosand, Aaron 264, 270, 309, 311, 338

Rosanoff, Marie Roemat 155, 156

Rosen, Max 37

Rosenbaums (Fels family friends) 99, 100, 109

Rosenstein, Arthur 107, 108

Rosenthal, Moritz 165, 181

Rossini, Gioacchino 125

Rostropovich, Mstislav 297, 298, 306, 312

Rothschild, Jacqueline 260

Rubinstein, Anton 30, 36, 39, 41, 48, 234

Rubinstein, Artur 85, 177, 195

Rubinstein, Isaak 85

Rubinstein, Nicholas 29, 36

Safonov, Vasili 29

Saidenberg, Eleanor Levin 224., 227–231

Saidenberg, Theodore 208, 210, 214–216, 217, 222–223, 224, 226–231, 232

Saint-Saëns, Camille 18, 172, 271, 283, 285

Saleski, Gdal 90, 292

Salin (professor) 5, 7, 9

Salmond, Felix 174, 248, 252, 255

Samaroff, Olga 122, 123, 150, 258, 282

Sammons, Albert 75, 98

Santley, Sir Charles 70

Saperton, David 251–252

Sarasate, Pablo de 14, 21–22, 54, 56, 72, 77, 98, 116–117, 118, 122, 171, 191, 205, 216, 261–262, 285, 330

Sarnoff, David 171

Sauer, Emil von 47

Sauret, Émile 21, 78, 223

Scalero, Rosario 275

Scheiville, Herman 197

Schelling, Ernest 154, 161–162, 163, 173, 335

Schenk, Frieda 259, 289, 290

Schiff, Jacob 112

Schildkraut, Rudolf 50

Schloezer, Tatiana 28, 29, 83

Schmuller, Alexander 90, 91

Schnabel, Artur 166

Schnitzer, Germaine 154

Schoettle, Enid 314

Schoenberg, Arnold 335

Schonberg, Harold 105–106, 237

Schubert, Franz 92, 129, 171, 191, 254, 319

Schulman, Julius 205, 264, 338

Schumann, Elisabeth 251, 255

Schumann, Robert 78, 87, 92, 125, 216, 221

Schumann-Heink, Ernestine 100

Schwarz, Boris 54, 263

Scott, Cyril 73, 95, 110, 335

Scotti, Antonio 70, 116

Scriabin, Alexander 28

Seidel, Toscha 14, 144–145

Seidl, Anton 62

Sembrich, Marcella 128, 134, 165, 251, 307

Senofsky, Berl 265

Serber, Michael 265

Serkin, Rudolf 249, 282, 296, 301, 307, 310

Ševčik, Otokar 21, 41, 43–46, 52, 75, 76

Sewell, Frederick 338

Shakespeare, William 50, 246

Shapey, Ronald 338

Shapiro, Eudice 212, 217, 242, 324, 325, 338

Shaw, George Bernard 73, 130, 246, 254

Shefeluk, Marie 338

Shostakovich, Dmitri 222, 224, 278, 281, 297, 312, 335

Shumsky, Eric 328

Shumsky, Oscar 87, 172, 207, 237, 239, 248, 263, 309–310, 311, 316, 334, 338

Sibelius, Jean 18, 83, 84, 95, 122, 139, 149, 211- 212, 222–223, 260–261, 268, 276, 335

Siegfried, Franklin 314, 338

Siloti, Alexander 5, 18

Silverstein, Joseph 263, 264, 265, 314, 321, 323, 338

Simms, John 286

Simon, Abbey 248

Simon, Henry 253

Simpson, Claire 338

Sinding, Christian 39, 46, 48, 52, 54–55, 62, 274

Singher, Martial 307

Sirota, Gershon 127

Sitjar, Felix 338

Slatkin, Felix 219, 338

Smith, Anne 287

Smith, George 225–226

Snyder, Florence Frantz 218, 219

Sokoloff, Eleanor 255, 321

Sokoloff, Nikolai 232

Sokoloff, Vladimir 52, 58, 172, 217, 218, 232–236, 238–239, 242–243, 245, 247, 255, 260, 263, 268, 269, 271, 274, 283, 285, 287, 288, 293, 296, 302, 310, 313, 316, 321, 323, 325, 326–327, 328–329

Spalding, Albert 171, 213

Spivakovsky, Tossy 272

Spohr, Ludwig 10, 12, 59, 125, 137, 219

St. Petersburg Quartet 10

Stalin, Joseph 221–222, 228, 281

Stanislavsky, Konstantin 224

Stasoff, V. V. 39

Stasseivich, Paul 166–167

Stein, Bogutska, Mme. 145, 149

Steinbach, Fritz 65

Steinberg, Maximilian 223

Steiner, Diana 241, 309, 316, 325, 338

Steinway, Frederick 106, 169, 181, 184, 186, 299

Stephens, James 323

Stern, Isaac 272

Stock, Frederick 139, 148, 163, 173, 208, 214, 335

Stoeckel, Carl 139

Stojowski, Sigismund 154

Stokowski, Leopold 121, 122, 129, 143, 150, 165, 211, 213–214, 261

Stoliarsky, Piotr 220–221

Stradivari, Antonio 67, 109, 145, 175, 176 186, 225–226, 235, 254, 299

Stransky, Josef 105–106

Straus, Oscar 46

Strauss, Johann 161

Strauss, Richard 47, 50–51, 62, 74, 92, 129, 233, 253, 272, 335

Stravinsky, Igor 17, 214

Strecker, Wilhelm 130, 136

Strok, Artur 18 -19, 75, 183, 184, 186, 198, 209, 226–227

Sugitani, Takaoki 314, 338

Suk, Josef 171, 316

Sutherland, Robin 324–325, 328, 329

Suzuki, Hidetaro 264, 279, 290, 314, 338

Suzuki, Shinichi 305

Swastika Quartet 237

Szell, George 262

Szgelnick, Jacoblevich 225

Szigeti, Joseph 121, 195, 216, 280

Szymanowski, Karol 85, 173, 335

Tamagno, Francesco 18

Taulovw (conductor) 223

Tchaikovsky, Peter Ilyich 12, 19, 29, 35–36, 37, 39, 40, 58, 62, 64, 65–66, 67, 70, 74, 78, 88, 89, 92, 93, 105, 110, 115, 146, 167, 179, 216, 221, 226, 272, 274, 277–279, 297, 305, 306

Tertis, Lionel 73
Tetrazzini, Luisa 18
Thibaud, Jacques 137
Thompson, Randall 248–249
Thomson, Llewellyn 278
Thomson, Virgil 253, 336
Thornton, Edna 70
Tiomkin, Dimitri 188
Tokugawa, Yorisada 185, 190, 192
Toscanini, Arturo 106, 107, 161–162, 211, 229, 237, 242
Tosti, Paolo 70
Tree, Michael 172, 264, 269–270, 278, 338
Trio Classique 242
Troyanovsky, Alexander Antonovich 228, 242
Tsumura, Mari 338

Valentino, Rudolph 154
Van Emden, Harriet 206
Vanderbilt, Cornelius II 106, 112, 113
Vanderbilt, Grace 106, 112, 113
Vaska, Bedrich 231
Vécsey, Franz von 79, 80, 87, 91, 148
Vengerova, Isabelle 18, 268
Venuti, Joe 164
Verzhbilovich, Alexander 5, 10, 32
Vestay, Pamela 201
Viardot, Pauline 96
Victoria (princess) 69

Vieuxtemps, Henri 5, 12, 14, 22, 116, 125, 333
Viotti, Giovanni 12
Vitali, Tommaso 52, 233
Vivaldi, Antonio 166–167, 314
Vogelgesang, Frederick 217, 299, 314, 338
von Warlich, Reinhold 150, 162

Wada, Keiko 338
Wagner, Gottfried 314
Wagner, Richard 19, 65, 66, 171, 314
Waldo, Elizabeth 338
Wallach, Eli 243
Walska, Gana 230
Walter, Bruno 242
Walter, William 165
Walther (Auer student) 10
Weber, Carl Maria von 61, 63
Weingartner, Felix 46
Wells, H.G. 73
White, Roderick 37
Whiteman, Paul 160, 163–164
Wieniawski, Henri 10, 11, 12, 52, 90, 171, 218, 220, 302, 333
Wile, Oscar 115
Wilhelmj, August 59, 78, 116, 171–172, 191, 223
Wilson (masseur) 299, 304, 311, 326
Wilson, Woodrow 136
Windt, Paul 285, 338

Wippler, Harold 338
Witek, Anton 54
Wolf, Andrew 329
Wolff (impresaria) 48–49, 51, 52, 53, 54, 55, 58, 59, 61, 76, 88–89, 91, 127
Wolff, Hermann 48
Wood, Henry 62, 75
Woodruff, Marilyn 338
Woollcott, Alexander 155
Wright, Frank Lloyd 184–185, 190
Wurlitzer, Rembert 175, 197, 202
Yamada, Koscak 191
Yamamoto, Kyusaburo 185
Yampolski, Abram 220
Ysaÿe, Eugène 14, 22, 56, 75–76, 95, 106, 119, 143, 149, 159, 202, 222, 233, 271, 279, 283, 302, 304, 333–334, 335
Ysaÿe, Theophile 22

Zanuck, Darryl 174
Zeitlin, Lev 15, 83, 84, 220, 224
Zelig, Tibor 238
Zeppelin, Count Ferdinand 91–92
Zimbalist, Alexander (Aron) 1–5, 7, 15, 20, 27, 29, 41, 75, 84, 147, 223
Zimbalist, Edna 147

Zimbalist, Efrem, Jr. (Merfe)
    147, 148, 168–169, 196, 201,
    209, 211, 227, 228, 231–232,
    240–241, 242–243, 246,
    249, 264, 275, 283, 287,
    293, 296, 303, 306, 312, 314,
    320–321, 322, 330
Zimbalist, Efrem, III
    (Skipper) 264, 305, 314,
    321
Zimbalist, Efrem, IV 327
Zimbalist, Emily 264, 275
Zimbalist, Flora 147
Zimbalist, Helen 147
Zimbalist, Jane 141, 264, 296,
    303, 313
Zimbalist, Luba 147
Zimbalist, Maria 1–4, 7–9,
    16, 27, 147, 210
Zimbalist, Maria Virginia
    141, 142, 147, 148, 149, 196,
    227, 228, 231–232, 242, 249,
    264, 291–292, 296, 298,
    300, 301, 303, 307, 308–
    309, 310, 312, 313, 321, 324,
    325, 328, 329
Zimbalist, Mary Louise
    Curtis Bok 164–165, 180,
    202, 248–250, 252, 254, 255,
    256–257, 258–259, 269,
    277, 287, 289–290, 292,
    293, 295, 315, 316, 328
Zimbalist, Nancy 169, 264,
    298, 314
Zimbalist, Samuel 84, 147
Zimbalist, Sascha 29, 84, 90,
    147

Zimbalist, Stephanie ('Big')
    296, 303
Zimbalist, Stephanie
    ('Little') 303, 314, 321, 327